Adult and Higher Education
in Queer Contexts:
Power, Politics, and Pedagogy

Robert J. Hill, André P. Grace, and Associates

Published by Discovery Association Publishing House
Chicago, Illinois

Library of Congress Control Number
2009933139

Adult and Higher Education in Queer Contexts: Power, Politics, and Pedagogy
by Robert J. Hill & André P. Grace

ISBN: 1-931967-14-8

Manufactured in the United States of America
Printed by CSS Publishing Company, Lima, OH

Cover illustration by: James C. Savage
Copy Editor: Carolyn Law
Design: Tana Stith
Adult Education Editors: Joanne Sandelski and Dr. Keith B. Armstrong
(Discovery Association Publishing House).

Acclaim for This Book

Bob Hill and André Grace have made a unique contribution to the field of adult education. This book makes available to faculty and students a resource on a subject that was not even mentionable in most of our classrooms fifteen years ago. The fifteen chapters authored by nineteen researchers help the reader deconstruct the experiences and the environments as well as the way adult learning and education are encountered and utilized by the LGBT community. This book invites all of us to lay aside any fears or prejudices and to explore what it means to be informed allies fully engaging in this discourse.

Phyllis M. Cunningham
Professor Emerita, Presidential Teaching Professor, Northern Illinois University
International Adult and Continuing Education Hall of Fame
Outstanding Adult Educators Award Recipient,
American Association of Adult Continuing Education

Grace and Hill have produced an excellent, groundbreaking, and relevant book—Excellent because the writing, the research, and the argument are all just that; groundbreaking because they and their colleagues examine adult education from a Queer perspective (a first); relevant because the issues discussed are isolation, identity, prejudice, pain, struggle, progress, setback, and success, and these themes have significance for us all.

Michael Newman
Research Fellow of the Centre for Popular Education and
Honorary Associate, University of Technology, Sydney, Australia
Cyril Houle Award Recipient, Outstanding Literature in Adult Education

This much-awaited book by two of the most influential scholars in the field of adult and higher education is a must read. Grace and Hill are historians, environmentalists, critical pedagogues, and even popular educators. This time they have given us the world's first full and authoritative text on adult education, queer theory, and transformative practice. This book will inform the work of all those who believe in an education for a better world.

Budd L. Hall
Office of Community-Based Research, University of Victoria, Canada
International Adult and Continuing Education Hall of Fame

It is important to note two things about the early origins of this text: the bravery of those who initiated and sustained the [Queer] pre-conference meetings and the relevance of those meetings to the growth and development of the field of adult education. In the first instance, it is significant that these meetings took place in the context of a harsh and unforgiving environment. Stories told in the meetings were vile. They were accounts of lives lived in a milieu of hostility, humiliation, silencing, and personal danger.…The field has been irrevocably changed for the better because of those pre-conferences. Those of us who consider ourselves to be concerned about social justice and oppression were challenged to face our silences, avoidances, and rejections of the LGBTQ&A agendas. The pre-conferences offered us an annual, unrepentant, unremitting, and very necessary self-assessment of our prejudices and homophobia. They asked us not just to "talk the talk" but also to "walk the walk." In doing so, they brought the field closer to its historical roots as a social movement and thus questioned the pressure to equate adult education with functionalist training and vocationalism.…

This text …continues to challenge us to confront both ourselves and the field of adult education for our homophobic assumptions and actions. More importantly, it challenges us to act to change those situations. On the other hand, for those of us who live in countries where the tyranny of heterosexism remains strong, this text offers an alternative dialogue. I would venture to say that all of the world's adult educators live in countries that could benefit from this dialogue. Homosexual behavior is illegal in over eighty countries, but in many more it is, though not illegal, neither accepted nor acceptable. Thus, we can use this text to introduce issues, dilemmas, and possibilities around the lives of LGBTQ&A persons. Although it professes to be a partial record of everything that has happened in LGBTQ&A pre-conferences and caucuses, the book's introduction promises a wide-ranging exploration of LGBTQ&A issues.…I congratulate Bob Hill and André Grace on their continuing efforts to raise LGBTQ&A issues and for their indefatigable commitment and energy to strengthen the field of adult education with their insights and their challenges to act to create a better world.

Joyce Stalker
Policy, Cultural, and Social Studies in Education,
School of Education Te Kura Toi Tangata
University of Waikato, Te Whare Wananga o Waikato
New Zealand Aotearoa

Robert Hill and André Grace are to be congratulated on producing a unique insight into Queer. While others have written about Queer in higher education, and individual articles and chapters about Queer in adult education have appeared, there has to date been no comprehensive account of the variety of perspectives and understandings of Queer from the point of view of adult learning. This systematic collection addresses for the first time the complex political and pedagogic issues for adult and higher education in thought-provoking, challenging, and sometimes infuriating ways. All books which try to change the world should be like this one - maddening, contradictory, argumentative, and ultimately inspiring!

Miriam Zukas
Professor in Adult Education, Director of the Lifelong Learning Institute
University of Leeds, United Kingdom

As children, it is certain Bob Hill and André Grace were punished for talking in class. However, what they said there was nothing compared to what they thought and said on the way home from school. Now, years later, they are still flirting with fire, and in this book their task was to create a space for Queer voices in adult education. This collection dispenses with the notion that adult education is a benign or neutral process and shows how sexual identity lies at its heart and soul. Grace and Hill hope readers will be shocked, provoked, enlightened, and cajoled into asking hard questions about Queer perspectives. Contrary to rumors suggesting otherwise, the emancipatory impulse in adult education is not dead. By fossicking with the forbidden, exposing the unspoken, and poking around hidden topics, the contributors bring a fresh and needed perspective to an understudied aspect of adult education.

Roger Boshier
Professor Emeritus
Department of Educational Studies
University of British Columbia

DEDICATION

To Phyllis Cunningham and to the students with whom I work and learn

More than 15 years ago Phyllis Cunningham penned words that are as fresh now as they were then: "For me adult education is about critically assessing our reality, to name that reality, to devise strategies through adult education to change that reality, and to help students to do the same thing" (1993, para. 7). Phyllis has taught us that action, advocacy, and activism begin with people critically reflecting on their conditions and developing strategies to bring about democratic social change. To do this, we must not promote the existing hegemony, but rather, we must develop counter-hegemonic struggle. We must not simply attain knowledge, we must understand the politics of knowledge. We must not preserve the status quo and elitism, we must engage in the democratization of power relationships (Cunningham, 1993). It is hoped that this book aids in building Queer democratic possibilities.

I continue to be moved by Phyllis's lines: "Twenty years ago most of us nontraditional educators were trying to reform the university. This is not my goal today. I operate within the university to make ideological space for students and me to do our intellectual work. First we must cease being keepers of the gate and become keepers of the dream" (quoted in Hill, 2007, p. 156). Thanks are sent to the students who have helped me to Queer this ideological space and from whom I continually learn.

Phyllis's teachings have given shape to our dreams; they have given us permission to cultivate unruly perspectives and to expose oppressive "truths." I'm delighted to dedicate this work to Phyllis for her unflagging revolutionary zeal and inspiration and to the many students with whom I journey in and out of the academy.

Robert J. Hill
Athens, Georgia, USA

To the spectral community of Queer Others and our allies

To the many Queers erased from existence by suicide, murder, the tragedy of AIDS, and other horrors. To the many Queers still walking wounded on this earth, and to those who have been able to find a way forward in the light of hope and possibility. Gain strength from the caring work of contributors to this book, and transgress a history of erasure by sharing this Queer life lesson: We are bodies to be without apology, not bodies to cure or erase. Also gain strength from the work of caring educators and allies for social justice, like Phyllis M. Cunningham, a social educator and cultural worker extraordinaire. Like Paulo Freire, Phyllis is driven by just ire that motivates her work for social change and cultural transformation. Thank you, Phyllis. And thank you to so many other supportive allies in our field of study and practice. We are finding place, and we do belong!

André P. Grace
Edmonton, Alberta, Canada

References

Cunningham, P. M. (1993, Fall). Let's get real: A critical look at the practice of adult education. *Journal of Adult Education, 22*(1), 3-15. Retrieved August 2, 2008, from http://www.nl.edu/academics/cas/ace/resources/PhyllisCunningham_insight.cfm

Hill, R. J. (2007). Breaking open our times (and other liberatory acts). In K. B. Armstrong, L. W. Nabb, & A. P. Czech (Eds.), *North American adult educators: Phyllis M. Cunningham archive of quintessential autobiographies for the twenty-first century* (pp. 153-158). Chicago: Discovery Association Publishing House.

TABLE OF CONTENTS

Section II. Higher Education

Section III. Adult Learning

Section IV. Community

FOREWORD

Forewords are difficult things to write. You don't want to give the story away by revealing too much of the book's central theme or to signal the book's ending. You don't want to lavish praise for fear of seeming to be the uncritical mouthpiece of the book's publisher or authors. Yet you want to feel proud of any book you write the foreword for and to believe that the world is better for its appearance. This is a book I am proud of and for which adult and higher education can feel grateful. It took me a nanosecond, or whatever is the smallest amount of physically measurable time, to respond enthusiastically to the request from its co-editors to write this foreword. In writing it I see no necessary contradiction between scholarly objectivity and passion. It is my scholarly opinion, rendered with all due clarity and objectivity, that the past decade has proved overwhelmingly the need for Queering culture and politics—for an unyielding and unapologetic challenging of what passes for normality and business as usual and for the placing of human desire at the center of decision making.

I am proud that this book represents a perfect example of the praxis of radical adult education. It is more than a work of scholarship (though its scholarship is impeccable). Its very existence represents over fifteen years of activism by its co-editors within the field of adult and higher education research, particularly within the context of the Adult Education Research Conference (AERC). Insisting that the field focus on LGBTQ matters has involved the co-editors, the book's contributors, and many other AERC presenters in taking risks and taking stands in a cultural environment that for most of this decade has been overwhelmingly militaristic and suspicious of difference and the Other. In their acknowledgements, the co-editors refer to the routine harassment of Brenda and Wanda Henson of Camp Sister Spirit in Mississippi. There may not be many gunshots ringing out at AERC, but a more subtle, often equally effective, harassment has been felt by many who research Queer issues—being told by senior colleagues that such research is an academic dead-end, that it will not be taken seriously by the field, that it is a mistake to waste valuable time and academic capital on what is a single-issue stream of political work, that it can wait until after tenure has been earned, and so on.

To focus on researching Queer matters was an imperative for many of the contributors to this volume rather than a carefully weighed decision. A decision implies you have the opportunity to choose among multiple courses of action; an imperative is something you feel you *must* do, no matter what the cost might be. I think of this book as the realization of an imperative. It had to happen, no matter what the cost to its contributors to travel the road that ended (only as a temporary resting pause) in these pages. It cannot be stressed enough that if Queer terrain comprises "a site of transgression," as the co-editors note in the introduction, then researching that terrain has been a transgressive act. Those of us who have been involved with the AERC for much of its history can be proud that this strange, fluid, ever-shifting nomadic caravan of motley researchers has refused to be co-opted and controlled by any professional body or association and that it has remained open to consistently expanding the boundaries of what comprises the legitimate study of adult education. In its constant self-questioning of how adult education should be defined, its delightful and playful reframing of what counts as research and praxis, and its desire (mostly) to side with those challenging voices that act up and act out in the field, the AERC has practiced its own form of Queer politics (mostly) without being aware of that fact.

These days it is fashionable to lament the passing of adult education's transgressive spirit. The historical myth that exercises considerable influence on the field is that adult education used to be a radical expression of the democratic spirit, but it has been tamed, moved to the dark side, become the lapdog of workplace learning, sold its soul to the devil of professionalism in a misguided attempt to be taken seriously by more powerful branches of education. This myth is just that – a myth. I have never believed it. The radical, transgressive spirit of adult education has endured and constantly reconfigured itself, doing its best to escape and outwit those who would contain and neutralize its energy and surfacing in ways that constantly take adult educators by surprise. The colleagues I work with in adult and higher education and the learners I serve and study with are neither tamed nor ideologically hoodwinked. This volume of spirited commitment—defiantly hopeful, seriously playful, and placing matters of desire and resistance at its center—is an apt representation of the enduring radical spirit of the best of adult education.

Stephen D. Brookfield
Distinguished University Professor, University of St. Thomas
Minneapolis-St. Paul, Minnesota

PREFACE

In this collection, we collaborate with our associates to produce a conspectus of the emergence of a lesbian, gay, bisexual, trans-identified, Queer, and allied (LGBTQ&A) place, albeit an often contested one, at the national Adult Education Research Conference (AERC) from 1993 to the present. Interestingly, this quest for a Queer place was happening at AERC at a time when queer theory, as a cultural and political theory that interrogates heterosexism, homophobia, and transphobia, was emerging in academe. During the 1990s, our Queer work at AERC sought to link research to advocacy and educational and community practices. It was about Queer social activism and cultural work, transgression and transformation, vocality and visibility. What we wanted to achieve was far more action-oriented than the tamer textual analysis that was the preoccupation of queer theory throughout much of the 1990s. This book provides various details of our efforts.

While not a complete record of everything that has transpired since 1993 in LGBTQ&A caucuses and pre-conferences at AERC, this collection is nevertheless a substantial record of key moments in that history. It also provides a representative survey of the breadth and depth of the Queer research, activism, and cultural work presented during our meetings. It makes clear that we are here and, moreover, we are here to stay. Some of us have been making Queer waves for decades; others are exuberantly new to the venture of Queer educational and community research and advocacy that are contextually and relationally shaped in intersections with transformative learning, community development, grassroots research, and other heart-and-soul aspects of theory, research, and practice found in adult education as a complex field of study and practice. As readers work through the chapters in this book, there will be ample opportunities to gauge issues, concerns, and trends in adult and higher education in Queer contexts that will be valuable to those concerned with directions in social, cultural, and radical education in our field today. The book is an engagement with history, politics, power, multiple-perspective theorizing, the parameters of Queer inclusive education, institutionalism, social education, cultural education, inclusive pedagogy, praxis in contextual and relational contexts, social justice, community engagement and community building, ethical practice, the local and the global, and the political ideals of modernity: democracy, freedom, and social justice.

This book can be used as a text in university and college courses that examine adult education as a field of study and practice in social, political, and cultural contexts. It can be used in courses that are foundational in nature, such as the history or sociology of adult education. It can be used in courses that are postfoundational in nature and designed to explore the impact of hierarchies and structures on issues like access and accommodation in adult education. It can also be used in courses that take up such issues as social movement learning, cultural work to transgress exclusions, and community education and development for disenfranchised groups. It would be courageous to use *Adult and Higher Education in Queer Contexts* as a text or to include it on a reading list in any of these courses or in a course that is an introduction to adult education. This book contributes to the knowledge base in adult education by raising critical questions about the degree to which adult education as a field of study and practice is inclusive, ethical, just, democratic, and capable of dealing with differences and diversity. It also provides readers with an opportunity to explore the degree to which they may be heterosexist, sexist, homophobic, or transphobic. Hopefully the book will embarrass some, outrage others, and leave everyone with a sense of Paulo Freire's just ire as a motivation to make a more welcoming and inclusive place for sexual minorities in our field of study and practice.

For some, to engage these issues will be an exercise in risk taking. Yet, in his last book, *Pedagogy of Indignation,* Paulo Freire (2004) encourages social educators to be cultural workers who take risks:

> [I]t is important that education, rather than trying to deny risk, encourages men and women to take it. It is by taking on risk, its inevitability, that I become prepared to take this given risk that challenges me now, and to which I must respond. It is fundamental that I know that there is no human existence without risk, of greater or lesser danger. Risk implicates the subjectiveness of the one who runs it. (Italics in the original, p. 5)

Let reading this book be the given risk that challenges you now and to which you must respond. As you explore this book, take up Freire's challenge to go further and explore your own subjectivity and the degree to which you are making a difference to make space for Others, including Queer Others, in adult and higher education.

References

Freire, P. (2004). *Pedagogy of indignation*. Boulder, CO: Paradigm Publishers.

ACKNOWLEDGEMENTS

This work would not be possible without the past and current support of people far too numerous to name here. In separate autobiographical chapters—"Breaking Open Our Times (and Other Liberatory Acts)" (Hill) and an untitled autobiography (Grace)—in *North American Adult Educators: Phyllis M. Cunningham Archive of Quintessential Autobiographies for the Twenty-First Century,* edited by K. B. Armstrong, L. W. Nabb, and A. P. Czech (2007), we each mention many individuals who have been a part of our professional growth and to whom we are deeply grateful. Regarding this text, thanks are due to Keith Armstrong, who recognized early that the papers presented at the Adult Education Research Conference (AERC) and the Lesbian, Gay, Bisexual, Transgender, Queer, and Allies pre-conferences deserved a wider distribution than that provided by the conference *Proceedings*. The careful guidance and enthusiastic encouragement provided by Joanne Sandelski at Discovery Association Publishing House helped to carry us forward with ease. An enormous debit of gratitude goes to Carolyn Law for proofreading the text. Her skills have significantlyly enriched our book.

Queer[1] discourse has been gaining acceptance in adult education since Elizabeth J. Tisdell and Robert J. Hill founded the Lesbian, Gay, Bisexual, Transgender, Queer, and Allies Caucus at the 1993 AERC, which was held at the Pennsylvania State Univerity. In the early years we enjoyed the active, enthusiastic, and sustained support of folks such as Phyllis Cunningham, Fred Schied, Joyce Stalker, Michael Law, Budd Hall, Michael Welton, Stephen Brookfield, and Michael Newman.

At the 1994 AERC meeting at the University of Tennessee (where Bob and André first met), Roger Boshier exclaimed after Bob's presentation of the first adult education research paper in a Queer voice, "This is a historical moment."

---

1 "Queer" is used in at least two distinct ways. One is as a means to avoid the cumbersome acronym LGBTT, standing for "lesbian, gay, bisexual, transgender, and Two-Spirit," an umbrella term for the collection of sexual minorities. This usage of the word has value, including establishing an identifiable "we" that generates political and personal identity. Another use of "Queer" suggests that identities are always multiple, fluid, mobile, contingent, unstable (labile), and fragmented. It challenges fixed notions such as gay, lesbian, and straight. Queer in this formation "attempts to transform an epithet into a label of pride and militance…." (Rosenblum & Travis, 2003, p. 7).

Roger offered encouragement and support. Other voices prompting us to move forward included Ron Cervero, Paul Armstrong, Sharan Merriam, Rosemary Caffarella, Meriam Zukas, and Brenda and Wanda Henson of Camp Sister Spirit. Brenda and Wanda have been especially significant people in the unfolding of a Queer voice in our lives and in the field.

Brenda Henson visited Bob and his companion, Jim Savage (the graphic designer of the cover of this edition), at their home in metro Atlanta, where they sat around the kitchen table discussing her refusal to be a refugee in her own country. Rather than move to a more progressive and "safer" location, she and Wanda were hell-bent on remaining "on the land" at their lesbian-feminist retreat and folk education center in the midst of conservative Ovett, Mississippi. Brenda and Wanda remained unperturbed when gunshots rang out around their home in acts of fear mongering and intimidation. Not even waking up one morning to a dead puppy draped over their mailbox, its stomach blown out and stuffed with sanitary napkins, could budge them. Sadly, Brenda passed away before this volume was completed. The Hensons remain archetypes of courage and defiance, of resistance and struggle, and most important, of the refusal to be victims of hatred and homophobia.

We hope that the spirit of these pioneer advocates, and indeed the many unnamed advocates for a Queer presence in the field of adult education, stirs you as much as it has us.

Robert J. Hill
André P. Grace

References

Armstrong, K. B., Nabb, L. W., & Czech, A. P. (Eds.). (2007). *North American adult educators: Phyllis M. Cunningham archive of quintessential autobiographies for the twenty-first century*. Chicago: Discovery Association Publishing House.

Rosenblum, K. E., & Travis, T.-M. C. (2003). *The meaning of difference: American constructions of race, sex and gender, social class, and sexual orientation*. NY: McGraw-Hill.

INTRODUCTION

Queer Silence No More— Let's Make Some Noise

Robert J. Hill
André P. Grace

Adult and Higher Education in Queer Contexts: Power, Politics, and Pedagogy is largely the product of several years of research and scholarship that have been presented at the premier adult education research meeting in North America—the annual Adult Education Research Conference (AERC). In 2003, Robert J. Hill and André P. Grace organized the first Lesbian, Gay, Bisexual, Transgender, Queer and Allies (LGBTQ&A) Pre-Conference at AERC. The year 2003 also was the 10th anniversary of the founding of the AERC Lesbian, Gay, Bisexual, Transgender, Queer and Allies Caucus. After a decade of informal meetings with invited guest speakers, our community organized its own gathering of researchers to present results related to our in/queeries into the field. The pre-conferences, in addition to an occasional Queer paper at the regular AERC meetings, were highly successful. As a result, we received numerous requests to select representative papers and edit a book so that this scholarship could be available beyond the limited distribution of conference *Proceedings*. Thus, this book was born.

This introduction traces the journey, surveying key themes, concepts, and ideas that were presented and deliberated at AERC and our pre-conferences. We offer this construction as a quest for voice as well as the result of the conquest of being heard. In this introduction, we provide a conspectus of significant adult education work at the intersection of sexual orientation and gender identity, variation, and expression.

The chapters in this book are, like the concept Queer, eclectic, dynamic, flowing, turbulent, enraging, engaging, encompassing, unyielding, unapologetic, and still they provide just a limited purview of all that is Queer in adult and higher education, lifelong learning, culture, and society. Nevertheless, the sum of these chapters provides readers with an intricate and informative pathway to learn about Queer politics, culture, and sociality and to explore sexual minorities—including lesbian, gay, Two-Spirit,[1] bisexual, intersexual, transsexual, transgender, and Queer persons—and their issues into the present moment. This collection explores identities, subjectivities, positionalities, and socialities that comprise the spectral and fluid nature of Queer. These aspects of Queer being, becoming, belonging, and acting in the world inform and energize a politics of hope and possibility that make Queer terrain a site of transgression and potential change in which social and cultural transformation are the primary composite goals.

In our writing, we tend to capitalize Queer to respect the spectrum of sexual orientations and gender identities it is considered to include in the ebb and flow of sex, sexual, and gender differences. As you engage in what we hope will be a troubling trek through these chapters, we invite you to interrogate Queer oppression and disenfranchisement, as well as the exclusionary systems and traditions that sustain them. More importantly though, in the spirit of Paulo Freire's (2004) politics and pedagogy of indignation, we invite you to be open to being angry. We want you to use your anger, as Freire did, as a motivation for taking a stand and working for change. We want you to believe and insist that change is possible for Queers so we are respected, recognized, accepted, and accommodated (Grace & Wells, 2007). With delight, we introduce you to the chapters in this book as you begin your learning journey to enhance the motivation to "know."

The book is comprised of three topical areas or sections. Section I, Chapters 1 through 3, covers the breadth and depth of our fight for visibility and voice. It begins with a historical overview and then wends its way through thoughts about intimacy, ending in a chapter on arts-based inquiry—discovering "truth" without "facts." Section II, Chapters 4 through 7, explores the world of higher education at the crossroads of Queer meaning making. Materials in this section span notions of what it means to be an ally, the history of campus climate surveys,

---

1 "Two-Spirit," a term used by some North American Indigenous peoples to describe nonstandard gender systems, is found globally in native cultures. Thus, in some Aboriginal groups, men/boys are permitted to assume roles and behaviors typically restricted to women/girls, and vice versa (see Lang, 1998). Like much that surrounds sexual orientation and gender identity, it is not without controversy. Jacobs (1997) offers that it is complex and has, like so much surrounding Native Americans, been appropriated for ends other than its original intention. In this case, by White gay men to justify their lives by invoking an original authentic and natural primal condition. See Waller and McAllen-Walker (2001) for a discussion of its complex nature.

academic citizenship, and Queering the curriculum. Section III is an exploration of lesbian, gay, bisexual, transgender, and Queer adult learning. Chapters 8 through 11 make up this portion of the text. Here the reader will find challenging notions of identity development, aging as a Queer person, learning to be/come a member of a particular gay community related to sobriety (abstinence from alcohol), and the adult learning that takes place in gender identity transitioning—in this case from male to female. The final section, IV, delves into issues of Queer community education. In Chapters 12 through 14, the authors take us on an awe-inspiring tour of communities as diverse as those involved in international Queer peace building, positive HIV prevention, and building Queer culture in urban environments. The book concludes with Chapter 15, which offers a challenge to us to create Queer-inclusive histories and to be open to future possibilities of hope and promise.

In Chapter 1, entitled "Positioning Queer in Adult Education: Intervening in Politics and Praxis in North America,"[2] André P. Grace and Robert J. Hill review more than a decade of attempts to achieve Queer presence and place in North American adult education. They examine the formation and comprehension of Queer knowledge in adult education and in larger sociocultural contexts and explore the need to position Queer in adult education, mindful of how Queer is historically and currently positioned in culture and society. In doing so, Grace and Hill articulate "Queer"—a term representing a spectral community that incorporates a diversity of sex, sexual, and gender differences—and "Queerness"— Queer ways of being, believing, desiring, becoming, belonging, and acting in life-and-learning spaces. In a turn to Queer history and Queer studies, they also investigate Queer knowledge as fugitive knowledge integral and informative to a Queer project to transgress the social and to reconstitute the cultural in adult education as a field of study and practice. Grace and Hill locate Queer knowledge as an antecedent to Queer praxis, and they focus on inclusive Queer praxis as a transgressive practice-expression-reflection dynamic and a site of transformative learning.

In Chapter 2, "Que(e)rying Intimacy: Challenges to Lifelong Learning," Robert J. Hill takes up the political and pedagogical task of making sense of five contemporary intersecting arenas related to the intimacy of learning within sexual-minority communities: sexual minorities' struggles for equality and justice,

2 Previously published as Grace, A. P., & Hill, R. J. (2004). Positioning Queer in adult education: Intervening in politics and praxis in North America. *Studies in the Education of Adults*, 36(2), 167-189. Reprinted with permission of the publisher.

the complex nature of social movements of which sexual minorities are often a part, sexual-minority intimacy, democracy and citizenship for sexual minorities, and learning across the lifespan within our communities. Hill's efforts here are premised on the notion that the democratization of intimacy is a natural consequence of the principles of human freedom and equality as well as the human ability to reason. Hill relates that while formal venues of adult education and learning have been relatively silent on this fundamental human right, sexual-minority communities engaged in and outside of social movements have a long history of struggling for radical democratic inclusion, recognition of intimacy, and for the same citizenship rights afforded to heterosexuals. In this light, Hill maintains that sexual-minority adults are always involved in some measure in adult learning or lifelong learning that occurs through the mobilization of human desires for love, belonging, intimacy, and yearnings of the heart, regardless of social determinism. Hill concludes that sexual minorities are fully attuned to these matters of being, belonging, and becoming.

Chapter 3 is entitled "Art as Anti-Oppression Adult Education: Creating a Pedagogy of Presence and Place." In this chapter André P. Grace, Robert J. Hill, and Kristopher Wells recount their experiences of a deliberate act that attempted to erase the presence of sexual minorities at the 46th annual Adult Education Research Conference, which was held at the University of Georgia, Athens, in 2005. The co-authors reflect on their feelings and the politics and pedagogy of resistance inspired by the use of a crimson curtain by university staff to hide a Queer art installation from public view. Participants at the LGBTQ&A Pre-Conference had started to create the installation as part of an undertaking called *The Triangle Project,* and participants in the main conference had been invited to contribute to it. As Grace, Hill, and Wells reflect on this attempt to disenfranchise Queers at AERC, they speak to the importance of public art in the political and pedagogical task of building Queer knowledge. Each co-author provides a critical reflection on what transpired from the politics of his location in the conference. Collectively, the co-authors address the issue of Queer dismissal and defilement; the consequences when private morals are allowed to displace public ethics; the implications for critical Queer research and possibilities for transformative social learning in the face of exclusion; and the issues of spatiality, place, and the politics of Queer geography at AERC. The co-authors' collective reflections conclude with a perspective on the importance of public art as a political and pedagogical tool in fighting oppression.

In Chapter 4, "Lesbian, Gay, Bisexual, and Transgender Campus Climate Assessments: Current Trends and Future Considerations," Needham Yancey Gulley explores a relatively recent development: research on the impact of college campus climate on the everyday realities and safety of LGBT students. He uses the climate survey as a research medium to assess the reality for the broad and encompassing LGBT community on college campuses at a time when many students are coming out and coming to terms with their sexuality. Gulley begins with a historical conspectus of college campus climate surveys before speaking to the contemporary status of these surveys and how they might be better framed and utilized to build knowledge to inform inclusive institutional changes in the future. His work provides insights into the contemporary realities of LGBT college students in their search for respect and accommodation in the places where they have come to learn, to live, and to recreate.

In Chapter 5, Ann Brooks, Dawn Robarts, and Ronnie Lozano address a key question encompassed in their title: "LGBTQ Allies on Campus: Do They Have a Role?" These co-authors explore the role, place, and activities of LGBTQ campus allies in relation to matters of personal identity, professional group identity, experience as a minority, and family role models. In noting the need to delineate the ill-defined ally role now that allies programs are becoming more commonplace, the co-authors call for more studies of the positionalities of allies in terms of their motivations, cultural locations, commitments, enabling characteristics, and interpersonal dynamics. In addition to stressing the need to examine these research participant scripts, Brooks, Robarts, and Lozano also call for studies that examine how allies enact their roles as they build alliances and advocate for LGBTQ students on campus.

In Chapter 6, "Where Is Our Citizenship in Academia? Experiences of Gay Men of Color in Higher Education," Mitsunori Misawa examines the influences of two socially significant factors—race and sexual orientation—on the college experiences of students who identify as gay men of color. Misawa's aims are to better understand what experiences gay male students of color have had and how these experiences have influenced their campus life. He examines these factors within a larger focus on academic citizenship and possibilities for its formation in the intersection of race and sexual orientation. In doing so, Misawa addresses how important it is for higher education institutions to create and provide space for Queer students of color, space that could enhance the confidence of students and help them obtain full academic citizenship. To provide insights in this regard, he explores how sexual orientation and race emerge, develop, and intersect in a certain college environment; how the two identities influence the campus lives of gay male students of color; and how their sociocultural identities impact the larger learning environment. In the end, the author hopes to advance discussions on creating "Queer-Race Spaces" that attend to race and sexual orientation as complements so gay people of color may find space and place in their pursuit of higher education.

Chapter 7 is entitled "Successfully Queering the Business Curriculum: A Proposed Agenda for Process as Well as Content." In this chapter Julie Gedro provides an agenda for interrupting the heterosexist assumptions that permeate the higher education curriculum, particularly the assumptions that are operationalized and reinforced through both deliberate and unintentional neglect in the business school curriculum. Here Gedro draws on autoethnography as a business professor and director of a management education program at a public liberal arts college. From personal and professional perspectives, she explores the complexities that continue to exist in relation to coming out in academic and business cultures. Gedro explores what is necessary to revitalize teaching management education courses; she also speaks to using textbooks and curricula that counter heteronormativity. Gedro discusses how she crafts successful strategies and interventions designed to challenge heterosexist assumptions in higher education. In doing so, she takes up the urgent call to Queer the business curriculum to defy the ubiquitous and systemic oppression of LGBT people in society as well as in the microsociety of the corporate environment.

Chapter 8 is called "Crossroads for Creating My Space in the Workforce: Transformative Learning Helps Understand LGBTQ Sexual Identity Development Among Adults." In this chapter Kathleen P. King presents her LGBTQ transformative learning (TL) model, which she argues can be used effectively to understand the many crossroads that LGBTQ adults face as they attempt to create authentic space in the workforce. She elucidates how she developed her LGBTQ TL model with reference to transformative learning theory and Wishik and Pierce's (1991) model called the Sexual Orientation and Identity Continuum Diagram. King considers how her model provides a valuable perspective for LGBTQ adult learners as she describes its incorporation of coping strategies so these adults can frame their varied journeys of sexual identity development. King notes major benefits of the model, including its ability to confirm the dynamic and continuing characteristics of adult sexual identity development among LGBTQ people. As well, she relates that using the model as a tool to explore context and conflict helps LGBTQ adults witness commonalities of experience and eliminate the stark isolation that many of them experience. King also relates that the model aids the heterosexual workforce in developing an understanding that LGBTQ adults, as a non-mainstream constituency, must navigate difficult and risky decisions made in the workplace. King concludes that her model and related instructional strategies emphasize a framework that is critically reflective and potentially transformative when it is used to build understanding of self, colleagues, sexual identities, and socialities.

In Chapter 9, "LGBT Lessons from Midlife: An Unpicked Harvest," Thomas V. Bettinger highlights the contemporary need for research on sexual minorities at midlife. Bettinger positions this group as one that has witnessed and experienced massive societal shifts in relation to LGBTQ visibility, media representations, and progress toward civil rights. He also locates this group as one whose coming-out processes were, for the most part, void of engagements with Queer history, a Queer socialization process, or a supportive Queer culture. As Bettinger relates, sexual minorities at midlife have stories to tell, scars to show, and lessons to share. In this regard, he asks a troubling question: Is anybody listening? Bettinger uses his research both as an opportunity for intergenerational sharing with younger members of the LGBT community and as a chance to educate the larger society. He turns to adult education as a field of study and practice to provide context and a framework to guide his study. In doing so, he speaks to the importance of critiquing the heteronormative nature of adult educational research.

Chapter 10 is called "Sobears: Gay Bears, Sobriety, and Community." In this chapter, John P. Egan reminds us of the complex stratification and diversity within Queer communities when he researches the place and needs of "sobears," whom he describes as furry and full-bodied gay males pursuing sobriety from alcohol. In investigating their positionalities and their ways of mediating their lives, Egan describes how sobears turn to "cybearspace" to find a safe space that is free from the temptations of gay bars and the pervasive risks associated with going to homophobic straight bars. In his research, Egan speaks to how online bear culture has evolved and how sobears have turned to cyberspace to find and experience community. In particular, Egan considers how sobriety impacts the degree to which sobears feel part of the larger bear culture and community as well as the degree to which sobears seek solace and safety in online communities. He provides us with new insights into Queer geography as he explores how many sobears are supplanting the traditional gay-bar scene with "cybear" journeys that offer entrance to new and more comfortable communal spaces as well as new adult learning possibilities.

Chapter 11 by Robert J. Hill and Debra Davis is entitled "Transsexuality: Challenging the Institutionalized Sex/Gender Binary." It is a unique work in that the primary author is a gay adult educator who conducted a research study on learning to transition with male-to-female transsexuals. As an outsider to this community, issues of etic and emic accounts arise since Hill as researcher can only be an observer. In order to grasp the meanings of learning to transition, he invited a transgendered woman educator to comment on his research. The result is a sojourn into two particular phenomena: adult learning and education in the male-to-female (MTF) transsexual community as a social movement and the ways that some MTF transsexuals construct a form of feminism, called transfeminism, in their struggle to define the boundaries of what it means to be a "woman." The chapter challenges the reader to explore the sedimented male/female binary (whether gay or straight) and to open the possibilities that there are as many ways of being gendered as there are ways of being human.

In Chapter 12, called "When the Down-Low Becomes the New High: Integrating Queer Politics and Pedagogies Through Critical Community Education in Kosovo," Robert Mizzi explores his own role as an outsider educator involved in peace education and community health education. As the chapter unfolds, he develops an international perspective on issues of community/communities education, creating linkages among mutual respect, understanding, conciliation, and camaraderie. Mizzi engages the notion of community/communities education to reflect the fact that adult learners crisscross diverse communities and may hold membership in more than one of them. He argues that community/communities education can: acknowledge variously positioned Queer people within actions focused on connection, care, and making contributions; challenge heteronormative, sexist, racist, or able-bodied assumptions; and nurture Queer existence so that Queer citizens can openly claim their citizenship and human rights. In this exploration, Mizzi considers how community/communities education could offer pluralistic refuge and encourage learners to speak from their multiple subjectivities and positionalities.

In Chapter 13, "Posi+ive Prevention for Gay Men: Dismounting Missionary Positions," Francisco Ibáñez-Carrasco and Peter Hall speak to how Posi+ive Prevention needs to walk the talk. In this regard, they elaborate the concept and practice of Posi+ive Prevention, which has been the primary task for over five years in their work to inform and enhance everyday Posi+ive Prevention as praxis. For Ibáñez-Carrasco and Hall, their professional experiences interweave with their life experiences—they are contemporaries in age; one is HIV positive and the other is HIV negative. In this chapter, these co-authors juxtapose and integrate expertise and experience as they bring forward some necessary concepts and practices in this new approach to tackling HIV. Focusing primarily on Posi+ive Prevention in the lives of Canadian gay men, they query what comprises a strong gay men's health movement in the face of the ubiquitousness of HIV. In this regard, they ask a key ethical question to guide our thinking and analysis: Where lies the agency of gay men in their sexual health today? In answering this question, Ibáñez-Carrasco and Hall engage in analysis of impinging individual and sociocultural contexts. In their analysis, they take up issues of language and power in HIV discourse, and they discuss the social aspects of Posi+ive Prevention. Ibáñez-Carrasco and Hall conclude by discussing the educational dimension of their work, which is integral to building community dialogue and enlightenment.

In Chapter 14, "Just City Life: Creating a Safe Space for the GLBTQ Community in Urban Adult Education," Tonette S. Rocco, Hillary Landorf, and Suzanne J. Gallagher begin by speaking about the demographic reality of a higher concentration of sexual minorities in urban areas, with the anonymity and complexity that density and diversity of the urban population bring. The co-authors relate that urban environments are attractive to GLBTQ people as safe spaces to be anonymous, to facilitate identity development, to find other people like themselves, and to have a sense of belonging. They also relate that GLBTQ people experience urban areas as places of contradiction, where greater opportunities to be welcomed, enter desired careers, and be politically involved, for example, exist alongside oppression that includes symbolic and physical violence, discrimination, and marginalization. From these perspectives, Rocco, Landorf, and Gallagher juxtapose exploration of urban opportunities and oppressive forces using the four normative virtues of just city life, as proposed by Iris Young (1990): 1) social differentiation without exclusion, 2) variety, 3) eroticism, and 4) publicity or open and accepting public places. The co-authors present the virtues in the context of GLBTQ urban space, leading to a critique of the ideal of community. Rocco, Landorf, and Gallagher end by suggesting Young's vision of a just city life provides a means of creating a greater sense of identity, belonging, and justice for GLBTQ people in urban centers and urban adult education.

Finally, in Chapter 15, "No End to History: Demanding Civil Quarter for Sexual Minorities in Heteronormative Space," André P. Grace and Robert J. Hill consider the importance of the historiography of homosexual/lesbian and gay/ Queer lives in an effort to highlight the importance of history for building understanding of the state and status of sexual-minority lives today. The co-authors also incorporate a conspectus of the emergence of queer theory and then critique queer theory for dislocating gay history as this new political and cultural theory developed new language, new politics, and new understandings of Queer cultural literacy. To speak to the importance of studying history in relation to advocating for sexual minorities in contemporary times, Grace and Hill explore the more recent history of Queer invisibility and exclusion at CONFINTEA V, the fifth international adult education conference held in Hamburg, Germany, in 1997. They use this example as a vivid reminder that there is still history to be made to include sexual minorities within the social, cultural, political, and economic contexts shaping full citizenship. In concluding their chapter, Grace and Hill turn to a pivotal interview with Cornel West, published in the first issue devoted to lesbian and gay/Queer studies in the *Harvard Educational Review* in 1996, to consider what might be done to make queer-inclusive history a reflection of creating place for sexual minorities in the years ahead.

References

Freire, P. (2004). *Pedagogy of indignation.* Boulder, CO: Paradigm Publishers.

Grace, A. P., & Wells, K. (2007). Using Freirean pedagogy of just ire to inform critical social learning in arts-informed community education for sexual minorities. *Adult Education Quarterly, 57*(2), 95-114.

Jacobs, S.-E. (1997). Is the "North American Berdache" merely a phantom in the imagination of Western social sciences? In S.-E. Jacobs, W. Thomas, & S. Lang (Eds.), *Two-Spirit people: Native American gender identity, sexuality, and spirituality* (pp. 21-43). Chicago: University of Illinois Press.

Lang, S. (1998). *Men as women, women as men: Changing gender in Native American culture.* (J. Vantine, Trans.). Austin, TX: University of Texas Press. (Originally published as *Männer als Frauen, Frauen als Männer*)

Waller, M. A., & McAllen-Walker, R. (2001). One man's story of being gay and Diné (Navajo): A study in resiliency. In M. Bernstein & R. Reiman (Eds.), *Queer families, queer politics: Challenging culture and the state* (pp. 87-103). NY: Columbia University Press.

Wishik, H., & Pierce, C. (1991). *Sexual orientation and identity: Heterosexual, lesbian, gay, and bisexual journeys.* Laconia, NH: New Dynamics.

Young, I. M. (1990). *Justice and the politics of difference.* Princeton, NJ: Princeton University Press.

SECTION I:
GENERAL QUEER DISCOURSE

CHAPTER 1

Positioning Queer in Adult Education: Intervening in Politics and Praxis in North America

André P. Grace

Robert J. Hill

Queer discourse now permeates social consciousness. The discursive formation of "Queer" has complex roots, and while it only infrequently appears in adult education, Queer is expressed in multiple ways in culture and society. It is employed as an umbrella term for the indeterminate array of identities and differences that characterize persons in relation to sex, sexuality, gender, desire, and expression. As a pervious concept, Queer disturbs essentialized notions of male and female, heterosexual and homosexual, masculine and feminine, and lesbian and gay. Queer is about redeploying, twisting, and challenging these notions as stable, intact, and unitary categories (Butler, 1993; Gamson, 2000; Sedgwick, 1990), which, as we will explore in this paper, has implications for adult education. In order to engage these notions as discursive formations, we employ the constructions "w/e" and "u/s" to symbolize the notion of a diverse and, at best, loosely configured spectral community of Queer Others (Grace, 2001c). There is not a unitary we or us that adult educators can talk about. Thus w/e and u/s symbolize that LGBTQ (lesbian, gay, bisexual, trans [transgender and transsexual], and Queer) persons have different histories, identities, and needs as well as different ways of being, believing, desiring, becoming, belonging, and acting—ways that constitute Queerness—that not only set u/s apart from heterosexuals but

Previously published as Grace, A. P., & Hill, R. J. (2004). Positioning Queer in adult education: Intervening in politics and praxis in North America. Studies in the Education of Adults, 36(2), 167-189. Reprinted with permission of the publisher.

also from one another. The sociocultural and political threads that connect the w/e (or u/s) for purposes of resistance in particular times and spaces are aimed at achieving the rights and privileges of full citizenship, which translates as recognition, respect, access, and accommodation across sociocultural sites, including adult education.

Our Queer sociocultural and political project in education for adults aims to expand contemporary parameters and possibilities for inclusive and transformative adult education. For u/s, this means building adult education as a lived and knowable community that involves deliberate and deliberative engagements with Queer—a term representing our spectral community that incorporates a diversity of sex, sexual, and gender differences—and Queerness—our ways of being, believing, desiring, becoming, belonging, and acting in life-and-learning spaces (Grace, 2001c).

These engagements help construct Queer knowledge that informs inclusive Queer praxis as a practical, expressive, and reflective encounter with sex, sexual, and gender differences historically considered taboo terrain and relegated to fugitive spaces. This "education of adults which is analytical and dialectic leads inevitably to a liberation from taboos. … [It is] real adult education, [which] is far more radical than training guerrillas" (Ivan Illich, as quoted in Ohliger, 1971, p. 2). When w/e connect it to the Queer lifeworld, w/e can "smile the social system … and violence apart" as w/e interrogate formative aspects of culture, language, identity, and difference at the intersection where secrets, silences, misinformation, and mystification impede the way of truth and life (Ohliger, p. 6).

In this essay, w/e examine the formation and comprehension of Queer knowledge in adult education and in larger sociocultural contexts, and w/e use Queer knowledge to inform an inclusive Queer praxis where we reflect and express Queerness. First, w/e deploy Queer knowledge as a composite of sociocultural and political activities for social transformation. Proceeding from a conspectus constructing adult education as social education, w/e consider the *social* in North American academic adult education, investigating the degree to which this field of study has been inclusive across relationships of power. W/e focus particularly on the degree to which this located form of academic adult education has recognized, respected, and fostered presence and place for Queer persons. Then w/e highlight moments of resistance and visibility intended to build Queer knowledge and transform this field of study by affirming Queer integrity and acknowledging and accommodating Queer expression.

Second, w/e address the need to position Queer in adult education, mindful of how Queer is historically and currently positioned in larger sociocultural contexts. This involves articulating Queer and Queerness, which w/e cast as both an intellectual and practical project with epistemological, political, and strategic purposes aimed at inclusive praxis. To help u/s build a Queer knowledge base, w/e turn to Queer history and Queer studies to investigate ways of knowing Queer and Queerness. W/e locate this fugitive knowledge as integral and informative to our project to transgress the social and reconstitute the cultural. In this light, w/e take up the politics of building community from Queer perspectives and w/e discuss how this knowledge can inform tactical and transformative adult educational practices.

Third, using Queer knowledge as an antecedent to Queer praxis, w/e focus on Queer praxis as a site of transformative learning. As w/e deliberate, w/e assert that Queer knowledge and interventions inform the practical and political questions that adult educators need to ask as they interrogate exclusionary forms of adult education and revise praxis. W/e conclude by situating inclusive Queer praxis as a transgressive and transformative practice-expression-reflection dynamic that opens an in-between learning space of immense possibility in culture and society.

Deploying Queer Knowledge in Adult Education as a Political Activity for Social Transformation

Adult Education as Social Education: Moments from the First Fifty Years of Modern Practice

The thread that links learning to social justice has a long and venerable history in the discipline of education, including adult education. Starting with John Dewey and the progressives of the 1920s, the goals of education have been couched in social terms. In adult education, Eduard Lindeman focused on the field of practice as the most reliable instrument for social action, and he wrote that all successful adult education groups eventually become social action collectives (Brookfield, 1987; Lindeman, 1926/1961). The 1919 Report of the Adult Education Committee of the British Ministry of Reconstruction, which is symbolically taken to herald the era of the modern practice of adult education, promoted adult education as "an inseparable aspect of citizenship" (Knowles & Klevins, 1972, p.

7). It located social education for adults within a "vision of adult education as 'the way out' from … ineffectual democracy" (Cotton, 1968, p. 2). In the foreword to the 1948 *Handbook of Adult Education*, Alain Locke, who was instated as the first Black president of the American Association for Adult Education in 1945-1946 (Stubblefield & Keane, 1994), cautioned adult educators not "to forget the social aim of adult education" in the rush to individualism and corporatism (Knowles & DuBois, 1970, p. xxi).

While some adult educators may be aware of Locke's national role as a Black social educator in the United States, perhaps few would be aware that Locke likely made his most significant contribution to social and cultural education as a gay man and integral cultural worker during the Harlem Renaissance. That cultural renaissance was a pivotal historical moment that intersected the histories of Black segregation and Queer disenfranchisement in the United States. Garber (1989) writes that Locke made significant contributions to Black culture and gay life during the Harlem Renaissance period (circa 1920-1935). Within that period, "the blues reflected a culture that accepted sexuality, including homosexual behavior and identities, as a natural part of life" (p. 320). In general, the Harlem Renaissance provided an informal and communal public pedagogical Queer space for a coterie of musicians, artists, writers, and intellectuals. This coterie included homosexuals and bisexuals in its array of sexual nonconformists. In a revealing description of Locke's efforts to enable the Harlem Renaissance, Garber recounts:

> *A small, dapper, fair-skinned professor from Howard University, [Alain] Locke edited the important 1926 anthology, The New Negro, which focussed international attention on Harlem's emerging cultural renaissance. He channeled white patronage to Afro-American artists and provided essential intellectual and critical support. His influence was immense, but his young charges often found there were strings attached to his assistance. Locke was homosexual and was known to aggressively pursue his favorites. (p. 327)*

Thus Locke's impact on the Harlem Renaissance was immeasurable. However, it would appear that his involvement was not always altruistic.

As modern practice continued to emerge, other adult educators promoted social and cultural education focused on inclusion, justice, and democracy. For example, during the social upheaval marking the 1960s, Paul Bergevin (1967) perceived adult education as fostering democratic ideals. Robert J. Blakely (1967) asserted that adult education assists adaptation and leads the individual to a better, more fulfilling personal life while making the world a better place to live.

As social educators, they reminded field colleagues that the field of study and practice has a historical mission: to work for forgotten citizens in contesting their lives of exclusion and dispossession and fighting the difficult battle to "even get to a tributary of the mainstream of American life" (Rauch, 1972, p. 9).

+ ·· ᴤ·ᴦ ·· +

Replicating Heteronormativity: The Struggle for Inclusion in North American Academic Adult Education

Queer persons and citizens are still immersed in the difficult battle for mainstream presence and place. Thus, in contemporary adult education, a focus on the social has to be expanded to give space and place to a *Queer social*. This requires that the field of study and practice revise its predominant focus on heteronormative society, which, with its structures and strictures, constitutes what Corrigan (1990) calls "a certain kind of 'The Social.'" He explains how the dominant social works against difference:

> *"Society" (as a working fiction) is held together by coercive encouragements (aka values) through Social Forms which provide a set of proper, appropriate, approved expressive behaviours. But this holding is a co-ordinated set of regulating activities, a form of constructing, and sustains a certain kind of "The Social" through legitimated authorities whose repertoire extends through mundane routines, technical procedures, and magnificent rituals. (p. 219)*

While Corrigan believes that dominant social forms—variously constructed as sites that subordinate, exploit, and oppress—function to control behavior, he also believes that they cannot totally regulate an individual or group within dominant politics or discourse. In other words, "people have cognitive, affective, and, above all, somatic senses, perspectives, longings, hopes, desires, which cannot be fitted into the ways they are coercively encouraged to behave. It really is as simple and as complex as that!" (p. 219). It is this belief that undergirds a politics of resistance, and it helps explain why Queer individuals, negotiating the dominant society as a working fiction for u/s, resist heteronormativity as a certain kind of "The Social" that has historically ignored or dismissed Queerness. It also helps to explain why Queer persons have fought back in strategic ways in diverse heteronormative social spaces and heterosexualizing cultural spaces that deny u/s presence and place.

North American academic adult education is one such space. With its entrenched tendency to replicate heteronormativity, fighting back has proven an arduous task requiring the courage and persistence of Queer adult educators and graduate students. Our struggle, however, has not been solitary or isolated. It has been part of a larger struggle for inclusion by various disenfranchised groups, which is exemplified, for example, by the efforts of Vanessa Sheared and Peggy A. Sissel (2001) to get their groundbreaking edited volume—*Making Spaces: Merging Theory and Practice in Adult Education*—published. In the foreword to *Making Spaces,* social educator and activist Phyllis M. Cunningham describes the struggle to publish the text as a poignant moment in the emergence of North American academic adult education as a field of study. She relates that the book had been preceded a decade earlier by another, entitled *Adult Education: Evolution and Achievements in a Developing Field of Study* (Peters, Jarvis, & Associates, 1991). The U.S. Commission of Professors of Adult Education (CPAE) and its parent group, the American Association for Adult and Continuing Education (AAACE), had envisioned *Adult Education* as a new "black book" that would describe the emergence of graduate adult education since the publication of the first black book— *Adult Education: Outlines of an Emerging Field of Study*—edited by G. Jensen, A. A. Liveright, and W. Hallenbeck in 1964 (Cunningham, 2001). Specifically, the book by Peters, Jarvis, and Associates was intended to provide a status report on the accomplishments, parameters, and possibilities of adult education as a field of study. However, as Cunningham recounts, the new black book provoked intensely felt and strongly voiced reactions among many academic adult educators. Supporters and detractors alike began calling the edited compilation the "black-and-blue" book. While *heterosexist* was not specifically included in the list of adjectives describing omissions, the book was widely critiqued as "Eurocentric, racist, gender insensitive, elitist, and exclusionary" at the 33rd annual Adult Education Research Conference (AERC) held in Saskatoon, Saskatchewan, Canada, in May 1992 (Sissel & Sheared, 2001, p. xi). A resolution at the conference's business meeting summed up the general sentiments of discontent:

The 1991 Black Book, endorsed by the [U.S.] Commission of Professors of Adult Education, claims to represent the whole field of adult education. However, it is a book that reproduces the status quo and silences the voices that would challenge that perspective. These silent voices represent the future of the field. (Quoted in Sissel & Sheared, 2001, p. xii)

In passing the resolution, AERC participants requested that the Publications Standing Service Unit of the AAACE consult with the leadership of the Feminist Caucus of the AERC to publish a new, inclusionary book that would represent the voices, knowledge bases, realities, interests, visions, commitments, and diversity of all members of the field of study and practice.

However, the road to publication of *Making Spaces* was initially rocky and twisted. Sissel and Sheared (2001) relate:

> *Despite being sanctioned by the various oversight committees, when it was turned over to the paid AAACE staff that would oversee the production, they clearly expressed their disapproval of the book, labeling it as unimportant and uninteresting. In fact they openly derided it for including the voices of gays and lesbians. … Subsequent to this, we also discovered apparent attempts to block its full consideration by appropriate publishers. Thus, in the spring of 1996, and with the assistance of the CPAE board, we disengaged the project from the auspices of AAACE. (p. 8)*

Following the "process of review, approval, and then disapproval" (Sissel & Sheared, 2001, p. 8), which amounted to exercises in gatekeeping and censorship, Sheared and Sissel decided to proceed independently with work on the book. The result is *Making Spaces,* which they offer as a "dialogue and critique of our social, political, economic, and historical forms of hegemony operating in the field [of adult education]" that limit "the participation of some people because of their language, sexual orientation, race, [ethnicity,] gender, and class" (p. 3). As a testament to Sheared and Sissel's determination to help build a field of study and practice in adult education that is truly about inclusion and transformation across identities and differences, their milestone book includes Grace's (2001c) chapter, "Using Queer Cultural Studies to Transgress Adult Educational Space." This chapter takes readers beyond familiar ways of knowing, seeing, thinking, and acting to explore Queer cultural studies as a countercultural and sociopolitical way of reading what Freire (1998) calls "the word and the world." It also explores possibilities for positional adult learning outside the heteronormative box.

Apart from the struggle for inclusion in adult education represented by the difficulties in publishing *Making Spaces,* the AERC itself has been a sometimes exclusionary site epitomizing the struggle for space and place in our field. Regarding the Queer struggle for inclusion, a review of printed annual AERC conference proceedings and an examination of ephemera such as brochures and letters from past organizers indicate that until 1993 no adult education researchers presenting at AERC had addressed lesbian, gay, bisexual, trans, and Queer (LG-BTQ) topics, issues, or interests (Hill, 2003). This suggests that LGBTQ adults, as a spectral community representing diverse sex, sexual, and gender differences, were either an unknown entity to adult education researchers or a group they chose to ignore in their work in adult education.

However, this no-quarter scenario has changed significantly during the last decade. Three moments have been situated as pivotal periods of resistance and visibility that now define Queer vision and voice in the history of the AERC (Hill, 2003). The first moment was the formation of the Lesbian, Gay, Bisexual, Transgender, Queer, and Allies Caucus (LGBTQ&AC) at the 34th AERC held at the Pennsylvania State University (PSU), State College, in 1993. During that conference Robert J. Hill, then a PSU graduate student, spoke to AERC participants at the business meeting and announced the formation of a caucus for LGBTQ persons. The announcement was greeted by a mixture of comments, mostly receptive, but some critical of the initiative. Those with reservations made various remarks to Hill (2003, pp. 16-17): "The time isn't just right yet for this sort of thing!" "We need time to accept your ideas!" And in a year when President William Jefferson Clinton was still advocating a kind of open policy for lesbians and gays in the U.S. armed forces, Hill was told, "Slow down, you're moving too hard, too fast—like Clinton and the military!" These statements against social usefulness that suggest the time wasn't right or the people weren't ready have common elements of neutralization, denial, and avoidance expressed in previous civil rights struggles (Paul, 1982). Such struggles continue in spite of such comments. In this case the AERC LGBTQ&AC was formed, albeit in a humble way, when three conference attendees came to a 7:00 a.m. meeting the next morning.

In the years since, the caucus has made a deliberative space available to those who wish to reflect critically on LGBTQ identities and differences and the politics and processes in adult education and the larger culture and society that impact them. To support its work and communicative capacity, the LGBTQ&AC launched its AERCQueerSpace website in 2001 during the 42nd annual AERC at Michigan State University. The site (http://www.arches.uga.edu/~bobhill/AERC-QUEERSPACE), which is hosted by the University of Georgia, includes an extensive bibliography of references on Queer topics in education, with an emphasis on adult education.

The second moment of resistance and visibility was the inaugural LGBTQ&AC Pre-Conference exploring fugitive forms of social knowledge, which was held at the 44th annual AERC in San Francisco in 2003. The caucus promoted this milestone event as a time for a resilient, persistent, growing, and dedicated group of LGBTQ and allied educators and learners to celebrate its tenth anniversary as a visible and vocal contingent at AERC. The pre-conference provided a dialogical space to explore what counts as knowledge and what knowledge counts in adult education. Participants interrogated notions such as family, community, citizenship, democracy, and adult learning, exploring LGBTQ conceptualizations and perspectives that alter the meanings and parameters constituting such categories. Now the LGBTQ&AC is looking forward to the next ten years with cautious optimism, anticipating the challenges, barriers, and possibilities that lie ahead.

The third moment of resistance and visibility is an ongoing one that began when Robert J. Hill presented the first LGBTQ-themed paper—"Heterosexist Discourse in Adult Education: A Gay/Lesbian Critique"—at the 35th annual AERC held at the University of Tennessee, Knoxville, in 1994. In subsequent years, a growing number of LGBTQ-focused presentations have been part of the main program at AERC conferences (Hill, 2003). This list includes the symposium, *Tabooed Terrain: Reflections on Conducting Adult Education Research in Lesbian/Gay/Queer Arenas*, held at the 39th annual AERC in San Antonio (Edwards, Grace, Henson, Henson, Hill, & Taylor, 1998).

Collectively, these events have functioned to "catalyze hopes and aspirations of some AERC members, as well as to provoke a mild backlash" (Hill, 2003, p. 13). For the most part, the backlash has taken the form of subtle policing of AERC borders by certain resistant individuals. It is not illustrative of the majority of experiences where w/e have been affirmed, enabled, and supported by AERC organizers and participants. However, such policing when it occurs cannot be ignored, for it represents a shunning of LGBTQ participants by some at the AERC and an attempt to impede attendance at the LGBTQ&AC. As Hill (2003) relates, exclusion (or attempted exclusion) at different AERCs over the years has included:

- misnaming the LGBTQ&AC the "Social Action Caucus" in an AERC listing.

- omitting the LGBTQ&AC in the introduction of caucus groups during the opening plenary session of an AERC.

- scheduling our caucus meeting in a different building a 15-minute walk from the main conference site—the only caucus to be assigned a location outside the complex of buildings where all other AERC events occurred.

- scheduling our caucus against a presentation by a major figure in the field in order to keep, as a member of the host institution put it, the LGBTQ&AC from "standing out too much" (Hill, 2003, p. 17).

- "losing" our caucus brochures, resulting in their absence in AERC registration packets. (Following a vocal exchange, they were at last "discovered" in a cabinet and finally inserted.)

These incidents speak to the still-haunting perceptions of LGBTQ as taboo terrain and subversive power for some AERC organizers and participants. Moreover, they indicate that issues of access, accommodation, and community building are still concerns in our field despite a history of focusing on the social and the cultural. In a Tolley Lecture at Syracuse University on October 8, 1973, J. Roby Kidd, emphasizing the field's social purpose, spoke to the theme "learning to be, learning to become, learning to belong" (p. 4). In developing this theme, he expressed his concerns for *relentless verity* and the *whole* adult learner who functions fully as a participant in the adult education community. While his theme celebrated and affirmed the importance of building community, Kidd was still uncertain about what constituted adult education as a participatory learning community. More than three decades later, the notion of an inclusive learning community is still much deliberated at AERC. And while the LGBTQ&AC and other disenfranchised groups struggle for space and place at AERC, an inclusive learning community as a lived and knowable community will remain a fiction, a verity in waiting, a notion yet to be lived out.

The right and the freedom of the LGBTQ&AC to be public in terms of recognition, respect, access, and accommodation at AERC is embodied and embedded in Kidd's notion of inclusive community. However, a visible and vocal LGBTQ presence is challenging, even threatening, to some AERC participants because Queer life in critical public space not only interjects transgressive subject matter into contemporary social discourse, but it also intervenes in the knowledge-culture-language-power nexus to disrupt dominant power. From this perspective, Queer insurgency as a presence and praxis makes learning a part of the process of social change itself. The Queer movement has shifting, multiple, and overlapping sites in adult education (Hill, 1995, 1996). Most often they are constituted as sites of nonformal learning (for example, workshops on topics like the "coming-out" process or gay marriage offered through LGBTQ community centers) and informal learning (for example, everyday learning that happens in Queer bars, bookstores, and other public locations). These sites contextualize everyday life, contest hetero-hegemony, resist readings that exclude or defame Queer persons, allow the development of oppositional practices, and make possible the embrace of commitment to social change in an environment of hope and possibility. Furthermore, they confront silence and marginalization as well as exclusionary heteronormative structures, institutions, and texts in an effort to create a just society, equitable communities, and ethical accountability.

Ethnographic analyses, similar to the one w/e did for AERC, should be undertaken for national associations such as the American Association for Adult and Continuing Education (AAACE), the Canadian Association for the Study of Adult Education (CASAE), the National Institute of Adult Continuing Education (NIACE), and the Academy of Human Resource Development (AHRD) and for adult education journals such as the *Adult Education Quarterly* (*AEQ*), the *Canadian Journal for the Study of Adult Education (CJSAE)*, the *International Journal of Lifelong Education (IJLE)*, and *Studies in the Education of Adults (SEA)*.

Toward this end, with respect to CASAE, a review of proceedings from 1995 to 2003—there was no CASAE proceedings in 2000 when the association participated in an international AERC in Vancouver, Canada—indicates that there are no papers explicitly focused on LGBTQ issues prior to Grace's (2001a) paper, "Being, Becoming, and Belonging as a Queer Citizen Educator." In 2003, Grace's paper on Queer citizenship and Wells's paper on informal learning for Queer young adults complete the very short list of LGBTQ-themed CASAE papers over this nine-year period. Occasionally, Queer is a sub-theme in conference papers, such as Egan's (2001) paper on grassroots program planning. Interestingly, these papers are all written by gay academics and graduate students. To the CASAE's credit, John Egan received the inaugural CASAE Graduate Student Award in 2002, and another "out" gay graduate student, Kristopher Wells, received that award in 2003. However, w/e are waiting for more history to be made with the inclusion of a paper by a heterosexual ally engaged in Queer research. Such a moment will be important in further transgressing the comfort zone created by the hegemonic pervasiveness of heteronormativity at CASAE.

Regarding *AEQ*, Taylor (2001) conducted a content analysis of its pages for the decade 1989-1999. However, gender and diversity are lumped into a solitary category, and thus sexual orientation and gender identity are submerged. Our thorough re-analysis shows that no articles related to LGBTQ topics were published prior to 1995. The notion that sexual orientation iswas of interest or significance to adult education is not mentioned prior to articles in the early 1990s, where it sometimes appears in a list of subjugated subjectivities such as race, gender, and ethnicity. The identity marker "gay" appears in a few articles on AIDS, which, depending on how it is handled, can be a problematic association re-inscribing the misnomer that AIDS is a "gay disease" (e.g., Baumgartner, 2002; Boshier, 1992).

Correspondingly, Edwards (2001) determined that Hill's (1996) article on the gay lifeworld was the first Queer-themed article to appear in *Studies in the Education of Adults*. Speaking to the journal's record on engaging diversity, *SEA's* longtime former editor acknowledges that new forms of knowledge have been extended and appropriated over the years to embrace the interests of women, minorities, ethnic groups, and gay and lesbian communities. In general though, the history of the Queer quest for visibility and voice in *AEQ* and *SEA* is opaque. Given the growing pervasiveness of LGBTQ discourses in society and in some arenas of the academy, Queer's late arrival to adult education surely has a fascinating history yet to be narrated.

In performing this sociocultural and political work, it is the task of educators to look awry (Žižek, 1991). W/e argue that it is also the task of learners; Queer persons/learners offer a model for this aslant interrogation. Queer knowledge can help to build Queer praxis that peers sideways and raises questions about how adult education is embedded in/in bed with the colonizer. It disrupts the powerful and lethal heteronormative systems that communicate and educate to relegate sex, sexual, and gender outlaws to positions as outsiders. Deploying Queer knowledge in order to peer sideways permits radical inclusiveness and opens space for political activities for personal and social transformation. This can lead to Queer strategic actions that have the capacity to empower the marginalized Queer community with outcomes consonant with those posited as goals and objectives of adult education for personal and social transformation. Constituting both oppositional discourses and practices, Queer knowledge can be used to build inclusionary praxis in adult education. Of course, Queer does not involve fixed essences or rigid truth claims. Rather, as w/e have emphasized, it is a concept with complex dimensions that can inform adult education in (re) new(ed) and vigorous ways.

Engaging Queer History and Queer Studies to Transgress Adult Educational Space

Articulating Queer and Queerness

Eve Kosofsky Sedgwick's *Epistemology of the Closet,* published in 1990, is usually referred to as the founding text of queer theory (Gamson, 2000). In this text and its follow-up, *Tendencies* (1993), Sedgwick explicates two hypotheses as a way to theorize her work on the transitivity of sex, sexual, and gender identities. She submits that modern figurative, commonsensical constructions of these identities, which situate lesbians or gay men either between genders (inversion models) or as discrete genders (gender-separatist models), are meaningless tropes that fail "to think about lesbian, gay, and other sexually dissident loves and identities in a complex social ecology where the presence of different genders, different identities and identifications, will be taken as a given" (Sedgwick, 1993, p. xiii). She proposes that the failure to use the homosexual/heterosexual definition as a cultural site that includes the array of subjectivities and agencies associated with differences in sex, sexuality, gender, desire, and expression reduces to inutility, incoherence, and prejudice a conventional definition that has been used to think about distinctly straight male and straight female as well as distinctly lesbian or gay individuals. From these perspectives, Sedgwick (1993) engages the word "queer" as a more encompassing term to name and describe sex, sexual, and gender differences in the multifarious intersections of identities, identifications, desires, differences, and representations that lie inside and outside a pervasive, conservative heterosexualizing discourse: "Queer is a continuing moment, movement, motive—recurrent, eddying, *troublant*. ... [It is] transitive—multiply transitive. The immemorial current that *queer* represents is antiseparatist as it is antiassimilationist. Keenly, it is relational, and strange" (Italics in original, p. xii).

Sedgwick (1993) goes on to describe how Queer can organize (or at least has the potential to organize) the array of differences in sex, sexuality, gender, desire, and expression that lie within or beyond the heterosexist assumption:

> *That's one of the things that "queer" can refer to: the open mesh of possibilities, gaps, overlaps, dissonances and resonances, lapses and excesses of meaning when the constituent elements of anyone's gender, of anyone's sexuality aren't made (or can't be made) to signify monolithically. (Italics in original, p. 8)*

Sedgwick describes how Queer can be expanded beyond sex, sexual, and gender differences to include, for example, "identity-constituting, identity-fracturing discourses" (p. 9) on race, ethnicity, and postcolonial nationality that, on the one hand, lie beyond discourses on gender and sexuality and, on the other hand, intersect with such discourses. From this perspective, "the leverage of 'queer' ... [does] a new kind of justice to fractal intricacies of language, skin, migration, [and] state" (p. 9). In this social ecology, Queer can represent an intersection of relationships of power in a knowledge-culture-language-power nexus. As w/e move within this nexus, w/e can begin to understand resistance to naming and speaking Queer by exploring how Queer as a construct intermeshes problematically with constructs of race, class, and other relationships of power that have their own histories of excluding Queer. This exclusion contained in patriarchy and White supremacy extends beyond them in forms that are inextricably linked to them. For example, in an African American context, heterosexism and homophobia (and sexism) can be constructed as consequences of the assault on Black masculinity that is embodied and embedded in the history of slavery and in the subsequent history of subjugation that accompanied purported emancipation (Dyson, 1993; Eisen & Kenyatta, 1996; hooks, 2001; West, 1993/1994).

Articulating Queer and Queerness within a complex social ecology that collapses the heterosexist assumption suggests a need for a contextual and relational positioning of Queer in adult education. Thus positioning Queer in our field as an embodiment of challenges, risks, hopes, and possibilities is part of a larger history and politics of positioning Queer in mainstream culture and society. Our transgressive adult educational project includes engagements with this extended positional picture in which w/e explore:

- Queer knowledge formations built in life-and-learning locations that constitute fugitive educative spaces outside the mainstream,

- Queer social and cultural formations that give substance and meaning to Queer and Queerness, and

- Queer civil rights initiatives and other sociocultural and political projects tied to our efforts to attain the rights and privileges of full citizenship.

W/e engage in this work to assist adult educators and learners who want to know about Queer and Queerness to problematize larger social and cultural formations, including heteronormative adult education, that have historically relegated Queer persons to a sociocultural and political hinterland where w/e are left to struggle with issues of being, self-preservation, expectation, becoming, resistance, and belonging. Addressing these issues is integral to articulating Queer and Queerness, which involves analysis and comprehension of the formations, problems, and projects situating these constructs. It is also integral to assessing the degree to which adult education is an inclusive educational project and a lived and knowable community. Adult educator and cultural worker Raymond Williams believed that to live and know community involved reducing the distance between culture as knowledge that abets the kinds of performativity and productivity serving the status quo and culture as community that values the experiential knowledge associated with everyday life and work, popular culture, class, and community relationships (Grace, 1997; Grossberg, 1997).

It is a key aim of our project to have Queer and Queerness as lived and knowable aspects of an inclusive adult education community. To do this, w/e take up articulating Queer and Queerness as both an intellectual and practical project aimed at inclusive praxis. Slack (1996) contends that, methodologically, articulation offers ways to contextualize constructs like Queer and Queerness in order to fulfill epistemological, political, and strategic purposes in a sociocultural study. In this light, epistemologically, w/e articulate Queer and Queerness as a way of organizing Queer knowledge as an interaction of similarities, differences, tensions, and contradictions that impact possibilities for community building. Politically, w/e engage in this articulation as a means to bring power and the dynamics shaping relations of domination and subordination to the forefront in our Queer sociocultural analysis. Strategically, w/e use this articulation to shape actions designed to intervene—that is, to insert Queer and Queerness—in a specific context, relationship of power, social or cultural formation, or set of circumstances. For u/s, working to fulfill these purposes locates articulation as a means to confront and challenge ways that culture as heteronormalized knowledge and culture as heterosexualizing community exclude Queer persons from a lived and knowable community in our field of study and practice.

Building Fugitive Knowledge:
The Queer Struggle in a U.S. Context

Historically, in heterosexualizing culture and discourse, heterosexism and homophobia have been sociopolitical expressions of a public pedagogy of negation, erasure, and violence that violates Queer identities and assaults Queer integrity (Grace & Benson, 2000). A key consequence of this pedagogy for Queer persons is living with the uncertainty associated with a life demeaned and devalued and with a Queer reality that w/e are taught should be hidden or at least kept underground. Tierney (1997) speaks to this uncertainty: "The widespread notion that heterosexuality is normal and that everything that is not heterosexual is somehow aberrant has placed Queers in a constant existential state of questioning ourselves, our identity, and how we should act" (p. 39). Nevertheless, w/e have had a history of variously and vigorously fighting back—of being and acting Queer—in the decades subsequent to the three-day Stonewall Rebellion in New York City in June 1969 (Fone, 2000). While an earlier unique and militant grassroots activism had merged a local gay liberation movement with the city's gay subculture in post-World War II San Francisco (D'Emilio, 1989), it is the New York event that is usually taken as the birth moment of a U.S. gay liberation movement that, as D'Emilio (1992) recounts, had a global impact.[3] Police, with a long record of harassing and violating Queer individuals as persons and citizens, provoked the rioting when they raided a gay bar, the Stonewall Inn. In fighting back, a contingent of Queer persons, tired of the constant oppression and abuse, began a civil rights movement that continues to make inroads into the present moment. In academe, Stonewall has been inspirational to researchers exploring sex, sexual, and gender differences. As Tierney and Dilley (1998) chronicle, these researchers began to challenge a dominant notion of normality in the 1970s. In contemporary Queer research, which asserts that normalcy is a product of the Othering of Queerness, the contemporary challenge is intensely expressed as a transgressive politics of interrogating normal that supplants an earlier (and now rebuked) gay politics of normality focused on notions of assimilation or integration (Cohen, 2001; Tierney & Dilley, 1998).

In the post-Stonewall era, w/e continue to build what Hill (1996) calls "fugitive knowledge" as an integral part of our political and cultural work to trouble normal. Fugitive knowledge incorporates ways of knowing that have escaped the control of those who authorize and make legitimate dominant heteronormative discourse. They include histories of Queer persons and Queerness as well as studies of Queer culture. Fugitive knowledge is used to give presence and place to Queer social and cultural formations and, concomitantly, to confront heteronormative social constructs and heterosexualizing cultural contexts. Produced and distributed, for example, by Queer social activists and cultural workers engaged in civil rights initiatives, fugitive knowledge informs queer theory. Dilley (1999) observes, "The members and actions of Queer Nation and ACT-UP [AIDS Coalition to Unleash Power] influenced the formation of Queer theory and instilled in it a charge to change the dominant society" (p. 466). Current groups like the Lesbian Avengers keep this ambition alive as they challenge Queer women to "be the bomb you throw!" (Lesbian Avengers San Francisco, n. d., p. 2). Founded in New York City in June 1992, the Lesbian Avengers is a group of lesbian, bisexual, and trans women who engage in direct actions to fight homophobia, increase dyke

---

3   Further thoughts on this are presented by Grace and Hill below in Chapter 15, "No End to History: Demanding Civil Quarter for Sexual Minorities in Heteronormative Space."

presence, and abet Queer visibility and survival (Lesbian Avengers San Francisco, n. d.). For them, "direct action means turning our [energy, anger, and] political ideals into concrete confrontation [as public lesbians]. We conduct letter writing campaigns, visibility actions, and guerrilla publicity campaigns, all the while flaunting our lesbionic outrageousness" (Lesbian Avengers Chicago, n. d., p. 1).

Fugitive knowledge is built amid the similarities, differences, tensions, and contradictions that represent the diversity of differences in sex, sexuality, gender, desire, and expression constituting a spectral community of Queer Others (Grace, 2001c). This representation recognizes that lesbians, gay men, bisexuals, transgender persons, and transsexuals are not located in some cohesive community that meshes or blurs these differences within a fiction of generic or universal understandings of Queer and Queerness. However, it also recognizes that making space for Queer diversity, from political and cultural perspectives, means building at least some loosely configured community that acknowledges and accommodates an indeterminate array of differences in sex, sexuality, gender, desire, and expression as well as other relational differences. Some unity in Queer differences is needed for mobilizing the kind of collective or concentrated action needed to increase civil rights for Queer persons, perhaps most particularly right now for transgender and transsexual persons who face marginalization inside and outside the spectral community of Queer Others (Hill, 2000).

Queer histories coupled with contemporary Queer studies indicate that the spectral community of Queer Others has its own ontologies and epistemologies, its own mechanisms that explore how w/e know what w/e know and its own constructions of what defines it for the moment in Hall's (1996) sense of partial or arbitrary closure in particular times and spaces—"positionalities are never final, they're never absolute" (p. 264). Fuss (1991) puts Hall's perspective in Queer terms, suggesting that sex, sexuality, gender, desire, and expression may be perpetually reinvented performances: "The very insistence of the [ontological and] epistemological frame[s] of reference in theories of homosexuality may suggest that we *cannot* know—surely or definitively" (Italics in original, p. 6).

Collectively, Queer histories and Queer studies build fugitive knowledge that is about revelation of Queer and Queerness and defend of our interests and rights in public political and practical contexts. These discourses record the Queer struggle, which is an engagement with the political through a process of conscientization, rebellion, and resistance that is about understanding Queer and Queerness, transgressing the social, and reconstituting the cultural. Queer history is an engagement with a politics of memory that contests who is authorized to remember and under what conditions. Coupled with contemporary Queer studies, Queer history helps build fugitive knowledge that provides a basis for praxis that transgresses heteronormativity. This knowledge incorporates themes, constructs, languages, conventions, markers, and symbols that describe and give meaning to Queer lives and experiences (Edwards et al., 1998; Grace, 2001c). It includes historical and contemporary perspectives that help u/s understand how Queer and Queerness are constructed in relationships between language and action, knowledge and experience (Pinar, 1998). Fugitive knowledge emphasizes what Queer life really feels like and really is like. From a postmodern/poststructural perspective, it is a complex contextual, relational, and dispositional knowledge formation. It acknowledges its own partiality as it contests Queer exclusion and anti-Queer bias in concepts, ideas, and perspectives embodied and embedded in the partial and privileged heteronormalized knowledge and language used to convey them. Fugitive knowledge provides a basis to construct and affirm transgressive notions of Queer and Queerness. In doing so, it counters the culturally engrained notion that heterosexuality is *the* marker of normalcy against which Queer differences in sex, sexuality, gender, desire, and expression are to be gauged and judged (Dilley, 1999; Gamson, 2000; Tierney & Dilley, 1998).

The Politics of Queer Community: Building an Inclusive Lived and Knowable Community in Adult Education

Queer culture is a complex, diverse, indeterminate, and fluid formation shaped by history, politics, and relationships of power. Since change processes, internal inconsistencies, conflicts, and contradictions existing within and between cultures impact the range of acceptable and accepted identities and differences in any culture (Rosaldo, 1989/1993), culture is a contested construct made unstable by conflict over meaning (Agger, 1992; Giroux, 1992, 1993; Grossberg, 1997). Lonner (1994) concludes, "The concept of culture is human-made, abstract, and complex, and it seemingly defies precise and certain definition. However, we cannot understand human diversity without understanding how culture contributes to the substantial variations we observe every day" (p. 241). From these perspectives, Queer culture is a flexible formation that incorporates diverse understandings of "W/e're here! W/e're Queer! Get use to it!" These ways of knowing Queer refuse an essentialist epistemology of a unitary Queer and reflect the many fluid identities, differences, and positionalities of the sometimes-aligned, sometimes-competing members of a spectral community of Queer Others. Thus w/e need to ask particular questions as w/e attempt to make sense of this complex spectrum: How might w/e understand Queer identities, differences, and positionalities as partial and emerging and thus indeterminate constructs that shape a spectral Queer community and that, in turn, shape what Queer persons say, do, and create in our everyday lives? How do Queer persons see and remember one another, particularly those Queer Others whom w/e name and represent differently from our Queer selves?

Taking up these questions in a deliberate and deliberative engagement is vital for understanding the politics of Queer community and building a politics of resistance. Albert Camus (1960) believed that "the force of resistance, together with the value of freedom, gives us new reasons for living" (p. 242). In Queer cultural studies, the force of resistance is understood as an oppositional force whereby w/e inform and perform to counteract cultural forces that pathologize our being, desiring, acting, becoming, and belonging in this world. However, as resistance workers, w/e need to be careful actors who question what w/e say and do in our quest to live as whole persons and full citizens. W/e might ask: Are w/e being true to our Queer selves? Have w/e compromised our Queer integrity in any way to gain presence and place in a heterosexualizing culture that so often denies or resists Queer culture? If w/e mistakenly take what might be perceived as a step forward by assuming some "straight-looking and straight-acting" stance, then what should be our next step?

Perhaps it should be to step back and revise our politics to preserve Queer integrity. W/e need to interrogate and challenge understandings of normality that stifle our Queer selves and our Queerness. For u/s, being normal is not conforming or succumbing to heteronormativity. Indeed it is deviating from such "normality," which Marcuse (1968) describes as a mainstream construct intended to reduce the "healthy" person to one who supports the status quo. He provides this basis to understand why w/e must not succumb to a politics of conformity:

A harmony between the individual and society would be highly desirable if the society offered the individual the conditions for ... development as a human being in accord with the available possibilities of freedom, peace, and happiness (that is in accord with the possible liberation of ... [one's] life instincts), but it is highly destructive to the individual if these conditions do not prevail. Where they do not prevail, the [purportedly] healthy and normal individual is a human being equipped with all the qualities that enable

... [one] to get along with others in ... society, and these very same qualities are the marks of repression, the marks of a mutilated human being, who collaborates in ... [self] repression, in the containment of individual and social freedom. (p. 254)

Historically, Queer persons have been border crossers who learn about being, acting, and affiliating outside mainstream education through a pedagogy of survival enacted in the constituent learning arenas of the gay lifeworld (Hill, 1996). W/e turn to formerly hidden Queer histories as w/e continue our cultural and political work to challenge heteronormalized ways of naming, presenting, and representing Queer persons in learning spaces and other sociocultural sites. W/e also turn to defamatory anti-Queer mainstream histories and other literature in this work to interrogate normal. For example, as Tierney and Dilley (1998) recount, pre-1970s literature "framed [Queerness] in one of two ways: either by absence, or by defining the topic as deviant" (p. 50). This literature used the clinical term "homosexuality" to mark a homosexual orientation as errant sexuality; it labeled heterosexuality as apparently the only normal (accepted and acceptable) sexual positionality that may govern how w/e should be, act, desire, become, and belong in everyday life. As w/e have already noted, a new wave of research in the 1970s (albeit with a pervasive and problematic focus on assimilation or integration) investigated Queer persons as *normal* human beings (Tierney & Dilley, 1998). This kind of research followed pivotal Queer historical moments that include the aforementioned Stonewall Rebellion in 1969 and the removal of homosexuality from the list of pathologies of both the American Psychiatric Association and the American Psychological Association in 1973 (American Psychiatric Association, 1998; Norman Institute, 1999).

Since the 1990s, Queer research has focused on heterosexism and homophobia and the ways a heterosexualizing knowledge-culture-language-power nexus perpetuates them (Gamson, 2000). In pursuing this project, Queer studies analyzes the situated experiences and voices of Queer persons across an indeterminate array of sex, sexual, and gender differences and in terms of the cultural politics that shapes them. It takes up key questions: Why are there sex, sexual, and gender outlaws in the first place? How does the knowledge-culture-language-power nexus work to keep Queer persons positioned as outlaws despite moves forward in legal and legislative arenas? Why don't w/e enjoy the rights and privileges of full citizenship? Why are w/e still not truly able to live in communities of difference where w/e are respected and welcome, safe and secure?

As it takes up these culture/power questions, Queer studies explores matters of context, disposition, relationship, and language that shape heteronormative culture and the Queer counterculture that variously contests and resists it (Grace, 2001c). In this light, Queer studies can inform tactical and transformative adult educational practices. It can help u/s build adult education as an inclusive lived and knowable community that recognizes, respects, and accommodates Queer persons and Queerness. First, on a macro-level, adult educators can investigate and expose institutional and structural aspects of adult education that support and maintain heterosexualizing discourses and heteronormative learning climates to the detriment of the Queer educators and learners the field has tended to exclude. Second, on a micro-level, adult educators can strategize and develop policies, programs, courses, and activities that problematize anti-Queer perspectives, initiatives, symbols, and language in forms of adult education emulating and advancing a heterosexualizing knowledge-culture-language-power nexus. Third, to help accomplish this work, Queer studies can help u/s enhance communicative learning processes and critical analyses concerned with being, self-preservation, expectation, becoming, resistance, affiliation, and holistic living. Fraser (1994) believes that communicative interactions contribute further to possibilities for inclusion and transformation when diverse publics use a democratic, participatory model to engage in dialogue and deliberations about matters of public concern that include the concerns of different subaltern counterpublics. She concludes, "Democratic publicity requires positive guarantees of opportunities for minorities to convince others that what in the past was not public in the sense of being a matter of common concern should now become so" (p. 88). The knowledge and understanding gained from these communicative interactions involving a Queer subaltern counterpublic inform inclusionary adult education and provide lessons in participation, decision making, and action planning as aspects of strategic intervention.

⋆—⋯⋰⋱⋯—⋆

Using Queer Knowledge as an Antecedent to Queer Praxis/ Queer Praxis as a Site of Transformative Learning

The term "knowledge," while not easily defined, is freely employed in education. If knowledge is, at least in part, making sense of information and our experiences, then Queer knowledge incorporates the multiple ways that persons in the spectral community of Queer Others make meaning and sense in the face of what w/e know (Grace, 2001c). It includes multiperspective analysis of "the ways in which we narrate and, through reflection, give meaning to our everyday relations as well as to public life," and it emphasizes how "cultural and political discourse shapes our world through the power of socially situated language to signify as well as to form experience" (Aronowitz & DiFazio, 1994, p. 175). From these perspectives, Queer knowledge constitutes a site for learning and a basis for Queer praxis. It builds that praxis by challenging hierarchies, suspending classifications, and resisting dichotomization in regard to modes of intelligibility (ways of understanding the world). Acknowledging complex subjectivities, it rejects sorting, arranging, organizing, and systematizing identities.

Not only has the modernist project employed binaries as entrées into ways of understanding the world, but it has also tended to assign opposing values to each component of a dualism. Queer praxis, which is built on Queer knowledge in all its diversity and complexity, contests such privileging of male over female, straight over gay, and private acts over public ones. It works to dissolve such binaries and it resists either/or analyses. Additionally, Queer praxis complicates taken-for-granted cultural equations such as gender equals sex, active equals masculine, and sexuality equals private behavior. It challenges assumptions of a monolithic normative heterosexuality. As such, it even opens up the possibility of "straight Queers"—that is, heterosexuals on the margins of heteronormativity and its accepted and acceptable sexual and cultural practices (Cohen, 2001; Sedgwick, 1990). Queer praxis engages in the dissolution of identity-based politics and coalitions built on fixed identities. Alliances, when they appear, are centered on need, desire, or performance. Social constructions are viewed as mutable and shifting.

Queer praxis also challenges and reconstructs the meaning of conducting oneself with proper comportment. It rejects the truth claim that legitimate policies and norms arise only from certain inscriptions of reality. This is because Queer experiences can lead to a reading of truth claims as perilous myths, whereas acting freely can create opportunities for learning from a new (Queer) location that is always open to reformulation, rearticulation, renegotiation, and remediation. Thus Queer praxis, shown to be a site of learning in adulthood, offers potential for personal development (Hill, 1996). It offers possibilities for self-reinforcement and for Queer persons to write themselves into an alien (heteronormative) world. This is a process of becoming more fully human, which, in terms of Freirean praxis, requires u/s to dialogue and synthesize reflection and action in order to transform the world (Roberts, 2003).

Queer knowledge undergirds this praxis as w/e move beyond historical positions of invisibility and voicelessness where our experiences have been unheard and unwelcome. Such knowledge troubles the one-dimensional humanism that has been the coin of the realm in education since its formation as a field of study and practice. The familiar humanistic algorithm claims that the right use of reason produces truth and knowledge, which in turn are the authentic bases for value judgments, social norms, policies, and practices. Queer experiences raise a challenge to this notion and Queer practices subvert it. Like other postfoundational theoretical and political positions that include postmodern and poststructural feminist and postcolonial theories, Queer conceptualizations work against humanism's authorizations and exclusions (Haber, 1994; Honeychurch, 1996; St. Pierre & Pillow, 2000). They open up possibilities for actions that interrogate, celebrate, and acknowledge difference as fundamental to humanity. Central to this study of difference is querying categories. For example, transsexual Queer women and men engage in the dissolution of the boundaries constituting male and female while transgender Queer persons disrupt the social construction of what it means to be a woman/feminine or a man/masculine. Thus Queer being, desiring, and acting produce learning opportunities for richer understandings of human sexuality; they also politicize them. For instance, self-identified Queer lesbians may have sex with straight men, and straight-identified men may engage in sex acts with other men in a controversial condition called "heteroflexible" (Essig, 2000). In this sense, Queer identity may mean entering a bicurious space. Too, expressions of the erotic, affectional conduct, and personal endearment behavior—often deemed "private acts" within mainstream social norms—are often expressed publicly by members of the Queer community as well as by some heterosexuals who skirt the perceived boundaries of heteronormativity. These expressions confront assumptions, beliefs, and values that some would prefer not to know. Yet they restore sexual desire and rehabilitate erotic pleasure as essential to the human person. Moreover, they pry open possibilities that (re)make the world in more complicated ways than the flat renditions narrated by heterosexism and homophobia. In this light, Queer praxis—thinking Queer/expressing Queer/reflecting Queer—can impel the non-Queer Other to learn also.

As cultural work, Queer praxis opens an in-between learning space of immense possibility in culture and society. It identifies the complex notion of subjectivities. Recognizing the fluid nature of human sexuality, desires, and bodies, this action for transformation ruptures notions that essentialize lesbians as flannel-shirted dykes and gay men as limp-wristed fairies. As Dyer (1981) asks, "If that bearded, muscular beer drinker turns out to be a pansy, [then how are we to] know the real men anymore?" (p. 61). Queer individuals may self-express on a continuum that encompasses a complicated range including hypermasculinized and hyperfeminized males and females and comprises those with ambiguous gender and sexual identities. Queer behavior allows for uncertainty and partial truths. It jars and disrupts taken-for-granted truth claims by juxtaposing seemingly contradictory identities. For example, self-descriptors such as "homosexual Christians," "moral sexual outlaws," and "gay-cowboy rodeo stars" upset dominant notions of what it means to be "homosexual," "Christian," "moral," "masculine," and so forth.

From Queer perspectives, adults who belong to the spectral community of Queer Others occupy multiple and intricate sex, sexual, and gender positionalities and performative spaces. Having internalized hegemonic practices acquired in the classroom and in everyday life dominated by heterocentric discourses, they strategize and work from these spaces to interrogate normal, which includes learning to shatter patterns of self-alienation. This involves transgressing a history of formal learning in which the "performance of…openly gay and lesbian students is critically determined by their perceptions that mastery of school knowledge entails self-estrangement" (Aronowitz, 1992, p. 182). A turn to Queer knowledge is useful here. It helps to open up new performative spaces where w/e—society's historically constructed sex, sexual, and gender fugitives—can encounter and validate our complex selves as w/e confront an often hostile heterocentric world. It can proffer a location where identities grow and change, and it enables learners to challenge heterosexualizing discourses and heteronormative ways of being, believing, desiring, acting, becoming, and belonging. In doing so, Queer knowledge situates Queer performances within an alternative pedagogy that often forms new directions for personal development as it cuts across themes of postmodernity such as diversity, identity, representation, audience, textuality, body image/consciousness, and self-definition.

When Queer performances take the form of political interventions, they are aimed at social transformation in a conservative climate. These transgressive behaviors are tributes to the resiliency of the spectral community of Queer Others, for they are enacted in a climate of global neoconservative values that meld the moral and the political. The advent of religious fundamentalism with its right-wing, anti-gay, homophobic posturing has resulted in a new Queer political movement. In the southern U.S., this has led to a popular aphorism, "It isn't easy being Queer in the land of Jesus," and has spawned such automobile bumper stickers as "God save us from your followers."

The religious right has produced anti-Queer movements that function as sites of learning, knowledge construction, and opposition grounded in homophobia. Only a few adult educators and social scientists have investigated them. For example, Esterberg and Longhofer (1998) explore the responses of the Christian right to LGBTQ civil rights initiatives. They describe the religious right as a sundry collection of individuals and groups whose theocratic ambition is to problematize and demonize homosexuality and sex, sexual, and gender variations in political, cultural, and religious domains. Esterberg and Longhofer maintain that this ambition fires up a regressive social movement whose tactics position liberalism, secular humanism, feminism, and Queer civil rights activism as both the bane and foe of rightist Christian activists. Recently, Grace (2001b, 2002, 2008) has provided analysis of "reparative therapy" and "transformational ministry," situating them as alienating forms of a public pedagogy of negation that exist under the guise of transformative adult learning. These regressive pedagogies are attempts to convert Queer persons—supposedly an unhappy and miserable lot—to a heterosexual way of being and acting. Grace argues that both pedagogies assault Queer integrity and violate Queer identities when they suggest the scientifically unsubstantiated possibility of "transformation" to a heterosexual "lifestyle." He also argues that both anti-Queer learning projects employ tactics of cultural and pedagogical terrorism that fail to consider how Queer self-hatred and internalized homophobia have roots embedded in trying to live a life in a heterosexualizing culture and a heteronormative society. He provides critiques using educational and medical sources to make a case that "reparative therapy" (as an orthodox psychotherapy) and "transformational ministry" (as a conservative theocratic intervention) comprise forms of hetero-regulating pedagogies and sexist, homophobic cultural work that dismiss Queer being, acting, desire, history, and culture. These countermovements sanction hatred of Queer persons and Queerness as a legitimate form of public discourse.

Queer knowledge and interventions inform the practical and political questions that adult educators need to ask as they engage in strategic deconstruction of exclusionary forms of adult education and the construction of inclusionary, transformative pedagogies. How does adult education function? How are its various forms produced? Who regulates them? How is the teaching-learning interaction framed, executed, evaluated, and circulated in the intersections of differences in sex, sexuality, gender, desire, and expression and in the intersections of these differences with other relationships of power? How are these interactions impacted by the workings of the dominant knowledge-culture-language-power nexus and mainstream forms of adult education that maintain the status quo? Queer knowledge provides information and insights to those who take up these questions. It suggests ways to query truth claims, generate unruly perspectives, impeach what appears to be innocent, and probe hidden normative assumptions as actions for social and cultural change. It opens paths to educational pedagogies that are democratic, unsettling and unsettled, dynamic, inclusive, transgressive, and perhaps most important, transformative.

Concluding Perspective: W/e Want Cake

Queer praxis is built on contextual, relational, and dispositional analyses of multilayered oppressions. Queer persons hold multiple passports; seek to destroy normative sex, sexual, and gender categories; and celebrate unstable sexual identities and behaviors. That which is Queer is found in fluid sex, sexual, and gender identities and positionalities in the LGBTQ community and in the sexual outlaw status of those in the heterosexual community whose desires, choices, and expressions are perceived as nonnormative and unworthy of espousal by the straight world. Queer therefore encompasses alternative sexual representations and gender bending/gender blending. In mobilizing desire, Queer persons challenge the assumptions of heteronormativity in every aspect of our lives; thus w/e come in all stripes. W/e are "straight queers, bi queers, tranny queers, lez queers, fag queers, SM queers, [and] fisting[4] queers" (McIntosh, quoted in Cohen, 2001, p. 548). Our politics extend beyond the sexual arena (Warner, 1993).

Queer and Queerness call into question regimes of truth and systems of oppression that police people's lives through the construction of normalized space. It opens up a critique of the privilege, entitlement, and status obtained by obeying mandatory heterosexuality and other heteronormative behaviors. Queer praxis emerges in the intersection of lived everyday experiences, as Queer individuals navigate the pressures of domination and normalization. Queer does not mean gaining a seat at the table in a performance that merely exchanges privileges, but instead it demands an altogether new table arrangement. During a panel discussion on Queer cultural practice at the 2001 Social Movement Learning Conference, University of Toronto, one self-identified Queer participant put it bluntly, "W/e don't want a piece of the pie, w/e want cake!" The cyber-magazine *Mutate*

---

4   "Fisting" refers to inserting a hand into the sexual partner's anus.

Zine (http://www.mutatezine.com/index.html) asks the Queer question, "Have you genderfucked yourself today?" An affirmative answer to this interrogative opens up membership in the Queer community. While many adult educators might find answering such a question too intense an exercise in sex, sexual, and gender border crossing, w/e hope they will at least join in the refrain, "Let's all eat cake!" That would open up membership in the adult education community.

If adult educators are to engage in teaching-learning interactions in a lived and knowable community that includes Queer both in principle and in practice, then they have to unlearn social lessons and cultural practices that are expressions of a politics of complicity that perpetuates heterosexism and homophobia. Such unlearning requires that educators conceive of their educational project as an active engagement in a politics of hope and possibility (Giroux, 1994). From a Queer perspective, these politics constitute a social and cultural change force when they locate praxis as a transgressive and transformative practice-expression-reflection dynamic that builds fugitive knowledge and accommodates the spectrum of Queer positionalities. This is the substance of an inclusive and just learning process. This is having cake.

References

Agger, B. (1992). *Cultural studies as critical theory.* London: The Falmer Press.

American Psychiatric Association [APA]. (1998). *American Psychiatric Association rebukes reparative therapy.* Retrieved August 25, 2001, from http://www.psych.org/news_stand/rep_therapy.cfm

Aronowitz, S. (1992). *The politics of identity: Class, culture, social movements.* NY: Routledge.

Aronowitz, S., & DiFazio, W. (1994). *The jobless future: Sci-tech and the dogma of work.* Minneapolis, MN: University of Minnesota Press.

Baumgartner, L. (2002). Living and learning with HIV/AIDS: Transformational tales continued. *Adult Education Quarterly, 53*(1), 44-59.

Bergevin, P. (1967). *A philosophy for adult education.* NY: The Seabury Press.

Blakely, R. S. (1967). *Adult education in a free society.* Toronto: Guardian Bird.

Boshier, R. (1992). Popular discourse concerning AIDS: Its implications for adult education. *Adult Education Quarterly, 42*(3), 125-135.

Brookfield, S. (1987). *Learning democracy: Eduard Lindeman on adult education and social change.* London: Croom Helm.

Butler, J. (1993). *Bodies that matter.* NY. Routledge.

Camus, A. (1960). *Resistance, rebellion, and death.* NY: Alfred A. Knopf.

Cohen, C. J. (2001). Punks, bulldaggers, and welfare queens: The radical potential of queer politics? In L. Richardson, V. Taylor, & N. Whittier (Eds.), *Feminist frontiers 5* (pp. 540-556). NY: McGraw-Hill Higher Education.

Corrigan, P. (1990). *Social forms/human capacities: Essays in authority and difference.* NY: Routledge.

Cotton, W. E. (1968). *On behalf of adult education: A historical examination of the supporting literature.* Boston: Center for the Study of Liberal Education for Adults.

Cunningham, P. M. (2001). Foreword. In V. Sheared & P. A. Sissel (Eds.), *Making space: Merging theory and practice in adult education* (pp. xi-xiv). Westport, CT: Bergin & Garvey.

D'Emilio, J. (1989). Gay politics and community in San Francisco since World War II. In M. Duberman, M. Vicinus, & G. Chauncey, Jr. (Eds.), *Hidden from history: Reclaiming the gay and lesbian past* (pp. 456-473). NY: Penguin Books (Meridian).

D'Emilio, J. (1992). *Making trouble.* NY: Routledge.

Dewey, J. (1964). *Democracy and education.* London: MacMillan.

Dilley, P. (1999). Queer theory: Under construction. *International Journal of Qualitative Studies in Education, 12*(5), 457-472.

Dyer, R. (1981). Getting over the rainbow: Identity and pleasure in gay cultural politics. In G. Bridges & R. Brunt (Eds.), *Silver linings: Some strategies for the eighties* (pp. 53-67). London: Lawrence and Wishart.

Dyson, M. E. (1993). *Reflecting Black: African-American cultural criticism.* Minneapolis, MN: University of Minnesota Press.

Edwards, K., Grace, A. P., Henson, B., Henson, W., Hill, R. J., & Taylor, E. (1998). Tabooed terrain: Reflections on conducting adult education research in lesbian/gay/queer arenas (Symposium). In J. C. Kimmel (Comp.), *Proceedings of the 39ᵗʰ Annual Adult Education Research Conference* (pp. 317-324). San Antonio, TX: University of the Incarnate Word and Texas A & M.

Edwards, R. (2001). Editorial: Changing knowledge? Knowledge production in the education of adults. *Studies in the Education of Adults, 33*(2), 1.

Egan, J. (2001). Learning to change: A grassroots program planning model. *Proceedings of the 20th Annual Conference of the Canadian Association for the Study of Adult Education* (pp. 100-106). Quebec City, PQ: Laval University.

Eisen, V., & Kenyatta, M. (1996). Cornel West on heterosexism and transformation: An interview. *Harvard Educational Review, 66*(2), 356-367.

Essig, L. (2000, November 15). *Heteroflexibility.* Retrieved August 25, 2001, from http://www.salon.com/mwt/feature/2000/11/15/heteroflexibility/index.html

Esterberg, K., & Longhofer, J. (1998). Researching the radical right: Responses to anti-lesbian/gay initiatives. In J. L. Ristock & C. G. Taylor (Eds.), *Inside the academy and out: Lesbian/gay/queer studies and social action* (pp. 183-198). Toronto: University of Toronto Press.

Fone, B. (2000). *Homophobia: A history.* NY: Henry Holt.

Fraser, N. (1994). Rethinking the public sphere: A contribution to the critique of actually existing democracy. In H. A. Giroux & P. McLaren (Eds.), *Between borders: Pedagogy and the politics of cultural studies* (pp. 74-98). NY: Routledge.

Freire, P. (1998). *Teachers as cultural workers: Letters to those who dare teach.* (D. Macedo, D. Koike, & A. Oliveira, Trans.). Boulder, CO: Westview Press.

Fuss, D. (1991). Inside/out. In D. Fuss (Ed.), *Inside/out: Lesbian theories, gay theories* (pp. 1-10). NY: Routledge.

Gamson, J. (2000). Sexualities, queer theory, and qualitative research. In N. K. Denzin & Y. S. Lincoln (Eds.), *Handbook of qualitative research* (2nd ed.) (pp. 347-365). Thousand Oaks, CA: Sage Publications.

Garber, E. (1989). A spectacle in color: The lesbian and gay subculture of jazz age Harlem. In M. Duberman, M. Vicinus, & G. Chauncey, Jr. (Eds.), *Hidden from history: Reclaiming the gay and lesbian past* (pp. 318-331). NY: Penguin Books (Meridian).

Giroux, H. A. (1992). *Border crossings.* NY: Routledge.

Giroux, H. A. (1993). *Living dangerously: Multiculturalism and the politics of difference.* NY: Peter Lang.

Giroux, H. A. (1994). *Disturbing pleasures: Learning popular culture.* NY: Routledge.

Grace, A. P. (1997). Where critical postmodern theory meets practice: Working in the intersection of instrumental, social, and cultural education. *Studies in Continuing Education, 19*(1), 51-70..

Grace, A. P. (2001a). Being, becoming, and belonging as a queer citizen educator: The places of queer autobiography, queer culture as community, and fugitive knowledge. *Proceedings of the 20th Annual Conference of the Canadian Association for the Study of Adult Education* (pp. 100-106). Quebec City, PQ: Laval University.

Grace, A. P. (2001b). *Transforming pedagogy to engage a queer normal: Fracturing binaries, opening up sex-and-gender positionalities.* Paper presented at the 4th International Conference on Transformative Learning, OISE/University of Toronto, ON.

Grace, A. P. (2001c). Using queer cultural studies to transgress adult educational space. In V. Sheared & P. A. Sissel (Eds.), *Making space: Merging theory and practice in adult education* (pp. 257-270). Westport, CT: Bergin & Garvey.

Grace, A. P. (2002). "Transformational ministry" and "reparative therapy": Transformative learning gone awry. In J. Pettitt (Ed.), *Proceedings of the 43rd Annual Adult Education Research Conference* (pp. 123-128). Raleigh, NC: North Carolina State University. (ERIC Document CE084276)

Grace, A. P. (2003). Theoretical, legal, legislative, and educational policy perspectives on queer citizenship and welfare-and-work issues in Canadian education and culture. *Proceedings of the 22nd Annual Conference of the Canadian Association for the Study of Adult Education* (pp. 77-82). Halifax, NS: Dalhousie University.

Grace, A. P. (2008). The charisma and deception of reparative therapies: When medical science beds religion. *Journal of Homosexuality, 55*(4), 545-580.

Grace, A. P., & Benson, F. J. (2000). Using autobiographical queer life narratives of teachers to connect personal, political, and pedagogical spaces. *International Journal of Inclusive Education, 4*(2), 89-109.

Grossberg, L. (1997). *Bringing it all back home: Essays on cultural studies.* Durham, NC: Duke University Press.

Haber, H. F. (1994). *Beyond postmodern politics.* NY: Routledge.

Have you genderfucked yourself today? (2000). *Mutate Zine.* Retrieved August 25, 2001, from http://www.mutatezine.com/index.html

Hall, S. (1996). Cultural studies and its theoretical legacies. In D. Morley & K.-H. Chen (Eds.), *Stuart Hall: Critical dialogues in cultural studies* (pp. 262-275). NY: Routledge.

Hill, R. J. (1994). Heterosexist discourse in adult education: A gay/lesbian critique. In M. Hymens, J. Armstrong, & E. Anderson (Comp.), *Proceedings of the 35th Annual Adult Education Research Conference* (pp. 142-158). Knoxville, TN: University of Tennessee.

Hill, R. J. (1995). Gay discourse in adult education: A critical review. *Adult Education Quarterly, 45*(3), 142-158.

Hill, R. J. (1996). Learning to transgress: A social-historical conspectus of the American gay lifeworld as a site of struggle and resistance. *Studies in the Education of Adults, 28*(2), 253-279.

Hill, R. J. (2000). Menacing feminism, educating sisters. In T. J. Sork, V.-L. Chapman, & R. St. Clair (Eds.), *Proceedings of the 41st Annual Adult Education Research Conference* (pp. 176-180). Vancouver, BC: University of British Columbia.

Hill, R. J. (2003). Working memory at AERC: A Queer welcome … and a retrospective. In R. J. Hill (Ed.), *Queer histories: Exploring fugitive forms of social knowledge. Proceedings of the 1st Lesbian, Gay, Bisexual, Transgender, Queer and Allies Pre-Conference at the 44th Annual Adult Education Research Conference* (pp. 11-28). San Francisco, CA: San Francisco State University.

Honeychurch, K. G. (1996). Researching dissident subjectivities: Queering the grounds of theory and practice. *Harvard Educational Review, 66*(2), 339-355.

hooks, b. (2001). *Salvation: Black people and love.* NY: Perennial/HarperCollins.

Jensen, G., Liveright, A. A., & Hallenbeck, W. (Eds.). (1964). *Adult education: Outlines of an emerging field of study.* Washington, DC: Adult Education Association of the U.S.A.

Kidd, J. R. (1973). *Relentless verity: Education for being-becoming-belonging.* Syracuse, NY: Syracuse University Publications in Continuing Education.

Knowles, M. S., & DuBois, E. E. (1970). Prologue: The handbooks in perspective. In R. M. Smith, G. F. Aker, & J. R. Kidd (Eds.), *Handbook of adult education* (pp. xvii-xxiii). NY: Macmillan.

Knowles, M., & Klevins, C. (1972). Resume of adult education. In C. Klevins (Ed.), *Materials and methods in adult education* (pp. 5-15). NY: Klevens Publications Inc.

Lesbian Avengers Chicago. (n. d.). Retrieved August 25, 2001, from http://www.lesbian.org/chicago-avengers

Lesbian Avengers San Francisco. (n. d.). Retrieved August 25, 2001, from http://www.lesbian.org/sfavengers/old/index.html

Lindeman, E. C. (1926/1961). *The meaning of adult education*. Montreal: Harvest House.

Lonner, W. J. (1994). Culture and human diversity. In E. J. Trickett, R. J. Watts, & D. Birman (Eds.), *Human diversity: Perspectives on people in context* (pp. 230-243). San Francisco: Jossey-Bass Publishers.

Marcuse, H. (1968). *Negations* (J. J. Shapiro, Trans.). Boston, MA: Beacon Press. (Original work published 1965)

Norman Institute. (1999). *Psychiatric group discredits "reparative" therapy*. Retrieved August 25, 2001, from http://www.authenticity.org/v1no1/apa399.html

Ohliger, J. (1971). *Lifelong learning or lifelong schooling? A tentative view on the ideas of Ivan Illich with a quotational bibliography*. Occasional Papers No. 24. Syracuse, NY: Syracuse University Publications in Continuing Education and ERIC Clearinghouse on Adult Education.

Paul, W. (1982). Social issues and homosexual behavior: A taxonomy of categories and themes in anti-gay argument. In W. Paul, J. D. Weinrich, J. C. Gonsiorek, & M. E. Hotvedt (Eds.), *Homosexuality: Social, psychological, and behavioral issues*. Beverly Hills, CA: Sage Publications.

Peters, J. M., Jarvis, P., & Associates (1991). *Adult education: Evolution and achievements in a developing field of study*. San Francisco: Jossey-Bass.

Pinar, W. F. (1998). *Queer theory in education*. Malwah, NJ: Lawrence Erlbaum Associates.

Rauch, D. B. (1972). New priorities in adult education. In D. B. Rauch (Ed.), *Priorities in adult education* (pp. 1-24). NY: Macmillan.

Roberts, P. (2003). Knowledge, dialogue, and humanization: Exploring Freire's philosophy. In M. Peters, C. Lankshear, & M. Olssen (Eds.), *Critical theory and the human condition: Founders and praxis* (pp. 169-183). NY: Peter Lang.

Rosaldo, R. (1989, 1993). *Culture and truth*. Boston: Beacon Press.

Sedgwick, E. K. (1990). *Epistemology of the closet*. Berkeley: University of California Press.

Sedgwick, E. K. (1993). *Tendencies*. Durham, NC: Duke University Press.

Sheared, V., & Sissel, P. A. (Eds.). (2001). *Making space: Merging theory and practice in adult education*. Westport, CT: Bergin & Garvey.

Sissel, P. A., & Sheared, V. (2001). Opening the gates: Reflections on power, hegemony, language, and the status quo. In V. Sheared & P. A. Sissel (Eds.), *Making space: Merging theory and practice in adult education* (pp. 3-14). Westport, CT: Bergin & Garvey.

Slack, J. D. (1996). The theory and method of articulation in cultural studies. In D. Morley & K.-H. Chen (Eds.), *Stuart Hall: Critical dialogues in cultural studies* (pp. 112-127). NY: Routledge.

St. Pierre, E. A., & Pillow, W. (2000). Inquiry among the ruins. In E. A. St. Pierre & W. Pillow (Eds.), *Working the ruins: Feminist poststructural theory and methods in education* (pp. 1-24). NY: Routledge.

Stubblefield, H. W., & Keane, P. (1994). *Adult education in the American experience.* San Francisco: Jossey-Bass.

Taylor, E. W. (2001). *Adult Education Quarterly* from 1989 to 1999: A content analysis of all submissions. *Adult Education Quarterly, 51*(4), 322-340.

Tierney, W. G. (1997). *Academic outlaws: Queer theory and cultural studies in the academy.* Thousand Oaks, CA: Sage Publications.

Tierney, W. G., & Dilley, P. (1998). Constructing knowledge: Educational research and gay and lesbian studies. In W. F. Pinar (Ed.), *Queer theory in education* (pp. 49-71). Mahwah, NJ: Lawrence Erlbaum Associates.

Warner, M. (1993). *Fear of a queer planet: Queer politics and social theory.* Minneapolis, MN: University of Minnesota.

Wells, K. (2003). Queer young adults, informal learning, and the possibilities for an inclusive positional pedagogy. *Proceedings of the 22nd Annual Conference of the Canadian Association for the Study of Adult Education* (pp. 77-82). Halifax, NS: Dalhousie University.

West, C. (1993/1994). *Race matters.* NY: Vintage Books.

Žižek, S. (1991). *Looking awry: An introduction to Jacques Lacan through popular culture.* Cambridge, MA: MIT Press.

CHAPTER 2

Que(e)rying Intimacy:
Challenges to Lifelong Learning

Robert J. Hill

Overture

Practices that facilitate the art, knowledge, and skill of intimacy to take root in our Queer lives include unmasking the self, unleashing the heart, walking in harmony with the Earth, capturing the fiercely passionate and undomesticated side of our nature, taking control of our own bodies/emotions/relationships, the willingness to be disturbed, the recognition that "difference is a fundamental human right," and developing cultural and social competencies across difference. Sexual-minority experiences offer the opportunity to recognize intimacy as a process of weaving threads to others' hearts while not letting our judgments about "the Other" obscure the indispensable joy of learning.

Intimacy and Adult Learning: Profoundly Relational

This chapter argues that intimacy, in its affective, emotional, cognitive, physical, and spiritual embodiments—like learning itself—is profoundly relational. It also challenges the notion that intimacy—like education—is *truly* democratic. It offers evidence that sexual minorities (lesbian, gay, bisexual, transgender, In-

This paper was presented in a modified form as "Sexual Minority Intimacy: Challenge to Lifelong Learning," July 11, 2008, at Intimacy in Lifelong Learning: A Social Issue, Institute for Vocational Training and Continuing Education, University of Duisburg/Essen, Germany. It is based on nascent concepts developed at various AERC meetings. Thanks to Dr. Paul Bélanger, Université de Québec à Montréal, who initiated my thinking on the topic.

digenous/Two- Spirit and Queer people) must work against cultural, social, and political exclusions that daily deny us opportunities to authentic relationships, intimacy, the right to construct our own fluid identities, and full citizenship with equal privileges and responsibilities enjoyed by straight folks. One site of resistance and learning to this marginalization is within "gay and lesbian" social movements. These movements are inexorably linked to building a democratic social order. This chapter points to the failures of most formal lifelong learning strategies to develop "a democracy of intimacy" but recognizes that such strategies have emerged within sexual-minority communities, especially at the grassroots and within Queer social movements. Finally, it offers hope from experiences within sexual-minority communities to build connections between the joy of learning about and for intimacy that lead to "intimate citizenship." It also challenges sexual-minority strategies not only to democratize spaces for our Queer selves but also to address the universal human hunger for intimacy through building just communities with and for everyone.

"What's going on just now? What's happening to us? What is this world, this period, this precise moment in which we are living?" are questions raised by the French philosopher Michel Foucault more than one-quarter century ago (1982, p. 216). They remain relevant today! Answers to these questions have profound impacts on contemporary lifelong learning, the democratization of intimacy in general, and on learning within sexual-minority communities specifically. This chapter explores aspects of learning in current social movements and contributes to unpacking the Foucauldian probes about what is going on just now and what is happening to us in this precise moment.

⇤ ⫷✚⫸ ↦

"Lesbian and Gay" Social Movement(s)

Social movements often develop in response to oppression in order to construct, deconstruct, and reconstruct the identities of group members and to define the cultural roles of oppressors and the oppressed (MacNair, Fowler, & Harris, 2000). Frequently the result is social transformation through the introduction of new values, beliefs, knowledge, and skills that may eventually impact entire societies (Raschke, 1985). Perhaps most importantly, social movements are sites of learning, meaning making, and resistance (Finger, 1989; Habermas, 1981; Welton, 1993). Shor (1992) points out that the struggles of social movement actors transform society in an array of political arenas, from political campaigns to trade union organizing, from community action against discrimination to campaigns for peace, as well as for sexual rights, for environmental justice, and for civil and human equality. Shor bluntly claims that each movement is educational in and of itself. Movements are perhaps the most likely sites for learning across the lifespan in ways that lead to empowerment. Movements are "spontaneous commitment[s] to learning outside the walls of formal schooling….[This is learning that is] linked inexorably to building a democratic social order" (Heaney, 1996, p.1).

The United States, as in many places, has a long and complex history of learning in and through social movements. Because of space considerations, this chapter treats social movements as an empirical, monolithic unit of analysis that glosses over their complexities, but social movements, per se, are not the point of my argument. I recognize three historical "waves" of social movements. Sexual minorities have played roles in all three. Initially social movements arose in response to questions surrounding resource distribution and mobilization. The labor movement typifies this phase. Next, new social movements dominated the social scene beginning in the 1960s and continue to today. Identity based, they include the Civil Rights Movement, the Women's Movement, environmental movements, and sexual-minority ("gay and lesbian") movements, among many more. Finally, we are in the midst of a "new" new social movement that is:

> sustained by convergence activism, direct action, and civil disobedience. It is a "movement of movements" that has birthed new radicalism (Klein, 2002). It is based on multiple-issues of social justice, and has been prompted by such factors as globalization, the shifting boundaries between public and private space, the growing income disparity in the U.S. (and globally), U.S. Empire, the emergence of new personal identities, resistance to invisibility for the marginalized, and new information and communication technologies (ITCs) (See Shepard & Hayduk, 2002). It is about peoples' dignity and the refusal to accept being erased from the social equation. (Hill, 2008, pp. 84-85)

Many sexual minorities in the convergence movement, which is transnational, refuse to allow their expressions of intimacy and love to be silenced any longer. In some circumstances, such attitudes and concomitant behaviors are very consequential.

A thorough analysis of these three waves of social movements requires teasing apart the nuances and the significant differences within them. Regardless of their historical expressions, however, social movements give the pulse of an era. It is, therefore, not surprising to find emerging paradigms of learning in them (Hill, 2008)—including those that surround intimacy.

Intimacy

Mashek and Aron (2004) recall that the term "intimacy" is built on the Latin word, *intimus*, meaning "innermost." Intimacy is always about relationships—as is learning. While being intimate often refers to a close friend, *intim(us)*, it actually points to the interior landscape of our hearts. It connotes belonging, warmth, close association, and the joy and pleasure that these bring to those who possess them. Intimacy functions on multiple levels, including the emotional/affective, cognitive, physical (including, but not restricted to, sexual), sociocultural, and spiritual planes. An individual is healthiest when these aspects of the self are in harmony. Upon closer examination, we find the same is true of learning; we learn best when these aspects are in accord (Mackeracher, 2004).

The term "intimacy" is employed in many ways in contemporary society. It is the type of word that in fact eludes a conclusive definition. Rather than ask, "What *is* intimacy," I'd like to explore cognates that it conjures up and to discover some of the ways that intimacy *functions*. Intimacy has a component to it that we learn, so there must be pedagogical practices that enable the art, knowledge, and skill of intimacy (e.g., educational spaces where meaning around intimacy is constructed). Equally, there must be practices that are barriers to it! I am most interested in the behaviors and practices that release us into the embrace of (same-gender) intimacy and those that propel us away from it.

As a gay man, I am especially interested in interrogating how sexual minorities must work against social and political exclusions that deny us the right to intimacy, which is inextricably linked to being, becoming, and belonging—and ultimately to full participation in society as citizens with equal rights.[5] My experiences as a gay

---

5   As an aside to this essay, I am compelled to mention another group of people for whom intimacy is socially denied: those with disabilities, especially women. While not the focus of my work, Vansteenwegen, Jans, and Revell (2003) have shown that women with disabilities are far more likely to be unpartnered, unmarried, and far more socially disengaged so that intimacy eludes them. The public discourse surrounding disabilities and sexuality are linked to deviance. Tepper (2000) raises the question about the theft of intimacy for disabled people. There is, in fact, a loose connection with sexual-minority communities in that some disability activists, like sexual-minority activists, and other disenfranchised groups, are reclaiming the discourse of sexual pleasure. In a recent study, Decker (2008) reports a disabled participant exclaimed, "[P]eople will die if they don't get touched, if they don't have intimacy between them and another person. I don't understand people thinking that we [disabled] don't function in the same way [as able-bodied people]" (p. 21).

man and social movement activist lead me to believe that we not only learn (about) intimacy but also that theories and practices of intimacy are stand-ins—substitutions—for learning itself. The two are not only inseparable, in many instances when disambiguated and examined, they have many qualities in common.

Intimacy and Sustainability

Intimacy describes the ecology of the human soul. In many ways intimacy, and the much-used ecologically conscious word, "sustainability," are closely allied. Sustainability is a measure of harmony and balance. Like intimacy, it is nurturing and life giving when we open ourselves to it. It means utilizing a "resource" but never exhausting it, thus allowing its continuance. Intimacy is also linked to identities. We all bring our multiple identities into our intimate relationships. Like intimacy, identities too can be renewable resources that are never exhausted as we learn new ways of being, belonging, becoming, and behaving.

I recently spent time studying on the Navajo (also known as the Diné) Native American Nation in New Mexico. The Indigenous people who live there hold to a complex philosophy called *hózho*. A central concept within their cosmology, *hózho* expresses "order, the emotional state of happiness, the moral notion of good, the biological condition of health and well-being, and the aesthetic dimensions of balance, harmony, and beauty." [6] *Hózho* is the quintessential spirit of intimacy—a bonding with people, the environment, and other physical and spiritual realms (see Witherspoon, 1977, 1983; Witherspoon & Peterson, 1995). Learning in their culture is directly coupled with *hózho*. American Indian Indigenous pedagogy has an inherent "social bonding" (Allen, 2007, p. 44), an intimacy based on "principles of harmony, integrity, respect for all, and kinship" (p. 46). Recently this has been described as "indigenous critical pedagogy," which is a "rich social resource" (to use the language of Paulo Friere and Antonio Faundez, cited in Semali & Kincheloe, 1999, p. 15) that heals individuals, communities, and the sacred ground we walk upon, for justice's sake. It is an intimacy that extends beyond the self to connect with and to serve the community, resulting in sustainable lifeways, i.e., living freely now, with an openness and a hopefulness to the future.

Intimacy and the Unmasked Self

Intimacy functions in ways that allow an individual to unmask him or herself so as to be vulnerable in situations where the person feels safe. When I function in an intimate way, I feel united with the person, place, or thing in which I am

---

6   More found at http://www.uu9gt.org/documents/makeup/ResearchDine.htm.

sharing a deep experience. Fear of rejection or reprisal because of my identity or subjectivities is minimal or absent. I am recognized for the person I am, with all of the gifts, talents, and imperfections that make me human. Learning situations can be like this, too. Wanting to develop new capacities, beliefs, values, knowledge, and skills (or to confirm or reinforce current or former ones), I must unmask what I hold to be true. Intimacy and learning are both born of a sense of "honest closeness" to someone or something, acknowledging the consolations and desolations that accompany this nearness.

A person does not simply arrive at a state of intimacy, but rather one grows there in the process of human development. Learning across the lifespan is integral to this growth and progress. Equally fundamental for intimacy is participating in civil society where a sense of self and belonging often emerge as a result of engagement and participation. The Faure Report (*Learning to Be*, Faure et al., 1972) calls for a new level of respect for learning—learning *to be*—regardless of the means by which that learning occurs. "The report...weave[s] together learning arrangements toward...unique learning goals. What matters is...actual learning and the freedom to find one's own path along the way: There is no real freedom of choice unless the individual is able to follow any path leading to his [or her] goals" (p. 188). The work of Delors (1996) is as crucial to intimacy as it is to learning: individuals have a right to be, to belong, to become, and to take up agency. Intimacy and democracy—the free and equal right of every person to participate in society, community, organizations, and government—are thoroughly linked.

The Unleashed Heart

Paulo Freire (1999) reminds us that hope resides in each and every person—that "hope is an ontological need....[It] is the desire to dream, the desire to change, the desire to improve human existence" (p. 8). Pelias (2004) proposes a daily methodology wherein the heart, which "is never far from what matters" (p. 7), "finds its vocabulary in the senses" (p. 10). Without heart, relationships are empty and learning is soulless. Darder and Mirón (2006) offer that "love is a political principle through which we struggle to create mutually life-enhancing opportunities for all people....This is a love nurtured by the act of relationship itself" (p. 150)—what I would call intimacy. Darder and Mirón go on, "It cultivates relationships with the freedom to be at one's best without undue fear. Such an emancipatory love allows us to realize our nature in a way that allows others to do so as well" (p. 150). These attributes of the heart frequently emerge among and between members of social movements and spontaneously propel members to connect with other non-movement people.

But not all intimacy and love, at least in the public sphere, are democratic. Not all identities are deemed legitimate. Not all hearts are free to be unleashed. Not all selves are safe to be unmasked, at least not without consequences that at times are painful or even fatal. On a global scale, for most sexual minorities the Freirian ontological need for hope is suppressed, denied, or killed, and the emancipatory aspect of love remains unfulfilled in the dominant world. For us, the leanings and inclinations of our hearts are often stigmatized as criminal, immoral, or pathological. We habitually live in cultures that systematically invalidate our identities, our ways of constructing families and building communities. Yet hope and love—the products of learning to be intimate—can and do flourish and grow for those of us who have raw courage (or economic status, privilege, and social class) to dare to resist this oppression and to unleash our hearts' deepest yearnings. But setting our hearts free should always be done mindful of the consequences. We must be aware that doing so will produce unanticipated and unintended outcomes that can be either beneficial or detrimental to us and to others.

A "New and Strange Ally": Willingness to Be Disturbed

It is almost axiomatic that adult education must include teaching and training for social justice. In the past there have been numerous calls for a human rights agenda and intercultural dialogue in the field, yet inclusion of sexual minorities is often overlooked. Typical of the rhetoric is the orientation presented by UNESCO's Institute for Lifelong Learning, which claims that the critical importance of adult education and adult learning is "for fostering ecologically sustainable development, for promoting democracy, justice, gender equity, and scientific, social and economic development, and for building a world in which violent conflict is replaced by dialogue and a culture of peace based on justice" (UIE, 1997, cited in Imel, 2000, para. 2). Intimacy and sexuality are absent in this construction of adult education and learning.

We must ask, what has the social and cultural absence of discourses on intimacy and sexual and gender identity meant to the exercise of personal and communal rights, to learners, to learning, to training, to meaning making, to citizenship, to adult and community development, and to social justice? How have they stifled learners' capacities for expression, growth, and development? And, perhaps most important, what can we do to make a healthier future possible? Much of my own research, teaching, scholarship, and practice has been to foster the notion that *difference is a fundamental human right*. This difference includes variations on intimacy and sexuality. I believe that adult educators must be actively creating learning environments where people are challenged to be open to being disturbed on issues of intimacy and sexuality. Justice demands this of us.

Margaret Wheatley (2002) argues, "As we work together to restore hope to the future, we need to include a new and strange ally—our willingness to be disturbed. Our willingness to have our ideas and beliefs challenged by what others think" (p. 34). She goes on to spell out the joy in the relational and intimate nature of learning, saying, "We have to be willing to admit that we are not capable of figuring out things alone....I can't understand why we would be satisfied with superficial conversations where we pretend to agree with one another" (p. 35).

Her prescription is to listen for what shocks and surprises us during interpersonal communications; shock in the ideas and views of others reveals our own biases and beliefs. Inquiring about differences opens the door to the intimacy of learning. She concludes with the hope that this will develop better relationships, which ultimately will lead us to "laugh in delight as we realize how many unique ways there are to be human....The greatest benefit of all is that listening moves us closer. When we listen with less judgment, we always develop better relationships with each other. It's not difference that divides us. It's our judgments about each other that do" (p. 36). This seems especially true when learning about intimacy in sexual-minority communities.

In both instructional and occupational settings, the idea that difference is a fundamental human right means developing and implementing plans for cultural competence in order to educate people about sexual-minority issues, learning inclusive language, confronting language and behaviors that marginalize and oppress, recognizing anti-gay bias/violence, directing organizational publications to provide adequate and fair coverage of sexual-minority events and issues, and recognizing that diversity exists within diversity (i.e., sexual-minority identity and behavior are intersectional; they cross racial, ethnic, ability, age, etc., lines) (Hill, 2006a). Becoming culturally competent from the heart should be based on training that imitates the joy of learning and includes appropriate avenues for intimacy in human relationships. In society, the notion that difference is a fundamental human right means educating for *social* competence (Zwaans, van der Veen, Volman, & ten Dam, 2008).

Precariously Iconic: Not All Intimacy (and Not All Learning) Are Democratic

On the surface, the notions of intimacy, hope, and love described above seem so simple, so straightforward, so natural, and so inevitable in the course of life. This picture, however, is dangerously deceptive and unstable. When examined with a wide-angle lens, we see that intimacy, as presented in the dominant cultures of most societies, is actually an icon of heterosexuality, albeit one often reserved for married, conjugal, dyadic couples. Unpartnered heterosexuals also may face intimacy phobia and sex phobia in mainstream cultures. But the titanic reality is that sexual minorities occupy the very margins. Social institutions, popular culture, and media construct intimacy in the public sphere by and for specific heterosexuals in a very undemocratic manner. When intimations of intimacy are transferred to same-gender relations, it is alarming and threatening and habitually invites backlash (Hill, 2009). But as we shall see, sexual-minority communities have for years been fashioning a way "out," and social movements are at the heart of the exodus from pain and opprobrium to hope and freedom.

Queer Intimacy and Sexual Citizenship: Forging a Way Out

Lerner (1990) states that "intimacy means…we can be who we are in a relationship, and allow the other person to do the same. An intimate relationship is one in which neither party silences, sacrifices, or betrays the self and each party expresses strength and vulnerability, weakness and competence in a balanced way" (p. 3). A sense of democracy is inherent in this understanding of intimacy. The reality is, however, in most countries people are afforded full rights when they are, or appear to be, heterosexual. Lesbian, gay, bisexual, transgender, Indigenous/Two-Spirit, and Queer individuals are often asked to betray themselves. Human-rights violations occur because a person's sexual orientation or gender expression and associated intimacies are deemed transgressive.

Lerner (1990) offers that intimacy demands tireless self-learning (and also learning about "the Other"). We sexual minorities (and our allies) are engaged in lifelong learning processes, perhaps more so now than ever before in our history. The shear delight experienced in learning in general—and learning about the self in particular—offers us much hope at the personal level. And, at the level of society, it can open the way to learning for inclusive citizenship. The power of learning as an agent of transformation is glimpsed in the sea change of social policy during the past decade in a few countries that has resulted in positive gains for sexual minorities.

Queer Nationalism

The notion of establishing full rights for sexual minorities is clearly expressed in the philosophy of the decades-old movement, Queer Nation (see Seidman, 1996). Queer Nation is about reconceptualizing nationhood as an ideological space where same-gender intimacy has full authority and people can claim the delight and joy that attend it. The ideology of Queer nationalism focuses on sexual-minority civil rights, empowerment in the face of oppression, and visibility (Walker, 2008). Its "educational interventions…[allow] a relatively small number of activists to challenge dominant discourses and to facilitate rapid social change" (Walker, 2008, p. 47).

Queer nationalists contest traditional values about family, the police state, and the panopticon (surveillance) of authoritarian rule over our lives by religious, usually fundamentalist, institutions. It is a struggle to re/claim self-respect and self-esteem. It is a recovery process to salvage the intimacy that has been denied to us by the dominant culture.

Intimacy is inseparable from life itself; however, in the face of silencing and marginalization, it is difficult to publicly express. As a result, sexual minorities have developed underground (private and subversive) grassroots expressions of it. We have discovered, and at times have confronted society with, our intimacy and our menacing identities. As Hill (2004a) points out, men loving men and women loving women *are* revolutionary acts. Of course, this can be extended to transgender and bisexual relationships.

In the *Queer Manifesto* (1990), an anonymous activist wrote words worth quoting at length:

> *How can I tell you. How can I convince you…that your life is in danger. That everyday you wake up alive, relatively happy, and a functioning human being, you are committing a rebellious act. You as an alive and functioning queer are a revolutionary. There is nothing on this planet that validates, protects or encourages your existence. It is a miracle you are standing here reading these words. You should by all rights be dead….Straight people have a privilege that allows them to do whatever they please….Until I can*

enjoy the same freedom of movement and sexuality, as straights, their priv-
ilege must stop and it must be given over to me and my queer sisters and
brothers....Being queer is not about a right to privacy; it is about the free-
dom to be public, to just be who we are. Being queer [is] about gender-fuck
and secrets, what's beneath the belt and deep inside the heart; it's about the
night. Being queer is "grass roots" because we know that everyone of us...
is a world of pleasure waiting to be explored. Everyone of us is a world of
infinite possibility....[W]e are an army of lovers because it is we who know
what love is. Desire and lust, too. We invented them. We come out of the
closet, face the rejection of society, face firing squads, just to love each oth-
er!... Let's make every space a Lesbian and Gay space. Every street a part of
our sexual geography. A city of yearning and then total satisfaction. A city
and a country where we can be safe and free and more.... (n.p.)

We already have ways, often subterranean, subversive, and hidden, to be intimate—to learn how to be, to belong, to become, and to act—that are products of
learning in our social movements. These are most often expressed in the private
sphere where we are sexual and intimate citizens in a subculture that knows how
to delight in who we are and to relate to those like ourselves and our allies. To
the dominant world, however, we remain largely interlopers. We have yet to learn
how to move more effectively from "outsider to citizen" (Seidman, 2005, p. 225).

Being and Becoming the "Good Citizen"

Adult educators often promote citizenship and the concept of what constitutes the "good citizen." Westheimer and Kahne (2004) have explored the "spectrum of ideas about what good citizenship is and what good citizens do that are
embodied in democratic education programs" (p. 237). They have detailed three
perspectives that underscore the political implications of education for democracy: personal responsibility, participatory behavior, and justice orientation. They
argue that "many current efforts at teaching for democracy [reflect] not arbitrary
choices but, rather, political choices with political consequences" that often lead
to "narrow and ideologically conservative concept[s] of citizenship" (p. 237). Social movement learning in sexual-minority communities resists this, as we reinscribe notions of what constitutes the good citizen.

Johnston (2003) offers that "the role and possibilities of adult education in fostering citizenship…are often more aspirational than practical.…[It is] about a role for education which is not grounded in a realistic understanding of contemporary…cultural circumstances" (p. 53). This has certainly been the case in many regions of the world where same-gender intimacy is taboo and the construction of the good (sexual) citizen is a married heterosexual one (Seidman, 2005). Queer people, in fact, are typecast as "'bad sexual citizens'—inferior, immoral and dangerous to society. Bad sexual citizens become the targets of social control, which may include public stereotyping, harassment, violence, criminalization, and disenfranchisement" (p. 225). This has been well documented in organizational settings, including in civil society, the corporate/business world, and in formal, informal, and nonformal educational venues.

Very few places, including the most liberal democracies, offer comprehensive citizenship rights to sexual minorities. At best, a number of rights are simply denied; at worst, legal convictions and sentencing lead to imprisonment and death. On the one hand, gay theorists such as Weeks, Heaphy, and Donovan (2001) argue that we sexual minorities must command control of our own bodies, emotions, and relationships. Their chapter, "Towards Intimate Citizenship" (p. 180 ff), details possibilities, risks, and the practices of freedom for us. On the other hand, Biesta and Lawy (2006) show that a comprehensive construction of citizenship has given way to a more overtly individualistic approach. A remedy to this includes expanding our notion of citizenship by linking it to a broader human rights program, which is how contemporary gay and lesbian social movement learning constructs citizenship, as will be detailed below.

The many ways in which sexual minorities connect intimacy and learning "entail wildness, and mischief, conjuring up our more raucous nature.…The conflict that is sometimes generated by inserting sexual-minority content into the learning environment has the potential for growth and development for those who encounter it" (Hill, 2004a, p. 93). An appeal to our wild side evokes a call to "reject inhibitions imposed by assumed meanings and to cultivate in their place the fiercely passionate and undomesticated side of our…nature that challenges preconceived ideas" (Thomas, 1993, p. 7, quoted in Hill, 2004a, p. 93). That is a gift from sexual minorities to the world toward building the notion of what "intimate citizenship" might become.

The Democratization of Intimacy: A Declaration

The intersections of the unmasked self, the unleashed heart, the struggle for full citizenship and social justice for sexual minorities, and our willingness to be disturbed—coupled with the notion that heterosexism, homophobia, and transphobia place burdens on *all* people (not just lesbian, gay, bisexual, transgender, Indigenous/Two-Spirit, and Queer people)—are having seismic consequences in society today. In April 2006, a group of sexual-minority activists, community organizers, writers, artists, lawyers, journalists, scholars, and educators came together to challenge themselves (and us) to explore and debate issues of intimacy beyond the one-dimensional construction of what constitutes the sexual-minority community. They explored intersections of "race, class, gender and issue lines…to shape alternative policy solutions and to inform organizing strategies …[that] include the broadest definitions of relationship and family" (The April Working Group, 2006, para. 3). The result is a declaration on the democratization of intimacy built on restructuring the social justice agenda found in sexual-minority communities. The April 2006 meeting resulted in an invitation for us to radically declare ourselves:

> to be part of an interdependent, global community. [To] stand with people
> of every racial, gender and sexual identity…throughout the world, who are
> working—often in harsh political and economic circumstances—to resist
> the structural violence of poverty, racism, misogyny, war, and repression,
> and to build an unshakeable foundation of social and economic justice for
> all, from which authentic peace and recognition of global human rights
> can at long last emerge. (A New Strategic Vision for All Our Families and
> Relationships, 2006, para. 4)

This declaration is a personal and social cry—and a petition to governments—to be prophetic, visionary, and creative in democratizing intimacy. It makes difference a fundamental human right and allows various forms of love to find equal justice under the law.

The *New Strategic Vision* (2006) is a call to halt the "increasing shift of public funds from human needs into militarism, policing, and prison construction [that] are producing ever-greater wealth and income gaps between the rich and the poor" (para. 11). It is an intimacy of love recognizing that "people are forming unique unions and relationships that allow them to survive and create the communities and partnerships that mirror their circumstances, needs, and hopes… [where people]…are shaping for themselves the relationships, unions, and informal kinship systems that validate and support their daily lives, the lives they are actually living, regardless of what direction the current ideological winds might be blowing" (para. 11). It challenges sexual-minority strategies not only to democratize *our* lives but also to address the widespread hunger for authentic and just communities for *everyone*.

This declaration, together with unmasking the self, unleashing the heart, walking in harmony with the Earth, cultivating the fiercely passionate and undomesticated side of our natures, commanding control of our own bodies, emotions, and relationships, the willingness to be disturbed, and developing cultural and social competencies, makes up the pedagogical practices that enable the art, knowledge, and skill of intimacy to take root in our lives.

<hr />

A Few Vexing Thoughts

Unmistakably, sexual-minority movements are sites of learning and meaning making and are involved in the democratization of intimacy (as well as in the democratization of learning). It is vital to remember that most people do not intentionally seek to become movement members so that they may become intimate. And as sexual minorities we usually do not join movements as a means to establish the right to love in ways that are alternative to the dominant society; it is our loving that births the movements. The usual pattern is that lesbian, gay, bisexual, transgender, Two-Spirit, and Queer people self-identify forms of intimacy that are different (i.e., menacing) to the majority groups in their cultures and societies. Most, at least initially, do not focus on the fact that there are myriad people who are also same-gender loving or who express gender in ways not typical of their societies or cultures. This notion is poignantly developed in the award-winning documentary film, *Dangerous Living: Coming Out in the Developing World* (2003). Interviewees express that they did not one day simply wake up and proclaim, "I'm going to join the global movement for Queer human rights!" Their struggle was primarily in developing identities as sexual minorities and learning behaviors to be intimate and loving in their own special ways.

We must examine critically the notion, espoused especially by religious and political leaders in less developed countries, that the intimate desires and behaviors of sexual minorities are neocolonial projects. This argument claims that homosexuality and transgendered lives are Western perversions of traditional male-female (heterosexual) dynamics. We must be clear that, on a global scale, the practice of same-gender loving and multiple forms of gender presentation are *not* foreign or alien to most cultures. What is new is the movement for the right to live *openly* in ways that have always existed. Thus, sexual-minority identity and intimacy predate the colonial and imperial enterprises of Euro-American conquests. Sexual minorities have existed and have learned to be intimate in Africa (Murray & Roscoe, 1998), Islamic societies (Dunne, 1990; Khalaf & Gagnon, 2006; Murray & Roscoe, 1997), Asia (for a bibliography of literature, see Halsall, 1997), the Austral-Pacific and Oceanic regions (for a bibliography of literature, see Halsall, 1997), the Caribbean (Glave, 2008), and Latin America (Balderston & Guy, 1997; Murray, 1995)—that is, virtually everywhere!

The export of a specific Western (Euro-American) way of sexual-minority behavior is, however, a product of top-down globalization and the corruption of indigenous forms of homosexualities and gender role variations. Regarding this understudied phenomenon, Hill (2004b) has written that very little research has exposed the "McPinking" (a term employed to parallel global "McDonaldization") of the planet; the color pink is often associated with sexual minorities and the spread of Western sexual-minority constructions—including such tools of cultural hegemony as techno-beat music, the bar and nightclub scene, and the commercial paraphernalia that constitute the "material Queer" (Chasin, 2000; Morton, 1996). The role that these occupy in the democratization of intimacy remains unexplored. They may, in fact, be neocolonial projects, complicit with the genocide of indigenous alternative gender roles. Euro-American sexual minorities must be made aware of this.

Finally, que(e)rying the intimacy of learning leads us to ask vital (and contradictory) questions: Is democratic public space eroding? Is there ever too much democracy? (Hill, 2006b). I speak here of the ways that sexual-minority intimacy intersects with democracy. This is a democracy that is defined as more than a matter of voting. It is a *radical* democracy that includes the many ways that ordinary people govern their lives on a daily basis. Processes of democracy should be educative, dynamic, and most important, ongoing. The Queering of democracy, generated by sexual-minority intimacy, demands that people must:

be constituted through diverse experiences, needs, and desires as both individuals and members of communities. Thus, radical democracy is a form of politics that recognizes diversity, and invites participation from a variety of social spaces. But radical democracy does not simply "represent" this plurality, as if "diversity" were a static enumeration of "who" people are; rather, it fosters the continual proliferation of new voices, new communities, and new identities, as part of an ongoing process of democratization. What this means is the recognition that many struggles are "democratic." And that, to me, is radical democracy: a contestation of the universal, the particular, the public and the private to continually reshape the contours of what "the political" means. Radical democracy means, necessarily, broadening political participation in a meaningful way. It means fostering a variety of voices to contest "the universal," and fostering a recognition of a variety of struggles as specifically, and relatedly, democratic. A radical democracy is thus one which recognizes its own contingency, one which does not believe its processes and techniques to embody democracy "itself." It is, paradoxically, a form of democracy that can never claim itself to be fully "democratic." (Sandilands, 1993, para. 16, italics in original)

One the one hand, in the United States today there is a crisis in loss of democratic public space, especially after the attacks of September 11, 2001. In the name of (a false) "security," citizens have willingly allowed the government to diminish our civil liberties and to govern our lives for us, abdicating the right to make our own choices. Freedom is giving way to surveillance, discipline, and order. Some scholars claim there is "a frontal assault against all remnants of the democratic state [by the political Right]" (Giroux, 2006, para. 1). Giroux points out that we are losing a sense of a common good and of social justice. The State discourse of democracy is being used as a costume that cloaks fundamentalism. Cornel West (2004) has argued persuasively that just as we need to analyze the dark forces shutting down democracy, we must also be very clear about the visions that resist these forces. This is where gay and lesbian social movements are playing key roles.

On the other hand, I must ask (Hill, 2003a), Whose democracy are we discussing? Is it possible to resist a fixed meaning of democracy? Are there ever times when there is too much democracy? When is subversive education and revolutionary practice to undermine democracy called for? I talk about revolutionary practice in the sense of acting in ways that bring about momentous changes in social and cultural situations—e.g., drastic and far-reaching adjustments in ways of behaving and thinking, such as societal acceptance of men loving men and women loving women, which in most quarters remain revolutionary acts. The intimacy that this essay has addressed can be revolutionary. Likewise, by subversive I mean pedagogies that are in opposition to social policy. Many state governments in the United States have voted to alter their Constitutions so that sexual-minority rights become drastically limited through legislation that can be defined as the tyranny of the voting majority; sexual minorities become further entrenched as second-class citizens as a result of the democratic process as it exists in the United States today. The result of such legislation has been increased psychological stress and induction of ill-health for sexual minorities and their families.[7]

Conclusion

Intimacy, in its affective, emotional, cognitive, physical, and spiritual incarnations—like learning itself—is profoundly relational. Variations of the dominant (heterosexual) social paradigm on sexual orientation and gender identity often elicit visceral responses that negatively impact sexual minorities. It is imperative that educators and trainers, dedicated to the belief that difference is a fundamental human right, design learning opportunities and interventions that foster full citizenship for all youth and adults.

Democratic practices, freed from political manipulation, are necessary in the many spaces where everyone, including lesbians, gay men, bisexuals, transgender, and Iindigenous/Two-Spirit people, learn, study, work, and play. This is the type of radical democracy that allows for the constant creation of revolutionary voices, new communities, and pioneering identities. This is clearly articulated in the declaration, *A New Strategic Vision for All Our Families and Relationships* (2006). The sexual-minority "underground" already has informal and nonformal venues where intimacy has the freedom to delight and to take joy in human relationships, as cogently expressed in the *Queer Manifesto* (1990): "[W]e are all a world of pleasure waiting to be explored. Everyone of us is a world of infinite possibility....[W]e are an army of lovers" (para 7).

---

7 I previewed three papers in advance of a special issue of the *Journal of Counseling Psychology*, "Advances in Research with Sexual-Minority People," scheduled for January 2009 publication. These forthcoming papers are by Arm, Horne, and Levitt; Levitt, et al.; and Rostosky, Riggle, Horne, and Miller.

The demand for adult learning has focused in recent years on skills development, increased productivity, training, and market values, yet the field has historically supported adult learning for justice, human development, and empowerment (Grace 2004, 2005, 2007). Simultaneous with the human capitalization
of the field has been the call for human rights based on the right to be different
(Hill, 2003b). Bélanger and Federighi (2000) offer a vision of the adult learning
process as "the very meaning of empowerment sought by men and women, the
search for higher quality of individual and community life, self-expression, the
diverse expression of identities and the celebration of their difference. This process also involves...the democratisation of the quality of life" (p. 205). These lines
speak directly to the heart of sexual-minority hopes and dreams. Being open to
fully experiencing the world, in its spectral differences, *is* the way—and the social
movement actors who are lesbian, gay, bisexual, transgender, Indigenous/Two-
Spirit, and Queer offer experiences of how this can be done. Regarding sexual-
minority intimacy and sexual and gender identity, I concur with Wenger (1998):
"Learning cannot be designed. Ultimately, it belongs to the realm of experience
and practice. It follows the negotiation of meaning; it moves on its own terms. It
slips through the cracks; it creates its own cracks. Learning happens, design or
no design" (p. 225). It frequently happens through the mobilization of human
desires for love, belonging, intimacy, and yearnings of the heart, regardless of
social determinism; we sexual minorities are fully attuned to this. The literature
on learning is really one of delight and pleasure with intimacy as its foundation,
and the literature on desire and joy is profoundly a literature on the intimacy
of learning. The informal and nonformal learning for liberation with/in Queer
communities is a model.

This liberatory space is a radical democratically intimate space—indeed, a
spiritual space. Sr. Joan Chittister, Benedictine nun and activist, reminds us, "The
function of spirituality is not to protect us from our times. The function of spirituality is to enable us to leaven our times, to stretch our times, to bless our times,
to break open our own times" (2001, para. 10). Liberatory space includes the
Queer dimensions that are leavening the present moment in ever-changing ways.

As adult educators we are often not aware that we face questions of relevance
(Argyris & Schon, 1991) that include our openness to the democracy of intimacy
and sexuality. The choice is ours whether we will accept the opportunities and
challenges in the struggles over sexual-minority rights across the lifespan. Not to
do so is to miss an opportunity to weave threads to each other's heart, growing
together in new and consequential ways. By not allowing our judgments about

"the Other" to eclipse learning we can break open pedagogical practices that enable the art, knowledge, and skill of intimacy to re/create ourselves, our nations, and our world in a ground-breaking performance of radical practices. To do otherwise may mean to continue down the path to irrelevancy.

References

Allen, P. G. (2007). American Indian indigenous pedagogy. In S. B. Merriam & Associates (Ed.), *Non-western perspectives on learning and knowing* (pp. 41-56). Malabar, FL: Krieger.

The April Working Group. (2006). *Beyond marriage.* Retrieved November 25, 2008, from http://www.beyondmarriage.org/about.html

Argyris, C., & Schon, D. (1991). Participatory action research and action science compared: A commentary. In W. F. Whyte (Ed.), *Participatory action research* (pp. 85-96). Newbury Park, CA: Sage Publications.

Arm, J. R., Horne, S. G., & Levitt, H. M. (2009). Negotiating connection to GLBT experience: Family members' experience of anti-LGBT movements and policies. *Journal of Counseling Psychology, 56*(1), 82-96.

Balderston, D., & Guy, D. J. (Eds.). (1997). *Sex and sexuality in Latin America: An interdisciplinary reader.* NY: New York University Press.

Bélanger, P., & Federighi, P. (2000). *Unlocking people's creative forces: A transnational study of adult learning policies.* Hamburg: UNESCO Institute for Education.

Biesta, G., & Lawy, R. (2006). From teaching citizenship to learning democracy: Overcoming individualism in research, policy and practice. *Cambridge Journal of Education, 36*(1), 63-79.

Chasin, A. (2000). *Selling out: The gay and lesbian movement goes to market.* NY: Palgrave.

Chittister, J. (2001). Spirituality and contemporary culture II. Retrieved November 25, 2008, from https://www.tcpc.org/resources/articles/ spirituality_and_contemporary.htm

Dangerous Living: Coming Out in the Developing World. (2003). J. Scagliotti (Director). Human Rights Watch. Retrieved November 25, 2008, from http://hrw.org/ and http://firstrunfeatures.com/hrw4.html

Darder, A., & Mirón, L. F. (2006). Critical pedagogy in a time of uncertainty: A call to action. In N. K. Denzin & M. D. Giardina (Eds.), *Contesting empire/globalizing dissent: Cultural studies after 9/11* (pp. 136-151). Boulder, CO: Paradigm.

Decker, V. L. (2008). *Conversations with women with disabilities in regard to gender, relationships, and sexuality.* Unpublished master's thesis, University of Georgia, Athens.

Delors, J. (1996). *Learning: The treasure within.* Paris: UNESCO Publishing.

Denzin, N. K., & Lincoln, Y. S. (2008). Introduction. In N. K. Denzin, Y. S. Lincoln, & L. T. Smith (Eds.), *Handbook of critical and indigenous methodologies* (pp. 1-20). Los Angeles: Sage.

Dunne, B. (1990). Homosexuality in the Middle East: An agenda for historical research. *Arab Studies Quarterly, 12*(3/4), 1-23.

Faure, E., et al. (1972). *Learning to be: The world of education today and tomorrow.* Paris: UNESCO Publications.

Finger, M. (1989, Fall). New social movements and their implications for adult education. *Adult Education Quarterly, 40*(1), 15-21.

Foucault, M. (1982). The subject and power. In H. L. Dreyfus & P. Rabinow (Eds.), *Michel Foucault: Beyond structuralism and hermeneutics.* Chicago: University of Chicago Press.

Freire, P. (1999). *Pegagogy of hope.* NY: Continuum. (Original work published 1992)

Giroux, H. A. (2006). Cultural studies in dark times: Public pedagogy and the challenge of neoliberalism. *Firgoa – universidade pública - espazo comunitario.* Retrieved November 25, 2008, from http://firgoa.usc.es/drupal/node/25904

Glave, T. (2008). *Our Caribbean: A gathering of lesbian and gay writing from the Antilles.* Durham, NC: Duke University Press.

Grace, A. P. (2004). Lifelong learning as a chameleonic concept and versatile practice: Y2K perspectives and trends. *International Journal of Lifelong Education, 23*(4), 385-405.

Grace, A. P. (2005). Lifelong learning chic in the modern practice of adult education: Historical and contemporary perspectives. *Journal of Adult and Continuing Education, 11*(1), 62-79.

Grace, A. P. (2007). Envisioning a critical social pedagogy of learning and work in a contemporary culture of cyclical lifelong learning. *Studies in Continuing Education, 29*(1), 85-103.

Habermas, J. (1981). New social movements. *Telos, 49,* 33-37.

Halsall, P. (1997). *An online guide to LGBT history.* Retrieved November 25, 2008, from http://www.fordham.edu/halsall/pwh/index-wld.html

Heaney, T. (1996). *Adult education for social change: From center stage to the wings and back again.* Columbus, OH: ERIC Clearinghouse on Adult, Career, and Vocational Education. (ERIC Information Series No. 365)

Hill, R. J. (2003a). Inclusion of sexual minorities in the discussion on gender justice: The GEO virtual seminar. In Paz Alonso (Ed. coordinator), *Education for inclusion throughout life: The GEO virtual seminar* (pp. 130-134). Montevideo: The Gender and Education Office of the International Council for Adult Education.

Hill, R. J. (2003b). Turning a gay gaze on citizenship. Sexual orientation and gender identity: Contesting/ed terrain. In C. Medel-Anonuevo et al. (Eds.), *Citizenship, democracy and lifelong learning* (pp. 99-139). Hamburg: UNESCO, Institute for Education (UIE). Available at http://www.unesco.org/education/uie/pdf/ uiestud35.pdf

Hill, R. J. (2004a). Activism as practice: Some Queer considerations. In R. St. Clair & J. A. Sandlin (Eds.), *Promoting critical practice in adult education* (pp. 85-94). New Directions for Adult and Continuing Education, No. 102. San Francisco: Jossey-Bass.

Hill, R. J. (2004b). Going global: Internationalizing LGBTQ resilience and inclusion. In A. P. Grace, K. W. Wells, & M. Holcroft (Eds.), *LGBTQ Resilience and Inclusion: Being, Becoming, Belonging—The 2nd Annual LGBTQ&A Pre-Conference of the 45th Annual Adult Education Research Conference—Canadian Association for the Study of Adult Education (CASAE/ACÉÉA)* (pp. 16-30). Victoria, BC: University of Victoria.

Hill, R. J. (2006a). Editor's notes. In R. J. Hill (Ed.), *Challenging heterosexism and homophobia: Lesbian, gay, bisexual, transgender and Queer issues in occupational settings* (pp. 1-6). New Directions for Adult and Continuing Education, No. 112. San Francisco: Jossey-Bass.

Hill, R. J. (2006b). The war on democracy: A perspective from the USA. *Convergence, 38*(2-3), 167-176.

Hill, R. J. (2008). Troubling adult learning in the present time. In S. Merriam (Ed.), *Third update on adult learning theory* (pp. 83-92). New Directions for Adult and Continuing Education, No. 119. San Francisco: Jossey-Bass.

Hill, R. J. (2009). In/Corporating queers: Blowback, backlash and other forms of resistance to workplace diversity initiatives that support sexual minorities. In T. S. Rocco, J. Gedro, & M. B. Kormanik (Eds.), *Gay lesbian, bisexual, and transgender issues in HRD: Balancing inquiry and advocacy. Advances in developing human resources, 11*(3) 37-53. Bowling Green, OH: Academy of Human Resource Development and Sage.

Imel, S. (2000). International perspectives on adult education. Education Resources Information Center (ERIC) Clearinghouse on Adult, Career and Vocational Education. *Trends and Issues Alert, No. 14*. Retrieved November 25, 2008, from http://www.calpro-online.org/eric/docs/tia00082.pdf

Johnston, R. (2003). Adult learning and citizenship: A framework for understanding and practice. In P. Coare & R. Johnston (Eds.), *Adult learning, citizenship and community voices* (pp. 53-67). Leicester, UK: NIACE.

Khalaf, S., & Gagnon, J. (Eds.) (2006). *Sexuality in the Arab world*. London: Saqi.

Klein, N. (2002). The vision thing: Were the DC and Seattle protests unfocused, or are critics missing the point? In B. Shepard & R. Hayduk (Eds.), *From ACT UP to the WTO: Urban protest and community building in the era of globalization* (pp. 265-273). NY: Verso.

Lerner, H. (1990). *The dance of intimacy: A woman's guide to courageous acts of change in key relationships*. NY: Harper & Rox/Perennial Library.

Levitt, H. M., Ovrebo, E., Anderson-Cleveland, M. B., Leone, C., Jeong, J. Y., Arm, J. R., Bonin, B. P., Cicala, J., Coleman, R., Laurie, A., Vardaman, J. M., & Horne, S. G. (2009). Balancing dangers: GLBT experience in a time of anti-GLBT legislation. *Journal of Counseling Psychology, 56*(1), 67-81.

Mackeracher, D. (2004). *Making sense of adult learning*. Toronto: University of Toronto Press.

MacNair, R. H., Fowler, L., & Harris, J. (2000). The diversity functions of organizations that confront oppression: The evolution of three social movements. *Journal of Community Practice, 7*(2), 71-88.

Mashek, D. J., & Aron, A. (2004). *Handbook of closeness and intimacy*. Mahwah, NJ: Lawrence Erlbaum Associates.

Morton, D. (Ed.). (1996). *The material queer: A lesbigay cultural studies reader*. Boulder, CO: Westview Press.

Murray, S. O. (1995). *Latin American male homosexualities*. Albuquerque, NM: University of New Mexico Press.

Murray, S. O., & Roscoe, W. (Eds.). (1997). *Islamic homosexualities: Culture, history, and literature*. NY: New York University Press.

Murray, S. O., & Roscoe, W. (Eds.). (1998). *Boy-wives and female husbands: Studies in African homosexualities*. NY: Palgrave/St Martin's Press.

A New Strategic Vision for All Our Families and Relationships. (2006). Retrieved November 25, 2008, from http://www.beyondmarriage.org/full_statement. html

Pelias, R. J. A. (2004). *A methodology of the heart: Evoking academic and daily life.* Walnut Creek, CA: Altamira.

Queer manifesto. 1990. Retrieved November 25, 2008, from http://www.sterneck. net/gender/queer-manifesto/index.php

Raschke, J. (1985). *Soziale Bewegungen:Ein historisch-systematischer Grundriß.* Frankfurt: Campus.

Rostosky, S. S., Riggle, E. D. B., Horne, S. G., & Miller, A. D. (2009). Marriage amendments and psychological distress in lesbian, gay, and bisexual (LGB) adults. *Journal of Counseling Psychology, 56*(1), 56-66.

Sandilands, K. (1993, Winter). Radical democracy: A contested/ing terrain. *Synthesis/Regeneration: A magazine of green social thought online, 5.* Retrieved November 25, 2008, from http://www.greens.org/s-r/05/05-13.html

Seidman, S. (Ed.). (1996). *Queer theory sociology.* Malden, MA: Blackwell.

Seidman, S. (2005). From outsider to citizen. In E. Bernstein & L. Schaffner (Eds.), *Regulating sex: The politics of intimacy and identity* (pp. 225-245). NY: Routledge.

Semali, L. M., & Kincheloe, J. L. (1999). What is indigenous knowledge and why should we study it? In L. M. Semali & J. L. Kincheloe (Eds.), *What is indigenous knowledge? Voices from the academy* (pp. 3-57). NY: Falmer.

Shepard, B., & Hayduk, R. (Eds.). (2002). *From ACT UP to the WTO: Urban protest and community building in the era of globalization.* NY: Verso.

Shor, I. (1992). *Empowering education: Critical teaching for social change.* Chicago: University of Chicago Press.

Tepper, S. (2000). The missing discourse of pleasure. *Sexuality and Disability, 18*(4), 283-290.

Thomas, J. 1(993). *Doing critical ethnography. Qualitative Research Methods, Vol. 26.* Newbury Park: Sage Publications.

Vansteenwegen, A., Jans, I., & Revell, A. T. (2003). Sexual experience of women with a physical disability: A comparative study. *Sexuality and Disability, 21*(4), 283-290.

Walker, W. (2008, June 4). Adult learning in the Queer Nation: A Foucauldian analysis of educational strategies for social change. In T. V. Bettinger (Comp.), *Transcending the rhetoric of family values: Celebrating families of choice and families of value. Proceedings of the 6th Lesbian, Gay, Bisexual, Transgender, Queer and Allies Pre-Conference at the 49th Annual Adult Education Research Conference* (pp. 47-52). St. Louis: University of Missouri-St. Louis. (ERIC Document ED503480)

Weeks, J., Heaphy, B., & Donovan, C. (2001). *Same sex intimacies: Families of choice and other life experiments.* NY: Routledge.

Welton, M. (1993). Social revolutionary learning: The new social movements as learning sites. *Adult Education Quarterly, 43*(3), 152-164.

Wenger, E. (1998). *Communities of practice: Learning, meaning, and identity.* NY: Cambridge University Press.

West, C. (2004). Finding hope in dark times. *Tikkun, 19*(4), 18-20.

Westheimer, J., & Kahne, J. (2004). What kind of citizen? The politics of educating for democracy. *American Educational Researcher, 41*(2), 237-269.

Wheatley, M. J. (2002). Willing to be disturbed. In *Turning to one another: Simple conversations to restore hope in the future* (pp. 34-37). San Francisco: Berrett-Koehler.

Witherspoon, G. (1977). *Language and art in the Navajo universe.* Ann Arbor: University of Michigan Press.

Witherspoon, G. (1983). Language and reality in the Navajo world view. In W. C. Sturtevant (Ed.), *Handbook of North American Indians* (Vol. 10). Washington, DC: Smithsonian Institution.

Witherspoon, G., & Peterson, G. (1995). *Dynamic symmetry and holistic asymmetry in Navajo and Western art and cosmology.* NY: Peter Lang.

Zwaans, A., van der Veen, I., Volman, M., & ten Dam, G. (2008). Social competence as an educational goal: The role of the ethnic composition and the urban environment of the school. *Teaching and Teacher Education, 24*(8), 2118-2131.

CHAPTER 3

Art as Anti-Oppression Adult Education: Creating a Pedagogy of Presence and Place

André P. Grace

Robert J. Hill

Kristopher Wells

Let yourself be angry that the price of our [Queer] visibility is the constant threat of [symbolic and physical violence], anti-queer violence to which practically every segment of this society contributes.

Frank Browning (1994, p. 27)

At the 46th annual Adult Education Research Conference in 2005, lesbian, gay, bisexual, trans-identified, Queer, and allied participants once again witnessed a deliberate act intended to erase our presence as sexual minorities at a conference where we had already struggled for space and place for more than ten years (Grace & Hill, 2004). The third annual Lesbian, Gay, Bisexual, Transgender, Queer, and Allies (LGBTQ&A) Pre-Conference held at AERC 2005 was entitled Hear Me Out: Queer Narratives, Moral/izing Discourses, and the Academy. Participants at the LGBTQ&A Pre-Conference initiated an art as anti-oppression pedagogy undertaking called *The Triangle Project*. They invited participants in the main conference to contribute to the art installation. At one point during the main conference, the staff of the Center for Continuing Education at the host university, the University of Georgia, Athens, used a crimson curtain to hide the art installation from public view. Apparently parents of children attending an enrichment reading class in a nearby classroom had complained about our Queer presence. AERC participants responded variously.

What follows are our reflections on this attempt to disenfranchise us. Speaking to the importance of public art as a political and pedagogical tool in fighting oppression, we provide our critical reflections on what transpired based on our participation in the event. André begins, providing a description of the crimson-curtain incident as a marker of the dismissal and defilement that resulted when an educational institution enabled a conservative faction to place limits on what was not only an interactive artistic site but also a public pedagogical site. He reflects on the nature of the incident in which private morals were allowed to displace public ethics. He also considers the feelings it stirred, the collective action it provoked, and what it all means for AERC. Kris follows with a critical reflection on his experience of this incident. He speaks as a gay graduate student who engages in critical Queer research to explore the possibilities for transformative social learning in the face of exclusion and the heartfelt and generative emotions such exclusion fuels. Then, in his reflection, Bob focuses on spatiality, place, and the politics of Queer geography at AERC. He discusses how disciplinary behavior and spatial isolation were the responses of the custodians of the host space to the art installation. He frames this as an imposition of political territoriality on the conference landscape. Our collective reflections conclude with a perspective on the importance of public art as a political and pedagogical tool in fighting oppression.

⊷⊷ ▣▰▣ ⊷⊷

André's Reflection: When Private Morals Forget Public Ethics and Negate the Right to Be More

It was Saturday, June 4, 2005. Returning from a session to the conference book display and refreshments area, I anticipated enjoying the morning break with colleagues who were also attending AERC at the University of Georgia, Athens. As I came around the corner to enter this area, I was shocked to see that a crimson curtain shrouded the LGBTQ&A art installation that we had created at our pre-conference. We had placed this installation in a corner near the book displays. We had also placed a table with art supplies near it so that conference participants might add drawings, poems, or other artistic expressions to this emerging, collective visual statement that spoke to Queer history, resistance, and resilience. What we had wanted to be a political and pedagogical site of LGBTQ&A representation where conference participants could dialogue and interact had now been hidden from view.

What had happened this time? Well, apparently some parents whose children were attending an enrichment reading class in a room across from the art installation had found the Queer arts-informed, communal display to be an offensive reminder of what they no doubt perceived as some sort of pervert incursion. Pictures of Queer couples and Queer-led families, pictures of Queer heroes, and pictures of Queer culture must have made our presence too visible, too provocative, and just too much for them to handle. While I wasn't there for their verbal tirade with staff at the Center for Continuing Education (CCE), I can imagine the self-righteousness and bigotry that fuelled their remarks. Enrichment for their children would not include any interaction with representations of sexual-minority differences. Their reaction had prompted a nervous and compliant CCE staff to submit to their wishes. They put up a crimson curtain to hide the art installation, which constituted a reminder of our presence among them. This denial of Queer space and place amounted to engaging in a debasing politics of Queer exclusion that attempted to erase the reality of our presence because some were offended by it. In this moment of blatant oppression, I felt what Paulo Freire (2004) called legitimate anger or just ire in the *Pedagogy of Indignation,* the book he had been working on just before his death. Freire, who used his legitimate anger to infuse a politics and pedagogy of just ire, described the notion in these proactive terms:

> *I have the right to be angry and to express that anger, to hold it as my motivation to fight, just as I have the right to love and to express my love for the world, to hold it as my motivation to fight, because while a historical being, I live history as a time of possibility. … My right to feel anger presupposes, in the historic experience in which I participate, that tomorrow is not a "given," but rather a challenge, a problem. My anger, my just ire, is founded in my revulsion before the negation of the right to "be more," which is etched in the nature of human beings. (pp. 58-59)*

As his words suggest, Freire used his legitimate anger as an energizer in his social and cultural work for change in a dehumanizing world. He clearly inserted himself into this world and dared to "imagine a world that is less dehumanizing, more just, less discriminatory, and more humane" (Macedo, 2004, p. ix). Freire chose anger over cynicism, and he used his anger as his motivation to fight so he could live history as a time of possibility soaked in hope and freedom (Macedo, 2004). Macedo pinpoints that, for Freire, the expression of anger was the "eruption of just ire" (p. xi). This eruption had to follow denunciation with annunciation: "Changing the world implies a dialectic dynamic between denunciation of the dehumanizing situation and the announcing of its being overcome" (Freire, as quoted by Macedo, p. xi). At AERC, LGBTQ&A participants have continually denounced debasing Queer exclusion (whether subtly or overtly instigated) and announced a presence and place to our conservative colleagues through our caucus, pre-conference, and the growing number of presentations in the main conference (Grace & Hill, 2004; see Chapter 1 above). In all these spaces, we always make it clear that when there is an assault on our right to be or a betrayal of it, those who assault or betray are unfaithful to our humanity, their humanity, and indeed all humanity. Ultimately, they erode their own integrity as they batter Queer identities. When it is colleagues who jilt us, they unsubscribe to notions they may have valued in word – notions like adult education as community and adult education as social education.

Later, when speaking to Kris about the crimson-curtain incident, a colleague related, "When I looked at André, he was 38-hot!" In the moment when I saw the closed curtain, I was at least that. I was so very angry. I was angry because once again I had to deal with yet another group who had defiled and dismissed all of us who are LGBTQ. I was angry because CCE staff had acted unilaterally in submission to a group that was not part of the AERC conference, without consulting the LGBTQ&A Caucus. I was angry because many AERC colleagues milling about the book display and refreshments area didn't seem to notice or care. I was angry because some of them would call themselves social educators.

In my moment of legitimate anger, I had to act. I had to make other conference participants aware. I needed to create the kind of pedagogical moment that I tell my students about in my critical adult education classes. So I went to the middle of the common area and shouted loudly to attract everyone's attention. I told those gathered what had happened, and I reminded them that AERC prided itself as a conference that made space and place for disenfranchised groups. In the interest of this much-touted commitment to inclusive social education, I invited colleagues to write notes and attach them to the curtain to express their disdain for what had happened. In that moment the art installation started to become the site of dialogue and interaction that we had hoped it would be at the conference. Many colleagues – professors and graduate students alike – and several employees of the University of Georgia moved toward the curtain that we had now opened but wanted left in place as a reminder of the shame that those who had disenfranchised us had brought upon themselves. Supporters posted heartfelt comments that began a process of healing and recovery from one more rightist assault.

This engagement constituted a moment of informal, critical social learning focused on awareness and accommodation of sexual minorities as members of at least a temporary construction of adult education as community (Grace & Wells, 2007b). In this moment there was consideration of sexual orientation, gender identity, and the contexts in which they were taken up at AERC 2005. There was also a collective desire to transgress the art installation as a problematic cultural project and to reconfigure it as a cultural formation and critical Queer learning project focused on identities, differences, histories, survival, and collective action (Grace & Wells, 2007b). Ultimately, the art installation became a medium to advance an aesthetic intelligence that promoted the value of pursuing alternative learning as well as different possibilities and choices via expressive, relational learning (Eisner, in Grace & Wells, 2007b). Collectively, the dialogic interaction constituted a public pedagogy that denounced the exclusionary act and announced the strength and activism of our presence. Some of the shared thoughts, anonymous and signed, posted on the crimson curtain as an offensive wall of censorship included:

Walls shut down voices, shut out people, and hide truths – for shame.

Censorship offends, hurts, is wrong. We need all voices.

The public square should be public – all voices heard equally.

Gay and lesbian people are everywhere. Get use to it.

Ally is NOT a label – It's an action.

The GLBT "cover up" is entirely inappropriate. We too are citizens of this community, society, world. Everyone (at every age) needs to know and, at a minimum, tolerate this human reality.

UGA – please take down your barriers.

I find this wall of censorship extremely offensive. This is symbolic violence!
André P. Grace

UGA – a public apology is needed for this act of symbolic violence.
Ian Baptiste

To "shield" (exclude, ban, outlaw) this is an act that is offensive and a hurt to us all.
Stephen D. Brookfield

In every class I teach I speak about how important it is to put public ethics before private morals. I tell students that it is vital in social, cultural, political, and psychological terms to be there for every individual across differences, including LGBTQ differences that take us into the intersection of the moral and the political. The sum of the sentiments that people posted on the open crimson curtain provided not only affirmation but also a wonderful expression of resist/stances that demonstrated critical social education in action (Grace & Benson, 2000). Such education primarily focuses on ethical practices of inclusion and the political ideals of modernity: democracy, freedom, and social justice. Most importantly in this case, the expression constituted a public pedagogy that reminded everyone present that LGBTQ individuals are persons, too. In my poem, "I Am a Good Person," I speak to this fact.

I Am a Good Person

André P. Grace

Hard to be respected
In this dehumanizing world
Even harder to be queer and respected
In this dehumanizing world
You can tell how hard it has been for me
When I talk about the guilt I have felt
When I talk about the shame I used to endure

It was never my guilt though
And it was not my shame
Those are feelings that righteous bigots
Would force upon my person
With their heterosexual privilege
With their immoral morality
Fixed by tradition and cultural hetero-norms
Fixed by hollow forms of rightist religions
That tried to cover me like an irritating hair shirt
To mortify me
To tell me that I'm nothing
Beyond the sexed-up stereotypes
Etched in pictures or captured in words
In bibles and catechisms
And on public washroom walls

Still I am worth something
In fact
I'm worth a lot
I'm a person
I'm a queer person
Working to change my social tomorrow
So leave me to be
Leave me to become
Leave me to belong
And if you can't be in my life
That you see as untenable
Then at least stay out of it
And stop disrespecting me
Because I am a good person
I am a good person

In 1996 Cornel West was interviewed in an insightful piece that recognized the integrity of Queer for the first ever Queer-themed special issue of *Harvard Educational Review (HER)* (Eisen & Kenyatta, 1996; see Chapter 15 below for further analysis). In this article, West challenges people to understand how lives are Queered at the intersections of homophobia, White supremacy, and patriarchy. I remembered what West had said about the need for work in this intersection as I reflected on why other caucus or affinity groups of the variously and historically disenfranchised at AERC had not publicly and collectively supported us during the crimson-curtain incident. In his *HER* piece, West insists that work in this complex intersection is crucial to strategic coalition building, which is necessary to dismantle compulsory heterosexuality and other normative forms of containment. West reminds us that it is politically and culturally difficult to build coalitions because it is difficult to build trust among disenfranchised groups. Trust building requires honest confrontation of the fear, insecurity, and anxiety that we associate with other people. Reflecting on West's perspective, I wondered about the degrees to which fear, insecurity, and anxiety function at AERC not only to keep the mainstream distant from caucus or affinity groups but also to keep these groups distant from one another. It appears that we have a long way to go to make AERC a truly inclusive space and place. In this regard we would do well to remember this slogan from a contributor to the art installation: *Humanization requires representation.*

Kris's Reflection: Turning Rage
into Transformative Social Learning

As I walked out of a morning conference session, I felt encouraged and in-spired by the words of the leading adult educator I had just heard. Since I am pur-suing a doctoral degree focused on social justice, community development, and educational activism, I also felt hopeful that I had chosen the right field of study and practice. In my graduate degree program, I have been learning about the rich social justice narrative that is interwoven in the fabric and history of adult educa-tion. The words of Myles Horton and Paulo Freire (1990), Phyllis Cunningham (1988), Paula Allman (2001), and others have inspired me and strengthened my conviction to contribute to the creation of a more just and humane world. The critical perspectives of this collective of social educators fuel my passion and adherence to the Freirean belief that history is a time of possibility and not a pre-determined context in which action is futile. As a participant at AERC, critical deliberations have buoyed my learning and reinforced another Freirean belief: the mutuality between critical theorizing and critical action. These thoughts were swirling in my head as I turned the corner into the common area. That's when I first saw the crimson curtain. My body seemed to shrink at the sight. I was wounded. I was diminished.

For me, the curtain was an act of symbolic violence that not only covered up our perceived "obscene" pre-conference art installation but also assaulted my identity as a Queer person. I no longer felt safe at AERC. Perhaps it was foolish of me to think that I would find safety in this group. A history of symbolic and physical violence against LGBTQ persons has taught me to be constantly vigi-lant, to be continuously ready when the next gay-basher strikes (Fone, 2000). I scolded myself for being so naïve. Why would AERC be any different? The crim-son curtain was just another ominous fence, one that I saw as similar in purpose and intent to the barbed-wire fences that the Nazis used to confine LGBTQ per-sons in concentration camps to await the "final solution" (Grau, 1995).

As I looked around the conference book display and refreshments area, I watched adult educators whom I admire walk by as if nothing were amiss. Few, if any, seemed to notice the offending curtain. Indeed, they appeared oblivious to the erasure of our LGBTQ presence. Why didn't they notice the pain etched on the faces of those of us who had been so publicly defiled? However, such main-stream obliviousness is not unusual. It is marked indelibly in our LGBTQ history that exposes the persecution of persons whom culture and society deem to have unacceptable sex, sexual, and gender differences (Fone, 2000). Still, I was angry. Shouldn't these adult educators know better? How could you live in the U.S. and not know about Matthew Shepard, the openly gay college student who had been mercilessly beaten and left to die, tied to a buck fence in an isolated area outside Laramie, Wyoming? How many Queer crucifixions do these people need to witness before they begin to see them for what they are?

André, Bob, and I instantly gathered together. We could see the hurt in each other's eyes, even if few others saw it initially. However, it wasn't long before our collective hurt turned to rage. This was not a blind rage, but the kind of rage that West (1994) describes as an important and generative emotion that puts the focus where it belongs: "on any form of racism, sexism, homophobia, or economic injustice that impedes the opportunities of 'everyday' people to live lives of dignity and decency" (p. 150). After André spoke to those gathered in the area, others became very aware of this rage. André had moved to the center of the space where he spoke loudly and assertively, capturing the attention of many. His emotional-laden words not only sent a clear message to AERC participants, they also gave voice to Bob, me, and other LGBTQ persons who had been demeaned by the crimson-curtain incident.

When André finished speaking, the tide started to turn, and we found ourselves in a new moment of shared informal learning when a group of AERC participants recognized and affirmed our presence. Indeed, this group responded quickly. Some walked toward the crimson curtain. One professor shouted that we should tear down the wall. Others took construction paper and began to write statements that they affixed to the curtain. The art installation had taken on a life of its own, and the moment became one of transformative social learning. In that moment the art installation became a site of collective learning in which the complicated, contentious, and value-laden nature of Queer being, becoming, belonging, and acting in the world could be explored (Grace & Wells, 2007a). Both educational work and cultural work were enabled by this response to the attempt to hide the art installation. Indeed the collective learning constituted a public and performative act that reminded those present that the moral and political innervate everything Queer. Thus the crimson curtain, which had been meant to hide our LGBTQ presence, now provoked a pedagogical moment that confronted the symbolic act of erasure that the crimson curtain represented. In Freire's (1998) terms, this public pedagogy had fired up a contingent of AERC participants to read the LGBTQ word *and* the LGBTQ world.

AERC history will gauge the impact of this pedagogical moment. Will lessons on LGBTQ inclusion be learned? Will AERC participants use this moment as a double-edged opportunity to critique adult education's own exclusionary practices and expand the parameters of our field of study and practice? As a doctoral student nearing the completion of my degree, I will be watching the field closely to see if lessons are learned that help us move into a more inclusive and just future.

Bob's Reflection: Spatiality, Place, and the Politics of Queer Territory at AERC

Introduction

Darlene Clover (2000) reminds us that "over the years, the arts, and in particular community arts, have become important learning tools for adults, feminists, and popular educators world-wide to nurture the 'spirit,' to encourage 'conscientization' and to mobilize the community" (p. 19). She outlines the history of scholarship between art and adult education: adult educators use public art as a community-building tool (Farkas, 2000, see pp. 15-17), an opportunity to challenge orthodox forms of teaching adults (Bappa & Bello, 1981, see pp. 24-35), and as a means to excite, challenge, anger, threaten and outrage (Overton, 1994, see p. 94).

Community and public art can be dangerous, reinscribing public space with new, and sometimes menacing, meanings. Art is a communication system that allows the expression of people's values and beliefs to surface and points to what is important (McFee & Degge, 1977)—sometimes when it is unwelcomed. The Sixth World Assembly of the International Council of Adult Education (Ocho Rios, Jamaica, 2001) provides an example. At that meeting the North American Alliance for Popular and Adult Education (NAAPAE) organized a mural project (NAAPAE Bulletin No. 17, 2). The mural became an art "attack" when gay symbols were included (Hill, 2001). This was described by popular educator Larry Olds (n.d.) as causing an "uproar [that produced] sharp conversations...in the corridors and rooms of the conference.... The mural turned out to be an outstanding example of art as education doing its job" (p. 127).

In recognition of lesbians, gay men, bisexuals, trans-identified individuals, Queers, and our communities, the third annual LGBTQ&A Pre-Conference in

2005 undertook an art as pedagogy project entitled *The Triangle Project*. The initiative included a 6-foot pink-and-black triangle upon which pre-conference and, later, main conference participants were asked to inscribe words, images, picture cut-outs, and objects from a collection provided to express their experiences of life in a moralizing environment. The shape of a triangle was employed because the triangle has become a universal symbol of both the persecution and the resiliency of sexual-minority communities. The origin of the triangle as a symbol of lesbians and gay men lies in the persecution of our community groups in Nazi Germany, where homosexual men were sent to concentration camps and forced to wear pink triangles on their prison garb. This designated them as homosexuals and signalled their "crime." Women cast as sexual deviants, including lesbians, were assigned black triangles (see Grau, 1995; Heger, 1980; Plant, 1986).

During the conference, participants adorned the triangle canvas with many gay and lesbian visuals. The art space for the triangle was located in the vicinity of a classroom where parents and children were gathered for a reading class not associated with AERC. Apparently offended by the large, colorful triangle canvas, parents complained to the CCE staff about the project. In response, the staff placed a crimson-curtain screen around the art piece, blocking the view. It should be noted that none of the images were sexually explicit. Clearly, the triangle had challenged orthodoxies and had Queered the landscape in an unsettling way for some people. The censorship of *The Triangle Project* proved the point of the exercise, which was to illustrate the haunting experiences of LGBTQ people in the moralizing environment that characterizes our moment in history.

A Queer Geography

Geography must indeed necessarily lie at the heart of my concerns.

Michel Foucault (1980, p. 77)

Geography is central to my interests. In the classes that I teach, I frequently ask students to analyze such things as the geography of power, the geography of desire, and the geography of oppression and emancipation. Geography is about space and place and the politics of territoriality. Space and place are never neutral but rather constitute the shifting terrain of cultural conflict. As an out gay man and an academic, geography is a critical aspect of life both within and outside of the academy.

Space can be conceptualized as the physical landscape—the literal environment. It can be safe—defined as an accepting, supportive, and permissive location—in the sense of allowing us (sexual minorities, i.e., members of LGBTQ communities) to be who we are, who we desire to be, and whom we desire to become. Secure landscapes present visual texts of affirmation: pink triangles, rainbow flags, bear paws, images of same-sex couples, or lesbian and gay icons. Of course, this description of a safe space is both romantic and naïve because space can be transgressed and is open to diverse inhabitants with no guarantee that they will honor the ways the space has been inscribed as safe for us. In the context of *The Triangle Project*, the academic space we entered proved unsafe when we morphed (colonized?) a putatively neutral environment into a Queer one. Disciplinary behavior and spatial isolation were the responses of the custodians of the space. Indeed physical space can truly be unsafe for LGBTQ people, meaning that it can be the perilous location where sexual minorities are unwelcome and meet confrontation, aggression, violence, and death. The murder of junior high school student Lawrence King on February 12, 2008, provides yet another example of the ultimate consequence of being so unsafe and at risk. Larry's murder indicates that Queer youth who transgress silence and invisibility are a particularly vulnerable population in this era when "the shrinking closet" suggests supposedly greater acceptance of sexual minorities (Setoodeh, 2008, p. 1). Setoodeh provides this description of Larry's comfort with his gender identity and expression and the resulting tragedy that befell him:

> *At 15, Lawrence King was small – 5 feet 1 inch – but very hard to miss. In January, he started to show up for class at Oxnard, Calif's E. O. Green Junior High School decked out in women's accessories. On some days, he would slick up his curly hair in a Prince-like bouffant. Sometimes he'd paint his fingernails hot pink and dab glitter or white foundation on his cheeks. … He bought a pair of stilettos at Target, and he couldn't have been prouder if he had on a varsity football jersey. …*
>
> *[On the morning of February 12, Brandon McInerney] quietly stood up. Then, without anyone noticing, he removed a handgun that he had somehow sneaked to school, aimed it at Larry's head, and fired a single shot. … Brandon fired at Larry a second time, tossed the gun on the ground and calmly walked through the classroom door. Police arrested him within seven minutes, a few blocks from school. Larry was rushed to the hospital, where he died two days later of brain injuries. (p. 1)*

While this case is a complex one surrounding the life of a troubled youth, the fact remains that the comfortably Queer youth ended up dead. This tragedy once again reminds us that there are many dangerous spaces for sexual minorities.

If space is understood as the literal physical environment, then place can be conceptualized as the imagined and discursive landscape. It too can be safe—defined as salubrious and utopic. It can also be hazardous and distopic. Place has multivocality and, like space, it has texture as well. To some, space as well as place consists of "socially constructed worlds that are simultaneously material and representational" (Jones, 2001, p. 122). The space and place of *The Triangle Project* incorporated these characteristics and obviously represented taboo sentiments and notions (taboo terrain) in both material and representational ways. Consequently, marginalization became the response to LGBTQ participants who violated powerful social norms in the academic milieu we entered, especially those norms related to reproduction (sex and sexuality) and cultural (including religious, medical, educational, and legal) institutions. This description of unsafe space and place, of course, can be contested too. After all, we did find refuge within the hostile space when supportive colleagues came forward to contest the presence of the crimson curtain as a marker of Queer exclusion.

The concepts of space and place are not totally strange to adult education. By way of example, *Making Space: Merging Theory and Practice in Adult Education* (Sheared & Sissel, 2001) is a play on the intersections of space and place in adult education. It is an exploration of worlds not routinely charted. Interestingly, it contains only the "cultural perspective [of] one gay white man" (Sissel & Sheared, 2001, p. 11) in a paper by Grace (2001, pp. 257-270). Queernauts (Queers in space) and our allies occasionally navigate LGBTQ inclusion, once *terra incognita* in adult education. Between 1994 and 2005, Chris Parker (personal communications) documented 15 papers based on LGBTQ themes in that decade's *AERC Proceedings*. Some of us see these as a sign that someday we will have a rich and full life in the field and practice of adult education.

Mapping Resistance, Disruptions, Partialities, Contradictions, and Difference

There is never one geography of authority and there is never one geography of resistance.... The map of resistance is not simply the underside of the map of domination—if only because each is a lie to the other, and each gives the lie to the other.

Steve Pile, *Opposition, Political Identities, and Space of Resistance*
(Quoted in Halberstam, 2005, p. 1)

Spatiality can be constructed as the total of all conditions (the geographical situations) and practices (the social interactions) of the lifeworld that connect individuals and groups to one another. The North American Adult Education Research Conference has a geography and a spatiality. In many ways AERC constitutes a geography of desire: a desire to claim a history, a voice, a presence, respect, recognition, identity, appreciation, and equality as we share our realities. Since the time of my first attendance in 1992 there has been a diversification of discourses to include sexual minorities—one that has not been uncontested as we struggle to be more than a footnote in the history of the field (Grace & Hill, 2004; Hill, 2003). The production of space to be used for specific purposes imposes a political territoriality on the landscape. We Queer Others and our allies have worked the margins in ways that have opened up space for our silent and silenced voices to be heard.

The materiality/physicality of space, not just the mental or imagined notion of space (which we can call place), was at play at AERC 2005, as it always is. Like most institutions with which I am familiar, the host site, the University of Georgia, is a site of Queer resistance, contradictions, disruptions, fragmentation, and difference. A campus climate survey revealed significant homophobia, but the university has a modestly successful Safe Space program (Hill et al., 2002). It has an embattled president who for several years refused to act on the University Council's recommendations to add sexual orientation to the university's nondiscrimination and anti-harassment policy or to provide "soft benefits" to same-sex couples (for example, borrowing privileges at the library, reduced ticket prices for events, and the use of physical space such as the swimming pool). Signs of homophobia and heterosexism appear episodically on campus. For example, some culprit(s) etched numerous anti-gay graffiti—and potentially racist, if the Confederate battle flag is seen as a signifier of conflicting Black/White social relations in the southern United States—on the whitewashed-glass window panels in a campus greenhouse. Shibboleths included, "JRL is gay" and "turtle balls." Dated the day after Christmas 2000, this verbal violence continues to be displayed to the university community. Additional graffiti included, "T-H-O-M/S-O-D-O-M-Y" and "Thom is Gay." Graphic sketches of male genitalia and other anti-gay scrawling such as "Jacob Sucks Larry's Dick" accompanied the large, bold graffiti.[8]

Despite this, the university has a recently well-funded LGBT Student Center,

---

8 The greenhouse graffiti was removed in 2008 when Hill, as a member of the university's Anti-Bias Advisory Group, complained about the university's intransigence and distributed pictures to the Associate Provost for Institutional Diversity and others.

with a newly appointed director at the level of Assistant to the Vice President for Student Affairs. The campus location is one of resistance, contradictions, and differentiation marked by Queer networks, "the Old Boys" syndrome, homophobic athletics, LGBT organizations, and a complicated "Greek life" that sponsored a speaking engagement featuring Judy Shepard, mother of Matthew Shepard, and the airing of a film on Matthew's life.

Curtains and Ex/Posing the Cover-Up

Rules that disallow certain statements to be made provided the impetus that allowed for the draping of *The Triangle Project* space. This constituted an act to deny our presence and thereby wipe away our history. It is of interest that resistance to our presence in that location manifested itself in the form of curtains—symbols of the cultural logic of invisibility and death. Metaphors such as the "Iron Curtain" and Hitchcock's film *Torn Curtain* (the compulsion to discover what lies hidden and secret behind the curtain) come to mind. In theatre, the term "final curtain" is used to announce the end of the show or the closing of a series of shows. And, of course, the sinister, "It's curtains for you!" signals death itself.

In many ways, it is difficult to ex/pose the cover-up. Objections to *The Triangle Project* were problematical to ascertain since the host of the conference refused to allow access to the protests that were received and would not identify the objectors. However, when discussing the triangle canvas, one person with whom I spoke raised the point that a biracial gay couple, two men embracing, was offensive. This person seemed to object more to the racial profile of the actors than to the action itself, which is perhaps a response to the historically volatile social race relations in the southern U.S. (one aspect of the geography of the event). The image of a biracial gay couple was at once de-familiarizing (disrupting the normalized male-female dyad) and re-familiarizing (reacquainting the observer with racial tensions). Both processes created a dangerous intersectional space.

The Reassertion of a "Just" Space and Place

Evidences of a radical rethinking of purpose, motivation, and reassertion of a "just" space and place—ones that are inclusive, tolerant, and democratic—emerged when AERC participants intervened in the silencing. The landscape became a site for intercultural learning and assertion of a kind of intercultural competence. Supporters penned (and pinned onto the curtain) signs. Others, in addition to those noted earlier by André, included:

Teach your children tolerance and acceptance.

There is no possible justification for intolerance.

Silence = Death.

One dimension of the political geography of intolerance emerged in a sign that stated, "This [Georgia] is a RED state," implying that it is numbered among the right-wing, conservative Republican states in the U.S.

Concluding Perspective: A Curtain Call on Ignorance

Public art can be a tool for nurturing the spirit, an expression of people's values and beliefs, an encouragement for conscientization, and a mobilizer of the community. It has the potential to be a community-building tool, an opportunity to challenge orthodoxy, and a means to educate, resist, excite, anger, and outrage. The third annual LGBTQ&A Pre-Conference was marked by all of these characteristics.

The *Triangle Project* was initiated as a way to show that art can have an inherently anti-oppression pedagogical dimension. In the dialectic between censorship and approval, a revolutionary hope emerged at the AERC 2005 Pre-Conference. The activism of conference-goers and colleagues revitalized the dream that we hold for building a more inclusive adult education community.

References

Allman, P. (2001). *Critical education against global capitalism: Karl Marx and revolutionary critical education.* Westport, CT: Bergin & Garvey.

Bappa, S., & Bello, A. (1981). Popular theatre for adult education, community action, and social change. *Convergence, 14*(2), 24-35.

Browning, F. (1994). *The culture of desire: Paradox and perversity in gay lives today.* NY: Vintage Books.

Clover, D. (2000). Community arts as environmental education and activism: A labour and environment case study. *Convergence, 33*(4), 19-31.

Cunningham, P. M. (1988). The adult educator and social responsibility. In R. G. Brockett (Ed.), *Ethical issues in adult education* (pp. 133-145). NY: Teachers College Press.

Eisen, V., & Kenyatta, M. (1996). Cornel West on heterosexism and transformation: An interview. *Harvard Educational Review 66*(2), 356-367.

Farkas, S. (2000,). *Women artists creating space for healthy communities.* WE International, Summer/Fall, 15-17.

Fone, B. (2000). *Homophobia: A history.* NY: Metropolitan Books, Henry Holt and Company.

Foucault, M. (1980). *Power/knowledge: Selected interviews and other writings 1972-1977.* (C. Gordon, Ed.). NY: Pantheon.

Freire, P. (1998). *Teachers as cultural workers: Letters to those who dare teach.* Boulder, CO: Westview Press.

Freire, P. (2004). *Pedagogy of indignation.* Boulder, CO: Paradigm Publishers.

Grace, A. P. (2001). Using Queer cultural studies to transgress adult educational space. In V. Sheared & P. A. Sissel (Eds.), *Making space: Merging theory and practice in adult education* (pp. 257-270). Westport, CT: Bergin & Garvey.

Grace, A. P., & Benson, F. J. (2000). Using autobiographical queer life narratives of teachers to connect personal, political, and pedagogical spaces. *International Journal of Inclusive Education, 4*(2), 89-109.

Grace, A. P., & Hill, R. J. (2004). Positioning Queer in adult education: Intervening in politics and praxis in North America. *Studies in the Education of Adults, 36*(2), 167-189.

Grace, A. P., & Wells, K. (2007a). Everyone performs, everyone has a place: Camp fYrefly and arts-informed, community-based education, cultural work, and inquiry. In D. Clover & J. Stalker (Eds.), *The art of social justice: Re-crafting activist adult education and community leadership* (pp. 61-82). Leicester, UK: NIACE.

Grace, A. P., & Wells, K. (2007b). Using Freirean pedagogy of just ire to inform critical social learning in arts-informed community education for sexual minorities. *Adult Education Quarterly, 57*(2), 95-114.

Grau, G. (1995). *Hidden Holocaust?* NY: Cassell.

Halberstam, J. (2005). *In a queer time and place: Transgender bodies, subcultural lives.* NY: NY University Press.

Heger, H. (1980). *The men with the pink triangle.* Boston: Alyson Publications, Inc.

Hill, R. J. (2001). Contesting discrimination based on sexual orientation at the ICAE Sixth World Assembly: 'Difference' is a fundamental human right. *Convergence, 34*(2-3), 100-116.

Hill, R. J. (2003, June 5). Working memory at AERC: A Queer welcome...and a retrospective. In R. J. Hill (Ed.), *Queer histories: Exploring fugitive forms of social knowledge. Proceedings of the 1st Lesbian, Gay, Bisexual, Transgender,*

Queer and Allies Pre-Conference at the 44ᵗʰ Annual Adult Education Research Conference (pp. 11-28). San Francisco, CA: San Francisco State University.

Hill. R. J., Childers, J., Childs, A. P., Cowie, G., Hatton, A., Lewis, J. B., McNair, N., Oswalt, S., Perez, R. M., & Valentine, T. (2002, April 17). *In the shadows of the arch: Safety and acceptance of lesbian, gay, bisexual, transgendered and Queer students at the University of Georgia.* Athens, GA: Department of Adult Education. Available at http://www.uga.edu/globes/CCRG_report.pdf and http://www.redandblack.com/vnews/display.v/ART/2002/10/22/3db552ca16da4

Horton, M., & Freire, P. (1990). *We make the road by walking: Conversations on education and social change.* Philadelphia, PA: Temple University Press.

Jones, J. P., III. (2001). Introduction: Segmented worlds and selves. In P. C. Adams, S. Hoelscher, & K. E. Till (Eds.), *Textures of place: Exploring humanist geographies* (pp. 121-128). Minneapolis: University of Minnesota Press.

Macedo, D. (2004). Foreword. In P. Freire, *Pedagogy of indignation* (pp. ix-xxv). Boulder, CO: Paradigm Publishers.

McFee, J. K., & Degge, R. M. (1977). *Art, culture and environment: A catalyst for teaching.* Belmont, WA: Wadsworth.

NAAPAE. (2001, August). Special edition for the World Assembly of Adult Education, Jamaica, August 9 – 11, 2001.

Olds, L. (n. d.). *A memoir of my journey in adult education: The making of a popular educator.* Unpublished manuscript.

Overton, P. (1994). The role of community arts development in nurturing the invisible culture of rural genius. In *Artspeak to artaction: Proceedings of a community arts development conference* (pp. 87-97). Saskatoon, Saskatchewan: University of Saskatchewan (Extension Division).

Plant, R. (1986). *The pink triangle: The Nazi was against homosexuals.* NY: Henry Holt and Company.

Setoodeh, R. (2008, July 19). Young, gay, and murdered. *Newsweek.* Retrieved July 28, 2008, from http://www.newsweek.com/id/147790/output/print

Sissel, P. A., & Sheared, V. (2001). Opening the gates: Reflections on power, hegemony, language, and the status quo. In V. Sheared & P. A. Sissel (Eds.), *Making space: Merging theory and practice in adult education* (pp. 3-14). Westport, CT: Bergin & Garvey.

West, C. (1994). *Race matters.* NY: Random House.

SECTION II:
HIGHER EDUCATION

CHAPTER 4

Lesbian, Gay, Bisexual, Transgender Campus Climate Assessments: Current Trends and Future Considerations

Needham Yancey Gulley

Introduction

For many lesbian, gay, bisexual, and transgendered (LGBT) individuals, it is during college that they first begin to accept and embrace their sexuality (Evans & D'Augelli, 1996). The process of coming to terms with and becoming open to one's own sexual identity as not heterosexual is referred to as "coming out." Although the coming- out process is difficult in itself, this time can be made more dramatic when members of the college community feel that being perceived as homosexual puts them at risk for physical or psychological abuse. College is marked by homosexual students' acceptance of themselves, yet the college campus has not traditionally been a welcoming environment for such discovery (D'Augelli & Rose, 1990; Evans, 2002; Evans & D'Augelli, 1996; Rhoads, 1995). In light of this information, college/university administrators, staff, faculty, and students are faced with challenges particular to this setting as it relates to LGBT members of the community. These challenges are compounded because LGBT students "often find campus environments to be unwelcoming and even hostile" (Evans, 2002, p. 522). To better understand these situations, institutions of higher education have begun to focus on campus issues for LGBT students. Research on the campus climate for these students is a relatively recent development, as is literature on how best to work with such students (e.g., D'Emilio, 1990; Evans & Wall, 1991; Schreier, 1995; Wall & Evans, 2000; Walters & Hayes, 1998).

Early studies in this area have focused on issues related to housing, programming, teaching, and the establishment of LGBT resource centers. Assessments of campus climate for LGBT persons began in the early 1990s, and the number of studies conducted has increased over the years. The focus of such projects has varied, as have the types of data produced and the ways in which that data are used to create change on the campuses that participate in them.

This chapter outlines a brief history of LGBT campus climate assessments and the theoretical foundations of such projects and offers critical insights into the current state and future of this type of research as well as the implications for change in how these assessments are conducted and framed. The outcomes of this chapter are to assist those who are unfamiliar with these projects to become informed, further support those who wish to conduct such assessments on their campuses, and challenge those who are conducting these assessments to expand their scope to further the production of knowledge in this area.

History of Campus Climate Assessments

In the late 1980s and early 1990s research began to emerge on the climate of college and university campuses for LGBT members of those communities (e.g., D'Augelli & Rose, 1990; D'Emilio, 1990; Evans & Wall, 1991; Reynolds, 1989). During this time, the National Gay and Lesbian Task Force (NGLTF) undertook the first large-scale effort to understand the experiences of LGBT college students. This organization began to document reports of harassment on campuses that stemmed from issues related to sexuality and sexual orientation. The results indicated that harassment and violence against LGBT students were significant and increasing issues. In response to this information, other researchers began to explore how members of the LGBT community experience the campus climate of colleges/universities in contrast to how that climate is experienced by their heterosexual peers. D'Augelli (1989) and Reynolds (1989) both point out discrepancies in how LGBT students on the campuses they studied experienced the campus as opposed to their heterosexual counterparts. Independently, they found that the climate was significantly less welcoming and in fact more hostile toward LGBT students than for students perceived to be heterosexual.

Based on these findings, research branched into how coming out in college and the overall collegiate experience work to serve each other, as well as how they may be mutually exclusive. Studies (Evans; 2002; Evans & D'Augelli, 1996; Renn; 2000;

Rhoads, 1997) tended to be the work of scholars from academic disciplines created as part of larger research agendas. Many studies took place across multiple campuses as opposed to on one campus, focusing on individual experiences more than campus climate. Various researchers raised questions about how LGBT students felt about their college experiences, how they dealt with harassment when it was encountered, and where they turned for support (see, for example, D'Emilio, 1990; Evans & D'Augelli, 1996; Herek, 1984; Rhoads, 1995.) A growing body of literature on the subject has repeatedly pointed to homophobia and the harassment of LGBT persons on college campuses that is exacerbated by a lack of resources to support these students (D'Augelli, 1989; Eliason, 1996; Rhoads, 1995). Consequently, some college administrators tuned in to the issues and some institutions began to implement the suggestions for change formulated by these researchers, such as the creation of LGBT resource centers. However, most administrators were left with more questions than answers. They struggled to answer a key question: What is the campus climate like for LGBT students on my campus?

In turn, some colleges began to assess their own campus climates in terms of LGBT student experiences. In some cases, the motivation for such investigations came from upper administration, but a more common occurrence was that one office or group of faculty and staff (often led by student affairs professionals) came together to manage the project and make suggestions for change where necessary. Rankin (1998) indicates that "the impetus for conducting a campus climate assessment is in response either to incidents of harassment or to an awareness of a lack of equity" (p. 280). In this way, these assessments reflect grassroots efforts to determine whether results are applicable at specific campuses. At the time, no definitive national standard or assessment instrument existed, so researchers conducting campus climates assessments had to develop means by which to assess LGBT student experiences. The result was a myriad of methods for gaining information that, while helpful for institutions to better understand their students' experiences/needs, provided little insight into the larger context or a national perspective. Both qualitative and quantitative methods have been used as researchers explore the campus climate for LGBT students. Most assessments focus on discovering the actual experiences of LGBT students, the places where this population of students feels least comfortable, and where LGBT students feel unsupported.

In the late 1990s and early 2000s, several researchers began to hypothesize that there was value in collectively analyzing the results of the individualized campus climate assessments that had been conducted to that point (Gulley, 2003;

Rankin, 1998). The Consortium of Higher Education LGBT Resource Professionals (2008) had tracked 54 such assessments through October 2002, but little had been done in terms of comparative analysis of the results. Rankin (1998) published a meta-analysis of the results from 30 assessments in order to compare and contrast the findings of each. Similar undertakings followed, pointing to several common themes, most notably that LGBT students do not feel empowered on college campuses. In fact, they often feel unwelcome and silenced.

Rankin continued her work with campus climate assessments by partnering with the Policy Institute of the National Gay and Lesbian Task Force to publish the largest LGBT campus climate assessment to date (Rankin, 2003). This survey project was conducted in 2000 and 2001 with participation from 1,669 students, faculty, and staff/administrators from 14 colleges throughout the United States. Rankin used a standard instrument across campuses in an attempt to better understand the national campus climate as well as to test the instrument for future use on multiple campuses. Like most individualized assessments, the survey asked participants to engage in self-reflection regarding "campus experiences as members of the GLBT community, their perception of the climate for GLBT members of the academic community, and their perceptions of institutional actions, including administrative policies and academic initiatives regarding GLBT issues and concerns on campus" (Rankin, 2003, p. 4). Results of this assessment were used to gain a better understanding of issues facing LGBT members of the collegiate community throughout the country. Participating colleges were also provided with analysis of results for their campuses so that they could have insight into the climate on the local level.

Since the 2003 report, individual campuses have continued to develop assessments that focus on their unique cultures. Likewise, Rankin and others have continued efforts to develop national instruments to gain information on campus climate for LGBT students, as well as faculty, staff, and administrators. Consulting agencies have also emerged that assist institutions in conducting these projects (Rankin & Associates Consulting, 2002/2006).

Theoretical Foundations of Campus Climate Assessments

Most researchers conducting assessments of campus climate for LGBT people use concepts from the coming-out process, discrimination politics, lesbian/gay identity development, and queer theory in order to inform their studies. The

following is a background of the literature that has and continues to be foundational for many of these campus climate assessments.

The Coming-Out Process

The discovery of one's sexual orientation is at the root of "coming out," and
this concept is central to the purpose behind many campus climate assessments
for LGBT students. Rhoads (1997) noted that the process of coming out and the
degree of visibility related to it varies among individuals. The fear of negative
reaction to a student being homosexual is founded in a history of discrimination against LGBT persons. Schreier (1995), noting the writings of R. L. Quack-
enbush, asserts, "[W]hen heterosexist beliefs are challenged by the presence of
individuals who are gay, lesbian, or bisexual a reactive attitude is formed as an
attempt to maintain the belief" (p. 20). This assumption is further supported by
D'Augelli (cited in Renn, 2000), who implies that students are at a higher risk of
experiencing anti-gay attitudes and behaviors the more "out" they are. However,
he also states that being out is a way of gaining support from students, faculty,
and staff. In this way, being out is a catch-22; it opens an individual up for discrimination while offering the freedom to express one's true feelings. It is argu-
able, then, that once one is out, the negative reactions to that orientation can be
less damaging due to the increased sense of self. One of the key purposes for
these climate assessments is to discover the methods used by members of the
campus community to deal with the dilemma of being out on campus, focusing
on the individual versus the culture of systematic institutional change.

Discrimination Politics

Discrimination against LGBT persons is prevalent throughout most college
campuses (Eichstedt, 1996; Hill, 1995; Rankin, 2003; Rhoads, 1997). Discrimination is a direct effect of certain individuals or groups being identified by specific
factors, such as race, ethnicity, social class, and sexual orientation, and then being excluded in the heteronormative, White, masculinist culture (Gerschick &
Miller, 1994). Dominant or hegemonic ideals do not allow for participation in the
power culture by those who are different than the people in control of that culture. Marmor (cited in Herek, 1984) "identified [stereotypes and ignorance] as
the most important sources of hostility toward homosexual persons" (p. 8). These
two components create false fears and negative ideas regarding LGBT individuals. Herek (1984) notes that discrimination against LGBT persons is perpetuated
by social structure, specifically the current policies found in business and govern-

ment that do not allow LGBT persons equal participation. Cornel West had this to say on the topic of discrimination against LGBT persons: "[I]t seems to me that to talk about the history of heterosexism and the history of homophobia is to talk about ways in which various institutions and persons have promoted unjustified suffering and unmerited pain" (quoted in Brandt, 1999, p. 290). Researchers conducting LGBT campus climate assessments use this type of background to support the implementation of their projects and to further validate their findings. These claims can, however, lead to further "Othering" of LGBT people when researchers use such assertions to separate these students from the heteronormative culture and group all LGBT people under one experience.

Queer Theory

The term "Queer" has widely been considered a negative term, as it has often been used to refer to gays and lesbians in a harmful and oppressive manner. However, scholars such as Grace, Hill, Johnson, and Lewis (2004) discuss the difficulty in defining Queer this way. They assert that it cannot be defined as a single category of sexual orientation, but the word is a more inclusive term relegated to people they designate as sexual outlaws. These scholars further indicate that Queer can never be completely defined but rather is a perennially shifting way of knowing the world and being in it. Queer transgresses the normative sexual values of the culture at large. In this way, Queer has been reclaimed by those who have previously been harmed by it.

Queer identity development is the process of recognizing and accepting one's place in the world based on a non-heterosexual orientation as well as on how one interprets the world from one's Queer location in it. Although a variety of theories exist around the topic, most include the common components of experiences, senses, and sensibilities (Dilley, 2002). This is to say that these theories focus on what happened to an individual, how they understood it, and the meaning they have associated with that experience. While a significant amount of literature exists on the topic of sexual identity development (Laumann, Gagono, Michael, & Michaels, 1994/1997; Rubin, 1984/1993)[9] and some literature exists on the topic of Queer identity development (Eliason, 1996; Sedgwick, 1993; Talburt, 2000), until relatively recently there has been little effort to examine how college attendance specifically impacts this development. In one contribution, Dilley (2002)

---

9   For additional information, see also Kathleen King, "Crossroads for Creating My Space in the Workforce: Transformative Learning Helps Understand LGBTQ Sexual Identity Development Among Adults," Chapter 8, this text.

investigated the impact of the college experience on the Queer identity development of gay men. He provides this summary:

> *College environments most certainly impacted both the process and the product of these men: postsecondary institutions created environments (both positive and negative), provided structures for socialization and organization, gathered together like-minded peers, and offered the idea of not only the prerogative to determine through the college experiences whom one was but also, in time, the right to do so openly and publicly. (p. 215)*

In terms of linguistics, it is worth noting that while Queer identity development and queer theory are often foundational in the framework of campus climate assessments, the term "Queer" is surprisingly absent from the studies and reports themselves, often because of the politically charged nature of the word itself.

Current Perspectives and Future Considerations

Assessments of LGBT campus climate have traditionally focused heavily on student populations who identify as not heterosexual. This has often, but not always, been done while neglecting their heteronormative counterparts on campus. Brown, Clarke, Gortmaker, and Robinson-Keilig (2004) note, "GLBT students are the primary respondents in campus GLBT climate studies with most reporting having experienced harassment or discrimination" (p. 8). Studies often found that the experiences of LGBT-identified students were not positive. Moreover, most studies (at lease the earlier ones) failed to sample the referent student population, namely, heterosexuals. Thus, researchers were forced to make assumptions about the quality and type of heterosexual experiences, which were then juxtaposed with research claims about LGBT students. In order to compare the climates of the LGBT and heterosexual communities more accurately, researchers must begin to include non-LGBT people in these assessments. Likewise, in current studies, when LGBT participants report being harassed or discriminated against, there is a void in examining from where that harassment comes (Brown et al., 2004; D'Augelli & Rose, 1990; Rhoads, 1995, 1997), often leading readers to assume that such activity comes from members of the heterosexual community. With the prevalence of internalized homophobia and historic tensions between subgroups of the non-heteronormative culture, it is worth investigating the origins of such incidents beyond assumption or presumption.

Another shortfall of early campus assessments was that they typically focused on students and not on other members of campus communities such as staff, faculty, or administrators. Certainly some assessments have broadened their scope to include a full range of the campus stakeholders. However, these projects often fall short of developing a clear understanding of the specific lived experiences of each group or the collective campus. Investigators would serve themselves and their institutions well by focusing their assessment projects on specific populations while developing a plan to include studies on each subset of the campus community (students, faculty, staff, and administration). This approach would allow for specific data gathering on each group. Findings could be comparatively analyzed. Knowing how students, faculty, staff, and administrators feel individually can assist school officials in developing plans to support these groups more effectively versus assuming their needs are the same across campus. This type of research acknowledges that participants' primary identities may not rest in their sexual orientation and that members of these areas of campus are at different life stages.

Many of the campus climate assessments that have been conducted thus far attempt to understand issues pertinent to the LGBT community as a whole. The separate identities of those captured by the LGBT label are often merged into one as researchers choose to focus on the common experiences of those with non-heterosexual identities. This does not lend itself to the discovery of the needs, experiences, or lives of specific groups who make up the LGBT community. Herek (2002) asserts that considering the climate for the lesbian, gay, bisexual, and transgender subgroups as one experience under LGBT may not provide a full picture. There is a need to understand both the collective lived experiences and the differences between these groups (Johnson & Kivel, 2007; Longerbeam, Inkelas, Johnson, & Lee, 2007). Studies that focus more on individualizing the experiences of these subgroups may offer greater insights into how different members of the LGBT community gain access to heteronormative privilege and experience the campus climate differently. Knowing how different subgroups feel about their campus as well as what issues are most relevant to them can have theoretical and pragmatic implications. These potential differences should be explored more fully as we continue to assess campus climate. This may have significant implications for how a campus climate assessment impacts the programming and/or practice of a particular campus.

Longerbeam et al. (2007) offer another critical observation of current climate assessments, stating:

Research about the ways in which lesbian, gay, and bisexual students experience the college environment has focused on homophobia and heterosexism, particularly in residence halls and classrooms. What is unknown relates to LGB students' broader college experiences, particularly their overall co-curricular involvements and academic and social outcomes. (p. 217)

A variety of factors contribute to why campus climate assessments primarily focus on understanding student experiences in these two settings, one being that the people who conduct this research on individual campuses often work in these areas. However, in order to know how the entire institutional culture contributes to the climate perceived around LGBT issues, a broader picture is necessary. Developing studies with specific emphasis on a more diverse range of campus settings will help to produce this breadth, but the effort must be intentional. On a pragmatic level, asking questions such as, "Do you feel supported in the classroom based on your sexual orientation?" offers less room for this expansion than more open-ended questions about locations where one may or may not feel supported. Collecting information about more areas of campus will allow researchers not only to suggest change in those places where needed but also to praise those who are nurturing the LGBT community. They can also offer those settings as positive examples to others.

LGBT campus climate assessments have highlighted the negative experiences of LGBT people. When introducing the findings of her 2003 assessment, Rankin led by saying, "[I]t will examine the anti-GLBT experiences described by participants, their general perceptions of anti-GLBT sentiments and activity on campus" (p. 24). This statement is indicative of most studies that typically highlight findings of harassment and discrimination in order to better argue for more tolerance of the LGBT community. While the results of assessments have certainly encouraged this method, the reporting of findings in this way fails to provide a full picture of the lives of LGBT people. Future assessments should be intentional about researching the positive experiences around LGBT issues and reporting those instances as well. Knowing the locations and instances of support around these issues can provide opportunities for mentorship and mirroring behavior within an institutional setting that can bring about even greater nurturance than focusing on what is perceived to be wrong.

A significant number of LGBT campus climate assessments have been conducted. However, very few institutions have conducted follow-up studies. Even then, the schools that have done so often have not been as thorough in their follow-up investigations as in the preliminary research. Secondary studies tend to focus on how new initiatives fostered by the first assessment have been received, not the current overall campus climate during that moment. Scholars in this area note that long-term studies need to be used to investigate the impact of programming in addressing concerns of the LGBT population (Rankin, 2003), but this does not necessarily allow for discussions and findings of new issues that may have arisen. Campuses should be conducting these assessments in a routine manner and evaluating programming outcomes separately. These two distinct types of research will inform each other and together create a stronger picture than using only one approach to further investigate any change that may be occurring.

In recent years, efforts have been made to develop one standard assessment tool to measure the campus climate for the LGBT community at colleges and universities so that results may be used by individual campuses while also providing data on a national level (Rankin, 2003). However, this approach falls short of meeting the goals of many campuses, as such instruments are not designed to accommodate the vast differences of individual campuses in terms of campus culture, organizational structure, academic emphasis, geographic location, institutional mission, campus size, or other factors. Assessment instruments of this nature provide a breadth of knowledge in terms of "national trends, but the staff of each campus must study their own campus climate to determine campus needs and evaluate the effectiveness of interventions" (Brown et al., 2004, p. 21). Creating assessments based on the specific nature of one's campus and institutional mission allows researchers to investigate cultural experiences specific to that campus, thus making findings much more pertinent and meaningful to members of that campus. Institutions should make every effort to assure that assessments are as meaningful to their own communities as possible, including creating studies that take into account these individual factors.

Equally important is to continue the work of Gulley (2003) and Rankin (1998) by collectively examining individual campus climate assessments, thus yielding greater understanding of issues facing LGBT people in collegiate settings. Through the use of collective analysis and interpretation of original assessments conducted by individual institutions, the body of knowledge surrounding issues facing sexual minorities in higher education can be advanced. Recognizing that a wealth of data exists, the condensing of these studies and results can lead to the understanding of trends through comparing and contrasting not just results, but the very form of assessment.

Conclusion

Those conducting LGBT campus climate assessments have often been critical of the implicit and explicit institutional practices and policies that they find have fostered harassment and discrimination against LGBT members of the campus community. It is time to be equally critical of how these assessments are developed, structured, and framed in the politically charged settings of college campuses. The motivation for these assessments, as well as their implementation, needs to be more sophisticated in the future, focusing on the experiences of multiple campus stakeholders around issues of sexuality and sexual orientation, regardless of the sexual orientation of those participating. By reframing these studies, researchers can move LGBT administrators, staff, faculty, and students from a victimized mass to equal partners in the campus community. The critiques expressed in this chapter offer a starting place for this shift.

References

Brandt, E. (Ed.). (1999). *Dangerous liaisons: Blacks and gays and the struggle for equality.* NY: New Press.

Brown, R. D., Clarke, B., Gortmaker, V., & Robinson-Keilig, R. (2004). Assessing the campus climate for gay, lesbian, bisexual, and transgender (GLBT) students using a multiple perspectives approach. *Journal of College Student Development, 45,* 8-26.

Consortium of Higher Education Lesbian Gay Bisexual Transgender Resource Professionals. (2008). Retrieved March 22, 2008, from http://www.lgbtcampus.org

D'Augelli, A. R. (1989). Lesbians' and gay men's experiences of discrimination and harassment in a university community. *American Journal of Community Psychology, 17,* 317-321.

D'Augelli, A. R., & Rose, M. L. (1990). Homophobia in a university community: Attitudes and experiences of heterosexual freshmen. *Journal of College Student Development, 31,* 484-491.

D'Emilio, J. (1990). The campus environment for gay and lesbian life. *Academe, 76,* 16-19.

Dilley, P. (2002). *Queer man on campus: A history of non-heterosexual college men, 1945-2000.* NY: RoutledgeFalmer.

Eichstedt, J. L. (1996). Heterosexism and gay/lesbian/bisexual experiences: Teaching strategies and exercises. *Teaching Sociology, 24*(4), 384-388.

Eliason, M. J. (1996). Identity formation for lesbian, bisexual, and gay persons: Beyond a minoritizing view. *Journal of Homosexuality, 30*(3), 31-58.

Evans, N. J. (2002). The impact of an LGBT safe zone project on campus climate. *Journal of College Student Development, 43*(4), 522-539.

Evans, N. J., & D'Augelli, A. R. (1996). Lesbians, gay men, and bisexual people in college. In R. C. Savin-Williams & K. M. Cohen (Eds.), *The lives of lesbians, gays, and bisexuals: Children to adults* (pp. 201-226). Fort Worth, TX: Harcourt Brace College Publishers.

Evans, N. J., & Wall, V. A. (Eds.). (1991). *Beyond tolerance: Gays, lesbians and bisexuals on campus.* Alexandria, VA: American College Personnel Association.

Gerschick, T. J., & Miller A. S. (1994). Gender identities at the crossroads of masculinity and physical disability. *Masculinities, 2*(1), 34-55.

Grace, A. P., Hill, R. J., Johnson, C. W., & Lewis, J. B. (2004). In other words: Queer voices/dissident subjectivities impelling social change. *The International Journal of Qualitative Studies in Education, 17*(3), 301-324.

Gulley, N. Y. (2003). So you know about the queers: What campus environment studies say about queer knowledge production. In A. Grace & R. J. Hill (Comp.), *Lesbian, Gay, Bisexual, Transgender, Queer & Allies Caucus of the Adult Education Research Conference* (pp. 57-61). Seattle: University of Washington.

Herek, G. M. (1984). Beyond homophobia: A social psychological perspective on attitudes toward lesbians and gay men. *Journal of Homosexuality, 10*, 1-21.

Herek, G. M. (2002). Heterosexuals' attitudes toward bisexual men and women in the United States. *Journal of Sex Research, 39*, 264-274.

Hill, R. J. (1995). Gay discourse in adult education: A critical review. *Adult Education Quarterly, 45*(3), 142-158.

Johnson, C. W., & Kivel, B. D. (2007). Tracing the origins of queer theory to advance leisure and sport research. In C. Aitchison (Ed.), *Gender and sexuality in sport* (pp. 93-105). NY: Routledge.

Laumann, E., Gagono, J., Michael, R., & Michaels, S. (1994/1997). The social organization of sexuality. In W. Rubenstein (Ed.), *Cases and materials on sexual orientation and the law* (pp. 19-28). St. Paul, MN: West Publishing Co.

Longerbeam, S. D., Inkelas, K. K., Johnson, D. R., & Lee, Z. S. (2007). Lesbian, gay, and bisexual college student experiences: An exploratory study. *Journal of College Student Development, 48,* 215-230.

Rankin, S. R. (1998). The campus climate report: Assessment and intervention strategies. In R. L. Sanlo (Ed.), *Working with lesbian, gay, bisexual, and transgender college students: A handbook for faculty and administrators* (pp. 277-284). Westport, CT: Greenwood.

Rankin, S. R. (2003). *Campus climate for gay, lesbian, bisexual, and transgender people: A national perspective.* Washington, DC: The National Gay and Lesbian Task Force Policy Institute.

Rankin and Associates Consulting. (2002/2006). Retrieved March 22, 2008, from http://www.rankin-consulting.com/

Renn, K. A. (2000). Including all voices in the classroom: Teaching lesbian, gay, and bisexual students. *College Teaching, 48*(4), 129-136.

Reynolds, A. J. (1989). Social environmental conceptions of male homosexual behavior: A university climate analysis. *Journal of College Student Development, 30,* 62-69.

Rhoads, R. A. (1995, January 27). The campus climate for gay students who leave "the Closet." *The Chronicle of Higher Education,* p. A56.

Rhoads, R. A. (1997). Implications of the growing visibility of gay and bisexual male students on campus. *NASPA Journal, 34*(4), 275-286.

Rubin, G. S. (1984/1993). Thinking sex: Notes for a radical theory of the politics of sexuality. In H. Abelove, M. A. Barale, & D. M. Halperin (Eds.), *The lesbian and gay studies reader* (pp. 3-44). NY: Routledge.

Schreier, B. A. (1995). Moving beyond tolerance: A new paradigm for programming about homophobia/biphobia and heterosexism. *Journal of College Student Development, 36*(1), 9-26.

Sedgwick, E. K. (1993). Epistemology of the closet. In H. Abelove, M. A. Barale, & D. M. Halperin (Eds.), *The lesbian and gay studies reader* (pp. 45-61). NY: Routledge.

Talburt, S. (2000). Introduction: Some contradictions and possibilities of thinking queer. In S. Talburt & S. R. Steinberg (Eds.), *Thinking queer: Sexuality, culture and education* (pp. 3-13). NY: Peter Lang.

Wall, V. A., & Evans, N. J. (Eds.). (2000). *Toward acceptance: Sexual orientation issues on campus.* Lanham, MD: University Press of America, Inc.

Walters, A. S., & Hayes, D. M. (1998). Homophobia within schools: Challenging the culturally sanctioned dismissal of gay students and colleagues. *Journal of Homosexuality, 35*(2), 1- 21.

CHAPTER 5

LGBTQ Allies on Campus: Do They Have a Role?

Ann Brooks

Dawn Robarts

Ronnie Lozano

You know, someone like that would have been nice to have around the day my friend and I took a bus on our lunch break. We were holding hands, and a man came up behind us and began to yell and curse at us. As we sat there in embarrassment and fear, I looked around at the other people on the bus. Several people smiled at us sympathetically, but nobody stopped him. Finally, we got off the bus before our stop and ran away from the bus as quickly as we could, so no one would think we got off because we were afraid.

This story, told by the college-aged daughter of one of the researchers, highlights both the need for LGBTQ allies and the lack of a script for ally action existing in U.S. culture. Although individuals could "smile sympathetically," no one acted.

An ally is "a person who is a member of the dominant or majority group, who works to end oppression in his or her personal and professional life through support of, and as an advocate for, the oppressed population" (Washington & Evans, 1991, p. 195). We amend that definition of ally, based on the membership in the university allies program we studied, to include members of the oppressed population who advocate for themselves as well. Over 200 LGBTQ ally programs exist on college campuses, but the ally role remains ill-defined. In this study, campus allies based their role on personal identity as a lifelong ally, professional group identity, experience as a minority, or family role models. No culturally defined ally role script was evident for ally identity and action on college and university campuses, yet ally programs are becoming increasingly common. Typically housed in the Office of Student Affairs, these programs form to provide a supportive and nurturing college experience for lesbian, gay, bisexual, transgender and Queer (LGBTQ) students. Ally programs began in the early 1990s under such names as "Safe on Campus" and "Safe Zone." Slightly fewer than 200 college campuses today report having some form of ally program (Beemyn, Barnett, & Tubbs, 2006).

Research Design

The Human Rights Campaign Foundation, a major LGBTQ advocacy organization in the United States, writes, "Allies to racial, religious and ethnic minorities have been remarkably effective in promoting positive change in the dominant culture, and only recently has their instrumental position been extended to the area of sexual orientation. The past few years have witnessed the development of heterosexual Ally organizations which have attempted to make the culture of a campus or workplace more aware and accepting of gay, lesbian, bisexual and transgendered individuals" (2008, para. 1). But what motivates individuals to become allies and what is their role? How do they understand themselves in relation to their culture and society? This single-case study of a large public university in central Texas (Texas State University) explored these questions in order to contribute to the strengthening of ally organizations both on and off college campuses.

To explore these questions, we conducted life-history interviews with nine faculty and staff members (including two of the researchers) at Texas State University-San Marcos. Interviews focused on the question of why the interviewees became allies. In contrast to Washington and Evans's definition, the Texas State Allies Program includes LGBTQ as well as straight members. The three researchers each completed the university's allies training course before beginning the interviews. Two of the researchers have children who identify as lesbian or gay. Two of the researchers worked on the study as part of a three-semester course intended to introduce doctoral students to the research process at the beginning of their program. One researcher was the supervising faculty member.

We recruited study participants from among the faculty and staff using a snowball sampling technique, beginning with interviewing the director of the Allies Program on campus and asking him for names of individuals he perceived as especially committed members of the program. We asked our initial participants for the names of other allies whom they perceived to be stanch supporters. We transcribed the interviews and coded them according to the three research questions. Because we are looking at role and social identity, we further analyzed the data from the perspective of social scripts and cultural scenarios. We shared our findings with our interview participants in follow-up interviews a year later and revised our analysis and interpretation. The study also draws on Allies Program documents, such as promotional materials, announcements of activities, training materials, and planning documents, and the participant observations of the three researchers as employees of the institution and at Allies Program activities.

Theoretical Perspective

In his book, *Postmodern Sexualities*, William Simon (1996) describes cultural scenarios as instructing in the narrative requirements of particular roles by providing knowledge that makes role entry, performance, and exit believable for self and others. Narrative requirements of a role refer to the language we use, the clothes we wear, and the stories we tell about ourselves when we assume a particular role that communicates our role to others, signals how we see ourselves and, in turn, how we would like them to see and behave toward us.

Increased individuation leads to situations where others may not share the same cultural scenarios, so individuals improvise interpersonal scripts to shape the content of relevant cultural scenarios to fit particular contexts. However, when life at the level of cultural scenarios becomes very complex, conflicted, and ambiguous, interpersonal scripts become inadequate and greater demands are placed on individuals who "rehearse" significant alternative behaviors and outcomes. Although these concepts are usually applied to human sexuality (Gagnon & Simon, 1973), we are using them here to examine the sociocultural positioning of LGBTQ allies on university campuses.

LGBTQ Allies

The allies we interviewed at the university defined themselves as allies based on personal commitment to an ally identity in general, a professional or institutional role, or membership in another minority group.

"It is who I am."

All but one of the allies (a gay male) saw themselves as having taken the role of ally or advocate for persons who are the targets of discrimination before ever joining the university's Allies Program. They said such things as:

"I had been an ally before I even knew that I was an ally with the label of being an ally."

"It was just kind of a natural thing…it was not something I had to think about. It was just something I wanted to do."

"It just mirrors everything I have done throughout my life…for me it's such a natural thing. I never had to think about it. It is who I am."

One woman explained her identity as an ally in terms of a cultural scenario immortalized in the text of the U.S. Constitution: "I have always just been an advocate. I've always wanted to be a voice for anyone or anything that didn't have a voice, and I totally believe in equal rights for everyone—maybe I could do something." Another ally described her motivation as being very personal: "It just feels right for me. I feel like it's important for me personally to do this, to be true to myself, kind of a socially responsible thing to do."

"I was hired to do this work here."

Several of the allies also held positions at the university that provided them with a legitimating cultural scenario for acting as an ally. One of the allies with whom we spoke, Lisa, was enthusiastic that her job actually required her to act as an ally for LGBTQ students. As a bisexual Hispanic woman psychologist, she had explored her sexuality and, as she began to develop a workable interpersonal script as a sexual-minority psychologist, helped set up a safe place center at the university where she had earned her doctorate. She then found a position that incorporated her ally work at Texas State University, saying:

I was hired to do this work here, which is the awesome piece—this is actually a part of my job description…I'm very lucky because I work in a department that has created that space and said that it's important….Some of my role as a psychologist is where I have students come in who are struggling with sexual orientation issues and need someone to talk to them about it. I did a film festival this semester and would be down in the second-floor food court sitting at a table, and I've had students come down and say like, "Aren't you the one who did the film festival? Can I just sit down and ask you questions about stuff?" And I've only been here since the fall semester. I think it's because I am so visible.

For Lisa, in addition to the university's cultural scenario for LGBTQ advocacy, a similar scenario already existed within her profession as a psychologist. In 1975, the American Psychological Association adopted a policy in which it condemned discrimination against gay men and lesbians (in private and public contexts) and urged the repeal of all anti-gay legislation (Conger, 1975). However, from her statement, "I'm very lucky because I work in a department that has created space and said that it's important…," we can infer that in her experience not all university counseling centers are as supportive of their psychologists and counselors acting as LGBTQ allies and advocates as her current one.

Two of the allies, both faculty members, held positions that did not necessarily include an ally component. They developed interpersonal scripts for themselves. One of the faculty members, Jess, explained that she has worked to identify her own unconscious acts of discrimination as a professor:

I keep finding new things to do. For years I have supported sex, gender, and race minority students so that they can pursue identity-based research and scholarship. When I first started, other faculty sponsors had turned them down because they said the research wasn't important, so they came to me. Then one day, sometime in the early '90s, I saw a White guy stand up in a sociology conference general session and tell other White guys to stop dominating and discounting what women and minorities had to say. I started thinking about how people with more privileged identities can advocate for members of other groups. I started pointing out policies and practices that discriminate against members of "minority" groups during faculty and committee meetings and pointing out when Whites were overrepresented.

As a professor, Jess had no cultural scenario for her ally role, but she found her own ways and adopted actions she saw others model. However, straight-ally advocacy of LGBTQ persons is complex. While allies themselves may incur some risk for their advocacy (one of the allies we interviewed mentioned receiving hate mail from Christian groups for sponsoring a conference on LGBTQ scholarship), they may also accrue additional privilege, including awards and the admiration of others for their ally activities. This positive multiplier effect (Bonilla-Silva, 2006), first used in regards to White privilege, in the case of straight allies describes the additive privileges accorded straight persons and any rewards gained as a result of speaking out with relative impunity on behalf of LGBTQ persons.

"I was a member of a minority population."

Being a member of a minority population provided a store of personal, familial, and group experiences that served to induce empathy with members of other subordinate groups. A Jewish female faculty member, Ruby, told us:

I go back to probably when I started talking and walking. That's the way my whole family was. I was a member of a minority population in a majority neighborhood. I was the only Jew in a neighborhood full of Southern Baptists and a few other off-branches, so I knew what it was like not to be able to express who I was around other people. Also, my parents themselves had always, from the time they were growing up, placed themselves in the advocacy role. They were very involved in the Civil Rights Movement before anybody else. Back in the 1940s, they were participating in sit-ins and organizations. My grandfather was a union organizer back in the 1920s and 1910s, so this type of thing, this whole advocacy role, goes way back.

Ruby's family provided her with a cultural scenario of activism and protest through participation in civil rights and labor union movements. She personalized their activist scenario through her experience as a Jewish minority among a Southern Baptist majority.

"I would have liked to have had access to an ally."

Those participants who saw themselves as part of a subordinate group wanted to be allies because they had wanted an ally at some time in their lives. A gay male professor, Thomas, described going to college in Mississippi:

There are times, and especially when I was an undergraduate, when I would like to have had access to an ally, but [my university] never had a formal program....When I was at the University of Mississippi in 1990, to find the campus gay and lesbian support group you had to go through this call-in service and go through a screening procedure over the phone....The person who ran the group would know that you were okay, and you were genuine in your intent, and you weren't somebody who was out to gay-bash. So then you would be given the secret meeting location and time and place and all that. So it was a very elaborate process, and there was nothing like the Allies Program there.

Ruby also wanted an ally while growing up as a Jew in the South:

There were no allies available. All through elementary school we had prayer in school and the teachers would send me out of the room when they had their school prayers because they said, "Well, you're Jewish, you don't believe in God." ... Here I was in elementary school, and I was being held out in front of my whole class and being told that I was different, that I was unequal in some way...and then students' reactions to me—some would act like I had leprosy, you know.

She talked about the persistence throughout her family's history of such discrimination:

And some of these things happened to my daughter forty years later when kids found out she was Jewish. Kids would say, "My parents said I couldn't play with you." It still occurs today. My mother was kicked out of restaurants during WWII because she looked Jewish and that was in the United States.... It's very hurtful, but when you grow up with that, you learn to be everybody's advocate.

Ruby, like others who needed allies, believed an ally would have stood up for her and her family so that they would not have been in danger or singled out for different treatment.

"There is a tie between all those groups and all having similar struggles."

Finally, the allies who had institutional roles that included working with a subordinate group held a vision of all such groups across campus organizing together for equity. These allies seemed to have chosen their professional roles for the opportunity they provided them to act as allies and advocates for subjugated group members. Each of these "professional allies" was also a member of a minority group on campus.

Mandy, the director of disability services and herself a wheelchair user, felt her community has an "affiliation" or "tie" with other groups and likened the disability group's struggle for rights to that of African Americans and women:

In the disability community there was a struggle for us to get passage of federal laws to protect the rights of people with disabilities, and I saw that the African American community went through struggles to get the civil rights legislation passed and the Voting Rights Act passed, the women's rights. So when you view the struggles various groups have gone through, the disability community is another group....There is a tie between all those groups.

The Assistant Vice President in charge of Multicultural Student Affairs spoke of intentionally and strategically supporting all subordinate groups on campus:

In this office, we provide funding. We have an organization called Underrepresented Student Advising Council. We have student representatives from different communities, so we have an African American student rep, Latino, Asian, Native American, and LGBTQ. So, when I came to this position one of my strategic initiatives was to find a way to include the LGBTQ student community under this umbrella because previously we kind of focused on racial identity politics...but my vision was to kind of broaden that to be more inclusive of various cultural identities and various identities under the umbrella of multiculturalism and diversity.

Finally, a gay male professor articulated an ideal that called for breaking down boundaries between *all* groups, subordinate and dominant:

I saw an advertisement for it [the Allies Program] inside one of the buses recently. So it's just about creating the culture, really...I would like to see a natural progression where diversity was truly valued in all aspects of society and that we didn't need an Allies Program because it was a total non-issue.

Members of minority groups on campus see their own group's experiences as similar to those of other groups and envision a benefit in allying with each other. Nevertheless, except for some individual actions, such an alliance remains a vision.

Discussion

The LGBTQ Allies Program at Texas State University is institutionally legitimated, but it lacks a cohesive cultural scenario within which its members can act out an interpersonal script. A Safe Place placard and an Allies coffee cup symbolize membership, but these do not define a culture of advocacy or an ally role. Allies do not affiliate with each other because they are allies, nor do they define themselves as a community. They have no interpersonal script to guide them in their actions.

Instead, most of the allies defined their commitment to being an ally as coming from some other dimension of their lives, such as a family-derived identity, professional or institutional roles, or identity as a member of a minority group. The most commonly mentioned cultural scenario justifying the ally role came from the identity-based rights movements such as the Civil Rights or Women's Movements. Nevertheless, no broadly known script or ally story seemed to exist to provide an ally role model for members of dominant groups. Thus, the allies with whom we spoke at the university had to do significant interpersonal and intrapsychic processing of their experience to individually discern how to play the ally role.

Implications

This study suggests that for allies programs such as the one at Texas State University to be successful, the existing cultural scenario of movements such as the Civil Rights Movement need to be brought onto campus. Drawing on the strength of this existing and pervasive cultural scenario, work needs to be done to develop viable role scripts for allies that culturally legitimize actions they can take. Such scripts might have helped the "sympathetic smilers" act on behalf of Rachel and her friend as well as take action on behalf of other members of oppressed groups.

The Allies Program's training at the university, which focuses on helping allies develop an understanding of sexual identity, did not address how allies might enact their role. Developing an ally script requires addressing specific actions allies can take and gathering stories of ally actions from both the allies themselves and the LGBTQ persons whom they may have supported. This is cultural work that moves beyond the development of sensitivity to the active promotion of a culture of alliance and advocacy.

References

Beemyn, B., Barnett, D., & Tubbs, N. (2006). History of LGBT centers: Consortium Survey 2006 office history. Retrieved October 26, 2008, from http://lgbtcampus.org/about/studies-history.php

Bonilla-Silva, E. (2006). *Racisms without racists.* Lanham, MD: Rowman and Littlefield Publishers.

Conger, J. J. (1975). Proceedings of the American Psychological Association, Incorporated, for the year 1974: Minutes of the Annual Meeting of the Council of Representatives. *American Psychologist, 30,* 620-651.

Gagnon, J. H., & Simon, W. (1973). *Sexual conduct: The social sources of human sexuality.* Chicago: Aldine Publishing.

Human Rights Campaign. (2008). *Establishing an allies/safe zone program.* Retrieved October 26, 2008, from http://www.hrc.org/issues/342.html

Simon, W. (1996). *Postmodern sexualities.* NY: Routledge.

Washington, J., & Evans, N. J. (1991). Becoming an ally. In N. J. Evans & V. A. Wall (Eds.), *Beyond tolerance: Gays, lesbians and bisexuals on campus* (pp. 195-204). Alexandria, VA: American College Personnel Association.

CHAPTER 6

Where Is Our Citizenship in Academia?

Experiences of Gay Men of Color in Higher Education

Mitsunori Misawa

Introduction

Adult educators have identified that ableism, ageism, Eurocentrism, gender-ism, heterosexism, racism, sexism and other *-ism* constructions perpetuate discrimination and marginalization in academia (Johnson-Bailey, 2002; Rocco & Gallagher, 2004; Sissel & Sheared, 2001). These forms of oppression are "ways in which hegemony has constructed learning environments and limited the participation of some people because of their language, sexual orientation, race, gender, and class" (Sissel & Sheared, 2001, p. 3). Current approaches to understanding multiculturalism and diversity in educational curricula, though, ignore the intersection of these different identities in individuals (Kumashiro, 2002; Misawa, 2007; Newman, 2007). When adult learners come to a classroom, they bring their sociocultural and socioeconomic positions and social histories with them (Tisdell, 2001). These socially significant factors form the ways that people think and act towards each other in academia (Tisdell, Hanley, & Taylor, 2000). It is useful for adult educators to take into account the combination of identities in their learners when developing curricula to provide their learners with an effective academic environment.

One of the major reasons that discrimination occurs in higher education is because the mainstream discourse has been crafted mostly from a White heterosexual male perspective (Rocco & Gallagher, 2004). While many contemporary researchers are exploring sociocultural factors that give privilege to some and marginalize others, two of those factors, sexual orientation and race, are usually explored separately. The exploration of identities will not be complete unless these two identities are explored together as a whole.

When adult educators strive to develop a welcoming and inclusive learning environment, learning about their learners' backgrounds is one of the most important skills that adult educators should have (Brookfield, 2006). However, while adult educators may look at a specific identity to help them understand a learner's marginalization and inequality, they ought to remember that learners have multiple identities or sociocultural positions in today's society. Simply exploring one aspect of identity, even a key one, will not allow an adult educator to understand the full impact of inequality because "inequality has been revised to reflect a greater degree of complexity" (Collins, 2004, p. 249) in contemporary society. Collins (2004) and hooks (1989, 2003) have deconstructed the notion of inequality in the emergence of the second-wave Women's Movement, where feminists of color were underserved in a purportedly umbrella movement. Black women were not a primary focus in initiatives of White women, even though women of color were part of the overall movement.

However, the intersection of race and sexual orientation in contemporary society reflects the attitude in the early Women's Movement with respect to women of color. Collins and hooks may be right about gender and race inequality being treated as a more complex issue, but the discussion has not advanced in complexity with regard to sexual orientation and race. Spaces in higher education for gay people of color, or "Queer-Race Spaces," are rare, and each of these identities is treated separately in the classroom. This chapter attempts to bring to light the intersection of race and sexual orientation in the classroom by exploring the experiences of gay male students of color in the adult learning environment of college. It will allow a better understanding of experiences learners may have as gay male students of color and how these experiences influence their campus lives. It will also explore how sexual orientation and race emerged, developed, and intersected in a specific college environment and how their sociocultural identities impacted the larger learning environment.

Race and Sexual Orientation as an Intersection

This chapter deals with the intersection of race and sexual orientation in adult learning. One might ask questions such as: Why is it important to address race and sexual orientation in adult education? Why do adult educators need to focus on the intersection of race and sexual orientation? Many researchers and practitioners in adult and higher education have largely ignored these questions (Ferguson & Howard-Hamilton, 2000; Hill, 2005; Misawa, 2007, 2009).

There are at least three reasons why race and sexual orientation have not been widely discussed before. The first reason is that topics such as race and sexual orientation are mainly non-issues to conventional academics. Traditionally, educational contents in education, including postsecondary education, have mostly been knowledge and wisdom generated by White men who are heterosexual or who cover as such (Kumashiro, 2008; Tisdell, 1995; Yoshino, 2006). So, perspectives of minority people are not often addressed and, in fact, they were only added later as extracurricular activities or multicultural education, traditionally not considered mainstream education (Kumashiro, 2001). Then there are the teachers who are White and teaching a White audience for whom the racial issue becomes invisible (Delgado & Stefancic, 2001; Lawrence, Matsuda, Delgado, & Crenshaw, 1993). Following this, sexuality, too, is a non-issue to these heterosexual teachers who sustain heterosexist curricula in schools and institutions (Dilley, 2002). [10]

The second reason why race and sexual orientation have often been excluded is that it is difficult for academics who are White heterosexual men or who were trained under conventional academic curricula (by and for White male academics) to address the issues of race and sexual orientation in a classroom context. In contemporary education, White and heterosexual teachers are often too wary of these sensitive topics to address the issues on race and sexual orientation in the classroom. When dealing with multicultural education in school curricula, White teachers do not want to be perceived as racist (Dixson, 2006; Johnson-Bailey, 2002). Alongside that, when heterosexual teachers are covering topics that are related to sexual orientation or sexuality, they do not go into the topics too deeply because they do not want to be perceived as either homophobic or

---

10 For more thoughts on curricula, see Gedro, Chapter 7, "Successfully Queering the Business Curriculum: A Proposed Agenda for Process as well as Content," below.

gay (Birden, 2005; Jackson, 2007; Kumashiro, 2002; Sanlo, 1999). So, teachers who are White and heterosexual may, and often do, find that addressing race and sexuality can be risky to their professional lives.

The third reason race and sexual orientation are often invisible in academic discourse is because minority groups have difficulty creating a coalition to challenge the majority group. Misawa (2007) reflects on how minority groups have their own agendas to normalize and privilege their positions so they can be included in mainstream American society and fully function in that context. He provides this synopsis of reality in higher educational contexts:

> Across higher education institutions, most LGBTQ organizations operate under administrations where race is of little or no concern. Because these contemporary organizations and programs for LGBTQ populations mainly focus on sexual orientation, they often ignore issues such as race, gender, and class within the LGBTQ population. (Misawa, 2007, p. 78)

In one situation, Misawa (2009) relates how a racial-minority leader, a Native American man, imposed his own agenda in two meetings on racial and ethnic issues without considering sexual orientation within racial communities. That showed an example of how race and sexual orientation have been treated discretely in higher education and racial communities. Since groups that consist of people of color have their own agendas for racial equality, they oftentimes do not think sexuality should also be part of their work.

Some scholars of color have argued that homophobia exists in racial communities. For example, hooks (1989) described why Black communities may be perceived as more homophobic than other communities. She states that sociocultural aspects of Black communities have perpetuated homophobia. One reason is the Christianity in Black communities where "religious beliefs and practices... promote and encourage homophobia" (p. 122). Some Black people have been indoctrinated "in churches that it is a sin to be gay" (p. 122), and they have formed an ideology that "homosexuality threatens the continuation of black families" (p. 123).

In addition to hooks's (1989) reflection on homophobia in Black communities, other scholars of color have also stated that a homophobic attitude is deeply embedded in their cultures (Guzman, 2006; Lang, 1997; Watt, 2002). For example, Watt researched the segregation of racial and sexual identities in one community by focusing on gay Asian men, and he showed that all the participants had a strong sense of Asian identity and gay identity but the two were kept separate, segregated. Chan (1989) states that her gay Asian American research participants felt they were not fully recognized by either the gay community or the Asian American community. Watt's and Chan's findings are echoed by the students in my own study on gay male students of color.

Two questions deserve to be answered: How can people fully be themselves as both people of color and gay people despite the distance between racial and sexual groups? Can it even be done at all? Perhaps these questions are fundamental questions to ask when one studies the intersectionality of race and sexual orientation. The contemporary situation observed in adult education with regard to the intersection of race and sexual orientation could be something similar to what Yoshino talks about in his book, *Covering* (2006), when he describes how people "cover" or assimilate into American culture. According to Yoshino, covering is a human behavior "to tone down a disfavored identity to fit into the main stream" (p. ix) and, in contemporary American society, people feel obligated "to tone down their stigmatized identities to get along in life" (p. x). To be able to be themselves, gay people of color have to overcome the force of positionality and negotiate a myriad of sociocultural power dynamics.

The next section will address the intersection of race and sexual orientation from a larger study examining the intersection of race and sexual orientation in higher education. It will focus particularly on the issues of community, membership, and academic citizenship in higher education. The following experiences of gay male students of color demonstrate how their race and sexual orientation influenced their campus lives.

Where Is Our Place?
Looking for a Queer-Race Space to Be Ourselves

In the spring semester 2004, I conducted a qualitative study that investigated the intersection of race and sexual orientation in higher education. I interviewed seven self-identified gay men of color between the ages of 20 and 30. The research interview was designed to elicit information from the participants about their experiences at a university in the northwestern United States.

According to the school website and the research participants, the university allows students to form clubs (communities), which creates a diverse campus environment for students. There are two student organizations for minorities on the campus, one for Asians, Blacks, Hispanics, and Native Americans and one for lesbians, gays, bisexuals, transgender persons, and Queers (LGBTQ). Although the research participants were variously involved in these student clubs on campus, they did not really feel that they were fully accepted by the others in the clubs or the club members. Only two people mentioned the racial-minority student club on campus, but all mentioned the LGBTQ club in this study.

Sam, a 28-year-old Black gay man, said that he knew that there was a club for sexual minorities and that the members were nice. However, he was caught in his own struggle over his identity as a sexual minority, which caused him to avoid joining the LGBTQ club:

I know there is [a club for sexual minorities], which I don't attend, but it helps just to know that there are people I could go to, I guess, if I needed.... I went once.... The people were very caring and sincere. It just didn't, I mean, I was at this point where I was still struggling, and they were very comfortable.... I think that had a lot to do with my adequacy because they were very comfortable and I wasn't, so it was hard for me to think or to be around someone that was that comfortable.

Although Sam was struggling with how open he wanted to be in public, he felt better knowing that there was an LGBTQ student club on campus.

It is important for gay male students of color to feel comfortable because that creates a feeling of membership in the college environment. If he decides to be more comfortable with himself in the future, he knows that he has a place to go for support. Just the existence of student clubs for minority support helps those who have not yet understood their own identity, especially with regard to minority sexual orientation.

Although all participants of this study mentioned the LGBTQ student club on campus, only one of them was actively involved. Gary, a 25-year-old gay Native man, said:

I have never been involved with the Native clubs. Instead, I have been active with my own tribe. As an Alaska Native, I didn't feel much inclusion at the university. The Native club at the university reaches out to the traditional image of a Native person. I think that I felt included in the LGBTQ club when [one certain person] was actively involved. At that time, the club was very active, and she helped me as a mentor when I was not feeling well.

Gary also commented that he identified himself as a Native person even though he looks more like a White American. As long as he does not reveal his racial identity as a Native person, people assume that he is White. Unfortunately, his racial identity as a Native person did not allow him to feel included in the Native club on campus. Rather, he preferred to be involved in the LGBTQ club as a gay man. His prior experience of support from the LGBTQ club enabled him to continue to be involved in it. Such an environment helped him think positively about his sexual orientation.

The students also implied that they do not have full membership in the organizations for minority students on campus because those organizations support only one aspect of their identity. Matt, a 28-year-old gay Black man, commented:

I think it would be wonderful to have a person of color gay group—aside from the [current LGBTQ club].... [Groups for gay men,] that's different from [groups for] gay [men] of color, 'cause that's White people, Asians, Blacks, that's everybody.... I don't think they have anything specifically [for] gay men of [color]... gay men or women of color support, which is a different issue [than just having a group for gay men].... White people complain that they can't have just their own club, which they can't. So, you know, [gay men of color are] not allowed [to have their own group]. They can't segregate.... Some people of color want their own club, and that may not actually be... legal or constitutional or something like that 'cause White people can't have their own club.

Matt was pointing out the uneven distribution of races at the university. Even though clubs couldn't limit their membership to a particular race, in the end, White people dominated the non-racial clubs. It could be difficult for a gay man of color to feel included in such an environment because it feels like racial discrimination within the LGBTQ campus community.

The research seems to suggest that gay men of color are disconnected from the gay community on campus because it is mainly made up of White people, a phenomenon common in the more general American culture (Kumashiro, 2002). This disconnectedness may make the gay male students of color feel uncomfortable in their college lives. Having a common gay identity is not enough to make the students in this study feel comfortable in the LGBTQA student club.

Ed, a 20-year-old Latino gay man, said that "[gay] clubs for minorities would be very inclusive because those clubs would try to reach out towards all the minorities to help each other." Both Matt and Ed said that they hoped to have some kind of student club for both sexual and racial minority people, which I propose here to be called "a Queer-Race Space," a space for Queer people of color where their ethno-racial identities and sexual orientation are equally included in contrast to conventional spaces for single-identity organizations that focus on either race or sexual orientation (Misawa, 2007). Queer-Race Spaces for people of color would welcome both race and sexual orientation as integral parts of an attending person's identity.

Jim, who identifies himself as a gay Mexican, also offered a perspective similar to Matt's and Ed's. He pointed out that there needs to be some professional organization for gay male students of color:

> *Hopefully there will be an organization or a club outside of just the student club, but a university-initiated club, not a club [where] a bunch of gay people... create a student gay club [...] a university-oriented thing, that the university established.*

The university already had a Native organization that had been institutionally created to support Native people and improve relations between Native students and the mainstream culture on campus.

Sam had been experiencing a period of self-discovery while devoting all his time to higher education, even living on campus. He felt that he needed to belong to a group that would fully support his life as a racial minority and as a sexual minority. He noticed that he feels increasingly alone as he becomes more educated, reporting:

> *I have always kind of been the only African American male in my classes. And maybe that is because... a lot of African American men aren't interested in pursuing a degree in English or writing.... There is one aspect of me trying or finding a way to be comfortable with being the only African American sometimes, but sometimes the only African American male. Then, there is the aspect of being comfortable with being the only [sexual-minority student]. So, there are two things working there.*

Sam is depicting a common experience for people of color. Such loneliness occurs not only in the university setting but also in the real world. As Blacks pursue higher education, they become isolated from their sociocultural community (hooks, 1989; Johnson-Bailey, 2001). Given that, people who have multiple minority perspectives might experience more isolation as they progress through higher education.

Discussion

Ideally, all gay adult learners of color should have a space where they feel included, one that makes them feel whole regardless of internal and external tension between their identities. The voices in the study above (Misawa, 2004) describe a campus community that is not a place of belonging for students who are both sexual minorities and racial minorities. This indicates that the learning environment is not democratic for gay male students of color because of their minority positionalities. While the general campus makes an effort to include gays and people of color, gay people of color are marginalized in their racial communities where heterosexism is perpetuated and they are marginalized in communities based on sexual orientation where every community function is saturated by whiteness (Misawa, 2007). Individuals need to be a part of a community to feel included, but the community also needs to include all aspects of the individual (Tisdell, 1995).

The notion of community appeared on many occasions in the interviews in my 2004 study. It has been crucial for people with minority perspectives to belong to communities. These communities support and help them survive in the mainstream culture of higher education (Dilley, 2002; Kumashiro, 2001, 2002; Watt, 2002). Higher education reflects how society operates. As in politics, students are citizens of academia. Their citizenship in university support groups is a crucial aspect for democracy on campus. Gay adult learners of color must be able to complete their education without having to struggle to gain full-fledged citizenship.

During the interview process, two participants in the study told how they knew there was a support group for gay students and one for students of color but not one for people who are gay *and* people of color. They also said that there were different minority student groups, such as the LGBTQ student club, Native student services, and the Asian, Black, Hispanic, and Native American student organization. However, none of these clubs would give gay men of color the support they needed concerning the intersection of their identities; they could not feel wholly included on campus without such a group.

As previously stated, both gay people and people of color in the U.S. have strong feelings for their own communities (Watt, 2002). However, communities based on race and sexual orientation have not yet come together to combat societal oppression. As a result of this divergence of racial- and sexual-orientation-based groups, neither LGBTQ communities nor racial-minority communities embrace the intersectionality of race and sexual orientation, so gay people of color cannot obtain full citizenship in either community. These communities are based on particular minority aspects in the United States, so they do not seem to accept extra burdens or identities that are perceived to be negative, such as race in LGBTQ communities and sexual orientation in racial communities. We find this dynamic operating in the context of higher education as well. In the interviews, research participants stated that they could not find a place on campus where their sexual and racial identities could be integrated. They also felt that marginalizing their gay identity in classrooms where heterosexism is deeply embedded was difficult and repressive but often necessary for survival. The same students did not feel comfortable being the only gay students of color in the gay student club where racism (or at least color-blindness) existed. Delgado and Stefancic (2001) defines color-blindness as a belief that "one should treat all persons equally, without regard to their race" (p. 144); it can be a fundamental ideology of equality. Delgado and Stefancic called it "'formal,' [based on] conceptions of equality, expressed in rules that insist only on treatment that is the same across the board, [and] can thus remedy only the most blatant forms of discrimination" (p. 7). Some scholars and researchers have argued that color-blindness is a positive way of creating a democratic learning environment, but others have argued that it is a negative way because it denies differences among diverse racial groups, and it ends up further privileging White students (Chae, 2006; Misawa, 2007). In situations involving gay students of color, color-blindness does apply because it automatically gives Whites and heterosexuals more privileged status as they are generally accepted as the norm (it is hard to imagine an adult educator assuming every learner in the room is gay or a person of color, and even harder to imagine the assumption that everyone is a gay person of color).

In such hostile environments where a gay person of color must suppress being gay, the research participants in my study said that they were glad that there was a Queer Space program, even though most of them were not involved with it. They at least knew that their gay side was getting support on campus. Likewise, they were glad that there was at least one place where they could go to get racial support. However, a Queer Space for just anyone was not enough for them. Since people who were in the Queer Space group were mostly White, "anyone" more aptly referred to gay White people at their institution. The students implied that the current Queer Space catered only to White sexual minorities and openly gay people. Their comments suggested that a Queer-Race Space was indeed required so they could enjoy combined support for their two minority perspectives. Some thought that a Queer-Race Space would enhance the confidence of gay people of color. It might also help them rightfully obtain full membership in the academic community.

Implications for Educators of Adult Learners

Scholars have emphasized that creating an inclusive learning environment is important for students because positive learning experiences may improve their learning process (Misawa, 2006; Tisdell, 1995). In the field of adult and higher education, some scholars who emphasize racial equality have stated that race is a significant factor in U.S. society because society itself is influenced by race; in other words, race matters (Johnson-Bailey, 2002; Johnson-Bailey & Cervero, 2008).

Racial differences make a huge difference in terms of accessing educational opportunities, obtaining high-paying jobs, and living in safe neighborhoods (Sissel & Sheared, 2001). Because people in the United States are from different racial backgrounds, they are able to develop their own communities to support each other. That was particularly helpful during the Civil Rights Movement because people of color were able to obtain civil rights as a group; their community bonds helped shape the social movement. In the context of adult education, Peterson (1999) criticizes how Black American adult educators are not appropriately included in knowledge production in adult education and proposes that critical race theory could be a strong tool to utilize in examining race in adult education. However, since the last decade, the contributions of Black American adult educators have increased. For example, Troy's (2006) content analysis of AERC papers from 1995 and 2005 indicates that papers on race in North America was about 10% of the all papers published during the decade. About 47% of the papers that dealt with race were on African Americans; the rest were on other racial groups such as Asians, Latinos, and Native Americans. Although there is an encouraging number of papers on race at AERC, the number of research studies and publications on race is not sufficient for this complex topic and more are needed in adult education.

Sexual orientation is also an important consideration in higher education in terms of making a more equitable learning and cultural environment for students. Grace (2001) argues that adult education has not fully become a democratic field of study. He further emphasizes that contemporary adult education reflects mainstream American society where heterosexual values are normative and non-heterosexual values are sidelined or ignored. From this perspective, he argues that the field needs to draw on more diverse aspects of Queer cultural studies and other types of critical multicultural studies. Grace and Hill (2004) also describe how important it is to include Queer contents in education. They critique the pervasive exclusion of sexual orientation in the field of adult and higher education and suggest how inserting Queer into education could become a way of contributing to knowledge production regarding sexual orientation in adult and higher education.

So, how about people who are gay and of color? People with multiple oppressions, particularly racial and sexual minorities, need a safe space where their identities can be openly merged. In a college environment, membership in a support group and academic citizenship are fundamental rights. The concept of belonging to a group helps sexual minorities of color feel secure and comfortable (Varney, 2001). Yet mainstream learning environments for adults in the United States have underdeveloped the ways of creating an inclusive learning environment for their diverse students. To create environments where diversity and intersectionality are fully understood, educators and administrators in adult and higher education have to incorporate the identity intersection of race and sexual orientation into an inclusive support system instead of focusing separately on the two identities (Kumashiro, 2001). Once adult educators can ensure effective learning in educational settings by helping develop a Queer-Race Space, academic dialogues about this currently missing intersectionality of race and sexual orientation can finally begin. Hopefully, this dialogue will lead to safer and more inclusive learning environments for all learners.

References

Birden, S. (2005). *Rethinking sexual identity in education.* NY: Rowman & Littlefield Publisher, Inc.

Brookfield, S. D. (2006). *The skillful teacher: On technique, trust, and responsiveness in the classroom* (2nd ed.). San Francisco: Jossey-Bass.

Chae, H. S. (2006). Using critical race theory to explore Korean-origin working class youth's conceptualizations of identity. In C. C. Park, R. Endo, & A. L. Goodwin (Eds.), *Asian and Pacific American education: Learning, socialization, and identity* (pp. 219-240). Greenwich, CT: Information Age Publishing.

Chan, C. S. (1989). Issues of identity development among Asian-American lesbians and gay men. *Journal of Counseling and Development, 68*(1), 16-20.

Collins, P. H. (2004). Comment on Hekman's "Truth and method: Feminist standpoint theory revisited": Where's the power? In S. Harding (Ed.), *The feminist standpoint theory reader: Intellectual and political controversies* (pp. 247-253). NY: Routledge.

Delgado, R., & Stefancic, J. (2001). *Critical race theory: An introduction.* NY: New York University Press.

Dilley, P. (2002). *Queer man on campus: A history of non-heterosexual college men, 1945-2000.* NY: RoutledgeFalmer.

Dixson, A. D. (2006). What's race got to do with it? Racial identity development, and teacher preparation. In E. W. Ross & V. O. Pang (Gen. Eds.), H. R. Miller & E. W. Ross (Vol. Eds.), *Race, ethnicity, and education: Racial identity in education* (pp. 19-36). Westport, CT: Praeger.

Ferguson, A. D., & Howard-Hamilton, M. F. (2000). Addressing issues of multiple identities for women of color on college campuses. In V. Wall & N. Evans (Ed.), *Toward acceptance: Sexual orientation issues on campus* (pp. 283-297). Lanham, MD: University Press of America, Inc.

Grace, A. P. (2001). Using queer cultural studies to transgress adult educational space. In V. Sheared & P. A. Sissel (Eds.), *Making space: Merging theory and practice in adult education* (pp. 257-270). Westport, CT: Bergin & Garvey.

Grace, A. P., & Hill, R. J. (2004). Positioning queer in adult education: Intervening in politics and praxis in North America. *Studies in the Education of Adults, 36*(2), 167-189.

Guzman, M. (2006). *Gay hegemony/Latino homosexualities.* NY: Routledge.

Hill, R. J. (2005, July). *Making difference count: Queer cultural competency in lifelong learning.* Paper presented at the 35th Annual Standing Conference on University Teaching and Research in the Education of Adults Conference (SCUTREA), University of Sussex, Brighton, UK.

hooks, b. (1989). *Talking back: Thinking feminist, thinking black*. Boston, MA: South End Press.

hooks, b. (2003). *Teaching community: A pedagogy of hope*. NY: Routledge.

Jackson, J. M. (2007). *Unmasking identities: An exploration of the lives of gay and lesbian teachers*. NY: Rowman & Littlefield.

Johnson-Bailey, J. (2001). The power of race and gender: Black women's struggle and survival in higher education. In R. M. Cervero & A. L. Wilson (Eds.), *Power in practice: Adult education and the struggle for knowledge and power in society* (pp. 126-144). San Francisco: Jossey-Bass.

Johnson-Bailey, J. (2002). Race matters: The unspoken variable in the teaching-learning transaction. In J. M. Ross-Gordon (Ed.), *Contemporary viewpoints on teaching adults effectively* (pp. 39-49). New Direction for Adult and Continuing Education, No. 93. San Francisco: Jossey-Bass.

Johnson-Bailey, J., & Cervero, R. M. (2008). Different worlds and divergent paths: Academic careers defined by race and gender. *Harvard Educational Review, 78*(2), 311-332.

Kumashiro, K. K. (2001). Queer students of color and antiracist, antiheterosexist education: Paradoxes of identity and activism. In K. K. Kumashiro (Ed.), *Troubling intersections of race and sexuality* (pp. 1-25). NY: Rowman & Littlefield Publishers.

Kumashiro, K. K. (2002). *Troubling education: Queer activism and antioppressive pedagogy*. NY: RoutledgeFalmer.

Kumashiro, K. K. (2008). *The seduction of common sense: How the right has framed the debate on America's schools*. NY: Teachers College Press.

Lang, S. (1997). Various kinds of two-spirit people: Gender variance and homosexuality in Native American communities. In S.-E. Jacobs, W. Thomas, & S. Lang (Eds.), *Two-spirit people: Native American gender identity, sexuality, and spirituality* (pp. 100-118). Chicago: University of Illinois Press.

Lawrence, C. R, III, Matsuda, M. J., Delgado, R., & Crenshaw, K. W. (1993). Introduction. In M. J. Matsuda, C. R. Lawrence III, R. Delgado, & K. W. Crenshaw (Eds.), *Words that wound: Critical race theory, assaultive speech, and the first amendment* (pp. 1-15). San Francisco: Westview Press.

Misawa, M. (2004). *The intersection of race and sexual orientation in adult and higher education: Creating inclusive environments for gay men of color.* Unpublished master's thesis, University of Alaska Anchorage, Anchorage, AK.

Misawa, M. (2006). Queer race pedagogy in adult higher education: Dealing with power dynamics and positionality of gay students of color. In M. Hagen & E. Goff (Eds.), *Proceedings of the 47th Annual Adult Education Research Conference* (pp. 257-262). Minneapolis: University of Minnesota.

Misawa, M. (2007). Political aspects of the intersection of sexual orientation and race in higher education in the United States: A queer scholar of color's perspective. *Journal of Curriculum and Pedagogy, 4*(2), 78-83.

Misawa, M. (2009). The intersection of homophobic bullying and racism in adulthood: A graduate school experience. *Journal of LGBT Youth, 6*(1), 1-14.

Newman, D. M. (2007). *Identities and inequalities: Exploring the intersections of race, class, gender, and sexuality.* NY: McGraw-Hill.

Peterson, E. A. (1999). Creating a culturally relevant dialogue for African American adult educators. In T. C. Guy (Ed.), *Providing culturally relevant adult education: A challenge for the twenty-first century* (pp. 79-91). New Direction for Adult and Continuing Education, No. 82. San Francisco: Jossey-Bass.

Rocco, T. S., & Gallagher, S. J. (2004). Discriminative justice: Can discrimination be just? In L. G. Martin & E. E. Rogers (Eds.), *Adult education in an urban context: Problems practices, and programming for inner-city communities* (pp. 29-41). New Directions for Adult and Continuing Education, No. 101. San Francisco: Jossey-Bass.

Sanlo, R. L. (1999). *Unheard voices: The effects of silence on lesbian and gay educators.* Westport, CT: Bergin & Garvey.

Sissel, P. A., & Sheared, V. (2001). Opening the gates: Reflections on power, hegemony, language, and the status quo. In V. Sheared & P. A. Sissel (Eds.), *Making space: Merging theory and practice in adult education* (pp. 3-14). Westport, CT: Bergin & Garvey.

Tisdell, E. J. (1995). *Creating inclusive adult learning environments: Insights from multicultural education and feminist pedagogy.* Information Series No. 361. Columbus, OH: ERIC Clearinghouse on Adult, Career, and Vocational Education.

Tisdell, E. J. (2001). The politics of positionality. In R. M. Cervero & A. L. Wilson (Eds.), *Power in practice: Adult education and the struggle for knowledge and power in society* (pp. 145-163). San Francisco: Jossey-Bass.

Tisdell, E. J., Hanley, M. S., & Taylor, E. W. (2000). Different perspectives on teaching for critical consciousness. In A. L. Wilson & E. R. Hayes (Eds.), *Handbook of adult and continuing education* (pp. 132-142). San Francisco: Jossey-Bass.

Troy, L. (2006). Knowledge production at the cutting edge? A content analysis of AERC papers from 1995-2005. In M. Hagen & E. Goff (Eds.), *Proceedings of the 47th Annual Adult Education Research Conference* (pp. 409-414). Minneapolis-St. Paul: University of Minnesota.

Varney, J. A. (2001). Understanding the normal: Community efforts for queer Asian and Asian American youth. In K. K. Kumashiro (Ed.), *Troubling intersections of race and sexuality* (pp. 87-103). NY: Rowman & Littlefield Publishers.

Watt, E. C. (2002). *The making of a gay Asian community: An oral history of pre-AIDS Los Angeles*. NY: Rowman & Littlefield Publishers, Inc.

Yoshino, K. (2006). *Covering: The hidden assault on our civil rights*. NY: Random House.

CHAPTER 7

Successfully Queering the Business Curriculum: A Proposed Agenda for Process as Well as Content

Julie Gedro

Introduction

This article proposes an agenda for interrupting the heterosexist assumptions that permeate higher education curricula, particularly the assumptions that are operationalized and reinforced through both deliberate as well as unintentional neglect in the business school curriculum. As a business professor and director of a management education program at a public liberal arts college, I have experienced firsthand the complexity that continues to exist around the issue of coming out as a lesbian in the academy, about teaching management education courses with textbooks and curriculum that reinforce the silence that fosters heteronormativity, and about crafting strategies and interventions designed to challenge heterosexual assumptions in higher education. I began my academic career at Empire State College, which is a liberal arts college within the State University of New York system. Although Empire State College is located in New York State, our students come from all over the country. We are a nontraditional college that serves adult students, and the average age of our students is 38. The business curriculum of which I speak, therefore, is a national curriculum, and the purpose of this chapter is to identify the ways that heteronormativity is reified through existing business curricula. Additionally, the chapter will suggest ways that the

This chapter has been updated and modified from a presentation given at the AERC Lesbian, Gay, Bisexual, Transgender, Queer, and Allies Pre-Conference, Athens, Georgia, in 2005. That version may be found in the published *Proceedings* of that conference.

business curriculum may be broadened and deepened to include issues related to LGBTQ inclusion. The silence and ignorance around LGBTQ issues in business reinforce the dominant heterosexist paradigm of organizational America, and this chapter will propose ways to Queer the business curriculum.

— ——— ·≡·— ——— —

Heterosexism and the Business Curriculum

McQuarrie (1998) offered three reasons why sexual orientation is missing in management curricula: (a) There is a lack of visible or physical distinction of LGBTQ people; (b) issues of LGBTQ people go unidentified and unaddressed because of LGBTQ invisibility; and (c) the discussion of sexual orientation poses a threat to an instructor.

Instructors who are gay or lesbian may fear that teaching about sexual orientation may require them to disclose their own sexual orientation, even if they are uncomfortable in doing so or worried that such disclosure may affect their jobs or careers. In my own teaching practice, there are two fundamental locations for Queering the curriculum. First, as a lesbian faculty member as well as an administrator, I continually make decisions about coming out to students. In discussions with students, I have come to realize, however, that my decision to come out is one that is increasingly less of an issue over which I have control. To date, several of my students have confided in me that they already assumed that I was a lesbian. Second, as a business professor, I am often faced not only with decisions around self-disclosure but also with decisions around including LGBTQ issues in my studies and in my teaching. Sexual orientation complicates self-disclosure because of the stigma associated with orientations other than heterosexuality (Allen, 1995).

My presence itself in the classroom, therefore, interrupts heterosexist assumptions about the world of business. As a business professor, I teach studies that facilitate students' acquisition of capitalistic values, skills, and knowledge. I teach business, and I am an out lesbian. My lesbianism sometimes is a topic of discussion when I teach, and sometimes it is not. As I have become more comfortable negotiating the political landscape of the academy, I have also become comfortable introducing topics related to LGBTQ equality in the classroom. For example, with my dean I proposed, developed, and taught a course that explored women in sports. We offered the course as an elective in our business school, and the content of the course included the social construction of gender as well as the use of the term "lesbian" as a rhetorical and linguistic strategy to control women who might otherwise resist patriarchy. Joyce (2007) notes that LGBT academics face career risks by coming out; however, coming out is critical for LGBT faculty. This is because LGBT faculty can serve as change agents by modeling authentic behavior and by destabilizing "students' experiences of bodies as having unique, stable, unchanging, natural identities" (Schippert, 2006, p. 282). The risks inherent in coming out, while noteworthy, are becoming decreasingly significant. Joyce (2007) also observes that society has become increasingly knowledgeable and concerned about LGBT issues and that college campuses are becoming locations of student as well as faculty activism. The term "Queer" is now embraced by many as a term that proudly flouts its deviance from the norm, its ability to interfere with and to thwart established social, political, and philosophical conventions that privilege heterosexuality and all for which it stands (Carlin & DiGrazia, 2004). Queering the curriculum represents the emergent attempt by scholars and educators to make relevant the issues of silence, marginalization, awkwardness, and apathy related to LGBTQ voice and visibility in the environment of higher education.

Societal and Workplace Discrimination as a Mandate to Queer the Business Curriculum

The call to Queer the business curriculum is urgent because of the ubiquitous and systemic oppression of LGBTQ people in society as well as in the microsociety of the corporate environment. Lesbian, gay, bisexual, transgender, and Queer (LGBTQ) people continue to face employment discrimination in corporate America (Croteau, 1996; Fassinger, 1996; Miller, 1998; Swisher, 1996). This discrimination begins with the employment decision and continues throughout an LGBTQ employee's organizational life in both subtle as well as covert ways. LGBTQ people are handicapped by the stigma of being a sexual minority, and this stigmatization is replayed during hiring, transfers, promotions, and daily corporate life. Disclosing one's sexual orientation at work is one of the most difficult issues that LGBTQ employees face because it involves emotional turmoil and a fear of retaliation and rejection (Griffin & Hebl, 2002). Presently, LGBTQ workers face a double-edged sword when managing their stigmatized sexual identity in the workplace because they face problems if they come out and they face problems if they remain closeted (Griffin & Hebl, 2002). The problems of remaining closeted include co-worker perceptions of aloofness, stress, and a sense of self-betrayal.

The burden is squarely on the shoulders of LGBTQ employees to make decisions about personal (identity) disclosure and, just as important, to educate his/her manager(s) about issues related to being LGBTQ (Gedro, Cervero, & Johnson-Bailey, 2004). Despite the gains of the modern-day LGBTQ human rights movement, as manifested in the provision of domestic partner benefits by employers and in certain states, cities, and localities by the provision of legal protection to LGBTQ citizens and employees, there continues be to a collective silence that surrounds issues related to being LGBTQ. There continues to be a dearth of practical management education and adult education that provide opportunities for understanding and growth of the heterosexual majority in the workplace. Because LGBTQ individuals must continually make decisions about self-disclosure, they live with stress (Huebner & Davis, 2007; see also Mercier, 2007; Vincke, DeRycke, & Bolton, 2006). This stress could be reduced, if not eliminated, if management were educated and sensitized to the issues related to being LGBTQ. This lack of education among managers serves to reinforce existing feelings and systems of oppression, as LGBTQ employees expend significant energy managing their sexual orientation on the job and attempting to control whether, when, and to whom their orientation is disclosed (Schneider, 1982).

Queering the Business Curriculum: The Process

Including LGBTQ issues in the business curriculum involves both process as well as content. The process of Queering the business curriculum involves creating affirming classrooms and learning environments for LGBTQ students. In my own institution, for example, I generally know who the LGBTQ students are, which is a function of my own willingness to be out as a lesbian as well as of the nontraditional nature of our pedagogy at my institution. In other words, my visibility as a lesbian creates an environment whereby LGBTQ students feel comfortable and invited to come out to me. Because of the varieties of ways that we teach, which include guided independent study, online classrooms, group studies, and residency-based studies, there are opportunities for students to engage individually with professors as well as with each other. Wlodkowski and Ginsberg (1995) posit that in order to establish inclusion in a higher education setting, it is important to create a culture of respect as well as connectedness. Wlodkowski and Ginsberg suggest ways to create respectful, connected cultures that include collaborative learning, peer teaching, and opportunities for multidimensional sharing. Miller (2000) proposes a "caring education, an education rooted in face-to-face relationship, participation in community, and social responsibility" (p. 5). In my own teaching practice, I make it clear that all perspectives are welcome and valued in class, including varying positions on management and other related business issues such as outsourcing, globalization, technology, and even Affirmative Action. Wlodkowski and Ginsberg also note the importance of creating classroom norms that "create expectations for behaviors" (p. 64) and that norms can "provide the kind of atmosphere and understanding that allow highly charged feelings and responses to be buffered as well as acknowledged" (p. 64).

There is no shortage of conversation and specific suggestions within the academy about how to keep the business curriculum current and relevant. A search, for example, of EBSCO Host on the term "business curriculum" resulted in an array of articles encouraging the inclusion of sustainability, risk management, strategic thinking, globalization, ethics, and technology in the curriculum. A similar search on ProQuest yielded articles dealing with technology, ethics, and internationalization. LGBTQ issues are not on the agenda of business educators as an emergent theme in business education. Bohanon (2008) observes that there are four persistent themes in colleges of business: "content of business curriculum, professional nature of business and business schools, social responsibility of corporate managers, and integration of business curriculum" (p. 239). In the abstract, the themes of content, social responsibility, and integration lend themselves to LGBTQ issues. However, LGBTQ issues are unnamed in the article. As such, there is little guidance for fair-minded and well-intended educators who want to create inclusive classrooms or who want to include LGBTQ issues in their curricula.

Queering the Business Curriculum: Content

The range of studies that I teach spans human resources management, compensation and benefits, business ethics, business policy and strategy, employment law, organizational behavior, and training and development. When I began my career at Empire State College in July 2003, I conducted an aggressive review of textbooks that I would use in the various courses. Although my review consisted of scanning, reading, reviewing, and critically analyzing for content, breadth, clarity, and readability, it occurred to me several months into my position that there was a paucity of discussion around the issues related to LGBTQ employees in the organizational context. One might think that, given the subject matter that I teach, which prepares business managers and leaders to acquire skills in planning, organizing, leading, and controlling the work of other people in organizations, there might be a mention of this population of employees. Business curricula should foster critical thinkers, ethical leaders, strategic planners, and savvy managers. Braun (2004) identifies the ways that a capstone study of business should encourage and teach critical thinking; one of those facets includes teaching students how to question assumptions and traditions in organizations.

Corporations, as bastions of heterosexism (Gedro et al., 2004), are characterized and pervaded by assumptions of heterosexuality. Just as business itself requires a new set of skills to deal with technology and globalization, businesspeople must develop the critical ability to analyze socially constructed oppressive norms about sexual orientation. The following are some observations about the current state of certain business studies as well as suggestions for Queering them.

Management

Managers plan, organize, lead, and control. The study of management provides learners with opportunities to conceptualize management in a theoretical framework and to extend those theories into the workplace. One interpretation of current management theory and pedagogy includes the following contemporary issues: the Internet, globalization, knowledge management, and collaboration across boundaries (Bateman & Snell, 2004). Additionally, there is increasing focus on diversity in management texts, and there is even a brief mention of LGBTQ issues. For example, Jones and George (2006) make this observation in their chapter entitled, "Managing Diverse Employees in a Multicultural Environment":

> *Clearly, many highly qualified potential and current employees might happen to be gay or lesbian. An organization that does not welcome and support such employees is not only unfairly discriminating against this group but also is losing the contributions of its valued employees. Additionally, an organization that discriminates against this group risks alienating customers. Fifteen million consumers are in the GLBT group in the United States, and according to research conducted by MarketResearch.com, their purchasing power is around $485 billion. (p. 158)*

The emergence of LGBTQ inclusion in management texts holds some promise for the inclusion of LGBTQ content in the business curriculum. However, management research, teaching, and texts need to extend more practically into issues of understanding the invisibility of LGBTQ people and how easy it is to overlook or minimize these issues. While Jones and George (2006) introduce the fact that LGBTQ people do exist, the brief mention only cracks the metaphorical closet door. It neither invites straight management students into the world of LGBTQ employees, nor does it let closeted LGBTQ managers and employees out. It merely mentions their presence. It notes their buying and spending power. It presents the "what" of LGBTQ issues, not the "how" to include them in the study and practice of management.

The existing literature benignly describes the practical and global breakdown of the multilayered and complicated hierarchical systems of management. There is an explosion of research and practice that describes the emergence of teams, empowerment, and self-direction, and these are unquestionably valid and important aspects of management. However, despite the fact that LGBTQ issues are emergent and LGBTQ issues are gaining some visibility in society and in commerce, most treatment of LBGTQ issues is relegated to the closet of human resource management, employment law, and their troubleshooting cousin, "diversity." Queering management should include sensitivity training and education content for emerging managers about the issues that their LBGTQ employees face.

Labor Economics

Labor economics texts explore decisions of employment and income of "husband" and "wife." There is no current theory that examines the employment and income decisions made by two partners of the same sex. Queering labor economics would mean including discussions of employment decisions made by same-sex couples. For example, it might involve consideration of the tax consequences of domestic partner benefits. Infusing such LGBTQ issues into labor economics would not only broaden the perspectives of students, it may also sensitize educators and researchers about the myriad policy issues surrounding LGBTQ inequalities in the broader U.S. society. For example, even though over half of the *Fortune* 500 corporations provide domestic partner benefits to employees (Human Rights Campaign, 2008), those benefits are taxed. However, healthcare benefits for opposite-sex married couples are not. A crisp infusion of some education about LGBTQ employees and economics into the labor economics curriculum might help dispel the commonly held myth that the LGBTQ community is a "prosperous elite" (Hyman, 2002, p. 12). Moreover, it might provide a more accurate picture of LGBTQ people and counter other myths such as "those of privilege, of the ease and protection of being in the closet, of our conspicuous consumption, and of childlessness" (Badgett, 2001, cited in Hyman, p. 12).

Leadership

Leadership texts reinforce gendered binaries of "male" leadership styles and "female" leadership styles. Leadership literature and teaching prides itself on the deconstruction of essentialist notions that women lead in only feminine ways and that men lead in only masculine ways. Such discourse closets and impedes LGBTQ leaders who long ago had to self-determine—sometimes with bruises and scrapes on the front lines of the organization—which leadership styles will be accepted and which will not. Queering leadership would mean deliberately complicating the constructs of "feminine" leadership styles and "masculine" leadership styles and providing alternative perspectives to these constrictive, gendered binaries.

Business Ethics

"Business ethics is the study of what constitutes right and wrong, or good or bad, human conduct in a business context" (Shaw & Barry, 2006, p. 4). Sexual orientation inclusion, as a human rights issue, is also an ethical issue. The study of business ethics is an ideal place to inform business managers and leaders about issues related to invisibility, heterosexism, and homophobia. Shaw and Barry include a compelling article written by Richard D. Mohr, entitled "Homosexuality, Prejudice and Discrimination." The article unpacks some myths and stereotypes about homosexuality. It also identifies the lack of civil rights protection afforded LGBTQ people, and it argues for such protections: "Extending civil rights protection to gay men and lesbians is also justified as promoting general prosperity. Such legislation tends to increase the production of goods and services for society as a whole" (p. 502). The presence of one very good article in one very good text, or the fact that I highlight it here, is in no way meant to suggest that business ethics is LGBTQ-friendly. Rather, it is to celebrate one piece of curricular material and hold it up as an exemplar and a model for other texts to follow. Other texts that I have reviewed, and even some that I use, make no mention of LGBTQ issues at all.

Organizational Behavior and Human Resource Management

Organizational behavior is the study of how individuals, teams, groups, systems, and organizations interact. It is a multidisciplinary study that includes psychology, sociology, management, leadership, and systems thinking. Because this study deals so heavily with the perceptual process of people in systems, the topic offers an appropriate place to include discussions of LGBTQ issues in the workplace today. Yet current texts on organizational behavior are generally silent about LGBTQ issues, and professors have to look for creative mechanisms to include LGBTQ issues in their courses. In my case, I use my own anecdotes from my experience as a human resource practitioner in corporate America in order to highlight how heterosexism operates as a hegemonic system of dominance in organizations. Organizational behavior deals with how individuals create meaning and how groups, teams, and systems function. I share my own experiences as an out lesbian working in corporate America and my own experiences of how myths, prejudices, and stereotypes inhibit workplace effectiveness.

Clearly, human resource managers should have an understanding of the issues related to being an LGBTQ employee. Human resource studies hold great promise for preparing human resource practitioners to be responsible, enlightened stewards of the advancement of LGBTQ rights. Again, however, there is silence and invisibility surrounding LGBTQ issues in most HR textbooks. Because human resource management covers a variety of subfunctions, such as recruitment and selection, training and development, workplace safety, labor relations, employee relations, and compensation and benefits, there is a significant opportunity for human resource management curricula to be LGBTQ inclusive.

LGBTQ people face employment discrimination when they look for jobs (recruitment and selection); they face employment discrimination when they seek promotional opportunities (training and development); they face harassment and discrimination on the job (workplace safety); they often do not have allies within their Human Resource Departments (labor and employee relations); and they face wage and benefits discrimination (compensation and benefits). Badgett (cited in Hyman, 2002) found that lesbians and bisexual women earn 8% more than heterosexual women, but gay and bisexual men earn 35% less than heterosexual men (p. 12). Lesbians earn less than gay men, on the average, which represents both sexual orientation as well as gender discrimination. Indeed there are opportunities to include LGBTQ issues in the human resource management classroom, and to do so would only serve to increase the knowledge, skills, and competencies of students of human resource management.

In this regard, I developed what has proven to be a very successful course for Empire State College's Center for Distance Learning (CDL). Selected Topics in HRM: LGBTQ Issues is a 2-credit, advanced course offered in the Business, Management and Economics Area of Study (Empire State College's nomenclature for "Department"). The course proposal was shepherded with the help of straight allies who were in positions to help it move through the acceptance process, and I developed the course in 2006. Since that time, it has been a mainstay in the curriculum; over half of the students who enroll in the course are heterosexual human resource management practitioners who indicate a desire to learn more about LGBTQ issues. The primary text for the course is Dr. Nicole Raeburn's (2004) book, *Changing Corporate America from the Inside Out*; other readings include "How Lesbians Have Learned to Negotiate the Heterosexism of Corporate America" (Gedro et al., 2004)[11]. Students complete a variety of assignments on LGBTQ issues in corporate America, including an evaluation of local, city, and state laws that protect (or do not protect) LGBTQ people; a career-seeker project in which the student assumes the identity (of their own choosing) of a lesbian, gay, bisexual, or transgendered person and then develops a career search strategy; and a final project in which the student develops a strategic plan for a fictitious corporation to become LGBTQ inclusive. The course has had nearly full enrollments since its inception, and students indicate their increased knowledge as well as confidence in understanding LGBTQ issues and LGBTQ employees.

⊷ ⊷ ⊷

Recommendations and Conclusion

The issue of homophobia is the last frontier in the workplace where people can be intolerant and often get away with it (Krupat & McCreery, 1999). The business curriculum in higher education is uniquely positioned to interrupt societal and organizational prejudice, intolerance, discrimination, and homophobia. However, in all but a very few textbooks that I have adopted, there is no mention of LGBTQ employees. Instead of serving to disrupt pervasive societal heterosexism, the silence and invisibility of LGBTQ issues in higher education curricula reinforces its stigmatization. Faculty in higher education—particularly those in business—can advance the cause of the fight for LGBTQ equality by locating sources that provide insights about LGBTQ employees and by including discussions about LGBTQ issues in the business classroom. Allies of the advancement

---

11 Readers interested in additional source material should consult R. J. Hill (Ed.), *Challenging Homophobia and Heterosexism: Lesbian, Gay, Bisexual, Transgender and Queer Issues in Organizational Settings*, New Directions for Adult and Continuing Education, No. 112 (San Francisco: Jossey-Bass, Winter 2006); T. S. Rocco, J. Gedro, and M. B. Kormanik (Eds.), *Gay, Lesbian, Bisexual, and Transgender Issues in HRD: Balancing Inquiry and Advocacy* (Bowling Green, OH: Academy of Human Resource Development and Sage, 2009).

of the equal rights of LGBTQ people should strive to include LGBTQ issues in their courses. Additionally, faculty members who are LGBTQ have the opportunity to serve as activists inside the classroom by coming out. By claiming space, voice, and presence, LGBTQ faculty and allies are uniquely positioned to foster learning environments in which students can be exposed to issues of LGBTQ equality that might otherwise be ignored.

References

Allen, K. (1995). Opening the classroom closet: Sexual orientation and self-disclosure. *Family Relations, 44*(2), 136-141.

Badgett, M.V. L. (2001). *Money, myths and change: The economic lives of lesbians and gay men.* Chicago: University of Chicago Press.

Bateman, T., & Snell, S. (2004). *Management: The new competitive landscape.* NY: McGraw-Hill.

Bohanon, C. (2008). Persistent themes in colleges of business. *Journal of Education for Business, 83*(4), 239-245.

Braun, N. (2004). Critical thinking in the business curriculum. *Journal of Education for Business, 79*(4), 232-236.

Carlin, D., & DiGrazia, J. (Eds.). (2004). *Queer cultures.* NY: Prentice Hall.

Conrad, K., & Crawford, J. (1999). Passing/out: The politics of disclosure in Queer-positive pedagogy. *Modern Language Studies, 28*(4), 153-162.

Croteau, J. (1996). Research on the work experiences of lesbian, gay, and bisexual people: An integrative view of methodology and findings. *Journal of Vocational Behavior, 48,* 95-209.

Fassinger, R. (1996). Notes from the margins: Integrating lesbian experience into the vocational psychology of women. *Journal of Vocational Behavior, 48,* 160-175.

Gedro, J., Cervero, R., & Johnson-Bailey, J. (2004). How lesbians learn to negotiate the heterosexism of corporate America. *Human Resource Development International, 7*(2), 181-195.

Griffin, K., & Hebl, M. (2002). The disclosure dilemma for gay men and lesbians: "Coming out" at work. *Journal of Applied Psychology, 8*(6), 1191-1199.

Huebner, D., & Davis, M. (2007). Perceived anti-gay discrimination and physical health outcomes. *Health Psychology, 26*(5), 627-634.

Human Rights Campaign. (2008). *GLBT equality at the Fortune 500.* Retrieved on July 29, 2008, from http://www.hrc.org/issues/workplace/fortune500.htm

Hyman, P. (2002). Buying lesbians. *The Lesbian Review of Books, 8*(2), 10.

Jones, G., & George, J. (2006). *Contemporary management.* NY: McGraw-Hill.

Joyce, T. (2007). Lesbian, gay, bisexual and transgender issues on campus: Making the private public. *Journal of Curriculum and Pedagogy, 4*(2), 31-36.

Krupat, K., & McCreery, P. (1999). Homophobia, labor's new frontier? A discussion with four labor leaders. In K. Krupat & P. McCreery (Eds.), *Social text, out front: Lesbians, gays, and the struggle for workplace rights* (pp. 59-72), Durham, NC: Duke University Press.

McQuarrie, F. (1998). Expanding the concept of diversity: Discussing sexual orientation in the management classroom. *Journal of Management Education, 22*(2), 162-172.

Mercier, L. R. (2007). Lesbian parents and work stressors and supports for the work-family interface. *Journal of Gay and Lesbian Social Services, 19*(2), 25-47.

Miller, D. (1998). *Freedom to differ.* NY: New York University Press.

Miller, R. (2000). Caring education and meaningful democracy. *Lapis Magazine, 12,* 1-6. Retrieved December 3, 2008, from http://www.pathsoflearning.org/articles_ Caring_Education_Meaningful_Democracy.php

Mohr, R. D. (2006). Homosexuality, prejudice and discrimination. In W. H. Shaw, & V. Barry (Eds.), *Moral issues in business* (pp. 496-504). Belmont, CA: Thomson Wadsworth Press.

Raeburn, N. (2004). *Changing corporate America from the inside out.* Minneapolis, MN: University of Minnesota Press.

Schippert, C. (2006). Critical projection and queer performativity: Self-revelation in teaching/learning otherness. *The Review of Education, Pedagogy, and Cultural Studies, 28,* 281-295.

Schneider, B. (1982). Consciousness about sexual harassment among heterosexual and lesbian women workers. *Journal of Social Issues, 38,* 75-78.

Shaw, W. H., & Barry, V. (2006). *Moral issues in business.* Belmont, CA: Thomson Wadsworth Press.

Swisher, K. (1996). Coming out in corporate America. *Working Woman, 21,* 50-53.

Vincke, J., DeRycke, L., & Bolton, R. (2006). Gay identity and the experience of gay social stress. *Journal of Applied Social Psychology, 29*(6), 1316-1331.

Wlodkowski, R., & Ginsberg, M. (1995). *Diversity and motivation.* San Francisco: Jossey-Bas

SECTION II:
ADULT LEARNING

CHAPTER 8

Crossroads for Creating My Space in the Workforce: Transformative Learning Helps Understand LGBTQ Sexual Identity Development Among Adults

Kathleen P. King

Coming out is a struggle on many levels. Coming out to oneself and one's family, friends, and community all need to be addressed individually because they often involve different time frames, contexts, and relationships. These decisions represent many symbolic crossroads that often need to be navigated as individual decisions for lesbian, gay, bisexual, transgender, and Queer (LGBTQ) adults. Contrary to popular beliefs, LGBTQ adults do not often come out globally and with great fanfare. In fact, coming out is a series of choices, often made incrementally, based on trust, need, and opportunity, to name just a few. Additionally, LGBTQ people need to make these decisions continuously in societies where they do not have heterosexual privilege.

In the lifelong process of coming out, some people may stumble along their way, figuring out the decisions they need to make, seeking abundant support and resources to guide them, or making decisions based on situations, social climate, and need. To depict LGBTQ sexual identity development experiences as monolithic would contradict the nature of LGBTQ perspectives. Instead, one needs to be open to the rich and complex variability of human need, nature, experience, and uniqueness. A brief example reminds us of some of the intricacies that LGBTQ adults must cope with in the workplace as they seek to create space for their real selves.

Scenario: Miguel had been employed at the Cabriano Home Improvement chain for three years, and medical benefits for his partner, Manny, had never been a concern. But then Manny got laid off and, due to the recession, he was unable to secure employment. As a result, they struggled with the exorbitant COBRA medical costs (a provision for unemployed people to maintain health benefits). However, they finally realized they had to take the risk and apply for benefits through Miguel's employer.

Miguel went to Human Resources (HR) to handle the change in benefits quietly but discovered he needed his supervisor's signature. The jig was up! His supervisor would see Manny's name on the form, and Miguel would be outed. His mind raced through the questions yet again:

- Would his boss live up to the professional diversity standard of the company or would the heteronormative subculture of their department win out?

- Could they make ends meet without going through this ordeal?

- Was Manny likely to need medical coverage?

- Would HR support him if there were problems with the supervisor or staff?

- Once outed, would he have any chance to advance in his department in the future?

- Why did he have to stress over benefits he was due through his employment?

Overview

While most people speak openly about their husband, wife, or significant other, and co-workers nod in agreement, LGBTQ employees are confronted with constant questions and many second guesses about small talk. They need to evaluate whether or not it is worth the risk because they might not accurately predict the reactions, even when routinely mentioning their family members or family activities. Unfortunately, it is an exceptional situation when co-workers and supervisors appreciate LGBTQ lives as equitable and valued. Another level of persistent conflict is present whenever colleagues or organizations present obstacles, ridicule, or judgments of LGBTQ adults. Such confrontations cause LGBTQ adults to evaluate their coming out in various settings and situations as an ongoing process.

In fact, although LGBTQ persons may appear confident, their internal homophobia, self-doubt, and fear may resurface when they are publicly challenged. The destructive messages sometimes present at these crossroads remind LGBTQ people that, compared to non-LGBTQ colleagues, their lives are much more challenging to negotiate at work.

Turning to Theory in Meeting LGBTQ Needs

Several nations and communities have begun to protect and provide more equitable rights for LGBTQ people. In part, this is a result of:

- having seen LGBTQ people fight to express their sexual identity in mainstream society (Becker, 2006; Teal, 1971)

- realizing more fully the terror and proliferation of hate crimes due to LGBTQ identity (CBS News, 2006; Duberman, 1994; The National GLBT Taskforce, 2007; Matthew Shepard Foundation, 2008)

- understanding the harm caused by lack of civil rights and protection (Lambda Legal, 2004; Lester, 2007; Mule, 2007)

- allowing more successful and open LGBTQ people to be included in the mainstream media (Elton John, k. d. lang, Melissa Etheridge, Lily Tomlin, Ellen DeGeneres, Rachel Maddow, Suze Orman, and Carson Kressley)

However, in contemporary times, many countries, including the United States, still have gross inequities in civil rights, legal and legislative protections, legal matters, benefits, health care, and privileges for LGBTQ adults. Conservative religious groups, among other heteronormative and socially limiting institutions, exacerbate LGBTQ disenfranchisement. However, to mainstream society, the needs and obstacles that impede or deny LGBTQ living, care, and safety may remain invisible and of no consequence. Therefore, a theoretical model that describes how LGBTQ persons cope with prejudice, injustice, alienation, and contradictions is most informative for workplace training. Such a framework helps us understand the needs and processes by which LGBTQ people make decisions and navigate the crossroads of their lives in a heteronormative culture.

Recent literature and theory of adult learning and counseling helps to inform the topic at hand. Specifically, the Wishik and Pierce model (1991), as well as transformative learning, have served as a collective basis for the framework presented in this chapter: King's LGBTQ transformative learning model (LGBTQ TL model) (King, 2003).

The Wishik and Pierce Model

The continuing process of sexual identity development is vividly demonstrated in Wishik and Pierce's (1991) model, the Sexual Orientation and Identity Continuum Diagram. This model provides a continuum, or journey, for individuals in exploring their sexual identities. This continuum illustrates the many stages and events (or "crossroads") people encounter throughout their lives and their relationships to sexual identity development.

The model's structure is two pathways, which oscillate above and below the timeline of life events. The mainstream culture and expectations are defined as the "dominant" strand; the LGBTQ world is identified as the "subordinate" strand. Although other classic models of sexual identity development among LGBTQ adults have been recognized in the past, sexual identity is recognized as having a fluid nature that results in some adults moving from one identity to another, or more, over time (Taylor, 1999; Wishik & Pierce, 1991).

Within this model, the "dominant" strand is heterosexual life, the "subordinate" is lesbian/gay, and the middle ground, which appears at intermittent points, is bisexual. (The transgender perspective is not identified in this version of Wishik and Pierce.) The dominant and subordinate waves rise and fall along an individual's life, and at various points there are key questions and experiences. In some theoretical approaches to understanding sexual identity or cultural identity development, these questions create "pressure" and the need to "cope" with an individual's social and personal identities (Cass, 1984; Taylor, 1999). In Wishik and Pierce's model, these pathways are traced through personal questioning; learning of diverse cultures and perspectives; critical questioning; and new definitions, personal concepts, and personal and organizational relationships to embrace diversity in sexuality.

Transformative Learning

Transformative learning is a popular theory of adult learning that describes a significant shift in adults' understandings of their meaning perspectives (Mezirow, 1978), otherwise known as their frames of reference (Cranton, 2006).

In his introduction of this theory, Mezirow (1978; Mezirow & Associates, 2000) originally focused on the cognitive process adults experience as they examine long-held or never-questioned values, beliefs, and assumptions. The experience of transformative learning may begin with a *disorienting dilemma* and progress through many stages that include personal questioning, deliberation, re-examination, new perspectives, provisional adoption, and final reintegration of a significantly new frame of reference for understanding the world. Through the years, Mezirow's theory has been challenged and now stands not as iconoclastic or prescriptive, but rather as a descriptive and dynamic pathway (Cranton, 2006; King, 2005; King & Heuer, 2008).

Transformative learning has also been of interest in the study of LGBTQ identity development for some time. Brooks and Edwards's work (1997, 1999; Edwards & Brooks, 1999), followed by Donnelly's (2001) research and discussion of the transformative learning experience of lesbian women coming out, opened this door of research. Later King (2003) developed a working model for discussing these LGBTQ adult learning experiences.

The LGBTQ Transformative Learning Model (LGBTQ TL Model)

The connections between transformative learning and the sexual orientation and identity journey provide the opportunity for educators, learners, and LGBTQ adults to examine their lives and adult learning using a personal, empowering, and grounded heuristic. This approach enables a focus on critical questioning, understanding, and construction; continues these inward changes; and leads to decision for action. As LGBTQ adults better decipher their past experience and reflect on the decisions at hand, they may experience insights, freedom, and "change from the inside out" (King, 2003). This process is multidimensional and includes a spectrum of varied stages of understanding. Ultimately, LGBTQ adults move toward greater understanding, development, and expression of their sexual identities.

The goal of the LGBTQ TL model is to facilitate the valuing and embracing of multiple interpretations of sexual identity across individuals. The intent is never to predict behavior, "label," or "pigeonhole" an adult's sexual identity. And that is why it moves beyond the labels used in Wishik and Pierce's model. In fact, the LGBTQ TL model affords great opportunity to recognize and appreciate that bisexual and transgender (BT) adults often have more complex journeys than gay/lesbian adults in the areas of identity development and interactions with heteronormative and homosexual communities.

In fact, while bisexual and transgender adults face the rejection and oppression of traditional society, they may also face fear, isolation, and resistance from some members of the gay and lesbian community (Weiss, 2007). The model is inclusive and recognizes the similarities of all Queer (not heterosexual, not fitting social norms) experiences. Therefore, all LGBTQ adults are included in its design. Nonetheless, bisexual, transgender, and Queer adults may need to develop additional connections and extensions of the model, and further work in this area is much needed.

The Model Detail

In Table 1, the LGBTQ TL model is contrasted to the prior models. It blends Mezirow's ten stages with an outline of Wishik and Pierce's model to illustrate a composite process that dynamically shifts with frames, perspectives, or themes. Critical questioning, reflection about self and others, interpersonal understanding, and deliberation are foundational elements of the composite model. These elements are not always represented in other theories or models that are popularly used in counseling and psychology to address sexual identity development. A more dynamic macro-perspective of this process is represented in Figure 1. The diagram reveals that there are potentially four "framing perspectives": LGBTQ Exists, Coming Out to Yourself, Coming Out to Others, and Valuing and Embracing Different Journeys. These stages of the QRSAA process (Question, Risk, Strategy, Act, and Accept New Perspective) are repeated as adults experience the framing perspectives.

Each framing perspective identifies major themes of understanding that LGBTQ individuals construct and may one time or another hold as they cope with sexual identity development within a heteronormative society. The diagram's arrows point at the main figure in order to represent traditional expectations that continually confront LGBTQ adults. These messages include the following comments and thoughts:

- "Why is a nice girl like you are not married yet?"
- "You should settle down with a wife/husband by age 25."
- "Everyone is invited to bring their spouse or girlfriend/boyfriend to the company party!"

		Table 1		
		Comparison of Models (King, 2003)		
LGBTQ TL Process (King)	**Wishik and Pierce (1991)**	**Mezirow (1991, pp. 168-169)**		
	Opposition			
QUESTION	Encounter new views	1.	A disorienting dilemma	
	Question	2.	Self-examination with feelings of guilt or shame	
RISK		3.	A critical assessment of epistemic, sociocultural, or psychic assumptions	
		4.	Recognition that one's discontent and the process of transformation are shared and that others have negotiated a similar change	
	Deliberate			
STRATEGY	Learn content	5.	Exploration of options for new roles, relationships, and actions	
		6.	Planning of a course of action	
		7.	Acquisition of knowledge and skills for implementing one's plans	
	Deliberate			
	Learn in action	7.	(Repeated). Acquisition of knowledge and skills for implementing one's plans	
ACT		8.	Provisional trying of new roles	
		9.	Building of competence and self-confidence in new roles and relationships	
ACCEPT NEW PERSPECTIVE	New perspective	10.	A reintegration into one's life on the basis of conditions dictated by one's new perspective	

- "ALL people have the right to get married or not."
- "Anyone can list their retirement or insurance beneficiaries at work without fear of reprisal."

In fact, for some individuals a change could be a first-order or major perspective transformation; for others it could be a second-order change (less fundamental to the core of the individual's identity). The difference is entirely dependent on prior experience, one's threshold for risk and rejection, and the perceived safety of the environ-

Figure 1. The Proposed LGBTQ TL Model: Process and Framing Perspectives (King, 2003)

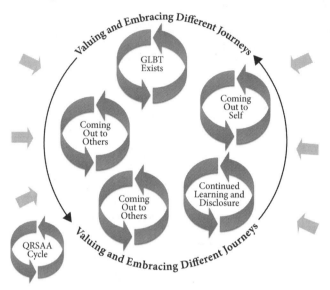

ment for action. LGBTQ adults may continue a QRSAA process as they learn about and critically examine concepts and situations throughout their lives. The experiences may not culminate in these specific major perspective transformations.

Situations are different, and external or internal catalytic events or moments may terminate each sequence and start a framing perspective for some people (Donnelly, 2001). However, it is also viable that individuals may, over time, just begin to question the many personal and societal assumptions surrounding them. A specific event is not required to catalyze the experience.

These framing perspectives have a fluid, dynamic relationship. Just as LGBTQ adults encounter new situations frequently, they never "finish" coming out in all the many aspects of themselves. In every situation, they have to navigate the crossroads of context, climate, risk, and response. Nonetheless, each of these successive comings out contribute to an individual's entire experience of valuing and embracing different journeys. When everyone realizes the rich variations incumbent in this multitude of experiences, we all have a greater realization of the larger map of variable and interwoven crossroads.

The progression of critical reflection, deliberation, learning, and action is an iterative cycle that moves toward each framing perspective. All individuals have their own journeys that unfold in their understanding and experience, and on their own timelines. And even as one reaches an integrated perspective, freedom to explore greater understanding along the journey provides room for LGBTQ adults to intersect desire and sexuality (Lemert, 1996, in Brooks & Edwards, 1999). Moreover, continually, reflectively, and authentically, they may explore new understandings and constructions.

Individuals also have their own contexts, personalities, and personal risks to navigate, and we should stay clear of "normative" expectations and experiences (Brooks & Edwards, 1997; Hill, 1996). Also, results will vary. Just as in queer theory, there is not a unified homosexual identity; therefore, one cannot expect a fully predictable experience of change, transformation, and perceptions (Brooks & Edwards, 1999; Hill, 1996). With this in mind, broad strokes of the images of each perspective are offered here as a guide. They may assist LGBTQ adults in considering their own journeys and understanding those of others. Conversely, the pattern provides heterosexuals an opportunity to understand the LGBTQ internal and external sexual identity development process. What follows are very brief descriptions of the stages in this process.

LGBTQ Exists. Adults become aware of the existence of LGBTQ individuals. They may start questioning their understanding as they consider risks of continuing, develop strategies for dealing with new perspectives, and act and accept the new "framing" perspective.

Coming Out to Oneself. Adults wrestle with their personal sexual identities and whether they may be LGBTQ. This perspective may be described by self-doubt, fear, anger, excitement, and anticipation, either variously or all at once.

Coming Out to Others. The LGBTQ adult continues to wrestle with coming out to other people. In a heteronormative society, these moments are considered by revelation and climax. In reality, adults repeatedly engage in coming out throughout their daily lives as assumptions or challenges to their sexual identity are pressed upon them. Finally, multiple experiences of this cycle may occur across the lifespan; therefore, there are many images of the cycle in Figure 1.

Valuing and Embracing Different Journeys. As LGBTQ adults increasingly resolve their sexual identity, coming out within themselves and to others, they continue the journey by understanding others' experiences. Rather than a monolithic "LGBTQness," they develop a more integrated perspective of sexual identity.

Because LGBTQ adults have to cope with so much more than the usual adolescent and adult development stages of individuation and young adulthood, there are many more complexities, dynamics, and possibilities to deliberate within themselves. Within a heteronormative society, marginalization is a consistent factor in the sexual identity development of gay and lesbian adults, and it is even more pronounced for bisexual and transgender adults. LGBTQ adults continually have to cope with and navigate these issues. The model provides a basis for validating individuals' questions and contexts; it suggests new directions and provides a basis for further dialogue about the many diverse experiences.

Applying the LGBTQ TL Model to the Workplace

As we intersect the coming out experience with the workplace, the model illuminates issues, patterns, and recommendations. In particular, one has to consider that coming out to self and coming out to others are dramatically different experiences. At times, it feels like professional Jeopardy because LGBTQ adults have to find the hidden questions, discern the risks versus rewards, map out the "return on investment" for their action, and hope they have the correct answer in time for the buzzer. This model provides a framework with which to consider those many imprecise parameters and to realize that LGBTQ adults hope for high-level algorithms to address the fuzzy logic of human behavior and attitudes successfully.

The Model in Action

We can return to our opening LGBTQ scenario and others like them (Baumgartner & Merriam, 2000) to consider the model in action. The LGBTQ TL model serves as a guide to frame the deconstruction of these situations by asking participants to:

- examine the experiences, values, beliefs, and behaviors included;
- consider the individual's current beliefs and concomitant desires to retain or release values and beliefs and endure the consequences;
- consider whether the person wants to explore a new perspective; and
- determine whether the person will keep or abandon engaged change and why.

"From the Inside Out"

The LGBTQ TL model extricates the intellectual, emotional, and social dimensions of human experience in sexual identity development. On the first internal basis, the intellectual, the perspective represents framing thoughts such as, "I can work through the situation and understand it." On the second internal level, the emotional, the view is, "I can know my feelings and feel the experience." And in the external dimension, the social, the individual asserts, "I can interact with other people about these issues, approaches, and decisions." Examining such cases and workforce situations with these dimensions and frames may illuminate many additional insights.

Another way to examine the model in the workplace is its relationship to shifts in career stages. Just as one experiences changes in one's life journey and sexual identity development, the same is the case in career development change. As professionals experience the different phases of job search, application, hiring, orientation, probation, advancement, and so on, there are a multitude of places to confront and assert their sexual identities as ongoing encounters in a heteronormative society. Although it is illegal in some states and organizations to fire someone because of sexual orientation, people need to be aware that sexual minority status is not a US federally protected right, nor is it supported by state law in many cases. That is, nondiscrimination in the workplace is not an iron-clad right (Lester, 2007; Muñoz & Thomas, 2006). Even with serious denials of protection, gay and lesbian people still have more rights and (albeit risky) assurances (Lambda Legal, 2004) than transgender persons who remain constantly threatened with termination, violent confrontation, and "no hire" (Lambda Legal, 2008). In addition to the many stages of a career at one job, adults today are expected to make five or six career changes on average. Even though many workplace skills may be transferable, new career pathways are fraught with stress, uncertainty, and risk.

Add the challenging formula of career stages to LGBTQ sexual identity development in the workplace, and then add on constant change in the 21st century, and you have a multitude of crossroads. Anyone can see there will be adjustments, relationships, disclosures, learning, and uncertainty careening in every direction. Such a navigational nightmare would seem to require a global positioning system to survive, but the LGBTQ TL model provides a theoretical and practical basis for pulling apart these multiple strands, sorting through, and coping with them from the inside out.

Recommendations for facilitating the LGBTQ TL model in workplace training provide many approaches for implementation. These suggestions emerge from the model and assist in "making space" and creating a climate of validation in the workplace for LGBTQ people. In addition, trainers and managers need to be mindful that many opportunities may arise based on specific needs, personnel responsibilities, industry-specific needs or culture, or the cultural identities of staff. In addition, interpersonal dynamics, specific work-related issues, or recent historical events provide prime opportunities to address diversity learning. Foundational training and communication are essential, and ongoing dialogue is an indispensable, valuable learning vehicle.

In order to dovetail the LGBTQ LT model with a diversity training program, the essential elements needed are information, attitude, communication, safety, and policy. Topics that are vital include those that are often skirted in corporate settings but are valuable for discussions that will impact staff perceptions and behavior; they include knowledge and discussion of heterosexual privilege, homophobia, LGBTQ bias, and LGBTQ discrimination. In addition to the information and issues presented and discussed are the critical elements of conduct: attitudes and communication. These topics include respect, word choice, communication skills, privacy, confidentiality, and related legal guidelines.

Safety is a critical issue for LGBTQ people for good cause. Heterosexuals need to comprehend the seriousness of this issue and how to respond in emergency situations. Finally, a complete discussion of and a strong emphasis on organizational policy demand that a high standard of behavior is not optional, but a condition of employment (Hornsby, 2006). All staff members need to know there is an absolute expectation of compliance with the policy.

Awareness encompasses several additional strategies needed to facilitate the model, which include a dedication to presenting, discussing, and validating the issues related to LGBTQ adult sexual identity development. The fact that the model offers both a different perspective on the LGBTQ experience and a common basis for understanding, dialogue, and interaction is a strong reason to emphasize the value of this learning for all staff. Whenever possible, according to religious and cultural mandates, this approach guards against the traditional sex-education mindset of separating genders for discussions behind closed doors and instead builds an open and equal workspace.

The staff needs to develop an understanding and awareness of this dynamic experience and model of sexual identity development. The focus on the issues related to LGTBQ adult sexual identity development may build on the diversity training discussions to enhance understanding of the constant need for coming out, the risks, dilemmas, reflection, and struggle. Emphasizing process rather than outcomes reinforces the concept of a continuing journey.

The most common and effective format for creating space in the workplace for LGBTQ people is through small-group training (Baumgartner & Merriam, 2000; King, 2005). Many instructional strategies are available to assist in working through sample work situations, complexities, variations, and alternatives. Role playing, simulations, group projects, collective action research, and self-evaluation tools are valuable approaches with which to explore and critically discuss complex situations (Wlodkowski, 2003). Strong ground rules for respect, non-bias, language, confidentiality, and equal time need to be established prior to starting all activities (Wlodkowski, 2003). The rules should reinforce organizational policy or a prescribed handbook, or the group might create one as part of the process.

Small-group experiences have multiple benefits. If facilitated well, such groups provide a safe proving ground for exploring new behaviors and responses. They may also provide validation of appropriate and constructive behavior. Many of these experiences may be missing from adults' formal training experiences.

An emphasis on communication skills has at least two major positive benefits for this situation. The first is improving communication and interpersonal relations among the staff, assuring that communication in all forms, including affective responses and body language, are appropriate to stated needs and policy. In addition, strengthening staff communication skills will create a workforce that is more effective in serving clients from diverse multicultural perspectives, including variations in religion, language, national origin, and sexual identity.

In the 21st century, we are challenged to be effective and sensitive communicators through text, video, and audio. Communication can happen without ever having to meet, see, or "talk" to a person. Realizing the meaning of words, actions, and minority cultural subtexts from a position of privilege is enlightening in the area of communications (Baumgartner & Merriam, 2000; Wlodkowski, 2003). As the staff works through communication with one another on this difficult topic, they will be much better positioned to handle daily client communications.

The final suggestion is to use narrative in empowering formats, such as self-study, research, journals, or written text, as a means of facilitating understanding of the LGBTQ adult journey in sexual identity development. Many individuals find that writing helps them process their thoughts and realize deeper understanding (King, 2005). This same format may be used in guiding individuals, small groups, or an organization in exploring their group or individual journeys in sexual identity awareness or development. Working on this project collaboratively may provide a tangible focus for dialogue, including group process and energy, rather than deep introspection or critique of "the Other." In the same way, many rich sources of primary data and content exist via the Internet. For example, LGBTQ podcasts, video, audio or conventional books, and blogs could be the basis for research, presentations, or discussion groups (King, 2008; King & Sanquist, 2008).

Conclusion

The LGBTQ TL model may be used effectively to understand the many crossroads that LGBTQ adults face as they attempt to create authentic space in the workforce. The model provides a valuable perspective and describes coping strategies for LGBTQ adults to frame their journeys of sexual identity development, some of which may be hostile (Muñoz & Thomas, 2006). Major benefits of the model include confirming the dynamic and continuing characteristics of adult sexual identity development among LGTBTQ people, which is confirmed in other literature (British Council, 2003). In addition, it eliminates the stark isolation that many people experience; instead, they witness commonalities of experience.

For the heterosexual workforce, the model aids in developing an understanding that LGBTQ adults, as a minority constituency, must navigate difficult and risky decisions. This model further highlights multiple layers, conflicts, and potentially perilous situations that LGBTQ adults must learn to move deftly through in their lives.

The model and related instructional strategies emphasize a framework that is critically reflective; has a transformative learning lens; builds greater understanding of self, colleagues, and one's own sexual identity; reveals societal expectations; and provides space and freedom to question assumptions. When LGBTQ individuals and allies explore these questions together, they find opportunities to build new constructions of understanding and acceptance. In fact, consistent with the tenets of diversity training, everyone may gain insight about themselves and about those who are different (Muñoz & Thomas, 2006). Safety and respect may be much enhanced in the workplace that is dedicated to this orientation of critical reflection and learning. Such a climate certainly is a much better place in which to cultivate vital employee retention, loyalty, dedication, productivity, and creativity for all.

References

Baumgartner, L., & Merriam, S. (2000). *Adult learning and development: Multicultural stories.* Malabar, FL: Krieger.

Becker, S. (2006). Many are chilled but few are frozen. *Journal of Gender, Social Policy and Law, 14*(2), 177-252. Retrieved June 18, 2008, from http://www.wcl. american.edu/ journal/genderlaw/14/becker2.pdf?rd=1

British Council: The Diversity Unit. (2003). *Sexual identity.* London: Author. Retrieved November 15, 2005, from http://www.britishcouncil.org/diversity/ sexual_ identity.htm

Brooks, A. K., & Edwards, K. (1997). Narratives of women's sexual identity development. In R. Nolan & H. Chelesvig (Eds.), *Proceedings 38th Annual Adult Education Research Conference Proceedings* (pp. 37-42). Stillwater, OK: Oklahoma State University. (ED 409 460)

Brooks, A. K., & Edwards, K. (1999). For adults only: Queer theory meets the self and identity in adult education. In A. Rose (Ed.), *Proceedings 40th Annual Adult Education Research Conference* (pp. 56-61). DeKalb, IL: Northern Illinois University. (ED 431 901)

Cass, V. (1984). Homosexual identity formation: Testing a theoretical model. *The Journal of Sex Research, 20*(2), 143-167.

CBS News. (2006, April 11). Gay rights group decries island police. Retrieved June 16, 2008, from http://www.cbsnews.com/stories/2006/04/10/world/ printable1487446.shtml

Cranton, P. (2006). *Understanding and promoting transformative learning* (2nd ed.). San Francisco: Jossey-Bass.

Donnelly, S. (2001). *Building a new moral, religious, or spiritual identity.* San Antonio: Texas A&M University.

Duberman, M. (1994). *Stonewall.* NY: Plume.

Edwards, K., & Brooks, A. K. (1999). The development of sexual identity. In M. C. Clark & R. S. Caffarella (Eds.), *An update on adult development theory: New ways of thinking about the life course* (pp. 49-57). New Directions for Adult and Continuing Education, No. 84. San Francisco: Jossey-Bass.

Hill, R. (1996). Learning to transgress: A sociohistorical conspectus of the American gay lifeworld as a site of struggle and resistance. *Studies in the Education of Adults, 28*(2), 253-279.

Hornsby, E. E. (2006, Winter). Using policy to drive organizational change. In R. Hill (Ed.), *Challenging homophobia and heterosexism: Lesbian, gay, bisexual, transgender and Queer issues in organizational settings* (pp. 73-84). New Directions in Adult and Continuing Education, No. 112. San Francisco: Jossey-Bass.

King, K. P. (2003). Changing from the inside out. In R. J. Hill (Ed.), *Queer histories: Exploring fugitive forms of social knowledge. Proceedings of the 1st Lesbian, Gay, Bisexual, Transgender, Queer & Allies Pre-Conference at the 44th Annual Adult Education Research Conference* (pp. 63-72). San Francisco, CA: San Francisco State University.

King, K. P. (2005). *Bringing transformative learning to life.* Malabar, FL: Krieger.

King, K. P. (2008). Slamming the closet door and taking control. In T. V. Bettinger (Comp.), *Transcending the rhetoric of family values: Celebrating families of choice and families of value. Proceedings of the 6th Lesbian, Gay, Bisexual, Transgender, Queer and Allies Pre-Conference at the 49th Annual Adult Education Research Conference* (pp. 81-87). St. Louis: University of Missouri-St. Louis. (ERIC Document ED503480)

King, K. P., & Heuer, B. P. (2008). Evolution of an educational research model. *International Forum on Teaching and Scholarship Journal, 4*(1), 13-20. Retrieved June 18, 2008, from http://www.americanscholarspress.com/content/IFOTS-One-2008.pdf

King, K. P., & Sanquist, S. (2008). Empowering underrepresented voices through new media. *Proceedings of the 49th Annual Adult Education Research Conference.* St. Louis: University of Missouri. Retrieved March 13, 2009 from http://www.adulterc.org/Proceedings/2008/Proceedings/King_Sanquist.pdf

Lambda Legal. (2004). *Why marriage equality counts.* Retrieved on June 18, 2008, from http://www.lambdalegal.org/our-work/publications/facts-backgrounds/page. jsp?itemID=31988962

Lambda Legal. (2008, April 4). *Court recognizes viability of Lambda Legal's sex discrimination claim on behalf of transgender woman.* Retrieved on June 18, 2008, from http://www.lambdalegal.org/news/pr/court-recognizes-sex-discrimination.html

Lester, T. (2007). Harassment, retaliation and relief. In M. V. Badgett & J. Frank (Eds.), *Sexual orientation discrimination: An international perspective* (pp. 293-305). NY: Routledge.

Matthew Shepard Foundation. (2008). Matthew's story. Retrieved on June 18, 2008, from http://www.matthewshepard.org/site/PageServer?pagename=mat_ Matthews_Story_Main_Page

Mezirow, J. (1978). *Education for perspective transformation.* NY: Teacher's College, Columbia University.

Mezirow, J. (1991). *Transformative dimensions of adult learning.* San Francisco: Jossey-Bass.

Mezirow, J., & Associates. (2000). *Learning as transformation.* San Francisco: Jossey-Bass.

Mule, N. (2007). Sexual orientation discrimination in health care and social service policy. In M. V. Badgett & J. Frank (Eds.), *Sexual orientation discrimination: An international perspective* (pp. 305-322). NY: Routledge.

Muñoz, C., & Thomas, K. C. (2006, Winter). LGBTQ in organizational settings: What HR professionals need to know. In R. J. Hill (Ed.), *Challenging homophobia and heterosexism: Lesbian, gay, bisexual, transgender, and Queer issues in organizational settings* (pp. 85-96). New Directions in Adult and Continuing Education, No. 112. San Francisco: Jossey-Bass.

The National GLBT Taskforce. (2007). *Task Force works toward passage of Local Law Enforcement Hate Crimes Prevention Act of 2007.* Retrieved on June 16, 2008, from http://www.thetaskforce.org/issues/hate_crimes_main_ page/2007_ legislation

Taylor, B. (1999). "Coming out" as a life transition: Homosexual identity formation and its implications for health care practice. *Journal of Advanced Nursing, 30*(2), 520-525.

Teal, D. (1971). *The gay militants.* NY: Stein and Day.

Weiss, J. (2007). *Transgender workplace diversity.* North Charleston, SC: Booksurge.

Wishik, H., & Pierce, C. (1991). *Sexual orientation and identity: Heterosexual, lesbian, gay, and bisexual journeys.* Laconia, NH: New Dynamics.

Wlodkowski, R. (2003). Fostering motivation in professional development programs. K. P. King & P. A. Lawler (Eds.), *New perspectives on designing and implementing professional development for teachers of adults* (pp. 39-48). New Directions in Adult and Continuing Education, No. 98. San Francisco: Jossey-Bass.

CHAPTER 9

LGBTQ Lessons from Midlife: An Unpicked Harvest

Thomas V. Bettinger

Public discourse, awareness, and visibility of sexual minorities have increased to a degree that would have been unfathomable a generation ago. This has contributed to heightened attention on the part of educators and advocacy groups to the needs of lesbian, gay, bisexual, transgender, and Queer (LGBTQ) youth. Preservice teacher training and a growing body of literature are addressing LGBT issues for K-12 educators, although LGBT curriculum models and related library books remain largely underutilized due to the lack of supportive school-district policies and the efforts of some parents and special-interest groups opposed to the use of such resources (Grace & Wells, 2007). Furthermore, a growing number of colleges and universities have initiated lesbian and gay studies programs, implemented safe space projects, and funded resource centers for sexual minorities. Two relevant chapters, "LGBTQ Allies on Campus: Do They Have a Role?" (by Ann Brooks, Dawn Robarts, and Ronnie Lozano) and "Lesbian, Gay, Bisexual, Transgender Campus Climate Assessments: Current Trends and Future Considerations" (by Needham Yancey Gulley) are found in this book. Concomitantly, community groups and human service agencies have begun to address issues of concern to LGBTQ individuals in later adulthood. While such initiatives are both welcome and necessary, midlife sexual minorities garner much less demonstrated interest and attention from researchers and academic institutions alike. Paradoxically, midlife sexual minorities may offer many, and perhaps unique, lessons not only for other LGBTQ cohorts but also for society at large. Sexual minorities currently at midlife have witnessed and experienced seismic societal shifts with regards to LGBTQ visibility, media representations, and progress towards human and civil rights. They have stories to tell, scars to show, and lessons to share—the vexing question is: Is anybody listening?

Like previous cohorts, sexual minorities currently at midlife have come out and matured with little historical experience and few cultural expectations to guide them (de Vries & Blando, 2004). Yet this pattern needn't continue for succeeding generations. While the impact of living as a sexual minority under heteronormativity is "profound and oppressive" (Herdt & de Vries, 2004, p. xvii), many midlife LGBTQ people have successfully maneuvered through the oppression of the larger culture and society. These oppressions include legal and political barriers to full citizenship, such as the denial of the right to marry or adopt; denial of access to housing; refusal to recognize partner benefits, including such fundamental issues as determination of medical care for one who is incapacitated; lack of societal support for major life events such as the loss of a partner; condemnation by religious institutions and politicians; and misrepresentations in the media such as the characterization of the self-absorbed, sexually obsessed gay-male stereotype, Jack, in the hugely popular American sitcom *Will and Grace*. In addition, the threat of homophobia-inspired physical violence is a real and constant presence for most LGBTQ individuals. These factors irrefutably result in different life experiences for sexual minorities than for their heterosexual counterparts. For some, the stigma and oppression may lead to long-lasting mental or emotional scarring with life-changing, devastating consequences.

Yet despite the relentless pressure of living in a heteronormative society, and not unlike previous cohorts of LGBTQ people, many now at midlife have developed resiliency in the face of ongoing struggle and are leading meaningful, fulfilling lives. However, this cohort is also qualitatively different from any previous LGBTQ cohort. They have lived through, and indeed created and were active in, movements for civil rights, women's rights, and gay rights and the emergence of what became known as the AIDS epidemic (Kimmel & Sang, 1995). These historical changes helped to transition gay and lesbian culture from isolation and fragmentation to group consciousness and collective identity (Cruikshank, 1992); they sowed the seeds for U.S. professional organizations focused on the achievement of equal civil rights such as Lambda Legal Defense Fund (now called Lambda Legal), the National Lesbian and Gay Task Force, and the Human Rights Campaign (Hunter, 2005). Thus, those currently at midlife have witnessed the progress made towards nondiscrimination laws and workplace equity and the shift (albeit slow) in societal support for LGBTQ equity such as growing public support for overturning the United States military policy known as "don't ask, don't tell." They've also seen media representations evolve from shadowy, clandestine, and ill-fated characters to engaging, thoughtful, and well-rounded individuals. Ellen DeGeneres serves as a salient example. Shortly after both she and her self-titled sitcom character came out as lesbian in 1997, ratings declined and the show was canceled. Less than a decade later, she became (and remains) widely admired as an award-winning host of a syndicated television talk show. As a whole, the current cohort of midlife LGBTQ people is substantially less closeted than previous generations (Kimmel & Sang, 1995). This sets the stage for inter-generational sharing of life lessons within the LGBTQ community and for those life lessons to inform the broader society—opportunities largely unavailable in previous generations when issues surrounding sexual minorities were relegated to silence and invisibility. Furthermore, the tremendous sociopolitical changes of which those currently at midlife have been a part will impact life opportunities and patterns of development for subsequent generations of LGBTQ people, with untold wider societal implications. Research in this endeavor has been insufficient and inadequate, but given that the lives of midlife sexual minorities "have spanned a unique period of history…it is important that this generation be studied now" (Kimmel & Sang, 1995, p. 208).

Learning and Development at Midlife

Adult education has long relied on the contributions that adult development theory has made to adult education theory and practice (Hoare, 2006; Merriam & Caffarella, 1999; Merriam & Clark, 1991). The two areas of study deal with similar questions, concerns, and interests such that engagement with one inevitably entails the other (Tennant & Pogson, 1995). Caffarella and Clark (1999) stress that adult educators need to help expand the adult development theory base to include other perspectives, lest they "continue to foster images of growth and change that fit only some of the people with whom they work" (p. 126). Over the past two decades, interest in how adults learn and how they develop has shifted from grand theories to specific dimensions and the influence of contextual factors, with more research attention on socially constructed notions of gender, race, and ethnicity (Guy, 1999; Hayes & Flannery, 2000; Lee & Sheared, 2002). However, adult development research has been almost exclusively heterosexual in its focus, and sexual orientation is generally not even considered (Kimmel & Sang, 1995; Merriam & Caffarella, 1999). As such, it reflects an inherent, unexamined heterosexist bias. Consequently, traditional notions and models of identity formation and adult development that fail to take into account historical events, social context, and lived experiences of sexual minorities cannot be presumed to be applicable to sexual minorities (Kertzner, 2001). This mirrors the field of adult education in which the experiences and concerns of LGBTQ persons remain largely invisible and unaddressed, leaving applicability of learning theories and models to sexual minorities an open question. Intentional study of aging and developmental processes in the lives of sexual minorities would lead to different questions being asked, new conceptualizations being constructed, more creative and inclusive research, and deeper understanding of adult development in general (de Vries & Hoctel, 2007). Once again, parallels can easily be inferred to the field of adult education. Deliberate and purposeful consideration of LGBTQ voices and experiences would add to the richness, depth, and utility of adult learning theories and models that reflect current understandings and undergird much of adult education practice.

Within human development studies, a long-standing tendency to concentrate on childhood, adolescence, and old age leads to misperceptions, misinformation, and myths regarding midlife. Many people have negative perceptions regarding midlife, fed largely by social constructs such as *midlife crisis* and *change of life*, as well as stereotypical images of graying hair, false teeth, sagging body parts, decreased libido, and incontinence. Such stereotypes also influence societal expectations of certain behaviors, rights, and responsibilities. Yet such widely shared cultural beliefs "stand untested, unvalidated premises on which millions of people make decisions" (Brim, 2001, p. xi). Nevertheless, midlife is commonly understood as a period of significant shifts in the social, psychological, and physical realms of life, although defining it (or its corollary, *middle age*) is problematic. For one thing, the concept of midlife as a distinct period of life is a recent one, and having so many middle-aged people in society is a relatively new phenomenon. Throughout much of human history, most people lived less than four decades. Even in the United States as recently as 1900, approximately one half of those who reached 20 did not live to be 65. As a result, there was no sense of a population as a whole moving through midlife (Brim, 1995). Demographic trends, including increases in human longevity, have resulted in new ways of thinking about the life course, and midlife in particular. Notions of midlife also vary between and within cultures and are influenced by various factors including one's current age, socioeconomic class, cultural background, education level, and geography (Lachman, 2001). In Western societies, midlife is commonly, though not universally, thought of in chronological terms as a span between specified age boundaries (ranging from 30 to 70), typically the ages of 40 to 60 years old. Although this is a relatively long period, it has yet to be divided into subperiods akin to the "young-old"/"old-old" distinction often used to describe later life (Lachman, 2001). In particular, given increased visibility and shifting cultural representations and societal views regarding LGBTQ persons, more narrow age groupings may be appropriate when investigating adult development and cohort effects for sexual minorities (Bettinger, 2007).

A growing recognition of midlife as worthy of study in its own right is underway due primarily to the Baby Boom generation—those individuals born between 1946 and 1967. In the year 2000, there were greater than 80 million baby boomers in the United States, or roughly 30% of the population (Lachman, 2001). This generation is the largest midlife cohort in U.S. history. From 1960 to 1985, those between the ages of 45 and 64 increased by 24%; by comparison, from 1990 to 2015, the same age group will increase by 72%. Furthermore, this group is the best educated and most affluent to pass through middle age. Such factors are salient given the ever-changing socially constructed meanings of midlife. Contemporary midlife is characterized by growing diversity in roles, resources, and relationships, and age-related paradigms and stereotypes are morphing or falling by the wayside as baby boomers discard obsolete notions about middle age and replace them with new knowledge gained from their lived experiences. Among those notions that need to be challenged are heteronormative assumptions and expectations foisted upon midlife sexual minorities.

The Intersection of LGBTQ and Adult Development Research

Research into LGBTQ-related issues in general does not have a long history, with the earliest literature dating to the 1950s and 1960s. Many early studies were geared towards determining the "cause" of what was considered, at least since the ascendancy of Freud's notion that homosexuality represented arrested development, a pathological phenomenon (Fone, 2001). Since the American Psychiatric Association's declassification of homosexuality as a mental disorder in 1973, research interest regarding sexual minorities has shifted from a preoccupation with etiology and pathology to a greater focus on characteristics and psychosocial concerns of sexual minorities as well as societal attitudes toward them. This has been accompanied by a concomitant shift from a deficit orientation towards a more holistic understanding of how sexual minorities live their lives (D'Augelli & Patterson, 1995). This holistic approach finds expression in examining the ways in which LGBTQ paradigms help to inform and reconceptualize broader psychological and social issues of sexuality, gender roles, identity, intimacy, family relationships, and lifespan development (Garnets & Kimmel, 2003).

Much early research also conflated the experiences of gay men and lesbians while virtually ignoring bisexuals and transgender persons. Contemporary researchers, particularly in research on human development and adult education, are less inclined to view sexual minorities as a monolithic group. Gender, regardless of sexual identity, is acknowledged as a crucial factor in shaping life experiences, development, and meaning making; thus, lesbians and gay men are now less likely to be considered an amorphous category. As an example, one phenomenon that seems to be much more prevalent among women than men is a change in sexual orientation over time—with many women not identifying as lesbian until midlife (Charbonneau & Lander, 1991). Similarly, the lived experiences and spectrum of gender identity/expression among transgender persons warrant consideration in themselves (Witten, 2003). Cook-Daniels (2006) underscores the need to consider unique health, legal, and employment issues faced by transgender people. Furthermore, she describes an anecdotal phenomenon in which many people who have struggled with gender questions all of their lives discover at midlife "a name for their feelings and courses of action they could take" (p. 23). Although identity development models often include it (Bilodeau & Renn, 2005), bisexuality remains a poorly understood and rarely researched phenomenon. Most scholarly research either does not address bisexuals at all or collapses bisexual subjects into the lesbian and gay subjects pool because of small sample size (Dworkin, 2006). Although relatively unexplored, aging bisexuals may differ in important ways from lesbians and gay men (Kimmel, Rose, Orel, & Greene, 2006). Kertzner and Sved (1996) speculate, "Adult development may vary widely among bisexual individuals and share features of both homosexual and heterosexual midlife" (p. 291).

Early LGBT research also tended to lump lesbians or gay men over a certain age (e.g., 35 or 40) into an "older" category. Given an increased appreciation of age-cohort effects, more distinct age ranges to differentiate among developmental groupings are now more typically the case. However, despite the increase in attention and interest in issues relating to aging and development of sexual minorities over the past two decades, related research tends to focus on youth, young adults, and those in later adulthood. Thus, despite Kertzner and Sved's (1996) assertion that "this generation [of sexual minorities] may be creating a unique developmental trail though the middle years of life" (p. 289), there remains a dearth of literature on midlife LGBTQ people, and much of what does exist is conceptual or anecdotal in nature (Bettinger, 2007; Hash & Cramer, 2003). Nevertheless, some lessons can be gleaned from the literature.

Lessons from the Literature

A key lesson is that, despite ongoing heteronormative messages to the contrary, it is possible for sexual minorities to lead happy, contented, and fulfilling lives. Probably the most common, widely held stereotype is that of the lonely, socially isolated, unhappy old gay man or lesbian—fearful of being "found out." Studies have consistently found that loneliness and unhappiness are no more prevalent in older LGBT people than in their heterosexual counterparts. Using a variety of psychological tests, Hooker (1957) found no differences in mental health functioning between gay and heterosexual men. Numerous studies since that time have found that older sexual minorities are psychologically well adjusted and tend to have high levels of self-esteem and strong friendship ties (Adelman, 1991; Berger, 1996; Friend, 1991). Furthermore, they tend to care less about "exposure" than younger counterparts (Berger & Kelly, 2001). Nonetheless, there remain "prevalent and deeply entrenched negative stereotypes…in spite of the growing evidence to the contrary" (Wahler & Gabbay, 1997, p. 16).

It is well established that individual differences in both learning and development are influenced by a host of social and cultural factors, including (but certainly not restricted to) family relationships, class, race, ethnicity, and geographic area. LGBTQ people face these and similar issues, as do their heterosexual counterparts. Furthermore, many contributing factors to successful aging are likely the same or similar across sexual orientation (e.g., education, social networks, financial security, intimate relationships), but sexual minorities face unique challenges in their daily lives. However, as a consequence of having endured the stigma of being a sexual minority in a heterosexist society and of working through the coming-out process, older LGBT people develop resilience and may be better prepared for the processes of aging than their heterosexual counterparts. Berger and Kelly (2001) refer to this phenomenon as *mastery of stigma* and explain that in Western cultures aging is stigmatized and aged people are devalued. LGBTQ people have already learned how to manage stigma. Thus, when they are faced with the stigma of aging, they are better able to adapt. A crisis of independence is a similar phenomenon in that LGBTQ people, who often cannot rely on traditional institutions for support, learn adaptive skills that later facilitate the process of aging. An understanding of such unique LGBTQ developmental issues and responses across the lifespan helps to explain why traditional models of adult development may not adequately address LGBTQ development patterns and pathways. Critical factors contributing to the wide diversity of adult development patterns for LGBT people include the age at which one comes out (Kimmel & Sang, 1995) and self-acceptance (Brown, Alley, Sarosy, Quarto, & Cook, 2001; Gabbay & Wahler, 2002).

Exposing Heteronormative Assumptions of Adult Development

Two prominent types of adult development theories are (a) stage (or phase) theories, which are premised on an individual progressing through various stages toward an ultimate developmental end point—that of a mature, psychologically healthy person, and (b) life event or lifespan theories in which development is viewed in terms of life events and transitions (Hayslip & Panek, 2002; Tennant & Pogson, 1995).

Erikson (1968), perhaps the most well known of the stage developmental theorists, proposed a series of eight psychosocial stages, each of which involves a "crisis" that can be resolved either positively or negatively. His model includes five stages of childhood and three stages of adult development: (a) young adulthood, (b) middle adulthood (midlife), and (c) late adulthood. Midlife is characterized as the resolution of the developmental crisis of *generativity* versus *stagnation*. Stagnation indicates a lack of psychological growth. Stagnated adults are self-centered, have difficulty looking beyond their own needs, and seek to maximize their pleasures at the expense of others. These individuals may be fairly happy until confronted with the onset of the physical and psychological consequences of aging—at which an identity crisis may ensue. Generativity, the opposite of stagnation, entails a concern for producing something that will outlast oneself or to commit to society and help guide the next generation; in Erikson's (1968) words: "I am what survives me" (p. 114). Despite the high degree of interest and attention that generativity has received, there is still uncertainty and lack of a common understanding as to what constitutes it. Ostensibly, the drive to be generative is as inherent in sexual minorities as it is in their heterosexual counterparts. Indeed, midlife sexual minorities provide fertile ground for exploring the dialogic process between person and social order with respect to generativity and contribute to "the broader study of adult lives within contemporary bourgeois society" (Cohler, Hostetler, & Boxer, 1998, p. 273). Furthermore, the analysis of generativity in the lives of sexual minorities "prompts the questioning of the heteronormative language" (de Vries & Blando, 2004, p. 18) associated with this and other developmental concepts. For instance, generativity is frequently interpreted in terms of child bearing and child rearing. However, Erikson never restricted the concept of generativity to parenthood. Rather, it can be expressed through a vast variety of life choices, beliefs, and commitments of midlife sexual minorities, including occupational or professional activities, volunteer activities, social group memberships, friendships, and even leisure pursuits. Obviously, many LGBTQ individuals are parents through previous marriages, adoption, and biological co-parenting or through *families of choice*—the heterogeneity of contemporary family forms and structures created by those who reject the hegemonic notion of the intact, heterosexual, two-parent norm as the only legitimate family structure (Bettinger, 2008; Wilson, 2007). Other expressions of generativity among LGBTQ people include career choices (such as teaching and mentoring), artistic pursuits such as dance or theater, restoration and preservation efforts often found in gay neighborhoods, and "perhaps political activism in many forms may also be seen as generative; these forms are creating social change to benefit others... in the service of creating for the self and others a better place to be" (de Vries & Blando, 2004, p. 17).

Life-event perspectives view developmental tasks occurring at different ages based on social expectations and biological development. Successfully achieving a task leads to happiness and success in later tasks, whereas failure results in societal disapproval and personal disappointment and adversely influences later tasks. Every society has a "social clock" (Neugarten, 1976) that sets the expectations regarding age-appropriate behavior or life events (e.g., marriage, career, retirement). The individual is seen as passing through a succession of socially delineated age statuses, each with recognized rights, duties, and obligations. Normative patterns are largely followed as most people check themselves against the norms they perceive for their age group. Thus, behavior, self-concept, and subsequent development are influenced by whether one perceives himself or herself to be "on time" or not with these life events. Such a perspective also reflects heteronormative underpinnings given societal expectations for heterosexual dating, heterosexual marriage, and heterosexual co-parenting. The study of LGBTQ midlife development must address this experience of being outside normative social timelines "without benefit of a gay-specific social timetable" (Cohler et al., 1998, p. 277). Yet another example of a heteronormative impediment to meeting societal expectations associated with a life-event perspective is that of career development in which some sexual minorities have faced "a choice between deceit and discrimination" (p. 278).

Conclusion

The literature reveals some lessons with respect to adult learning and development that the current cohort of midlife LGBTQ people has to offer. Considerably more could be gleaned and understood through increased attention to and engagement with this overlooked population. There remains a pressing need to explore and investigate the lived experiences and meaning-making processes of the generation of sexual minorities currently at midlife. Out of necessity, this entails examining and challenging the heteronormative nature of cherished theories and models within both adult development and adult education. Whether intentional or not, or whether through ignorance, homophobia, or mere oversight, continued invisibility of the needs and concerns of midlife LGBTQ persons is a disservice not only to those individuals but also to the larger society, which could benefit from a deeper understanding of the contributions and lived experiences of this unique sociohistoric cohort.

References

Adelman, M. (1991). Stigma, gay lifestyles and adjustment to aging: A study of later-life gay men and lesbians. *Journal of Homosexuality, 20*(3/4), 7-32.

Berger, R. M. (1996). *Gay and gray: The older homosexual man* (2nd ed.). NY: Harrington Park Press.

Berger, R. M., & Kelly, J. J. (2001). What are older gay men like? An impossible question? In D. C. Kimmel & D. L. Martin (Eds.), *Midlife aging in gay America* (pp. 55-64). NY: Harrington Park Press.

Bettinger, T. V. (2007). Gay men at midlife and adult learning: An uneasy truce with heteronormativity. *ProQuest Dissertations Express* (UMI No. 3266075).

Bettinger, T. V. (2008). For better, for worse, or not at all: Re-conceptualizing the meaning of family and valuing all families. In T. V. Bettinger (Comp.), *Transcending the rhetoric of family values: Celebrating families of choice and families of value. Proceedings of the 6th Lesbian, Gay, Bisexual, Transgender, Queer and Allies Pre-Conference at the 49th Annual Adult Education Research Conference* (pp. 9-13). St. Louis: University of Missouri-St. Louis. (ERIC Document ED503480)

Bilodeau, B. L., & Renn, K. A. (2005). Analysis of LGBT identity development models and implications for practice. In R. L. Sanlo (Ed.), *Gender identity and sexual orientation: Research, policy, and personal* (pp. 25-39). New Directions for Student Services, No. 111. San Francisco: Jossey-Bass.

Brim, O. G. (1995). MIDMAC Bulletin No. 4. Retrieved January 19, 2006, from http://midmac.med.harvard.edu/bullet4.html

Brim, O. G. (2001). Foreword. In M. E. Lachman (Ed.), *Handbook of midlife development* (pp. xi-xii). NY: John E. Wiley & Sons.

Brown, L. B., Alley, G. R., Sarosy, S., Quarto, G., & Cook, T. (2001). Gay men: Aging well! In D. C. Kimmel & D. L. Martin (Eds.), *Midlife and aging in gay America* (pp. 41-54). NY: Harrington Park Press.

Caffarella, R. S., & Clark, M. C. (1999, Winter). Development and learning: Themes and conclusions. In M. C. Clark & R. S. Caffarella (Eds.), *An update on adult development theory: New ways of thinking about the life course* (pp. 97-100). New Directions for Adult and Continuing Education, No. 84. San Francisco: Jossey-Bass.

Charbonneau, C., & Lander, P. (1991). Redefining sexuality: Women becoming lesbians at midlife. In B. Sang, J. Warshow, & A. Smith (Eds.), *Lesbians at midlife: The creative transition* (pp. 35-43). San Francisco: Spinsters.

Cohler, B. J., Hostetler, A. J., & Boxer, A. M. (1998). Generativity, social context, and lived experiences: Narratives of gay men in middle adulthood. In D. P. McAdams & E. de St. Aubin (Eds.), *Generativity and adult development: How and why we care for the next generation* (pp. 265-310). Washington, DC: American Psychological Association.

Cook-Daniels, L. (2006). Trans aging. In D. Kimmel, T. Rose, & S. David (Eds.), *Lesbian, gay, bisexual, and transgender aging: Research and clinical perspectives* (pp. 20-35). NY: Columbia University Press.

Cruikshank, M. (1992). *The gay and lesbian liberation movement.* NY: Routledge.

D'Augelli, A. R., & Patterson, C. J. (Eds.). (1995). *Lesbian, gay, and bisexual identities over the lifespan: Psychological perspectives.* NY: Oxford University Press.

de Vries, B., & Blando, J. A. (2004). The study of gay and lesbian aging: Lessons for social gerontology. In G. Herdt & B. de Vries (Eds.), *Gay and lesbian aging: Research and future directions* (pp. 3-28). NY: Springer.

de Vries, B., & Hoctel, P. (2007). The family-friends of older gay men and lesbians. In N. Teunis & G. H. Herdt (Eds.), *Sexual inequities and social justice* (pp. 213-232). Berkeley: University of California Press.

Dworkin, S. H. (2006). The aging bisexual: The invisible of the invisible minority. In D. Kimmel, T. Rose, & S. David (Eds.), *Lesbian, gay, bisexual, and transgender aging: Research and clinical perspectives* (pp. 36-52). NY: Columbia University Press.

Erikson, E. H. (1968). *Identity: Youth and crisis.* NY: Norton.

Fone, B. (2001). *Homophobia: A history.* NY: Picador.

Friend, R. A. (1991). Older lesbian and gay people: A theory of successful aging. In J. A. Lee (Ed.), *Gay midlife and maturity.* Binghamton, NY: The Haworth Press.

Gabbay, S. G., & Wahler, J. J. (2002). Lesbian aging: Review of a growing literature. *Journal of Gay & Lesbian Social Services, 14*(3), 1-21.

Garnets, L. D., & Kimmel, D. C. (Eds.). (2003). *Psychological perspectives on lesbian, gay, and bisexual experiences* (2nd ed.). NY: Columbia University Press.

Grace, A. P., & Wells, K. (2007). Victims no more: Trends enabling resilience in sexual-minority students. Education for Social Justice: From the Margin to the Mainstream, Canadian Teachers' Federation Conference, Ottawa, May 4-6. Retrieved November 1, 2008, from http://www.ctffce.ca/e/programs/pd/ social_justice/sjc_backgroundpapers_en_web.pdf

Guy, T. (1999). Culture as context for adult education: The need for culturally relevant adult education. In T. Guy (Ed.), *Providing culturally relevant adult education: A challenge for the twenty-first century* (pp. 5-18). New Directions for Adult and Continuing Education, No. 82. San Francisco: Jossey-Bass.

Hash, K. M., & Cramer, E. P. (2003). Empowering gay and lesbian caregivers and uncovering their unique experiences through the use of qualitative methods. In W. Meezan & J. I. Martin (Eds.), *Research methods with gay, lesbian, bisexual, and transgender populations* (pp. 47-63). NY: Harrington Park Press.

Hayes, E., & Flannery, D. D. (2000). *Women as learners: The significance of gender in adult learning.* San Francisco: Jossey-Bass.

Hayslip, B., & Panek, P. E. (2002). *Adult development and aging* (3rd ed.). Malabar, FL: Kreiger.

Herdt, G., & de Vries, B. (Eds.). (2004). *Gay and lesbian aging: Research and future directions.* NY: Springer.

Hoare, C. (2006). Growing a discipline at the borders of thought. In C. Hoare (Ed.), *Handbook of adult development and learning* (pp. 3-26). NY: Oxford University Press.

Hooker, E. A. (1957). The adjustment of the male overt homosexual. *Journal of Projective Techniques, 21,* 17-31.

Hunter, S. (2005). *Midlife and older LGBT adults: Knowledge and affirmative practice for the social services.* Binghamton, NY: Haworth Press.

Kertzner, R. M. (2001). The adult life course and homosexual identity in midlife gay men. *Annual Review of Sex Research, 12,* 75-92.

Kertzner, R. M., & Sved, M. (1996). Midlife gay men and lesbians: Adult development and mental health. In T. S. Stein & R. P. Cabaj (Eds.), *Textbook of homosexuality and mental health* (pp. 289-304). Washington, DC: American Psychiatric Press.

Kimmel, D., Rose, T., Orel, N., & Greene, B. (2006). Historical context for research on lesbian, gay, bisexual, and transgender aging. In D. Kimmel, T. Rose, & S. David (Eds.), *Lesbian, gay, bisexual, and transgender aging: Research and clinical perspectives* (pp. 1-19). NY: Columbia University Press.

Kimmel, D. C., & Sang, B. E. (1995). Lesbians and gay men in midlife. In A. R. D'Augelli & C. J. Patterson (Eds.), *Lesbian, gay, and bisexual identities over the lifespan: Psychological perspectives* (pp. 190-214). NY: Oxford University Press.

Lachman, M. E. (Ed.). (2001). *Handbook of midlife development.* NY: John E. Wiley & Sons.

Lee, M. Y., & Sheared, V. (2002). Socialization and immigrant students' learning in adult education programs. In M. V. Alfred (Ed.), *Learning and sociocultural contexts: Implications for adults, community, and workplace education* (pp. 27-36). New Directions for Adult and Continuing Education, No. 96. San Francisco: Jossey-Bass.

Merriam, S. B., & Caffarella, R. S. (1999). *Learning in adulthood: A comprehensive guide* (2nd ed.). San Francisco: Jossey-Bass.

Merriam, S. B., & Clark, M. C. (1991). *Lifelines: Patterns of work, love, and learning in adulthood.* San Francisco: Jossey-Bass.

Neugarten, B. L. (1976). Adaptation and the life cycle. *Counseling Psychologist, 6*, 16-20.

Tennant, M., & Pogson, P. (1995). *Learning and change in the adult years: A developmental perspective*. San Francisco: Jossey-Bass.

Wahler, J. J., & Gabbay, S. G. (1997). Gay male aging: A review of the literature. *Journal of Gay and Lesbian Social Services, 6*(3), 1-20.

Wilson, A. R. (2007). With friends like these: The liberalization of queer family policy. *Critical Social Policy, 27*(1), 50-76.

Witten, T. M. (2003). Transgender aging: An emerging population and an emerging need. *Sexologies, 12*(4), 15-20.

CHAPTER 10

Sobears: Gay Bears, Sobriety, and Community

John P. Egan

Queer discursive production has evolved over the last half century (Foucault, 1990). From a biomedical discourse constructed around (homo/bi/heterosexual) behavior to today's identity politics, Queer lingo has shifted from one that seeks simplistic typologies toward one where a rich vocabulary is needed to capture the experience and identity of all Queers. In the Queer male public sphere, the very notion about what the words "Queer," "gay," or "bisexual" mean is very much contested terrain. As Queers have asserted our entitlements as citizens, there is simply more energy—and space—to be ourselves. Whether markers of identity, affiliation, or mere description, we live in an increasingly diverse Queer discursive reality.

Rather hegemonic discourses remain among Queer men about what it means to be Queer and male. Today we live in an era where the lean, smooth, style-conscious young man (sometimes referred to derisively as *twinkies* because of their thinness and ostensive superficiality) is often the archetype proffered as the totality of Queer male reality, both in our own and mainstream society's media. The emergence of bear culture—the celebration of furry, full-bodied Queer men—offers many men, for whom twinkdom is either undesirable or unattainable, affirming space (Suresha, 2002; Wright, 1997). Bear culture represents a refutational stance—material and discursive—to notions of Queerness that permeate both mainstream and Queer public spheres.

Although dedicated magazines, books, venues, and online spaces abound for bears, there is no universally agreed upon notion of who is a bear or what attributes are requisite for genuine membership in bear culture. In discursive terms, words like "masculine," "manly," "regular," or even (sadly) "normal" are ubiquitous in bear culture. But even with these terms (and their embedded hegemonic masculinity [Connell, 2005], which teaches Queer men that conforming to mainstream notions of maleness is preferable and, perhaps, somehow superior), there is an absence of consensus regarding who is (and is not) a bear. Still, in a broad sense, the North American bear archetype is skewed toward solid physiques and facial and/or body hair. In Europe and Australasia, it is slanted toward overweight, even obesity—men who would be called "chubs" in the United States or Canada. There can be much scorn and derision between those whose understandings are different in regards to what it means to be a bear.

The existence of bear culture is noteworthy in terms of how it challenges both conventional notes of Queer male experience and masculinity. For many Queer men, integrating a sense of being Queer has traditionally involved locating an accessible gay milieu as a point of entrée, often a twinkie gay bar. Many bears find it difficult to make connections in such venues; rather than acceptance, they experience scorn, rancor, or rejection. Some leave with a sense that in order to acquire genuine membership in Queer culture they need to clipper the body hair, drop several pounds, and purchase a new and more fashionable wardrobe. Some find success doing this; others do not.

Bear Here, Queer Here

As a young man I remember feeling a need to "choose" what kind of gay man (we weren't quite Queer just yet) I was going be. In mid-1980s New York City there was a distinct stratification of the scene: twinkie bars, leather bars, drag bars, piano bars, Black bars, Latin bars, even one "Brooklyn Italian" bar (at the disco where *Saturday Night Fever* was filmed). I wasn't obese, but I certainly wasn't skinny or smooth back then—nor did I wish to be. My preferred dress outside of work was jeans and flannel, hardly the ensemble of a disco dude. In 1986 a leather bar was the closest analogue to my interests and inclinations, but those bars (not to mention leather pants, chaps, and harnesses) were still a significantly uncomfortable fit.

When I migrated to Canada in 1989, Vancouver had a rather low-key Queer scene—one disco and several bars—and an intermingling between Queer constituencies that was wonderfully perplexing after stratified New York.

To be clear, in both cities I had certain inclinations in terms of style and the sort of man I desired. But I hadn't quite found a niche in either city. I saw a few guys who seemed to be sort of like me—but only sort of. As a result, the Queer scene was a place where I participated from time to time, nothing more.

Today the role Queer bars play in building community remains significantly rooted in one clear fact: mainstream society is still virulently homophobic. We don't yet live in a world where one man can chat up another and invite him on a date without significant risk of a violent response. For many straight people, having a person of the same gender express a sexual or romantic desire toward them inspires fear, disgust, or anger. Until that fundamentally changes, Queers will continue to seek Queer spaces, often Queer bars. Perhaps now, virtual ones.

Cybearspace

For me, the discovery of bear space coincided with my initial forays online. In 1995, access to the Internet was expanding rapidly, and with it, online bear space. The Bear Mailing List (BML), an e-mail-based community forum, was my primary point of contact with other like-minded men. On the BML members could pose questions, participate in debates (who is or is not a bear, monogamy versus promiscuity, liberalism versus libertarianism, can women be bears), share information, organize social activities—in other words, forge community. Websites offering personal profile pages like Resources for Bears (http://www.rfp. org/) and bear.net (http://www.bear.net), both free sites founded by men committed to nurturing this emerging culture, had memberships into the thousands. Live, text-based conversations on Internet relay chat (IRC) networks also played an important role in the development of this emerging online bear culture and community.

As this bear space—cybearspace—has expanded, so have modes of delivery online. Many of the men I met through the BML back in 1996 use blogs or online journals to stay in touch via sites like LiveJournal.com. We also chat using text-based instant messaging networks such as AOL Instant Messenger (AIM), Yahoo, and Microsoft Messenger (MSN) or video conference using programs like iChat, Skype or ISPQ.

Meanwhile, the face-to-face bear scene in many North American communities often continues to be centered on bars, pubs, and clubs. In seeking out spaces known to be "safe," bears (like other Queers) often seek connection and validation there, insulated from a world that remains largely homophobic. Therefore, nights out on the scene bring a lot of bears together for fun and frivolity. But for *sobears*—bears who, for a variety of reasons, pursue abstinence from alcohol[1]— such ostensibly safe spaces can indeed be unwelcoming, even treacherous.

Methods

This exploratory, descriptive study examined the experience of sobears— self-identified bears either living sober or pursuing sobriety—seeking and experiencing community. In particular it endeavored to answer this question: *To what extent and in what ways does sobriety impact membership and participation in bear culture and community in both face-to-face and online communities?*

This study looked at the experiences of 22 sobears from across the United States and Canada. Participants were recruited via online newsgroups and bear-specific e-mail listservs in 2001. Inclusion criteria were participation (at some time, though not necessarily concurrently) in both face-to-face (F2F) and online bear culture and being abstinent (or pursuing abstinence) from alcohol, regardless of motivation. Each participant completed a self-administered qualitative questionnaire, which included some basic demographic questions.

The themes covered in the questions included:

- Reasons for pursuing sobriety
- Characteristics of each man's local F2F bear culture experiences
- Characteristics of each man's online bear culture experiences
- Any impact being a sobear has had on efforts to socialize with other bears, including friendship, dating, and sex
- Any moments or instances when being a sobear led to a feeling of "apartness" from bear culture/community, and
- Views on the relationship between bears, bear community, and alcohol.

Editors' note: Substance abuse is reported in queer communities, however, scholars point out that it pathologizes queers. It is not rooted in empirical, population-based research, and, the limited epidemiological research focuses mostly on major US cities. Some references on substance abuse are found at http://www.aidsprevention.org/ADAPT/facts.htm; http://www.alcoholmedicalscholars. org/gay-out.htm; "Gay, Lesbian, Bisexual Drug Abuse and Alcohol Abuse," by Jonathan Huttner (http://ezinearticles.com/?Gay,-Lesbian,-Bisexual-Drug-Abuse-and-Alcohol-Abuse&id=411956).

Respondents completed their questionnaires electronically and submitted them to me via e-mail. Qualitative data were analyzed using MAX/QDA qualitative analysis software (See Kuckartz, 2002 for this analytic tool).

Findings

Most of the men (19 of 22) identified themselves as gay; one self-identified as Queer; one stated that he preferred not to answer the question; another did not respond. Mean age was 38 years. Fifty-six percent were in relationships, including one polyamorous man with two partners. Most of the men lived in the United States, including California, Florida, Georgia, Massachusetts, Missouri, New York, Ohio, Oklahoma, Texas, and Washington State. Nearly 20% were Canadian, based either in British Columbia or Ontario. The median length of sobriety was 12 years, including one person (aged 45) who had never consumed alcohol in his lifetime.

Alcoholic. And Not

Half the men described themselves as "alcoholic," a complicated term they variously defined in relation to experiences and/or consequences. For some this was directly linked to the specific impact problem drinking had on their lives. For others, like Jack, it coincided with other important issues. He quit drinking in his mid-30s "after being hospitalized for the umpteenth time for damage inflicted" by his (then) partner, at which point Jack decided his "life needed a change."

Pat realized in his teens that he had a problem with alcohol. He described himself as a "bright, but angry" young man who drank vodka before class in high school. In hindsight, the tenor of Pat's life should have made it apparent that alcohol was a problem:

Aside from the horrific hangovers, the fact that my life was always a crisis and struggle should also have been a clue. Over the last five years or so [of his drinking], I blacked out nearly every time I drank. I drank instead of buying groceries, I drank instead of paying the rent. Eventually I lost everything: job, partner, home, most possessions. And any sense of community.

After school and after having come out as gay, Pat did much of his drinking in gay bars. For him, realizing he was alcoholic (and then deciding to pursue sobriety) meant letting go of the primary venue through which he found Queer community. This sense of letting go of community because of sobriety was common among most of the men who identified as alcoholic.

Another 14% cited a parent's alcoholism, most often the father, as their reason for living sober. Misha didn't drink because his father, grandfather, and uncle were all alcoholics. Having seen how alcoholism affected his family, Misha was not going to do the same thing. He saw abstinence from alcohol as the surest way to prevent that fate.

Another 10% cited health reasons for being sober, including Walter, who stopped drinking alcohol because of mounting health problems: "overweight, Type II diabetes, hypertension, and severe degenerative joint disease." Others cited a lack of enjoyment of alcoholic beverages (their taste or the effects of intoxication), religious prohibitions against alcohol consumption, and in one case, a political commitment to avoid mass-marketed products, including (but not limited to) alcoholic beverages, as reasons for pursuing sobriety. Thus, for a range of reasons—not limited to alcohol misuse—these bears all elected to live sober.

Support

Many participants accessed both professional and peer-based supports. The various forms of support listed in the questionnaire were not mutually exclusive; a participant could indicate participation in more than one. About one half did. Of those who considered themselves alcoholic, relatively few had participated in professional substance abuse services such as residential detoxification ("detox"), residential substance abuse treatment ("treatment"), or extended transitional housing ("halfway house"). Only 14% of respondents had attended residential treatment, with another 9% having participated in out-patient treatment; a similar number had been in detox. Only one participant had lived in a halfway house.

Many, however, sought other forms of support. More than half had attended meetings of Alcoholics Anonymous, for example. Over two-thirds of respondents had at some point sought individual counseling or therapy. Forty percent had participated in group therapy facilitated by a counselor or other helping professional. So, both peer-based and counseling services were more commonly accessed than traditional substance abuse/misuse programs. And those who had sought substance misuse services were often also those who found traditional bear spaces difficult to navigate.

Bear Space, Bear Community

A broad range of perspectives and experiences regarding socializing with other bears was found in the responses of the 22 participants in this study. Norman found that being sober "doesn't impact [his] efforts to socialize at all." Neither did Phil, who "still will go to bars" and who had "no problem with other people drinking." For men like Norman and Phil, traveling in the bear scene was largely unproblematic as a sobear.

After establishing a "solid, confident sobriety," Joseph found it "much easier to go to clubs/bars without the urge to drink." He would strategize how he would participate in advance as a way to keep his involvement personally manageable:

Initially, it was very difficult to spend time around alcohol-related places and events, but now I do fine with a bottle of water in my hand. At first I was compelled to explain myself when turning down the offer of a drink; now I just simply say, "I don't drink."

Bears whose reasons for sobriety were related to alcoholism or problem drinking (their own or others) were less likely to use bars as a venue for meeting other bears. Rory complained, "Everything seems to revolve around 'going to the bar.'" So did Tim, who remains on the periphery of his "large" local bear community because it "seems to center around the bar." Interestingly, Hal thought being sober in such spaces gave him an advantage; it taught him to be uninhibited and "to develop seduction skills, as opposed to merely relying on alcohol."

For some sobears, whose sobriety was not rooted in their own alcoholism, the conflation of bear space and bar space still presented personal and social difficulties. Larry viewed his local bear community's meetings in bars "negatively" because he "really [does] *not* like going to bars/heavy alcohol events." Jason was similarly uncomfortable, which impacted him both personally and professionally. As someone who worked in the local LGBT community services sector, there were pressures to participate in after-work drinking, where important networking happened. Even when he attended, his discomfort made fitting in a challenge.

Several men noted that in bear space some drink to the point of intoxication while others do not. It was with the former that they encountered most problems. For example, Peter found it hard to relate to anyone who was drunk and "probably wouldn't choose to socialize with" those who were. But Peter didn't mind at all "the man who drinks in moderation and stays in control."

For Barry, being a sobear proved to be a profound barrier to participating in the F2F bear community:

The fact that I do not drink tends to make others suspicious of me in social settings like bars and bear runs.[2] I have been treated as an oddity and even with disdain...that I was "too good" to drink beer with the guys. I know that when I have been out at a bar and someone offers me a drink as a come on and I order water or Diet Coke, the other person usually disappears before I finish the beverage. I know that "let me buy you a beer" is a crutch phrase often used to help someone meet someone they are interested in. When the answer is, "No thanks" or "Thanks, but I'll have water," it seems to throw these guys off and they do not know what to do.

Pat described why he wasn't very involved in his local bear club:

The bear scene here is totally bar focused. I haven't attended many bar days, which are often on Saturday afternoons, because I'm loath to spend daytimes in beer parlors. That's my old life. And the guys who thrive on it are often the ones who keep the local bear club going, so I guess it suits a lot of fellas. But not me.

[I prefer] the Internet.

Pat's comments reflect the experience of a number of the men who found that being a sobear and exploring the traditional local bear spaces can be challenging. As a result, the emergence of online bear space and community prove to be an important and more comfortable alternative. Most of the participants cited the Internet as an important space for socializing, both in the pursuit of romantic or sexual partners and friendship. Local and international chat rooms, instant messaging, and listservs are among the cyberspaces most often used. Like Pat, Barry also found that "meeting people on the Internet seems to work better" as a sobear. Barry's online profiles all indicate he is sober; as a result, other like-minded men can "approach [him] directly...no guessing is involved."

Cal lives in the San Francisco Bay area, where a "vibrant" bear community thrives. He is also active online, where he may "connect with a good number of bear buddies." Walter goes to his local bear club, including its meet-and-greets at the local leather bar, but otherwise finds "bear folk" online. Stephen "seeks bear

---

Editors' note: A "bear run" is a gathering or rendezvous of bears, often sponsored by a bear club or organization.

company outside [of] bars or clubs, usually online." In fact, Stephen has traveled "many miles to be with other bears that have the same feelings about alcohol." Whether in face-to-face space or cybearspace, most participants continue to seek and find bear community and culture, and they value it.

For many of the sobears, being sober led them to feel estranged from other bears. A number wrote at length about particular moments and events that crystallized this belief and described this experience in more generalized terms. Walter felt like an outsider sometimes, trying " to laugh it off." Sometimes James felt angry and distanced in the bar scenario where others "attempt to get you to drink because they think that will cause you to loosen up a little." For Mark, it seemed like many bear events he attended "revolve around the bar and drinking so that you are distanced by the fact that you don't partake." Likewise, Luke felt detached from the rest of the bear community because of his sobriety, especially in a bar. Paradoxically he believed the bear community has just as many conformity issues as any other subset of the gay community. He finds expectations that bears "are supposed to dress butch, be 'masculine,' and drink their beer" oppressive.

Conclusions

My entrée into bear culture was not accompanied by any of the intense emotions I felt coming out as Queer some ten years earlier. But many other bears do experience almost a second coming out when they discover bear culture, sometimes in ways more powerful—and empowering—than their coming out as Queer. For some young bears who sought Queer culture only to find rejection, what has been a niche for me has, in fact, been a lifesaver for them. For some men in this study, finding bear culture liberated them from isolation, shame, and self-loathing—even as, for others, bear culture remains largely just an interesting and fun aspect of their social lives.

With the advent of the Internet, many men (bears and not) are carving out Queer space and place in ways that transcend the traditional gay bar. Sobears in particular seem to be using the Internet as a space where their concerns about alcohol are largely assuaged. These men's experiences demonstrate that even in specific sectors of the Queer community, ostensibly carved out in response to hegemonic notions of "gay," other norms may emerge that are also exclusionary—or have the potential to be. All of this needs to be learned, largely through experiences. The knowledge acquired through (and meanings ascribed to) these experiences define what Queer community is for these men—and what it is not and how it works.

Sobears use support services and their own critical self-reflections to make sense of their lives. Although extra-institutional and largely informal, their experiences as sobears seeking community and acceptance speak directly to how adult learning occurs for those whose lives don't fit what is construed as "normal" in mainstream society at large. In sum, research into sobear lives speaks directly to how and where adult learning occurs for this marginalized group whose members mediate their lives against the difficulties of fitting into not only mainstream society but also the urban gay milieu and the "regular" bear scene.

References

Connell, R. W. (2005). *Masculinities* (2nd edition). Cambridge: Polity Press. Foucault, M. (1990). *The History of sexuality, Volume 1: An introduction* (R. Hurley, Trans.). NY: Vintage Books. (Original work published 1976)

Kuckartz, U. (2002). MaxQDA (Version 1.1) [qualitative data analysis]. Berlin: VERBI.

Software Consult. SPSS. (Version 10.0) (2000). Chicago: SPSS Inc.

Suresha, R. J. (2002). *Bears on bears: Interviews and discussions.* Boston: Alyson Publications.

Wright, L. K. (1997). *Bear book: Readings in the history and evolution of a gay male subculture.* Binghamton, NY: Haworth Press.

CHAPTER 11

Transsexuality: Challenging the Institutionalized Sex/Gender Binary

Robert J. Hill
Debra D. Davis

By Way of Introduction

This chapter is dialogic. It is a conversation between a gay, male, adult educator (Bob) and a transgender woman (Debra) who is an activist, author, and educator. The conversation centers on the unreported findings of a year-long study undertaken by the first author to explore learning that occurs within (mostly) male-to-female (MTF or M2F) transsexual communities. The second author transitioned fully in 1998. She is an award-winning trainer in transgender issues with over 20 years experience, giving more than 1,000 presentations and workshops on the topic. Even though she self-identifies as transgender, she is also transsexual, based on the definition of "transsexual" (TS) in this chapter, for she now lives fully, in all respects, as a woman.

This conversation about Bob's research explores two particular phenomena: (a) social movement learning in the MTF transsexual community and (b) the ways that some MTF transsexuals construct a form of feminism, called transfeminism—a term that frequently appeared during interviews conducted for the

Parts of this chapter were presented by Hill at the 41st Annual Adult Education Research Conference (AERC) in 2000 (see http://www.adulterc.org/Proceedings/2000/hillr1-final.PDF). Davis was an invited keynote speaker at the 4th Annual LGBTQ and Allies Pre-Conference, May 18, 2006, at the 47th Annual AERC, University of Minnesota. Her talk was titled, "Putting the 'T' in LGB." The research reported in this chapter was conducted before the first author was hired by the University of Georgia in 2001.

study. Transsexuals, arguably the least understood and most stigmatized individuals in society, are engaged in the United States in a profusion of learning dynamics, critical education, oppositional practices, and meaning making, all of which are at the heart of Bob's research and Debra's activism. One value of the conversation is that two different kinds of data are presented—etic (by Bob, always an observer) and emic (Debra, an insider). See Creswell (1998).

Negotiating Boundaries

Bob: In my research I have found that male-to-female transsexuals negotiate the socially and culturally well-policed boundaries of what it means to be a "woman." Their educational efforts are often focused on people who identify as subjects of a sedimented male/female binary (whether gay or straight). Feminists, at times, have been a particular target population for TS efforts. Does this resonate with your experience?

Debra: I believe that other transgender people (other than transsexuals) would also be interested in educational efforts. The fact that one may have the desire to change their body parts, a traditional definition of transsexual, eclipses the fact that what it means to be a "woman" is more than anatomy. Body parts—original or reconstructed—have little to do with what we actually think.

Bob: I found that there is a proliferation of MTF discourses that have resulted in a contested form of feminism, called *transfeminism*. At times transfeminism is menacing since it challenges the institutionalized sex/gender binary in a way that most discourses do not. It interrogates the rigorously policed links between biological sex and gender in ways that few discourses are capable of. These challenges have implications for adult learning, education and community development. In your experience, how is transfeminism constructed?

Debra: Many times I am questioned about the fact that I identify as a feminist and have many feminist beliefs. One immediately, particularly obvious thing about me is I tend to be very feminine and some in the LGBT community would call me a "femme." During my presentations and workshops I dress in skirts and heels. This is how I feel comfortable in professional settings. Many times I am criticized because of feminine attire and my feminine nature. "How can you claim to be a feminist and look like that," some have said to me. My answer is always the same.

One of the things we fought for as women throughout the years is the right to present ourselves any way we want. Jeans and shirts or skirts and heels. It is our choice and no longer dictated by a "male-driven society." I'm not sure I believe that there is a huge difference between transfeminism and feminism. They both are based on the belief that we have the right to be whomever we want to be as women and that is dictated by ourselves, not society or others. I'm not sure if this is a radical view or a simplistic one, but it's my belief.

⊷ ⩲⩲ ⊶

Methods of Inquiry: MTF Adult Education and Learning

Bob: A few years ago, I was engaged in a qualitative investigation exploring the ways that transsexual knowledges are produced, used, and distributed in MTF's contest for collective identity and control over their own lives in the context of United States culture. In fact, this research has shaped my notions that people may be far less interested in meaning making in life, but rather are concerned with the experience of being alive. In my research I looked at the relationships of trans people to "non-transsexual" discursive practices. Theoretical frameworks on which this research was based included new social movements as sites of learning where a pedagogy of contestation and rebellion are carried out, identity as a source of meaning—and perhaps more important—of experience, and critical analysis that explored power asymmetries. It deepened my exploration into the social, historical, and contextual nature of learning, thinking, and practice. The research was transdisciplinary and drew from the adult education literature, queer theory, feminist discourses, educational anthropology (the culture of learning and investigating intra-group and inter-group—trans and non-trans—encounters and dis/continuities), and critical cultural studies. The methodological components of my trans research included an extensive literature review, retrieval of information in databases and electronic postings on e-boards, with subsequent analyses. The results served as rich data sources. The study utilized distance technologies and interactive computer-mediated communications (the Internet and telephone) for interview purposes. I was particularly interested in learning in informal settings. A "centrepiece of lifelong education [is] learning in informal settings. In the 1970's, informal learning provided impetus for [numerous adult education initiatives]. The Internet has greatly facilitated informal learning and created a mechanism within which to negotiate life changes even more dramatic than those that preoccupied [early efforts]" (Boshier & Pisutova, 2002).

Boshier (1999) offers that the impacts Internet technologies are having on adult education have been underexplored in wholesale fashion. Ten years ago he asked, "To what extent does the Internet present adult educators with opportunities to enact their historic commitments to equity and social justice? With the enormous reach of the Web what will adult education look like twenty years from now? What is the relationship between adult education and 'distributed learning?'" He went on to remark that, "unlike teaching machines from yesteryear, the Internet is not a passing fad." It is vitally important "because of its scope and speed of deployment—and possible consequences for adult education" (para. 3). In the past decade, "Information and Communication Technology (ICT) has changed dramatically.... Now technology facilitates communication and the sharing of information, documents and images with a multitude of people in a host of new ways" (Kop, 2008, para. 1). In fact, technology-rich environments have been shown to promote higher order thinking skills (Hopson, Simms, & Knezek (2001-2002). Kop references Martin (2006) to illustrate that professional "adult educators have been very reluctant to engage with these technological developments and have more likely than not seen such developments as undermining the traditions of adult education" (para. 3). Yet the adult education literature shows a growing recognition of the values of computer technology for informal electronic learning (e-learning), social movement and activist learning, and meaning making, often in areas that are taboo in mainstream culture. This has led researchers to acknowledge the role of cyberspace in establishing new, often fugitive, knowledges. Fugitive knowledges are the cultural understandings and meanings that have escaped the sanitizing and domesticating actions of the official canonists of any disciplinary field (Hill, 2003).

Crowther, ScAndrétt, Martin, and Hemmi (2007) have written, in a research proposal, that "much is already known about...three main strands: learning, information and communication technologies (ICTs) and social movements. On the other hand, very little is known about what happens when these three elements come together" (para. 1). They go on to describe their research as "concerned to identify how knowledge is constructed, generated, critiqued and exchanged through the use of ICTs in social movements, and to clarify how this sustains and develops the identities of ICT users as movement-activists and influences their actions" (para. 1). They are also interested "in the role of ICTs in attracting participation in the activities of the movement, and in assessing its influence on the degree and quality of people's engagement" (para. 1). Some adult education research (e.g., Hollenbeck, 2005) has begun to delve into these areas. My study assisted in exploring the questions raised by Crowther et al. (2007) as they pertain specifically to informal learning.

I'd love to have you say a few words about the uses of the Internet, blogging, listservs, YouTube, e-mail, and websites on learning in the transgender community?

Debra: The use of the Internet, blogging, listservs, YouTube, e-mail, websites and those that you have listed have had a *huge* effect on learning in the transgender community. Now information is readily available to even the most isolated and alone community members. Not only is academic knowledge available, but access to hundreds of online social networks exists at almost anyone's finger tips. Computers are commonplace, not only in most homes, but most work sites and in nearly every library in the country. Coffee shops, book stores, and cyber cafés are now common in most cities, and anyone who has the desire to find information or communicate with other transgender people online has that opportunity. This was not the case ten years ago. When I was growing up, few resources existed for transgender people, even in large cities. Libraries had little information, social organizations were few and far between—and only in major cities—and the Internet did not exist. These developments have immensely aided our communities.

Bob: In my study, 26 transsexuals/intersexuals were initially interviewed. Informants were selected from organizations dedicated to transsexual/transgender education and through "snowball" techniques. Respondents represented more MTF transsexuals than any other group. The underrepresentation of female-to-male transsexuals is a serious critique of the study. I'm curious about your thoughts on FTM transgender people, for example; do those whom you know experience the world differently than MTFs, such as yourself, do?

Debra: Of course the FTM population would have views very different than the MTF population, just as women view the world differently than men. In many large cities, FTMs make up a population as large as MTFs. In Minnesota, my hometown, our FTM population is very active and on the forefront of social change and activism. In most organizations, both groups coexist and work together in harmony. This may be because in many ways Minnesota has always been on the cutting edge of what is happening politically and socially in the transgender community. Our state's Human Rights Act was amended to include transgender people in 1993 and it was another seven years before any other state included these protections for their transgender population. Even now, in 2009, less than 15 states offer these basic protections to transgender people within their state's human rights provisions.

Bob: In my study, interviewees were culled from the initial 26 to 10 key trans respondents who participated over a one-year period. They were located, one each, in Pennsylvania (Philadelphia), North Carolina (Raleigh), West Virginia (naming this rural small town could disclose the person's identity), New York (New York), Michigan (Ann Arbor), Indiana (Bloomington) and two each in Oregon (Portland) and Massachusetts (Boston). The respondents' digital signatures were often creative (and revealing) pseudonyms;[3] some chose to provide their legal names and phone numbers so that we could communicate by conventional landline. One eventually was interviewed in person. Several transsexuals revealed that they were engaged in formal educational studies, reporting, for example, "I am a female who has transitioned and am doing feminist doctoral transgender studies." Formal semistructured interviews, informal discussions, and noninvasive techniques (e.g., snagging public messages posted on Internet listservs) were used to capture data which were coded and analyzed for themes related to adult education and community development in the transsexual community. All participants were given multiple chances for ongoing critique and a draft copy of the study results for comments.

Words…Words…Words

Bob: Elsewhere (Hill, 2006) I provide a comprehensive vocabulary related to gender, sexual orientation, and gender expression. To briefly summarize, language does not simply communicate reality in either direct or naive ways; that is to say, language is not transparent (Lather, 1996). On the contrary, language aids in the construction, marginalization, or privileging of individuals. The situation thus makes definitions always provisional and untrustworthy, but define we must if we are to communicate.

---

3 In only two instances did respondents request that, in the event that material they provided was published, I furnish identifiers. In keeping with the informed consent statement, respondents remain anonymous.

Labels not only describe, they *inscribe*. With this awareness, the following terms are used in specific ways in my study.

For my purposes, *sexual orientation* deals with factors and conditions that mobilize affectional and sexual desires. It is about personal attraction to another. Gay men, lesbians, bisexuals, transgender and Queer (LGBTQ) people typically have an orientation toward another, as do "straight" people. To academics working in postmodern projects, the binary "gay" (homosexual) and "straight" (heterosexual) is problematic and seen as socially and temporally constructed; however, this binary holds considerable currency in mainstream culture. I believe that binaries limit our ability to think about gender and sexual orientation.

Gender is "a multilayered phenomenon that digs deep down into our guts.... it is a system of social relations that organize our world...that helps us make meaning of the differences between people" (Scott-Dixon, 2006, p. 17). *Gender identity* concerns a person's feelings about her or himself in regards to being a woman or a man. The way in which a person presents her or himself to the world constitutes *gender expression*. *Trans-* is a prefix describing persons whose gender does not conform to norms. It can be a "fluid descriptor which is [a] broad, yet specific reference depending on context" (Weiss, 2004, p. 229). When a person has an identity of a man or a woman that does not conform to his or her actual anatomy, we employ the term *transgender*.

Transsexuality is the state of being transgender, but taking some form(s) of action to affirm self-identity, an identity that many would claim actually chooses them rather than one they elect to enact. *Intersexuals* are individuals with a combination of male and female biology and physiology, sometimes incorrectly lumped together as "hermaphrodites." Fausto-Sterling (2005) offers that intersex conditions (note the plural, "conditions") contribute to "challenging ideas about the male/female divide" (p. 116). This study included several participants who subsequently learned that they are in fact intersexual. It must be clearly stated from the outset that the two communities have very different worldviews and epistemologies. Intersexuals are often strongly opposed to being included in the families of sexual minorities such as gay, lesbian, bisexual, transgender, or transsexual.

Finally, *Queer* is a term that generates much controversy. Queer is used in at least two different ways. One is as a means to avoid the cumbersome acronym, LGBT, i.e., as an umbrella term for the collection of sexual minorities (see Chapter 15, "No End to History: Demanding Civil Quarter for Sexual Minorities in Heteronormative Space," by Grace and Hill, in this volume). Another way in which it is deployed is to suggest that identities are always multiple, fluid, mobile, contingent, unstable, and fragmented. It challenges fixed, sedimented notions such as gay, lesbian, and straight. Queer is best understood not by the question, "What is it?" but rather by the interrogative, "How does it function?" Answers are often found in the destabilization and contestation it offers to the meaning of "normal," raising the possibility that there are straight Queers, too.

I'm curious about your response to the idea that we don't choose our gender, our gender chooses us, regardless of our anatomy (body parts).

Debra: The idea that we don't choose our gender, our gender chooses us, regardless of our anatomy (body parts), is a view that many people have, especially those of us within the transgender community. Most of us know that we were born with bodies that were incongruent with our hearts', souls', and minds' views of who we are as boys or girls, men or women. There has been no conclusive data as to what causes a person to be transgender. Theories exist, but they are just that, theories, and the larger studies of our community have been inconclusive.

Translating the Literature

Bob: Transsexuals and intersexuals are arguably the most marginalized group of gender outlaws. Authors such as Feinberg (1996) have explored this. Hate crime violence is rampant against these segments of society. There is currently a powerful surge of trans struggles positioning themselves within the borders of new social movements working for social change (Feinberg, 1992). A review of the literature shows that transsexual and intersexual communities are engaged in a profusion of learning dynamics, oppositional practices, and sense making. As women, MTF trannies struggle to write their own feminist narratives, called transfeminism or "difference feminism" (Shalit, 1999). In part, it rejects marginalization at the hands of society, including Othering done to them by the straight, gay, and lesbian communities. Some respondents in my study saw this new feminism as the latest development and further evolution of feminist thought. Trans/actional learning included educational dynamics within trans communities and outreach to "non-trannies," especially to mainstream women feminists who frequently reject MTF transsexuals' identity claims. Trans respondents noted that until recently few people asked, "Who counts as a woman?" Those who did often answered the question with the refrain, "Only biological women!" Terms like

GGs (genetic girls), women-born women (also spelled "womyn"), and ciswomen (a term for gender identity or performance of a gender role that matches societal expectations for a person's sex) support this notion. The literature on transfeminists reveals both striving for harmony *and* a fierce battle over identity, meaning, and naming.

Debra: Yes, there is some struggle over language. By the way, to some of us, the term that you use, "trannies," is offensive and degrading. It is used by those who wish to marginalize us. I do, however, recognize that some trans communities like the term. I'm wondering as I read your work if it is necessary. To those who read our chapter, I'd say that I prefer to use the terms "trans communities" and "non-trans communities." In a similar way, it would be incorrect to use the term "dyke" when referring to the lesbian community as a whole.

Bob: Data show that numerous organizations exist for education, support, and advocacy in the transsexual and intersexual communities, but little of the trans educational effort is recognized by educators. Transsexuals and intersexuals report that the mainstream lesbian and gay communities have been obstacles to transsexual liberation; many traditional feminists have been troubling for (and troubled by) transfeminists. I found that there is a transfeminist community that is actively creating a narrative space that has grown to be recognized in feminist, gay and lesbian, and other literature and scholarship. Transsexual and transgender educational efforts are often specifically oriented as outreach to "our sisters." The transgender social movement is polyvalent, encompassing enormous diversity within a unifying field surrounding gender. Additionally, transgender, transsexual, and intersexual communities have actually each built social movements of their own. The antagonistic tendency of new social movements to produce and simultaneously deconstruct group identity (Gamson, 1998) is operative in the transgender movement. There is a tension that exists between creating stable collective identities on the one hand through an essentialized educational discourse while blurring and deconstructing identity boundaries on the other.

Debra: For those of us who believe that change starts, and must happen, from within the heart of organizations (assuming an organization has a "heart"), separating from established mainstream organizations and the creation of "isolated self-community" do not help the process of creating change from within. Only by getting to know each other, not only as a community but also personally (we might even call this "being friends"), can we make this change happen on a larger scale. I founded the Gender Education Center in 1994 and am the executive director (see http://www.debradavis.org/gecpage/ gecwelcome.html). It is an organization of differently gendered people dedicated to support, advocacy, and education. We started doing this work even before the formal organization was formed. Over the last 20 years we have given over 1,000 presentations and workshops throughout the country. We consult employers, law enforcement, human rights agencies, and not-for-profit service providers regarding policies that affect transgender people, and we are especially effective in coordinating workplace transitions for transgender employees. Our clients have included large national and international companies such as Best Buy Corporation and Tenant Company, as well as smaller organizations having as few as a dozen employees. One of the factors that gives us credibility is the fact that I transitioned in May of 1998 as a transgender woman at Southwest High School in the Minneapolis Public Schools. This transition is believed to be one of the first successful transitions in the nation of a transgender person working with children in secondary education. Our work is now recognized nationally and we continue to be a resource for those who have an interest in the transgender community.

De/Constructing the Category "Women"

Bob: From my reading and research, I am aware that numerous individuals have engaged in the construction of feminist ideology since the 1960s, producing strands identified as liberal-, radical-, socialist-, Marxist-, Black-, lesbian-, cultural-, postmodern-, critical-, and cyber-feminism, to name a few (Brooks, 1997; Whelehan, 1995). In fact, so diverse is the family of feminisms, it has spawned new fields of study and practice such as the "womanist" paradigm, employed to describe the perspective and experiences of African American women. It is a concept derived from the work of Alice Walker, *In Search of Our Mothers' Gardens: Womanist Prose* (2003). Each of these has counter discourses, such as the work of Stein (1998) that decenters lesbian feminism. There are many commonalities among the feminisms, as well as significant differences. Several major similarities are that they are predicated upon the primacy of *experiences* of what it means to be a woman, shared views of the patriarchy as hegemonic, and "gender polarization"—the concept that females and males live mutually exclusive, scripted lives that are part of "the ubiquitous organization of social life [that oppresses women]" (Bem, 1993, p. 80). Salamon (2008) raises powerful questions on "the relationship between women's studies, feminism, and the study of transgenderism and other nonnormative genders" (p. 115). Could you comment on experiences of what it meant to you to be a woman when you were bodied as a male?

Debra: One of the interesting things about transgender women is that we too experience many of these things, the primary difference is that we experience them bodied as a male. Even though we may begrudgingly participate in "male-scripted" experiences outwardly, we are inwardly seeing this experience as a woman would, our male bodies only being a physical aspect of our anatomy. For many of us, we see ourselves as woman-bodied in our minds' eyes. I remember living with a male body and looking in a mirror and seeing only a woman, even though I might be naked. The male parts did not exist.

Bob: Although feminist notions are characterized by embodied reflexivity (Lather, 1991), defined as a "self-conscious, critical, and intense process of gazing inward and outward that results in questioning assumptions, identifying problems, and organizing for change (Gustafson, 1999, p. 249), seldom are male/female and man/woman binaries themselves interrogated. There are exceptions, such as found in a writing by Rose and Camilleri (2002), who pose the question, "What would it mean to be a femme and not a woman? What makes femme different than femininity?" (p. 12). They argue that "femininity is a demand placed on female bodies and femme is the danger of a body read female or inappropriately feminine. We are not good girls—perhaps we are not girls at all" (p. 13). The MTF participants in my study often expressed the desire to have their bodies read as female.

Debra: Even though this is true for many transsexual women, the more important factor is that we be accepted in *all* ways as the women we are, the physical only being a part of that. Who we are is just as important, and many times more important, than how we may look. Outward physical appearance just makes it easier to live in a society that values traditional male/female stereotypic physical appearances.

Bob: My studies have shown that MTF transsexuals and others who make up gender diversity pose unique challenges to these binaries, especially the category "woman," and to some contemporary constructions of feminism. They simultaneously reinscribe *and* trouble gender polarization. As a result, several forms of transfeminism have emerged. The text, *Trans/forming Feminisms: Trans/feminist*

Voices Speak Out, edited by Krista Scott-Dixon (2006) is a classic compilation. Transfeminisms are "liberatory border pedagogies" that decenter the "dominant configurations of power and knowledge" (Giroux, 1993, p. 246) found in the other families of feminism. Califia (1997) has pointed to the tensions that "nothing upsets the underpinnings of feminist fundamentalism more than the existence of transsexual" (p. 91). Of interest here is the way that "policing gender is sometimes used as a way of securing heterosexuality" (Butler, 1999, p. xii) and is apparent in most forms of feminism, except transfeminism. As an aside, a contrarian view would argue with Butler (1997) not to put the two in opposition—against "pitting minority communities against one another at an historical moment in which the struggles between them need to be put into a dynamic and empowering interplay" (p. 1). Recent literature on the topic of transfeminism includes works by Califia (1997), Rose and Camilleri (2002), and Scott-Dixon (2006).

<hr />

Sisters to the Rescue: Trans/itional Sites and Trans/actional Education

Bob: In my study, education was universally posited by the trans community as indispensable in the struggle for identity, acceptance, and building an equitable society. The terms "education" and "learning" emerged as key words in transcribed interviews, and concepts related to them dominated. The research located multiple trans sites and opportunities employed in the struggle for cultural authority against the hegemony of transphobic discourses. One participant wrote about the relationship between female transsexuals and other women: "There is no enemy. This is not war. This is a rescue mission." It is a sortie to liberate their sisters. Another penned, "I will not fight [genetic women]...I'll do my best to educate them...." The education was trans/actional; one MTF transsexual wrote, "The women who socialized me taught me that sisterhood is fierce, not demure." Another wrote that she would not engage in activist behavior that "broke rules," saying, "I'll educate, but I won't cross that line. Because my whole transition is about HONESTY [capitalized in the original]. That's another value I learned from women." One lamented that being excluded from women spaces deprived her of "places to heal and learn, places of safety and growth." Another MTF extolled the virtues of sister-space "because after thousands of years of patriarchy, we have found a special value in a place where women can be seen without the male gaze, and speak without the male ear." She went so far as to conclude that defending a space where genetic women gather was more important to her than admitting transwomen, if entering that space would cause grief to those in it. Feminist music and cultural festivals with women-born-women-only admittance policies were major arenas where the struggle for acceptance and identity recognition occurred. Educational programs and grassroots activism were key tools at these sites. It is important to note that not all festivals ban transsexuals and not all women attending festivals that prohibit them agree with exclusionary policies.

For several years, the annual Michigan Womyn's Music Festival (MWMF) had exclusionary policies and was a significant location for education and confrontation. Sreedhar and Hand (2006) ask, "Should a women-only event allow room for the transgendered, especially women who 'were once men'?" (p. 161).

Debra: In your last quotation, of course this person assumed that we were once "men"; however, many in our community believe that the only part of our previous existence that may have resembled "men" was possibly our physical body parts. We, as women born with such body parts, can change them. I have found that "women-only" organizations evolve, and they discover that the admission of transgender women not only enriches the fabric and sisterhood of their organizations, they begin not only to tolerate us but in fact reach out to us in order to add this new face of diversity to their numbers. This is an evolutionary process and the level of acceptance can depend on the liberalness of the area of the country in which an organization is located. In the larger cities of Minnesota, where I live, transgender women can be found in most major, local, and national women's organizations.

Bob: Several of the interviewees self-identified as activists and educators who participated in a counterhegemonic event, called Camp Trans, sponsored by the street action group, Transsexual Menace, at the MWMF. This group staged demonstrations and educational workshops across from the MWMF admission gates, getting "face-to-face and maybe femme-to-femme" with women-born-women "gender police." When organizing for Camp Trans, activists often focused on education. One wrote, "Here is my intention [for the next camp]...workshopsworkshopsworkshops...education inside from people who can get in [to the MWMF]." Another wrote, "I'd like to see educational programs, like the first Camp Trans [in 1994]. I think they were very helpful...." Additionally, a person listed future educational classes at Camp Trans: "Y2K workshops: Trans 101- what the hell is going on here? TransFeminism - De and Re Construction. Saving Spaces - Practical

Guidelines to Trans inclusion. Self Made Men - Boyz and Men and Michigan. Dares Not Speak - Trans eros read around the campfire."

Not all transsexuals agreed to resist non-trans policies at music festivals, saying it is "a mistake for the trans movement to target [exclusionary events]; they do not have the kind of institutional power that male establishments have. The real enemy of the trans movement should be the patriarchal system rather than womyn-only events." Another MTF transsexual questioned the value of activism by saying, "While I see lots of trans outreaching being done by hard working activist types, I have to admit I have become a bit jaded, I don't really think it helps much. I was thinking about that Saturday morning while helping to escort people into the local planned parenthood clinic. All my 'pro-choice' chants weren't really educating anyone, certainly the pro-lifers I was chanting to were not impressed. So in the [end], I guess I was just doing it for myself, which is an odd thought. I mean, if activism is just to make me feel good, why does it always have to happen so early in the morning?" Another wrote, "You can't be both In Your Face activist and at the same time [be] an educator. In Your Face activism puts people on the defense. Education must have some modicum of receptiveness on the part of the educatee."

Debra: As this person alludes, we need both activism that draws attention to the issues and also education. Unfortunately, too often in our quest to create understanding and change, we try to educate those who are unresponsive. I believe that as adult educators we know that this cannot only be futile but also a waste of time. As we find common issues with those who may feel that our message is not relevant to them, we can start to create and nurture the relationships that will foster interest in being more receptive to ideas and ideologies that may be different than what is considered mainstream.

Education as a "Right to Be Myself"

Bob: On asking if education plays a significant role in transsexual communities, one respondent bluntly wrote, "Where have you been for the last decade? The mission of [several organizations cited] is to educate society about Trans/Intersex issues." Another wrote, "I'm forwarding your msg to my beloved who is [an] Ftm [female-to-male transsexual] and very active in local and regional education." One respondent put it, "Education is about the right to be myself."

Another said, "Every time I had a chance to educate, I did." Targets of educational campaigns varied. In some instances it was "the feminist community"; in others it was education at "women's centers." One wrote that she was engaged in a project based on "feminists and trans sisters working together to educate." A forum was organized "to address the issue of Transwomen exclusion at a Women's Center…. [The people at the center] felt one of the main reasons they did not include Transwomen was [their] lack of education around trans issues." The forum was taped so that it could be used for "mandatory training for all their volunteers and staff at the center."

Debra: I have had some of the same experiences when training at traditional women's centers, domestic abuse centers, and women's shelters. I hear, "We really don't know very much about this subject (transgender women) so we don't deal with it/them." I'm sure this was also said when these organizations first started to help women of color, 60 years ago. What they many times do not understand is that not only is this training important and necessary to stay within the mission and purpose of their women's organizations—every women's organization's mission statement I have ever come in contact with includes diversity among women—but to be effective, training must be done by a person who self-identifies as transgender. Participants must deal with how they feel interacting personally with someone who has lived part of her life in the role of the opposite gender. I think that in most situations a video will not accomplish this goal.

Bob: At times, the expression "being myself" meant that participants took up "resistance identities" (Castells, 1998); stigmatized by the logic of domination, these individuals built walls of resistance and survival in the emergence of identity politics. At other times, "project identities" were expressed, building new identities that redefined their social roles while seeking social transformation. Pedagogical trans tools, in addition to collective action and protests at music festivals where genetic women gather, differed widely depending on the form that identity took. They included direct actions at National Organization for Women (NOW) conventions until 1997. Activists from Transexual Menace targeted the NOW National Conference in 1995. As a result, in 1997, NOW passed a trans inclusion resolution. The declaration was offered after three years of ongoing debate. This resolution stated that NOW affirmed and honored the right of people to self-identify. In its press release, NOW went on to acknowledge that the transsexual community is on today's cutting edge in the struggle for equality of all humans.

Debra: My experience with our local NOW organization in Minnesota has been very positive. In the late 1980s and early '90s I was involved with this group and spoke many times at their meetings and joined them when speaking out about civil issues that related to their work. My daughter and granddaughter accompanied me and 75 other women (and a few supportive men) when we demonstrated at a local Promise Keepers gathering of over 50,000 men. I was one of the women who, on a truck bed as a stage with a large amplification system, during their lunch break, spoke out against their policies of women being "subservient to their man." So, as you can see, genetic women and transgender women can and do join forces.

Bob: Additional strategies involve dialogue; effective use of the media, such as appearances on talk radio and TV shows; authoring columns for the pulp press and online journals; networking (especially electronically); linking with sympathetic non-trans organizations like the Lesbian Avengers; "camp behavior"; parading; transsexual and intersexual political activity; election to community boards of directors; joining peer groups at sexual-minority centers in some cities; forming panels/speakers bureaus to address schools, college classes, civic clubs, companies, and other gatherings; websites; and permeating reading groups at commercial bookstores. Many of the strategies employed, such as taking membership on boards of directors at community gay and lesbian centers, paralleled Gramsci's (1971) "war of position" in order to counter or replace the dominant hegemony. One group developed a successful education program that they planned to disseminate to others. Outreach education to trans youth has become an increasingly important endeavor as well. One respondent spoke of a trans friend who started a youth support group. He wrote, "[My buddy's] identification is somewhere in-between and she switches pronouns back and forth. [She] has done lots of education among her peer group at [youth] meetings

Debra: Again, here I agree with the idea that we must be out, proud, visible, and involved transgender people who are involved in organizations that are not necessarily LGBT. In this way others will get to know us on a personal level as we get to know them.

Education as a *Rite* to Be Themselves

Bob: I found that for MTFs, education in the trans community is a rite of passage into female adulthood. This is especially important given the absence of intervening stages that most genetic women travel during childhood and adolescent development and female social enculturation. For some adults, it is a crash course in the pursuit to appear as they feel—as a woman. Transgender magazines and websites are replete with ads to assist transitioning folks "to be the woman of your dreams" in ways that seem to support "gender polarization"—the social scripting of gendered lives (Bem, 1993) that is abhorrent to some women. Topics for self-directed learning projects, such as how to measure for a bra, voice lessons, and lessons in femininity including shopping tips, contemporary fashions, etc., are common at sites where learning takes place. To be "style-clueless" is a trans/gression to be avoided. Would you comment on this notion that transgender women want to reproduce the cultural construction of non-trans "woman," so they learn "to be feminine"?

Debra: In some situations, transgender women have the desire to reproduce the cultural construction of non-trans women and therefore strive to be "feminine" in all respects. This can be true for many of us as we have lived much of our lives hiding that feminine quality of our being. The coming-out process can unleash a desire to be "overly feminine" in every aspect of our lives. We sometimes feel and create an image that many genetic women would reject as conforming to what a male-dominated society would consider to be "gender polarized." Fortunately, as trans women become more comfortable in society and confident in society, our feelings and presentation become as diverse as that of most other women.

Bob: At the time of my study, the trans group, Renaissance, "an organization providing education and support," was but one example of many that were educating transsexuals. An issue of their newsletter stated, "It is interesting to keep in mind some of our overtly feminine gestures and postures we affect as part of our own ritual are actually designed to attract...partners" (Amberle, 1996, p. 8). Many MTFs challenge the objection of some women to becoming an object of desire; the art of promenading is a ritual that allows the actor to gaze *and* to be a spectacle, an object of another's gaze. Does this seem to align with your experience—that some trans women want to be the object of desire precisely because they are women—whether it's by another woman or a man? I think this is important for readers to understand since some people think that to be the object of another person's desire is always oppressive.

Debra: I believe that all beings have the desire to be "an object of another person's desires," or more simply put, to be "desirable," since the word "object" has other connotations. This is not just true of transgender women. The gender of the person whom we want to desire us is strictly a personal choice, depending on the sexual orientation of that being. I believe that all people want to feel wanted and loved. In my experience, most of us would choose to have a loving and caring partner rather than be alone. I believe that society has instilled that within us. The problem that many times occurs is that as transgender women we are not on a lot of folks' radar as a datable or desirable person.

Bob: I found that some MTF transsexuals exaggerate traditionally feminine traits and sex roles—traits and roles that some forms of feminism largely repudiate. Would you talk to me about what it means to "pass" as a woman?

Debra: Many transgender women put a lot of emphasis on what is commonly referred to in the transgender community as "passing." We believe that we need to look like and have people believe that we are, in fact, genetic women, not transgender women, in order to be truly successful in life and society. There are even websites that perpetuate the concept that "you can only be successful and happy" in your life if you "pass" as a genetic woman. I strongly disagree with this notion. I believe that this idea can actually create another closet that we must now try to live in, with the fear of people finding out that we are in fact transgender.

Bob: Califia (1997) points out that "passing" is critical to the process of transitioning. She writes, "[Transsexuals] must prove they are real before they are accepted for treatment. Thus the role of the medical-psychiatric establishment in reinforcing sex-role stereotypes is significant, and one that affects the deepest dimensions of the transsexual issue" (p. 96). As a result there is contention in expressing notions of beauty, femininity, and the construction of the "female body" between some people who reject the patriarchy and some transsexuals. Certain feminists, following Bordo (1993a), are opposed to the female body being "offered to a viewer purely as a spectacle...a visual commodity to be consumed" (Bordo, 1993b, p. 287).

Some feminists critique the construction of beauty, exercise and diet regimes, body enhancements, and commercial imperatives of pulchritude as erasing women's physical difference, promoting polysurgic addicts and "cultural plastic" and positioning women as objects of men's power-filled desires, subordinating them to men. Rejecting the marginalizing status of femininity, they challenge cultural and ideological formations of "the feminine." This was not the case for most of the transgender participants in my study. The MTFs seemed to worship normalized female beauty as they struggled to make their appearance coterminous with their self-perception and normalized social constructions of femininity. The transsexual cultural geography is different terrain; cultural geography, in the sense of Garrison (2000), means "material, political, social, ideological, and discursive landscapes that constitute the text, base or environment [of something]" (pp. 141-142). For transsexuals, their body inhabits specific social, historical, and discursive contexts not familiar to ciswomen. One pre-operative MTF informant claimed, "I l-o-o-v-e when a store clerk calls me *ma'am* even when I'm dressed as a man. I know [then that] I'm passing for [the woman that] I really am." Yet, another wrote, "If [people] think that looks make the woman, well, a little educational outreach will do them some good."

How do you feel about these two different positions: that one transgender person wants to be seen as an attractive woman and another one rejects the notion that appearances make the woman.

Debra: Both of these views are valid. The fact that one person may want to be seen as an attractive woman can easily coexist with the concept that appearances alone are not what makes us women. The complexities of who we are as multifaceted individuals make our appearance just a small, and actually relatively insignificant, part of our total being.

Bob: Carter (2006), a MTF transsexual, reminds us that "only transsexuals really and truly believe that they belong in the role of a woman (male to female, MTF) or a man (female to male, FTM) and live it twenty-four hours a day, every day of the year. This means the MTF transsexual has to cope using the skills and insights of a woman—or not at all" (p. 53). In her book, *Crossing: A Memoir*, McCloskey (1999) points to many reasons why MTF transgender individuals take up stereotypical feminine gestures and bodies. But ultimately her answer is simple: it's an act of deployment! To the charge that the gender crosser is perpetuating offensive clichés, she replies, "It's to keep from getting murdered, dear. Get it!" (personal communication, February 24, 2000). This transsexual notion of the body is similar to Merleau-Ponty's conceptualizations about the body as an "anchorage in the world" (1962, p. 144) and a "mediator of the world" (p. 145). "It is what opens [us] out upon the world and places [us] in a situation there" (p. 165). It is our "mode(s) of bodily being and the specificity of a given situation that we act meaningfully: we endow meaning on ourselves and our material and cultural situation" (Parkins, 2000, p. 60).

The discourse taken up by a large number of MTF transsexuals regarding femininity is especially troubling to Second Wave feminists[4] who regard it as a compromise or betrayal of feminism. From the social context of women's liberation of the 1960s and 1970s, femininity serves the interests of (biological) men. Second Wave feminists struggled to eliminate sex roles and gender-normative constructions in an effort to dissolve standardized gender categories. The struggle for women's equal rights in the battle over male oppression at times suggested a kind of cultural androgyny. Many Third Wave feminists, and those transsexuals who subscribe to beliefs held by Third Wave members, reject androgyny (the mixing of masculine and feminine characteristics) in favor of celebrating hardcore butch (masculinized) and sexy femme (highly feminized) roles. Would you comment on this? Do the trans folks you know reject the blending and blurring of male and female appearance?

Debra: Many of the transgender women I know would identify with Third Wave feminism, rejecting androgyny and adopting what might be considered more masculine or feminine roles. Depending on the social structure in which the trans woman was raised, including masculine and feminine expectations, geographic area, organizations that she may be a part of (both social and political), and expectations of her peers, this role could lead to the feminine or masculine. I find this to be just as true with those I know in the MTF community and even the lesbian community. I find it interesting that how we look or present ourselves *to* the world is even a topic of conversation or consideration in how we look *at* a person. I believe it is just superficial and in most cases has little to do with the ideology or beliefs of that person.

Bob: While not an intention—but clearly an outcome—MTF transsexuals help Third Wave feminists write over and remap the performance of femininity. In so doing, they rename things feminine—but no longer as respectable, rather, they become irreverent: that feminine person, constructed as an object of heterosex-

---

4 Feminism has been constructed as occurring in three waves. The First Wave was during the late 1800s into the 20th century. It involved the suffragettes and explored women's political rights, such as gaining voting privileges. The Second Wave was the rebirth of women's rights that happened in the 1960s and focused on equality in employment, society, and culture. This wave was identity-based and often assumed women and their experiences were essentially similar. The Third Wave emerged in the 1990s to contest the Second Wave's essentialist notions of femininity and rejected a monolithic image of "woman" and female identity. This wave is, in part, anti-identity and explores an intersectionality (with race, culture, sexualities, multiple ideologies, social movements, etc.) that emphasizes difference rather than similarity.

ual men's or Queer lesbians' desires, was once herself a biological man. Hetero-normative male sexual desire, in the face of feminized MTF transsexuals, has the seeds of its own unraveling. Gender is no longer a thing or reified but becomes a performance. Transsexuals reach into femininity to reclaim it and the result is not something normal or even heteronormalized, but something very Queer.

Debra: I would have to disagree that we reach into femininity to reclaim it and the result is not something normal. What is normal for one group or social structure can be very different for another group or social structure. We look at femininity from within a context of the internal construct of self, creating a whole person. Ask ten women what they would consider as feminine and you will get ten different answers. I believe our view of femininity is neither irreverent nor no longer respectable.

Bob: Some MTF transsexuals in the study related to the notions of the self-identi-fied mixed-race, White-trash, Queer girl, Amber Hollibaugh (2000), being "tired of whiny movement women who seem to want only what they [think] the men of their class already possess—rather than being amazed at the very privilege of their assumptions and their 'wanting' in the first place…sick at heart over a femi-nism and a Left driven by a deeply ungenerous disregard for difference" (p. 13). Amy Richards, co-author of *Manifesta: Young Women, Feminism, and the Future* (Baumgardner & Richards, 2000), points out, however, that not all transsexuals embrace femininity; some reject all gender labeling and present themselves more androgynously. Also, not all Third Wave feminists endorse feminine role con-struction. Would you comment on Amy Richards's thoughts?

Debra: I would have to agree with Amy Richards. Many transgender women have decided to reject societal roles and have adapted a mixture of femininity and androg-ynous nature that works for their particular beliefs, views, feelings, and situations.

Being "Out" as a Pedagogy of Presence, Reaching Out as a Pedagogy of Praxis

Bob: Presence, that is, being "out," was regarded as a quintessential educational expedient. This particular approach to adult education was not located in specific places or sites, but instead was based on a set of common understandings and prin-ciples precisely taught through exposure to new ideas, dialogue, and the shared experience of presence. For most, claiming an identity also included involvement in identity politics, either directly or in support of other trans folks who were agents of change. As one person opined, "The best gender-education ... [is for trans people to become] more common images." Talk to me, please, about "visibility."

Debra: I believe that the only person who can explain and truly understand what life is like living in the roles of both genders is a transgender person. I find it paramount in the credibility I have when presenting workshops or presentations on these issues, especially when I go into companies to coordinate a transition for a transgender employee. I can talk about my lived reality and experience. It is essential that we be out and visible people, taking part in our society as full participants, unashamed of who we are. There is power in self-acceptance, even when those around us are uncomfortable with who we are.

Bob: One informant said, "Finding ways to do trans-outreach has been very challenging." However, most respondents agreed that in addition to being out, "reaching out" was essential. Reaching out was about making connections to communities. One claimed, "As the partner of an MTF, every day is like educating the public just walking down the street." Out/reach was a key activity used to become known, ease fear, advocate for social change and challenge medical policy, provide or receive medical information, access information on constructing femininity, and seek justice and safety. The role of education in the emergence from gender confusion to personal responsibility was sometimes cited. Education was often couched in drag-culture "camp" or in activist rhetoric. Of significant concern to the transsexual participants was the frequency of hate crimes, including violent death, to which members were subject. Outreach often surrounded this theme.

Debra: Violence is common against members of the trans community. Even though much of this violence goes unreported, studies have shown that transgender people are one of the most discriminated-against groups and subject to a disproportional number of hate crimes. The transgender community even has a Day of Remembrance, when we remember the lives of those transgender people who were murdered each year. In 2008 we lost over 30 transgender people, murdered only because they were transgender. Information on this can be found at http://www.gender.org/remember/day.

Bob: Activist events, such as the Camp Trans incidents, were seen by some as "outreach rather than protest." As one put it, "Doing outreach to the Women's community is vital to me because, frankly, that's where i get my allies." A respondent claimed, "What I have done is to be my best, to act like a woman, the best I can and when the time is right to EDUCATE and that doesn't mean [an] IN YOUR FACE EDUCATION [capitalized in original]." Another wrote, "[Education] is mostly done at a one person at a time level." In an essay that was shared by a self-identified MTF transsexual lesbian, she wrote that walking into women's space "was one of the most affirming experiences of my life."

Balance and Unity

Bob: Multiple, and at times contentious, meanings emerged around the construction of a stable trans group identity that was produced for consumption and distribution in the public sphere. The term "educating" thus had various expressions and a fuller meaning than to provide learning opportunities for non-trans people. It also meant educating MTF transsexuals. After an activist event, one trans person wrote to me, "[This] was an important education for me about TG [transgender]/TS [transsexual] issues, and started me on my own path to transition." Education, too, did not exclude providing help and information to FTM folks. There was a strong effort not to privilege MTF transsexuals over FTMs.

Debra: In some parts of the country MTF and FTM groups work in harmony when educating and even when sponsoring social events. Groups exist that do not even have either identification, but rather just "transgender" groups. This takes time to develop. As with typical men's and women's groups, common goals, objectives, and ideologies must be combined and shared.

Bob: Some discussions focused on male privilege. In one series of repartees on a feedback website, a post-operative MTF "with a few decades of feminism behind [me]" responded to a self-identified "male member of the feminist community" that his attitudes were "so incredibly indicative of that you have yet to shed your male privilege," claiming that his was "not a respectful or feminist attitude...[but] reek[ed] of male privilege and entitlement."

A few self-identified masculine women were strident about *feminine privilege* and one transsexual wrote about genetic women's rejection of MTF transsexuals: "Last time I checked, feminism was about exactly this: GETTING TO DO WHATEVER THE GODDAMNED HELL YOU WANTED TO DO AND NOT ANSWER TO ANYONE FOR IT. A core notion of FEMINISM. Isn't it, after all, a radical idea that **WOMEN ARE NOT FAINTING FLOWERS??????**...Get over yourselves for gods sake. I've had it with being bullied by white females with awful hair and big words [capitalized and punctuated in original]." By adding the comment about "awful hair," the respondent was saying, "I'm more of a woman than you who have taken up the socially constructed expression of 'feminine' to mean 'woman.'"

Debra: Of course this tension exists between strong women with strong ideas and ideals—this is true of both trans and genetic women. I would have to say that the things we have been fighting for as women and feminists, for decades, include the idea that as women we can believe whatever we want, and no one has the right to dictate to us what we should believe, how we should live our lives, or what we should look like. Can it get any more basic than that? We are all individuals and should be accepted as just that – for who we are.

Bob: To counter male privilege, frequently FTM resources were noted in educational publications. One group, American Boyz (www.amboyz.org/) specialized in educational opportunities for tomboys, butches, drag kings, and others, especially people of color, Spanish-speaking FTMs, and SOFFAs (significant others, friends, and families of transsexuals).

Unity in sexual-minority communities was evidenced in many ways. One transsexual activist wrote to me, "To a person, we cannot agree on the simplest of things. That is why I believe that until we be united behind a common cause, we will continue to be marginalized, because we cannot be taken seriously." Appeals for unity are exemplified by activist Riki Anne Wilchins in *Queer Theory, Gender Theory* (2004). As a Camp Trans organizer Riki exclaimed, "We're calling on everyone -- Menace members, Lesbian Avengers, Riot Grrrls, stone butches, diesel dykes, high femmes, intersexuals, transfags and faggot-identified dykes, FTMs, genderbenders, gender-blenders, transwomen, leatherdykes and dyke daddies, passing women, drag kings, and gendertrash of all descriptions. Being gender-different is not just a 'trans right,' it's a woman's right too" (*Protest called for women's music festival discriminatory policy still in effect*, 1999, para. 8). The call to end marginalization of all women was often repeated in writings and in interviews. This suggested the need for unity within diversity and a willingness to collapse identity into similarities rather than differences. On the other hand, at least one respondent reacted to unity with the notion that similarities within difference mattered. She wrote, "I am hoping that more trans women would recognize their uniqueness as well as their similarities to non-trans women....Unity of women does not require [trans folks] to ignore our differences; we only need to appreciate and celebrate them." Evans and Gamman (1995) describe the "paradox of cohesive identity" for political communities to maintain a narrative space and the drawbacks that such a fixed identity produce. The simultaneous intersection of collective identity and difference adds to a critical postmodern theorization of transsexualism. Do you have any thoughts on what it means to be unique women as trans women and at the same time to look for unity with genetic women?

Debra: The fact that we are transgender makes us unique women. We cannot get around that. We have had experiences that most genetic women have never had, just as genetic women have had experiences that transgender women have never had. I believe we should combine these unique experiences and create an even stronger and more vital women's movement, using our experiences to work for common causes.

Differences: Generational, Regional, and Class

Bob: One of the participants in my study wrote, "We are accomplishing [acceptance, support, and enthusiasm] because of the power of our ideas and the truths of our individual lives." Another claimed, "I say just go and be your best and try to show and teach so that we can eventually make a change." There were frequent remarks about generational differences; some self-identified "older" transsexuals attributed progress to the attitudes of younger generations. Another wrote, "I notice that my younger friends accept gender-bending of all kinds more readily, so I think that there is generational change coming." This belief was echoed by a 41-year-old self-described MTF transitioning lesbian feminist: "Younger dykes play with gender with a breathtaking forthrightness which I find invigorating." Beam (2007) discusses the dizzying mix of typical youth drama with the far more uncharacteristic challenges that the younger trans generation face than their non-trans counterparts. Do you have any thoughts on generational differences within the transgender community? How are your experiences different than those of much younger trans people? In your traveling around the United States, do you see regional differences in the trans community?

Debra: There are many generational differences in how trans people within the transgender community think. The fluidity of gender seems easier to express and experience within our younger transgender brothers and sisters. The notion of only two genders is now rejected by many young transgender people and their organizations. Many young people now find comfort and acceptance floating somewhere in the middle of the gender spectrum. Older transgender people seem to gravitate toward a more traditional view of the concept of man or woman. Also, growing up, there was no Internet and few written materials about transgender people or our community. There were not even "out" gay and lesbian groups for those of us who grew up in years past. It has only been in the last decade or two that the transgender community has been visible at all.

Most transgender communities and organizations I came in contact with during my recent traveling throughout the country as a speaker and lecturer (over 400 campus and university presentations) were small and seem to depend on a single strong leader and organizer. Because of this, membership and activities could be quite different year to year, depending on who that leader is. Sometimes the groups would even disappear for a time. Most transgender people I met on campus tended to be active in the campus LGBT group, most times being one of their few out transgender members. With a few exceptions, it seemed like only large, liberal campuses had "transgender" organizations.

Bob: Regionalism appeared to play some role in the type of education in which transsexuals engaged. One transsexual, writing from rural North Carolina, stated, "Here, there is no education [going on]…education is something that occurs in larger cities with more diversity." Although this study did not examine class and economic issues, some respondents' comments and trans community literature suggest that both are topics that merit deeper exploration. For instance, in the June 1996 number of Renaissance's newsletter, *News and Views*, an article appeared about a "'community computer,' passed along to needy gender folk." The article goes on to describe what can be done to bring older, seemingly useless computers to function as an Internet educational tool for economically "needy" transgender individuals. Costs of hormonal and surgical transitioning preclude expensive computer purchases for some. For the economically disadvantaged, seemingly a disproportionate number of whom are people of color, money for identity and body reconstruction was out of reach. As one interviewee wrote, "Economics is a central theme in any trans activism."

Debra: As with all economically disadvantaged people, our transgender population is affected too. Just the necessities of being able to continue on a hormone regimen can be difficult. And medically, treatment should not be stopped once it is started. Also, the difficulty of continuing with monitoring of hormone levels and basic blood work can be cost-prohibitive. Gender reassignment surgery can be completely out of reach for most unless health insurance policies cover such procedures, as do most carriers in Minnesota and a few other progressive states. Assuming that the transgender person has access to health coverage, even the cost of working with a health professional to get *approved* for surgery can be out of reach. Fortunately, for finding and communicating with other transgender people, computers are commonly available. Access is easier than in 1996 when I transitioned; however, there is a significant problem in that these places offer little if any privacy.

Transfeminism

Bob: Western society seems to be structured such that there are "women by chance" (genetic/biological, women-born women), "women by choice"[5] (transgender and transsexual persons whose core gender identity differs from what is culturally associated with their biological sex at birth [Hogan & Hudson, 1998]) who elect to transgress expected gender presentation, and "women by force" (intersexuals whose anatomy is assigned at birth, or later, historically often by coerced "normalization" because medical discourse labels their genitalia ambiguous). Members of each of these categories have constructed registers of feminist discourse. Do you have any thoughts on the idea that you are a "woman by choice," as some might suggest?

Debra: This is an interesting concept, this "woman by choice." Does anyone really believe that transgender people would choose to live this kind of early life of shame and guilt, being classified by the medical profession as having a mental illness (DSM IV 302.85: "Gender Identity Disorder") with a suicide rate many times the average for other populations? Most of society looks on us as "very different" people. We are not welcome in most places of worship and looked on as abnormal by many. Many individuals feel the only real choice we have is when we stop hiding from ourselves and society and accept who we are as proud and

---

5 Some would argue that this is not a valid category because claiming female identity and the internal desire to be a woman, despite one's anatomy, is not about choice; transgender expression and appearance might be.

vital people and "come out" not only to ourselves but to society and to the world.

Bob: It was in the 1980s that "critical theorists became increasingly fascinated with ambiguity and, in particular, with bodies, genders, sexualities, and practices which appeared to defy traditional forms of categorization" (Sullivan, 2003, p. 99) predicated upon social constructions, experiences, history, and culture. This focus on ambiguity was taken up by Queer theorists, including those with trans-sexual bodies, which "transgress, and thus help to dismantle, binary oppositions such as male/female, nature/culture, heterosexual/homosexual, and so on" (p. 99). For a lengthy discussion of this, see "Transsexual Empires and Transgender Warriors," in Sullivan (2003, pp. 99-118).

One of the prospective educational avenues cited by a respondent was coursework in "transfeminism." Yet, with few exceptions, only a sparse number of the original 26 transsexuals/intersexuals interviewed could explain transfeminism. However, feminism too is a difficult term to describe. As Whelehan (1995) writes, "Feminism is itself problematic, because the theories that inform it are heterogenous" (p. 25). Yet, she has discovered that "all feminist positions are founded upon the belief that women suffer from systematic social injustices because of their sex and therefore, 'any feminist is, at the very minimum, committed to some form of reappraisal of the position of women in society'" (Evans, 1986, p. 2). One respondent offered, "What I experience as a transsexual woman is exactly what other women experience, but on a much deeper level, in my view. I could cite examples from employment discrimination to child adoption to rape and hate crime. I believe, and have for decades, that the experiences of transsexual women could be a great benefit to women everywhere. But this never gets articulated because we remain the 'bastard stepchildren' of the women's movement. We are an image problem and a public relations nightmare to them. It is sad, but true."

Debra: This concept that we are the "bastard stepchild" is not only true when talking about our relationship with the women's movement but also true within the LGBT community. This was especially true a few years ago when many local and national gay and lesbian organizations struggled with transgender people and our political issues. I was attending a national conference where the speaker was the president of a large, national, well-respected organization, and one of his statements was that he did not know much about the transgender community, so they did not deal with those issues. At that time I was the only transgender person at the conference, so, of course, I had something to say about that during the question and answer period. We are also not recognized many times when companies and other organizations talk about diversity and diversity training within their organizations. Even if they include gay and lesbian issues, unless the organization is truly on the cutting edge of what is happening with diversity training, transgender people and the discrimination and harassment issues that happen within many workplaces are still never addressed. The attitude also exists that "we don't have any of *those people* here, so we don't have to deal with *that*." I find this true even within the diversity training that happens in most universities and colleges around the country. For those of you who are reading this—have you had transgender issues included within the diversity training you have attended?

Bob: In contrast to the beliefs of the participant quoted above, another reflected, "It's futile [and flawed] to insist that we trans women are 'just like' non-trans women; as a group, we have distinct experiences...and are different in certain ways from non-trans women as a group. We are pretty unique, so to speak....However, we are not so unique that our experiences put us outside of the feminist constituency." For example, Koyama (1999), a respondent, wrote, "Transfeminism cuts through all of the major themes of Third Wave feminism: diversity, postmodern identities, body image/consciousness, self-definition, and female agency." It has been pointed out that this "is not merely about merging trans politics [with] feminism, but it is a critique of the Second Wave feminism from Third Wave perspectives." It is significant to note that the transsexuals in this study felt that of all female-born feminists, those most likely to support transsexuals' claims to womanhood are Third Wave feminists. For most, this discourse is happening outside the walls of academia and more traditional feminist institutions. As Orr (1997) claims, assuming a position in popular culture allows the Third Wave to venture onto the stage where "feminism [first] captured popular imagination—and thus political clout—in the 1960s and early 1970s" (p. 41).

Koyama (1999, 2004) also points to the diverse strands of "transfeminism." Transfeminism has at least two distinct expressions in the trans community. One is the application of feminist perspectives to the trans discourse, aptly called "transsexual feminism." The individuals espousing this are feminist transsexuals, people who bring feminist principles to transsexual discourse. The publication, *TransSisters: The Journal of Transsexual Feminism,* champions this perspective. In its statement of purpose, the journal reports, in part, to "[give] voice to the ideas, feelings, concerns, and perspectives of transsexual feminists...to end the misperceptions that transsexuality and feminism are antithetical...to end the invisibility and marginalization of transsexual persons within the feminist community...to promote feminist consciousness within the transsexual community ...[and] to [empower] transsexual persons through feminist principles." Jessica Xavier is another transsexual feminist who self-identifies as both a "feminist, transgendered political activist" and a "transfeminist." Her work (posted during the time of my study at http://www.annelawrence.com/jessica.html) states that her struggles paralleled that of non-transgender people, especially those who became strong-willed and tough-minded in order to survive.

A second manifestation of transfeminism is more than a transsexual reading of feminism. It is about establishing transfeminism within the mainstream of feminism with specific content that relates to transsexuals' experiences but which are applicable to all women. Transfeminism has characteristics unique and special to the trans community. When articulated, this trans/vision makes the family of feminisms (Marxist, radical, Black, lesbian, socialist, etc.) richer. A scholarly illumination of this is found in the evolution of the writings of Emi Koyama. Her work, titled *The Transfeminist Manifesto*, from 1999 (see http://eminism. org/readings/pdf-rdg/tfmanifesto.pdf) and its 2004 revision are insightful. In the original manifesto, Koyama contends:

> *Transfeminism is primarily of and for trans women who view their liberation to be intrinsically linked to the liberation of women as a whole. It is also open to other queers, intersex people, trans men [FTM transsexuals], non-trans women as well as non-trans men who are sympathetic towards the needs of trans women and consider their alliance with trans women to be essential for their liberation. (para. 4).*

In 2004, however, she writes:

> *The paper, "The Transfeminist Manifesto," is a radical feminist text that followed the radical feminist orthodoxy as closely as possible while attempting to make a pro-transsexual and transgender argument. The problem is that in the process I had to limit myself to defending only a certain *kind* of trans people, while remaining silent about others because they did not fit into the radical feminist worldview that I was basing my argument on. Its consideration of race, class, and other social factors was also weak, because at the time I did not feel confident enough to challenge the primacy of sexism as the fundamental oppression.*

At best, the paper was my attempt to reconcile the radical feminist views I had been taught at undergraduate Women's Studies courses and my frustration at a major bashing campaign against a transsexual woman friend that was happening at the time in Portland, Oregon lesbian community....I have since come to disagree with much of what I wrote in the "Manifesto" itself, as I became more confortable [sic] discussing trans issues (and anti-racism, anti-classism, and so on) on its own merit rather than from within a preconceived framework.... (para. 2-4)

She goes on to invite "more transfeminist manifestos to be produced."

Debra: I believe that this work needs to be done. My views, however, are those of inclusion and finding common ideologies and issues, the things that bring us together, not the things that may separate us.

Bob: The Feminist Conspiracy, a group that embraced transfeminism at the time of the study, was devoted to those feminists who were pro-sex, pro-porn, and pro-choice and was established for those who liked to call themselves "girls" while insisting to be treated like adult women. The Feminist Conspiracy was created to engage in direct action to empower women and girls to be autonomous, and to replace former feminist tactics. Koyama's (2000-2001) collection of essays is a crucial analysis in which trans liberation is defined as "taking back the right to define ourselves from medical, religious and political authorities" (p. 6). Transfeminist projects included organizing sex workers' rights. This issue intersects with Queer theorists' notions as well. For instance, Hollibaugh (2000), a non trans Queer feminist, writes that street work allowed her to make "real money for the first time in [her] life and [gain her] first sense of personal power over men" (p. 41). (For research on sex workers, originally presented at an Adult Education Research Conference, see Hill, 2005). Other transfeminist goals included trans and intersexual activism and education, education on domestic violence against women and Queer survivors, and expanding the reproductive choice movement, including the right of the poor to have children (also on the Third Wave feminist agenda, e.g., see Baumgardner & Richards, 2000, p. 279), defending rights to abortion and birth control, and issues of sterilization abuse against poor women.

Both strands of transfeminism challenge the rigorously policed links between biological sex and gender. The intersexual movement illustrates this best, and often most tragically. One of their educational goals is to change the medical community's attitude that a penis less than one inch at birth does not count. As intersexuals point out, being a "man" in society is like joining a strict club that has very stiff rules for membership. Likewise, they challenge the medical notion that a clitoris larger than three-eighths inch at birth must be altered. Intersexuals read the medical message to say that an enlarged clitoris is too much like a male organ and so must be "trimmed"—females must never be in possession of the ultimate symbol of male power, even a "defective" one. Biological males must not possess an "inferior" penis either; when the sex of the child is not in doubt, such as when the penis opening is on the undersurface base, "[the biological boy] routinely receive[s] surgery—on the premise that boys need to be able to pee standing up" (Nussbaum, 1999). One intersexual activist, altered by forced surgery and socialized as a female, recalls having medically defined ill-formed male organs, which were removed at age five. When she "asked the doctor where [her] thing was [after surgery] he said, 'We had to take it off because you want to look like the other little girls in your class'" (Cowley, 1997). Health-care practitioners worry that intersex children will never fit in and often feel obligated to create a "normal" appearance; the message is clear—gender, as well as one's biological sex, is attributable to genitals. What are your thoughts on the forced surgery that some intersexed people have experienced?

Debra: I have friends who have experienced this type of surgery. In one case the person had been altered to appear female and to function in most ways as a woman. When I knew her, she was identifying as an FTM transsexual. When exploratory surgery was performed, they found a penis tucked into her abdomen that would ache and give her much pain when she became sexually excited. During her gender surgery as an adult, this "penis" was used as the base of creating her "new" anatomy.

Many within the intersex community believe that the intersex child should be the person who decides which gender and sex they are. Most children have developed their sexual identities very early in their childhood.

To Some, a Menacing Feminism

Bob: The writings of Wilchins (2004) seem pertinent here. She argues:

> Feminists remain largely unsure what to make of transgender people. FTM transsexuals are simply confusing—they seem to be women who've given up the battle against patriarchy and joined the other side. And imitation may be the sincerest form of flattery[;] many feminists suspect the MTF transsexuals...are merely pretending to be women—enacting a parody of

sexism's worst excesses in makeup, high heels, and inevitably prodigious breasts. (p. 28)

In a flier distributed at the 1994 MWMF, two gender outlaws with divergent beliefs co-wrote, "In defying [a rigid, destructive, and archaic gender system] we learn to convert fear into anger [and] this makes us dangerous" (Dobkin & Wilchins, 1995). Califia (1997) notes:

Nothing upsets the underpinnings of feminist fundamentalism more than the existence of transsexuals. A being with male chromosomes, a female appearance, a feminist consciousness, and a lesbian identity explodes all of their assumptions about the villainy of men. And someone with female chromosomes who lives as a man strikes at the heart of the notion that all women are sisters, potential feminists, natural allies against the aforementioned villainy. (pp. 91-92)

MTF trans members are engaged in informal education for control and ownership of the meaning of "woman" and are employing transfeminist discourse as a counterhegemonic practice. Transfeminism is *pro-feminist* (supportive of) as well as *proto-feminist* (archetypal, a prototype of feminism). Transsexual feminists claim that transfeminism exemplifies the kind of self-determination that is a prerequisite of feminism. It is proto-feminist in that it critiques mainstream notions of masculinity. It is pro-feminist in that it takes up the sentiment that women are humans deserving equal rights in society and that gender is a patriarchal social construct used to oppress women. One transsexual wrote that "a feminist approach cannot stigmatize on the basis of a different class of women, it must also begin to be sensitive that **many** different kinds of people shelter under and live under that category of 'woman.'" One transgender activist articulates that being an outlaw is "something all women understand: our bodies being disrespected, our rights, our capabilities, our very lives being so devalued" (Feinberg, 1995).

Significance to Adult Education: Trans/actional Education

Bob: Adult education has a venerable and long history and commitment to political action and social transformation. My study, in part, positioned direct action (activism) as a pedagogical tool, located transsexuality and intersexuality as sites of learning in adulthood, and situated them as places for knowledge and meaning making. It captured an underinvestigated new social movement that takes up trans/gressive acts and constructs learning communities built on difference. Transsexual MTFs and intersexuals have bodily identities different than females by birth. I think that the transfeminist discourse emerging here provides unique opportunities to challenge the institutionalized sex/gender binary, perhaps in ways that other feminisms do not. Hird (2000) argues convincingly that the overall feminist project has depended on a heteronormative definition of "woman." She points out that even postmodern feminists, while focusing on the body as fragmented, in the end remain "conceptual and remote from the everyday material relations of 'gender,' where 'sex' is fully grounded" (p. 349). Only MTF transsexuals "focus the assumption that you need a particular morphological configuration to 'know' yourself as female" (p. 349), and intersexuals "radically confront the modern two-sex model of sexual difference, and medical accounts of their sex 'reassignment' [telling] a disturbing story of the literal reinscription of sex on to 'unruly' bodies" (p. 349).

Mainstream adult education has been heavily influenced by various feminisms. For a decade it has been challenged by the project of "troubling" the boundaries of sexual orientation (Hill, 1995, 1996), but it has yet to address gender identity, expression, and presentation in any significant way. bell hooks (1994) reminds us that the feminist movement has been notorious for its censorship and exclusionary behavior, and she proposes that it will grow and mature only to the degree that it passionately welcomes and encourages, in theory and practice, diversity of opinion, new ideas, critical exchange, and dissent. Eisenstein (1991) criticizes feminism for becoming respectable, drifting from its radical roots. Zita (1997), a self-identified Second Wave feminist, writes:

> *The most pressing task for the feminisms of our time, both inside and outside the academy, is [the] cross-generational moment [in dialoguing with Third Wavers]: a passage of legacy, wisdom, memory, and yet unanswered questions and unresolved conflicts belonging to political and intellectual struggles that are much larger than life itself and much too important to leave behind without dialogue across the generations. (p. 1)*

Transsexual feminism is surely a significant ingredient of the Third Wave's "rally to embrace the complications of power in a discursive space that brings together populist activism, communities of resistance, strategies of intervention, and academic production" (Zita, 1997, p. 1), not usually grasped by those in the Second Wave.

Unfortunately, many Second Wave feminists "don't see feminism unless it looks like their brand" (Baumgardner & Richards, 2000, p. 223). Such myopia hurts all women, especially at a time when the continued viability of feminist studies is questioned (Brown, 1997). Feinberg (1996) reminds us that "the development of the trans movement has raised a vital question that's being discussed in women's communities all over the [U.S.]....'How is women defined?' The answer we give may determine the course of women's liberation for decades to come" (p. 109). Transfeminism opens up new possibilities for feminist debate; it can help mainstream feminisms to regain their lost rebellious center and subversive quality. Too, it will reshape the impact of inclusionary feminisms on adult education.

What are your thoughts on the ways that transgender education can aid feminism?

Debra: For those who believe in change and the acceptance of diverse opinions and discourses, our views of feminism can and must transform with the times, possibly a "fourth wave" of feminism that encompasses the views of all who identify as feminists and believe that all who identify as women can and should be welcomed. We all believe that as women we should have complete control of who we are as people, physically, emotionally, and mentally. Our bodies, our minds, and our hearts are ours to do with as we choose. And no one "kind" of woman is any more important or valid than any other. As women we should strive to create a culture that is equal for all people in all ways. We must invest in the joy of who we are and celebrate that together.

Bob: The Internet and web-based learning play a vital educational role in transsexual and intersexual communities; electronic bulletin boards, listservs, web-based discussions, and website documents (e.g., newsletters, zines, public and private announcements) are sources of information, education, skills development, and learning. Web-based communications were explored from the perspectives of the content of conversations, material culture including products and services, the role of agency and activities including activism, and personal statements vital for the construction of new knowledges, identities, and avatars (a computer user's text construction that represents herself, an alter ego). Owing to the power of ICTs, some educational efforts were made by transsexual activists to educate members on how to access online information. Because ITCs and cyberactivism are critical to trans education, they are readymade tools for research.

Debra: Today computers and the Internet are commonplace. The isolation that most transgender people felt during the early part of their development and coming-out process is now ameliorated by hundreds, possibly thousands, of resources on the net available to all. The net is used as a communication tool for most organizations, and electronic newsletters are even more common than standard printed copy that formerly was available. Anyone with a computer can now develop a web presence that can be accessed by anyone online. The days of mimeograph newsletters have come and gone. If a person wants to find and communicate with others in her community, it is relatively easy to do online.

Bob: While the use of the Internet in research has been explored in limited ways elsewhere (Markham, 1998), this study suggests that online data retrieval (both through "lurking" and personal correspondence) and computer communications are instruments for data gathering with action-oriented subjects. Advantages of screen-based techniques include communication at unprecedented speed, adult educators unbounded by physical location or certain personal limitations, and meaningful expansion of social interactions. Disadvantages of electronic communications encompass the filtering out and alteration of much of the nuance, warmth, and contextuality that seem important to fully human, morally engaged interaction (Sclove, 1997), and the interviewees' environments, often read as a text by researchers, are missing. Authenticity can be an issue as well. This is powerfully discussed by Wesch (n.d.). Additionally, only those on the wealthier side of the "electronic divide" are reached.

—·— ≕✦≔ —·—

Trans/posing Myself in the Research

Bob: Reactions to my incursions into the trans community, as an outsider, varied. A consequential reason to cooperate was stated by one of those interviewed: "It's especially important given your position as an educator." One wrote, "I've always had the impression that we T*folk have few allies in the lesbigay community; I'm glad that you're one of them, and I appreciate your efforts on our behalf." Another asked:

I would like to know if you yourself are transgendered. I am a transfeminist (this is the only word that I have ever heard to describe it), and feel that we are being fed upon by researchers from all schools in academia. Hell you know it's bad when English scholars begin doing textual analyses of our identities and bodies. Anyway I would love to help if you are not just another non-trans bottom feeder. We as transgendered people are more than capable of producing studies of our own cultural development, and many of us are beginning to feel the way gay and lesbian people do about heterosexuals studying them.

My presence in the transsexual community's dialogues was most apparent in a brief interaction that I had with one who self-identified as "a full member of the National Organization of Women, and one of the most vocal transsexual feminists there is." At the beginning she wrote, "I detest the term 'transfeminist' because it not only marginalizes me as a feminist, but as a woman as well." For her, arguing "gender theory" was odd; she likened it to "sitting around while Rome burns." In a compelling essay, she wrote that the term "transfeminism" was discordant with her experiences. She penned, "It saddens me very much to see some women battle for so long to simply be women, then separate themselves." For her, being born a male was a "birth defect"; how could you be trans anything if you were, from the very start, what you ended up being? After a period of sharing with her the ideas expressed by self-identified transfeminists, she wrote, "Put in the proper context, there can be transfeminism. And, after considering [some] points, should be."

Do you have any thoughts on a gay man doing research about the transgender community?

Debra: My feelings are that anyone who has an interest in research should be given the opportunity to develop that research. Why should only those who are transgender be doing research on our own community. It would make no sense. At present there is little data or formal research being conducted on transgender people. Public funding for these studies is scarce and when research projects are funded, many times they are part of a broader, more mainstream topic such as HIV/AIDS within the transgender community. Very few mainstream professional journals include articles or studies about our community. Of course, our own professional transgender organizations are an exception to this.

Final Thoughts

Bob: A few of those interviewed expressed opposition to the notion that transsexuality had a strong political dimension. For others, the act of transitioning seemed to be an ultimate defiance of the "cultural gaze." In popular discourse, normalized bodies are objects of prescribed desires. The fact that MTF transsexuals at one time possessed male bodies challenges the structurally embedded gender system. One responded, "I do agree with what you are saying, but I don't think transsexuals themselves like being seen as challenging the dominant culture. Transitioning is a private act for me, and I don't use it politically even though I can think of many ways I could." Yet, others viewed the mere presence of an out trans person as an act of confrontation and activism, supporting Califia's (1997) statement that radical activism was the most important factor that impacted transgender identity in the nineties.

Do you think that transitioning is a public or a private act, or both? Is it political?

Debra: I believe that transition is both a private and public act. It is a private and personal decision to accept who we are as transgender men or women and no longer need to hide that fact from the world. In other words, come out, or transition. It is a public act in the fact that now the world, and those around us who may have known us in the opposite gender role, must deal with our new image—our new presentation. Of course, we are the same persons; however, sometimes it takes time for those who know us to realize and accept that fact.

The question whether transitioning is political or not is an interesting one. For me, it was a very personal and spiritual journey, and I needed to be honest with myself and those around me and let them know who I really was—that is, a woman. I also needed to live my life in every way as my true gender and never again to have to pretend to be a man. It was a very spiritual journey. But because of my situation and the circumstances around my transition, being one of the first secondary school educators in the country who worked directly with children to successfully transition on the job in the middle of the school year was considered very political. I was considered an activist even though I did not consider myself to be one. Many believe that the fact that we have transgressed gender roles in every way, we are indeed political.

Bob: It has been written that much is known about the obvious physical transition of transsexuals (Burns, 2003):

> *their path to the operating theater, and all of the tears, drama, and obstacles that have to be regarded as the natural rites of passage on the gender-crossing road. Far less seems to have been written about what lies beyond the knife—that time when the stitches have come out and the physical wounds have healed, and when the newly liberated person is set loose on the world with a blank canvas on which to paint a life. (p. 188)*

This chapter is, hopefully, a glimpse into how some transsexuals have drawn their portraits, even though not all had undergone surgical transitioning. Burns outlines her own crossing, ending with the notion that two crossings actually occurred. The first was the transition from a little girl into a big girl's body. The second was a "more spiritual transition into maturity as a new woman" (p. 202). That step was much harder than the first crossing. It was a "spiritual journey towards completeness" (p. 202) and one that led her to become an adult educator, "set out to teach people what [she] see[s]." Her goal is to help the world by assisting all of us to better "read and understand" (p. 202) it. This too is our goal as authors of this work.

References

Amberle, D. (1996). Vis a vis. *News and Views* (a Renaissance publication), *10*(6), 8-9.

Baumgardner, J., & Richards, A. (2000). *Manifesta: Young women, feminism, and the future*. NY: Farrar, Straus and Giroux.

Beam, C. (2007). *Transparent: Love, family, and living the T with transgender teenagers*. NY: Harcourt.

Bem, S. (1993). *The lens of gender: Transforming the debate on sexual inequality*. Binghamton, NY: Vail-Ballou Press.

Boshier, R. (1999). Adult education adrift in a net: Making waves or clutching a lifering? *Proceedings of the 40th Annual Adult Education Research Conference*. Retrieved December 14, 2008, from http://www.adulterc.org/Proceedings/1999/ 99symp_boshier.htm

Boshier, R., & Pisutova, K. (2002). Using the Internet for informal learning about joining the brain drain: A qualitative Central/East European and Pacific perspective. *Proceedings of the 43rd Annual Adult Education Research Conference*. Retrieved December 14, 2008, from http://www.adulterc.org/Proceedings/2002/papers/ Boshier.pdf

Bordo, S. (1993a). Feminism, Foucault and the politics of the body. In C. Ramazanoglu (Ed.), *Up against Foucault: Exploration of some tensions between Foucault and feminism* (pp. 179-202). NY: Routledge.

Bordo, S. (1993b). Material girl: The effacements of postmodern culture. In C. Schwichtenberg (Ed.), *The Madonna connection* (pp. 265-290). Sydney, New South Wales: Allen and Unwin.

Brooks, A. (1997). *Postfeminisms: Feminism, cultural theory and cultural forms*. NY: Routledge.

Brown, W. (1997). The impossibility of women's studies. *Differences, 9*, 79-101.

Burns, C. (2003). The second transition. In T. O'Keefe & K. Fox (Eds.), *Finding the real me: True tales of sex and gender diversity* (pp. 188-202). San Francisco: Jossey-Bass.

Butler, J. (1997). Against proper objects. In E. Weed & N. Schor (Eds.), *Feminism meets queer theory* (pp. 1-30). Bloomington, IN: Indiana University Press.

Butler, J. (1999). *Gender trouble: Feminism and the subversion of identity*. NY: Routledge.

Califia, P. (1997). *Sex changes: The politics of transgenderism*. San Francisco: Cleis Press.

Carter, L. (2006). Female by surgery. In K. Scott-Dixon (Ed.), *Trans/forming feminisms: Transfeminist voices speak out* (pp. 53-57). Toronto: Sumach Press.

Castells, M. (1998). *The power of identity*. Oxford: Blackwell.

Cowley, G. (1997, May 19). Gender limbo. *Newsweek*, 64-66.

Cresswell, J. W. (1998). *Qualitative enquiry and research design: Choosing among five traditions*. London: Sage.

Crowther, J., ScAndrétt, E., Martin, I., & Hemmi, A. (2007). Learning through ICTs in social movements: A case study of the environmental justice movement in Scotland. Retrieved December 14, 2008, from http://www.education.ed.ac.uk/ hce/learninginsocialmovements/

Dobkin, A., & Wilchins, R. A. (1995). Pink and blue...Not! *TransSister: The Journal of Transexual Feminism, 7,* 38.

Eisenstein, H. (1991). *Gender shock: Practicing feminism on two continents.* Boston: Beacon Press.

Evans, C., & Gamman, L. (1995). The gaze revisited, or reviewing queer viewing. In P. Burton & C. Richard (Eds.), *A queer romance: Lesbian, gay men and popular culture* (pp. 13-56). NY: Routledge.

Evans, J. (Ed.). (1986). *Feminism and political theory.* London: Sage.

Fausto-Sterling, A. (2005). *Two sexes are not enough.* In R. Fiske-Rusciano & V. Cyrus (Eds.), *Experiencing race, class, and gender in the United States* (4th ed.). Boston: McGraw-Hill.

Feinberg, L. (1992). *Trans gender liberation: A movement whose time has come.* NY: World View Forum.

Feinberg, L. (1995). Excerpts from "Sisterhood: Make it real!" *TransSister: The Journal of Transexual Feminism, 7,* 24-26.

Feinberg, L. (1996). *Transgender warriors: Making history from Joan of Arc to Dennis Rodman.* Boston: Beacon Press.

Gamson, J. (1998). Must identity movements self-destruct? A queer dilemma. In P. M. Nardi & B. E. Schneider (Eds.), *Social perspectives in lesbian and gay studies* (pp. 589-604). NY: Routledge.

Garrison, E. K. (2000). U.S. feminism—Grrl style! Youth (sub)cultures and the technologies of the Third Wave. *Feminist Studies, 26*(1), 141-170.

Giroux, H. (1993). *Border crossings: Cultural workers and the politics of education.* NY: Routledge.

Gramsci, A. (1971). *Selections from the prison notebooks of Antonio Gramsci.* (Q. Hoare & G. N. Smith, Trans.). NY: International Publishers.

Gustafson, D. L. (1999). Embodied learning. In M Mayberry & E. C. Rose (Eds.), *Innovative feminist pedagogies in action: Meeting the challenge* (pp. 249-273). NY: Routledge.

Hill, R. J. (1995). A critique of heterocentric discourse in adult education: A critical review. *Adult Education Quarterly, 45*(3), 142-158.

Hill, R. J. (1996). Learning to transgress: A sociohistorical conspectus of the American gay lifeworld as a site of struggle and resistance. *Studies in the Education of Adults, 28*(2), 253-279.

Hill, R. J. (2003). Working memory at AERC: A Queer welcome ... and a retrospective.

In R. J. Hill (Ed.), *Queer histories: Exploring fugitive forms of social knowledge— The First Annual LGBTQ&Allies Pre-Conference (pp. 11-28)*. San Francisco: San Francisco State University. (ERIC document CE085106)

Hill, R. J. (2005, Spring). POZ-itively transformational: Sex workers and HIV/ AIDS education. In J. P. Egan (Ed.), *HIV/AIDS education for adults* (pp. 75-84). New Directions for Adult and Continuing Education, No. 105. San Francisco: Jossey-Bass.

Hill, R. J. (Ed.). (2006). *Challenging homophobia and heterosexism: Lesbian, gay, bisexual, transgender and queer issues in organizational settings.* New Directions for Adult and Continuing Education, No. 112. San Francisco: Jossey-Bass.

Hird, M. J. (2000). Gender's nature: Intersexuality, transsexualism and the "sex"/ "gender" binary. *Feminist Theory, 1*(13), 347-364.

Hogan, S., & Hudson, L. (1998). *Completely queer: The gay and lesbian encyclopedia.* NY: Henry Holt and Co.

Hollenbeck, C. R. (2005). Online anti-brand communities as a new form of social action in adult education. *Proceedings of the 46th Annual Adult Education Research Conference.* Retrieved December 14, 2008, from http://www.adulterc. org/ Proceedings/2005/Proceedings/Hollenbeck.PDF

Hollibaugh, A. (2000). *My dangerous desires: A queer girl dreaming her way home.* Durham, NC: Duke University Press.

hooks, b. (1994). *Outlaw culture: Resisting representations.* NY: Routledge.

Hopson, M., Simms, R., & Knezek, G. (2001-2002). Using a technology-enriched environment to improve higher-order thinking skills. *Journal of Research on Technology in Education, 34*(2), 109-119.

Kop, R. (2008). Web 2.0 technologies: Disruptive or liberating for adult education? *Proceedings of the 49th Annual Adult Education Research Conference.* Retrieved December 14, 2008, from http://www.adulterc.org/Proceedings/2008/ Proceedings/Kop.pdf

Koyama, E. (1999). *The transfeminist manifesto.* Unpublished manuscript. See also, http://intermargins.net/repression/deviant/transgender/trans_book/tf-collection.pdf

Koyama, E. (2000-2001). *Transfeminism: A collection.* Retrieved March 28, 2009, from http://intermargins.net/repression/deviant/transgender/trans_book/tf-collection.pdf

Koyama, E. (2004, January 20). *Transfeminism revised.* Retrieved December 14, 2008, from http://eminism.org/interchange/2004/20040121-wmstl.html

Lather, P. (1991). *Getting smart: Feminist research and pedagogy with/in the postmodern.* NY: Routledge.

Lather, P. (1996). Troubling clarity: The politics of accessible language. *Harvard Educational Review, 66*(3), 525-545.

Markham, A. (1998). *Life online: Researching real experiences in virtual space.* Lanham, MD: Rowman and Littlefield (Altamira).

Martin, I. (2006). In whose interests? Interrogating the metamorphosis of adult education. In A. Antikainen, C. A. Torres, & P. Harininen (Eds.), *From the margins: Adult education, work and civil society* (pp. 11-26). Rotterdam, The Netherlands: Sense Publishers.

McCloskey, D. (1999). *Crossing: A memoir.* Chicago: University of Chicago Press.

McCloskey, D. (2000, March). Just like a woman. *Lingua Franca, 10*(2), 57.

Merleau-Ponty, M. (1962). *The phenomenology of perception.* NY: Routledge.

Nussbaum, E. (1999, May/June). The sex that dare not speak its name. *Lingua Franca, 9*(4), 42-51.

Orr, K. M. (1997). Charting the currents of the Third Wave. *Hypatia, 12*(3), 29-45.

Parkins, W. (2000). Protesting like a girl: Embodiment, dissent and feminist agency. *Feminist Theory, 1*(1), 59-78.

Protest called for women's music festival discriminatory policy still in effect. (1999, June 4). Retrieved March 28, 2009, from http://www.gpac.org/archive/news/notitle.html?cmd=view&archive=news&msgnum=0175

Rose, C. B., & Camilleri, A. (Eds). (2002). *Brazen femme: Queering femininity.* Vancouver: Arsenal Pulp Press.

Sclove, R. (1997, Summer). Cyberspace: Democracy and technology. *Initiative, 8*(1), 1-3. Retrieved from http://udallcenter.arizonia.edu/publications/initiative/8-1cybersociety.html

Scott-Dixon, K. (Ed.). (2006). *Trans/forming feminisms: Trans/feminist voices speak out.* Toronto: Sumach Press.

Shalit, R. (1999, Fall). Today's woman. *Lingua Franca, 9*(8), B33-B35.

Salamon, G. (2008). Transfeminism and the future of gender. In J. W. Scott (Ed.), *Women's studies on the edge* (pp. 115-136). Durham, NC: Duke University Press.

Sreedhar, S., & Hand, M. (2006). The ethics of exclusion: Gender and politics at the Michigan Womyn's Music Festival. In K. Scott-Dixon (Ed.), *Trans/forming feminisms: Transfeminist voices speak out* (pp. 161-169). Toronto: Sumach Press.

Stein, A. (1998). Sisters and queers: The decentering of lesbian feminism. In P. M. Nardi & B. E. Schneider (Eds.), *Social perspectives in lesbian and gay studies* (pp. 553-563). NY: Routledge.

Sullivan, N. (2003). *A critical introduction to queer theory*. NY: New York University Press.

Walker, A. (2003). *In search of our mothers' gardens: Womanist prose*. NY: Harcourt.

Weiss, J. (2004). Trans. In J. Eadie (Ed.), *Sexuality: The essential glossary* (pp. 229-230). NY: Oxford University Press.

Wesch, M. (n.d.). An anthropological introduction to YouTube. Retrieved December 14, 2008, from http://www.youtube.com/user/mwesch

Whelehan, I. (1995.) *Modern feminist thought: From the Second Wave to postfeminism*. NY: New York University Press.

Wilchins, R. (2004). *Queer theory, gender theory*. Los Angeles: Alyson Books.

Zita, J. (Ed). (1997). Introduction to the special issue: Third Wave feminism. *Hypatia, 12*(3), 1-6.

SECTION IV:
COMMUNITY

CHAPTER 12

When the Down-Low Becomes the New High: Integrating Queer Politics and Pedagogies Through Critical Community Education in Kosovo

Robert Mizzi

Working in foreign contexts certainly raises a number of unexpected issues and complications for adult educators trying to facilitate social change through their teaching strategies. Adjusting to the different living conditions, languages, social structures, and cultures can be overwhelming for some. However, the journey toward working through this adjustment may create opportunities to deepen knowledge around the critical issues that embody social change. My work in Queer adult education in foreign contexts certainly is one example of how meaningful change can take place through acquiring a deeper understanding of a new living context as a site of adjustment and mediation for the touring educator.

In this chapter, I use "Queer" as a catchall term to describe sexual minorities, including transgender persons, who challenge and rupture a number of social normativities through expressing their forbidden desires. In 2002, I was hired to work in Kosovo as a teacher educator who focuses on social development (Mizzi

---

This paper was originally titled, "In Solidarity: Using Community Health Education to Build Queer Peace in Kosovo and Japan." It was delivered at the 2003 LGBTQ&A Pre-Conference, Queer Histories: Exploring Fugitive Forms of Social Knowledge, on June 5, 2003, at San Francisco State University.

& Moo Sang, 2007). I arrived into Kosovo fresh from completing a graduate degree in international/global education from the University of Alberta. I believed that I was ready to follow Paulo Freire's assertion that the theoretical cannot be distanced from the practical (Freire, 1998), so I eagerly planned to take my acquired knowledge and use it to inform and infuse my practice. However, before I explain my experiences, it is best to provide a history of the context in which I was working.

Kosovo: A Brief Explanation

Kosovo's population of 2.2 million people includes Albanian, Bosnian, and Turkish inhabitants who are predominantly Muslim and a minority Serbian population who are Serbian Orthodox (Anderson & Humick, 2007; Malcolm, 1999; Sommers & Buckland, 2004). Between 1989 and 1999, Kosovar Albanians experienced severe oppression and violent assaults under the regime of then Serbian President, Slobodan Milošević. Albanian schools were banned, antigovernment protestors were arrested, and the flow of information was severely regulated (Malcolm, 1999). In the fall of 1999, after Serbian paramilitary forces began ethnic cleansing of Kosovar Albanians through brutal murder and torture, the North American Treaty Organization (NATO) organized a military assault against the Yugoslavian government, which led to the former country's defeat after an intense three-month battle (Sommers & Buckland, 2004). As a consequence of this defeat, Kosovo, which had been part of Yugoslavia, was designated a United Nations protectorate. Kosovo has since received massive amounts of reconstruction aid and development as well as a mandate to end hostile relations between ethnic groups (Anderson & Humick, 2007; Sommers & Buckland, 2004).

On February 17, 2008, Kosovar members of Parliament, with the exception of Kosovar Serbians, declared Kosovo a sovereign state after repeated failed negotiations with the government of Serbia (formally Yugoslavia) over Kosovo's status. Since then Kosovo has been approaching foreign governments to recognize its independence (British Broadcasting Corporation, 2008a). While there is still no clear uniform agreement among world nations on this issue, fifty countries, including the United States, Canada, and the United Kingdom, have already acknowledged Kosovo's declaration of statehood (British Broadcasting Corporation, 2008b). Currently, the United Nations Mission in Kosovo (UNMIK) is conceding administrative obligations and reconstruction protocols to the European

Union and is working to support the local government's mandate to improve living standards.

⟶⸺ ⚎⧫⚏ ⸺⟵

Critical Community Education

As any other Queer professional living in post-conflict Kosovo, I had many questions about how to meet other Queer persons, local and international, and determine what the "scene" (if any) looked like. Being overseas and away from vital supports and resources can cause a great deal of stress and loneliness (Britt & Adler, 1999), and adult educators like myself need to feel confident about their decision to work abroad so that they will not be overwhelmed when they begin their time away (Lynton, Pareek, & Shepard, 1992). For me, meeting other Queer persons wherever I'm living is crucial for addressing my social needs and ensuring that I have a supportive and positive network. After a few contacts made through a British social networking site for Queers, www.gaydar.co.uk, I was instantly welcomed into the local Queer community. I became involved in lending my emerging knowledge of adult learning, peace building, and community development to assist constructing a "gay rights movement" according to the wishes of local Queer Kosovars.

The unique privilege and ethical responsibility that adult educators face has been widely written about elsewhere and, as such, crystallizes issues relating to sexual diversity in adult classrooms (Brooks & Edwards, 1999; Grace, 2001; Grace & Hill, 2001; Hill, 2006; Kerka, 2001). However, very little has been written on sexual identity issues in adult education, as expressed through community education in non-Western contexts (Mizzi, 2008). By community education, I mean that educators create a space to "encompass a wide range of educational practices and intentions which derive from different traditions, including adult education, youth work, democratic schooling, and community participation" (Hunt, 2005, p. 131). According to Hunt (2005), community education takes shape in four different ways: a) *nonformal/informal education*, where educational activities complement learning outside of formal education; b) *community schooling/learning*, where educational activities take place under the auspices of "community centers"; c) *popular education*, which organizes political momentum to reclaim collective histories in order to change oppressive social and political arrangements; and d) *community organization/development*, which focuses on community self-help processes and is largely linked to adult education. It is the latter of these forms that defines the community education that is the focus of my work. However, like Hunt, I acknowledge that the term "community" is awkward; it is catachrestic in nature, as it seeks to define *commonality* across a group of individuals who possess *different* histories, life paths, practices, and identities (Godway & Finn, 1994). Godway and Finn question the search for community:

> *It is up to us to make community: to find it, build it, or encourage it to grow in our fragmented world. But can we? Or should we even try, when in spite of good intentions, the effects of community are often more divisive, more exclusive, and more oppressive, than the absence of community it originally intended to remedy or remove? (p. 1)*

To better reflect the diversity of communities that impact the goals of community education, and in order to adhere to the caution that Godway and Finn (1994) share, community education might possess a more accurate fit when referred to as *critical community education*. Central to this critical delineation would be recognition that adult learners usually hold membership in more than one community, which shapes how they connect, contribute, and care about the knowledge they are being taught. As well, critical community education could be self-reflexive, interrogating the concerns of false misrepresentation of the "community" notion and working to defy the establishment of competing hierarchies (Godway & Finn, 1994). Critical community education could also offer pluralistic refuge and encourage learners to speak from their multiple subjectivities and positionalities. For example, in the critical community education work in which I have long been involved, participants often speak from their racialized, sexualized, gendered, able-bodied, and classed communities by finding a space in curricula and classroom life to voice these positions that construct their realities. These dialogues include speaking to the ways that the term "community" deploys very different connotations for each person; a community could simply be geographical by nature, such as a neighborhood, or it could be based on shared social identities, such as being members of a Black community. While multiple goals and backgrounds could exist, there is a shared common belief in developing a more just world for its members.

When discussing critical community education through a Queer topological lens, what situates the "common" is a perceived need to redefine heteronormative gender roles to accommodate same-sex sexual practices and identities. Fulfilling this need concomitantly works toward recognizing the differences Queer persons possess. This basic understanding of critical community education through multiple Queer lenses is the pedagogical entry point I use in this discussion.

Brooks and Edwards (1999) relate, "As adult educators, we must help open spaces where sexuality can be explored rather than exploited" (p. 3). Keeping this in mind, in critical community education, especially in cultural contexts that marginalize Queer bodies, there are largely two educational landscapes that are required in order to develop a greater sense of Queer citizenship. One landscape centers on the self-help of Queer communities so that Queer persons are better able to organize their Queer rights campaigns more smoothly and efficiently. The other landscape focuses on the social help of the dominant heteronormative society with the intention to re-educate it to Queer realities, injustices, and struggles in order to evoke change in public opinion and policy. The two often work in tandem and seek to create human agency that works to improve Queer livelihoods. For example, by training members of the Queer community in Kosovo on peer counseling methods, I worked to create a mutually supportive and empowering atmosphere to enable social change projects to emerge in the public domain.

As a Queer foreigner to the community-building work in which I participated, I cannot ignore my Canadian citizenship. From this perspective, I need to take up Hill's (2004) insightful question: "What if the desire to know others is a colonial hope of speaking for (and possessing) the other?" (p. 92). Being an outsider excludes me from completely understanding local Queer lives and their anxieties while working in foreign contexts. For example, for me, openly discussing matters as a Queer citizen in a public space like a café is a privilege that Queer Albanians cannot afford. They would be unsure who is actually hearing the conversation and would worry about possible ramifications. Nonetheless, my involvement is paradoxical by nature. While I am not able to understand fully the construction and consequence of being gay, Albanian, Muslim, and Kosovar, I am able to take some initial, yet cautious, steps toward co-creating opportunities to discuss change. To say, however, that my own Queer body has been unaffected by local social norms would be untrue. Like my local counterparts, I have also found my sexual identity linked to issues of health, employment, education, housing, and security. My sexual identity becomes radically displaced as I navigate my personal and professional life between un/safe spaces while living abroad. Queer adult educators living in challenging places like rural Georgia or Indiana might identify with this premise. By choosing to teach abroad, I am opening myself up to reduced access to services and supports because of the linguistic, religious, and cultural differences. After all, the nation that I am living in is just as foreign to me as I am to the nation, and I might not entirely understand the highly contested political terrain that constructs the subversive Queer.

Project Background

This chapter reviews findings from a research project in which I interviewed six gay/bisexual male Kosovar Albanians between the ages of 21 and 40. I facilitated a follow-up focus-group session in order for everyone to contribute collaboratively to the critical discussions on this topic. The intention of this data collection was for these men to describe how Queer life has changed for them from the period prior to the 1999 conflict to the current state of post-conflict reconstruction. In doing so, I encouraged the Kosovars to identify their life challenges, needs, and goals. In this research, I wanted to explore connections among the research participants not only in terms of their experiences of same-sex desires but also in terms of the degree to which they experienced a supportive community as gay and bisexual (not heterosexual) men (McCormick, 2006). The research participants had learned to use "gay" and "bisexual" as self-descriptors largely from the Internet, other foreigners, and from each other, long before I even came to Kosovo. I am acknowledging here that these are Western-oriented terms that can be problematic in many non-Western spaces. "Gay" and "bisexual" import a Western understanding of sexuality differences that can silence indigenous forms of sexual identifications and inhibit examination of other forms of social arrangements. This "McPinking" of the world is further described in Chapter 2 above, "Que(e)rying Intimacy: Challenges to Lifelong Learning," by Robert Hill. In Kosovo, seeing that the general aim of Albanian Kosovars is to ensure Kosovo joins the European Union, expressing identities and social practices often translates to adopting Western European terminologies and social categories.

Establishing rapport with the participants proved paramount toward ensuring validity and critical analysis and rigor as well as enabling the identification of data limitations or weaknesses (Freebody, 2003; Patton, 2002). Through acting as cultural interlocutors, the gay/bisexual Kosovar Albanian men in my study generously provided me with a look into their daily lives and struggles, which required a history of earning their trust, respecting their boundaries, and encouraging local ownership over what is revealed to me and to others (Smith, 1999). Unfortunately, at that time I was not able to locate lesbians, bisexual women, or transgender persons in order to diversify my complement of research participants. For lesbians, bisexual women, and transgender persons, being doubly marginalized and living in a conflict zone translates into restricted freedom of movement. Reaching out to include them in my project was simply not possible at the time of this inquiry.

This chapter also reflects my experience as a clandestine adult educator who explored Queer issues as I engaged in voluntary work on evenings and weekends with the nascent Queer rights organization. Following the advice of Baptiste (2001), I wanted to provide a learning space that alleviated some of the social maladies of injustice against Kosovar Queer citizens as they began to construct human agency to resist oppressive structures and regimes effectively. Thus my mission was both educational and political as I engaged in cultural work to empower the Queers with whom I worked so they could make their lives better.

While independence is a significant milestone for this emerging democratic nation, it does not translate into absolute respect for all minorities in Kosovo, including its Queer citizenry. For example, a comprehensive study from COC Nederlands (van der Veur, 2003), a Queer Dutch international nongovernmental organization based out of Amsterdam, confirms that Queer Kosovars feel threatened to disclose their sexual practices despite UN promises of safety and specific mention of "sexual orientation" in Kosovo's antidiscrimination laws. As a result, living under the threat of homophobic violence has many Kosovars "living to hide/hiding to live" their true sexual desires. While my experiences living in Kosovo validate aspects of the COC Nederlands report, my research and participation suggest that critical community education may provide appropriate sociocultural space in which to address Queer concerns.

The "Down-Low" on the Data Findings

Given the recent discussion of same-sex attraction among "straight" Black American men, known as the "down-low" (King, 2004), I borrow the term since I find that it strikingly resembles the furtive and negotiated experiences of Kosovar Albanian gay/bisexual men, especially among those who are in cross-sex relationships. The interviews and focus-group discussion revealed three interconnecting themes that demonstrate how the social isolation of the Kosovar Albanian gay/bisexual men shapes the decisions they make. These three main points include a) heteronormativity is an embodiment of the nuclear family; b) lack of educational and resource support was pervasive during the pre-conflict period; and c) living was contextualized by hostile (inter)cultural conditions. I will explain each in turn.

Heteronormativity as an Embodiment of the Nuclear Family

Being patriarchical in nature, the Kosovar culture focuses on the lives of young men to continue and improve the socioeconomic status of their families. Regardless of sexual orientation, young Albanian Kosovar men are charged with the primary task to marry a woman and produce children. This social pressure does not consider their ability to support children financially or raise them nor their wish to develop their careers first. This finding echoes the COC Nederlands report, which states, "Many gays in Kosovo, as heard, claim it is good to stay in a heterosexual marriage as bringing stability and family life" (van der Veur, 2003, p. 21).

There are clear gender and sexual boundaries that must be adhered to if young couples are to become successful in their lives and continue to endorse their family's honor and status. Once the Kosovar Albanian male follows this path, the family secures and elevates its position in the community. Not to follow this "hetero-only" relationship route places both the Albanian male and his family at risk for shame and social expulsion. This life direction is common in predominantly Islamic cultures, as Dunne (1990) attests:

> In the Islamic worldview, male and female, masculine and feminine, represent different, complementary "orders." The harmony on the whole, of the complementarity of the sexual division, is achieved by men assuming their masculine roles and women assuming their feminine roles; the separate orders achieve unity only in the context of marriage as the realm of legitimate sexuality and affiliation. (p. 10)

As a result, perceived social deviances, such as homosexuality, are culturally prohibited. Homosexuality counters Islam's emphasis on marriage, family, and (hetero)sexuality and brings shame upon the family (Dunne, 1990; Moumneh, 2008). If a family has an openly gay/bisexual family member, then family business, external relationships, and public stature in the community are placed at risk (Barbosa & Lenoir, 2003). In Kosovo, the unmarried men I interviewed described the pressure to marry they experienced from their parents, extended family members, and neighbors as a "daily occurrence" that complicated their Queer desires, practices, and bodies. One participant stated, "The pressure I feel from my family to marry a woman is quite intense. At times I've had to fake illnesses just to avoid situations where I predict it will be difficult for me." This external pressure is ongoing until the covert gay/bisexual male enters heterosexual matrimony.

When offering a comparison to the West, "coming out of the closet" as a discursive formation does not work to describe and liberate gay/bisexual male Albanian Kosovars from their internal struggles with sexuality, ethnicity, and culture. Coming out of the closet in a Western context is understood as a necessary path towards attaining gay/bisexual male liberation, ultimately leading to shared celebration of identity and community (Whitney, 2005). Whitney adds, "Coming out is integral to developing a healthy sense of self" (p. 193). The living realities of gay/bisexual male Albanian Kosovars are, in contrast, fear-filled, fugitive, and secretive. Life-risking decisions to reveal identity and behaviors do not speak to "stepping out" of a life of secrecy and shame but evoke acts of "side-stepping" culture-bound realities in order to provide brief and intense glimpses of sexual freedom. To come out in the Western sense of the phrase would bind gay/bisexual male Albanian Kosovars to complicated lives of shame, guilt, and torment. Clearly, finding the vocabulary to transgress sexual persecution rests squarely upon a critical community education approach to (re)educate a society to respect sexual difference, rather than openly sharing and celebrating a person's sexual orientation with family and friends.

Lack of Educational Resources and Support

The second finding of this study places an emphasis on the lack of educational and technological advancement that Kosovo experienced under Milošević's regime. Not being able to engage in comprehensive learning about global events and newly discovered knowledge, learning became an unstable commodity that privileged only the select few who supported the oppressive regime. For example, when I first arrived in Kosovo, I talked about HIV to some Albanian gay men and learned that while some of them were familiar with the infection, there was still some confusion as to whether they were at risk for infection through having unprotected anal sex. Outside knowledge needs to weave itself into society so that crucial life-altering (and life-saving) discussions can take place. Further, such discussions may open up, as Rasha Moumneh (2008) explains, "a frank consideration of sexuality in public health initiatives, and through that can possibly lead to wider discussions about the social conditions that are necessary in order to implement effective interventions and programs" (p. 45). While international interventions are rapidly addressing knowledge gaps in Kosovo, ensuring comprehensive outreach and change in attitudes and behaviors requires a longer period of time. The interviews, the focus group, and my lived experiences point to an interest from the gay/bisexual male participants to "catch up" on what has taken place outside of Kosovo and, in part, to continue to rely on their own ingenuity. One participant stated, "I learned about the outside world through learning English. From that point, I was able to learn about gay rights in other countries. I then began to feel normal." At the same time, he acknowledged that few gay/bisexual Kosovar Albanian men have access to this much-needed affirmation: "We set up a gay organization to help those who cannot read English, yet need to locate some personal and social support." Generally, the need for increased information about ways to organize programs that educate and advocate for Queer rights was a concern expressed by research participants who also sought opportunities to network with other Queer Kosovars.

(Inter)Cultural Conditions

My interviews echoed the COC Nederlands report in revealing that most heterosexual Kosovars, unsurprisingly, are not respectful of sexual differences among men. For example, gay-bashings against "suspected" gay/bisexual men continue while local law enforcement agencies do little to stop anti-gay violence. During the focus-group session participants pointed out that local police officers treat gay-bashing as not worthy of a criminal investigation and victim support. More so, if the international police officer is from a country where homosexuality is not accepted, such as Nigeria or Jamaica, the gay/bisexual victim will simply not report the crime. This finding illustrates that international agencies, which are meant to maintain objectivity through their interactions, are not doing enough to reach out to Queer communities to ensure they feel safe to report bodily harm. Moreover, they are not accomplishing their goal to train their international police officers to handle concerns faced by the Queer community in at least an adequate manner.

The altered multicultural face of Kosovo has its effects on gay/bisexual males. Kosovo was once renowned for its multicultural make-up of Serbian, Turkish, Roma,[6] and Bosnian Kosovars (Malcolm, 1999). Gay/bisexual Kosovars, prior to the conflict, had frequent encounters and relationships with each other, regardless of their ethnicity. Since the conflict, very little ethnic mixing has been possible, since UNMIK seeks to minimize any possibility for ethnic tensions. One study participant commented that he missed meeting and speaking with Bosnian, Roma, and Serbian gay/bisexual male Kosovars: "We used to have a broken-down old house to meet other gay men. I made many friends there, and

---

6 Peoples of South Asian descent, including those who have been labelled with the pejorative term, "gypsy."

from different backgrounds. Ethnicity was never a problem. I miss these experiences as they brought us together." While the presence of international gay/bisexual males has replaced this loss to a certain degree, participants reflected that it was just "not the same" as meeting someone who shares similar attributes and histories but different ethnic roots. This shared sense of camaraderie might explain why I witnessed many friendly and respectful social gatherings between gay/bisexual Albanian and Serbian males but rarely saw social cohesion between the two ethnic communities within non-Queer contexts. It appears that non-Queer Kosovars have not developed such intricate multiethnic relationships as their Queer counterparts.

Additionally, without the law firmly on their side, participants described a tense atmosphere when trying to meet other gay/bisexual men. Often, the nascent relationship can take cautious tones, as the gay/bisexual man does not know if he will be "outed" or misled by his new acquaintance. Meeting someone on the Internet is risky business, as no one is absolutely sure about the true intentions of the man he is chatting with. In one stirring encounter, a gay Albanian Kosovar male went on national television to describe his "fugitive" gay life (in the sense employed by Hill, 1996) and was shunned after the interview by his community and family and, surprisingly, by the majority of his gay/bisexual male friends as well because they were afraid of being identified as gay/bisexual by mere association. In reference to his social ostracism, one participant reflected, "It was a brave step, but not a very smart one."

Conducting research that provides such findings as entrenched cultural heteronormativity, lack of educational resources, and difficult intercultural conditions helps inform programs relating to critical community education and those it serves. Through recognizing how heteronormativity is defined and shaped in Kosovo, and through acknowledging some of the structural and societal barriers, I was better prepared to work with the gay/bisexual male Albanian Kosovars to ensure that progress toward social acceptance of Queer Kosovars remains on track.

⊷ ⚌✦⚌ ⊶

Becoming the "New High" Through Critical Community Education

After completing the research, two critical community education programs were launched to "build learning communities on identities of difference" (Brooks & Edwards, 1999, p. 3) and to address some of the issues uncovered in the data. One opportunity came through working with a bisexual male Albanian Kosovar to facilitate a seminar for a group of physicians so they could learn to address safety concerns in the medical field for Queer persons. Safety in this context refers primarily to speaking openly about marginalized sexual practices without fear of losing confidentiality and to positioning a core team of physicians as helpful allies. Of course, taking a "sexual history" in a respectful and nonjudgmental way is not only a problem in Kosovo. Even in the developed world there are challenges to be met in this area (Bachmann, 2000; Tomlinson, 1998). However, my local counterparts felt it would be a positive first step. The second opportunity came through creating a curriculum for adult educators from a nonprofit organization to educate about developing healthy sexuality. This included educating secondary school students about Queer issues. While both opportunities might seem small in scale, they began to transgress homophobia and create a safe space to discuss sexual difference.

Much cultural learning was associated with both critical community education projects. First, in relation to training the physicians, while there was some keen interest from the female physicians, some of the male attendees would take several "cigarette breaks." This finding is not new, as a Canadian study concluded that female physicians are more likely to counsel patients on appropriate sexual behaviors (Maheux, Haley, Rivard & Gervais, 1997). However, the male physicians resisted learning the material that fervently challenged heteronormative values, despite repeatedly trying to structure time for their breaks. Learning how Queer citizens, who are considered perverts according to prominent Kosovar medical health professionals (Haxhiaj, 2003), are "wrongfully" persecuted and learning about the effects on their health and wellness implicate physicians and hold them accountable in their work. Some Kosovar physicians just could not handle this responsibility given their deeply rooted assumptions that are inherent in Kosovar culture about homosexuality. These assumptions were challenged by the Queer Kosovar representation and authenticity in the training session. Despite this, perseverance does have its merits, and the Albanians were able to reach out to more physicians at a later time.

In contrast, in the second project there was a much more positive response to notions of sexual difference, as the curriculum reflected the democratic ideals of a plural society. Underlying notions included that everyone was at risk for sexually transmitted infections and that, given how teenage audiences are diverse in nature, it is important to be inclusive in the programming. While homophobia is omnipresent, by approaching and including sensitive matters such as sexual difference, adult learners are better equipped to think through how society shapes everyone's lives and to determine outcomes that result from not living authentic lives. There is rupture when the Queer body is outcast. By adopting an integrative critical community education approach as a forum for discussing human moral development, an attempt to disrupt the segregating processes that attack Queer being is made. While resistances are most likely to take shape, local involvement and ownership of such interventions can help to sidestep the barriers as they present themselves.

Observations

There are three observations that stem from these experiences with critical community education. First, in order to include a Queer topography in adult education while working in developing countries, adult educators need to be aware of how being Queer is perceived and constructed in the wider cultural context. Learning about social expectations, such as familial obligations, informs adult educators about the hegemonic barriers that subvert Queer bodies. In addition, this work is subjective in nature; addressing Queer politics and pedagogies might differ greatly in other settings and cause the adult educator to change her/his approach radically. Learning the various local histories that embody Queer identities contributes to wider discussions on how meaningful changes could be defined and implemented.

Second, when working in intercultural contexts, there is a greater challenge initially of building respectful cross-cultural relationships that form a basis upon which to begin discussions of how change might take place. While living in Kosovo, I studied the Albanian language and learned about Kosovo's history, traditions, politics, and society. These were poignant factors to consider as I engaged in critical community education. Clearly, the intercontextuality of the work shapes and determines each experience differently, which calls for constant communication and a determination shared with local counterparts.

Third, trustworthiness is extremely crucial in order to embark on any kind of critical community education project. For example, if someone maliciously "outs" a gay or bisexual male, then his family life becomes altered, which might cause him to drop out of school or quit his job. If a gay or bisexual male does not continue with his in/formal learning, then he might begin misreading his sexual practices as shameful and engage in unsafe relations affecting the health of his family as well as how he is perceived in Kosovar culture. Combined, cultural norms, disrespect, and distrust work to isolate and prevent gay and bisexual

Kosovar Albanian males from active transgression into living authentic lives. As subversive bodies, some seek ways toward finding some kind of conciliation with their culture. Still, the key to building on Queer strengths, in this instance, lies within creating an inner life support that respects diverse knowledges, behaviors, histories, and attitudes both on a personal and social basis.

Concluding Thoughts

I began this chapter by speaking about my Queer interests and work in community education in foreign contexts. My interest in this topic has not diminished since presenting my initial thoughts on the subject a few years ago. To help nurture a responsive informing/transforming program where Queer people from the global South can educate Queers in the global North and to provide access to much-needed resources for their community development work, I began an organization called Queer Peace International in 2004. This organization facilitates critical community education projects abroad based on adult learning principles, social development, and peace building. It provides opportunities for like-minded foreigners to engage in continuous learning about the emerging issues that face Queer persons in challenging cultural exclusion in their nations and generating spaces for intercultural dialogue. By remembering that speaking for others might reflect cultural appropriation, I work to place the local Queer citizenry in control of the interaction. This is one way to maintain respectful relations and minimize North-South power dynamics.

Engaging in critical community education, given its mission to create a "better-informed citizenry" (Hunt, 2005), is one way I suggest that we can challenge heteronormative structures and improve how Queer persons are treated. The experiences of the gay/bisexual male Albanian Kosovars whom I interviewed and befriended over my two years in Kosovo by no means represent the experiences of the vast population of Queer Kosovars. Still my work points toward meaningful and respectful ways an adult educator may encourage Queer knowledge production in challenging places. Being mindful of how ability, class, ethnicity, language, and gender all work in together to shape a (homo)sexual identity creates pedagogical points of entry for critical inquiries by adult educators and forms the basis of their cultural work. Essentially, there are emerging opportunities for the "new high" to include Queer issues in critical community education in international contexts, which might give some much-needed relief to those who operate on the "down-low."

References

Anderson, G., & Humick, B. (2007). The educator development program in the Balkans, 2001-2007. In G. Anderson & A. Wenderoth (Eds.), *Facilitating change: Reflections on six years of the educator development program* (pp. 1-23). Ottawa: Universalia.

Bachmann, G. (2000) The importance of obtaining a sexual history. *American Family Physician, 62*(1), 52.

Baptiste, I. (2001). Educating lone wolves: Pedagogical implications of human capital theory. *Adult Education Quarterly, 51*(3), 184-201.

Barbosa, P., & Lenoir, G. (Directors). (2003). *I exist: Voices from the lesbian and gay Middle Eastern community in the U.S.* [Documentary]. United States: AFD.

British Broadcasting Corporation. (2008a, February 17). *Kosovo MPs proclaim-independence.* Retrieved February 17, 2008, from http://news.bbc.co.uk/2/hi/europe/7249034.stm

British Broadcasting Corporation. (2008b, October 10). *Kosovo receives recognition boost.* Retrieved October 10, 2008, from http://news.bbc.co.uk/2/hi/europe/ 7662149.stm

Britt, T., & Adler, A. (1999). Stress and health during medical humanitarian assistance missions. *Military Medicine, 164*(4), 275-279.

Brooks, A., & Edwards, K. (1999). *For adults only: Queer theory meets the self and identity in adult education.* Paper presented at the 40th Adult Education Research Conference, University of Minnesota, Minneapolis, MN.

Dunne, B. (1990). Homosexuality in the Middle East: An agenda for historical research. *Arab Studies Quarterly, 12*(3/4), 1-23.

Freebody, P. (2003). *Qualitative research in education: Interaction and practice.* London: Sage.

Freire, P. (1998). *Teachers as cultural workers: Letters to those who teach.* Boulder, CO: Westview Press.

Godway, E., & Finn, G. (Eds.). (1994). Introduction: Community: Catechresis: Community. In E. Godway & G. Finn (Eds.), *Who is this "we"?: Absence of community* (pp. 1-9). Montreal: Black Rose Books.

Grace, A. (2001). Using Queer cultural studies to transgress adult educational space. In V. Sheared & P. Sissel (Eds.), *Making space: Merging theory and practice in adult education* (pp. 257-270). Westport, CT: Bergin & Garvey.

Grace, A., & Hill, R. (2001). *Using Queer knowledge to build inclusionary pedagogy in adult education.* Paper presented at the 42nd Annual Meeting of the Adult Education Research Conference, Michigan State University, Lansing, MI.

Haxhiaj, S. (2003, April 5). Experts say: "This is moral descent...." *Zëri Magazine,* 12.

Hill, R. J. (1996). Learning to transgress: A sociohistorical conspectus of the American gay lifeworld as a site for struggle and resistance. *Studies in the Education of Adults, 28*(2), 253-278.

Hill, R. J. (2004). Activism as practice: Some Queer considerations. In R. St.Clair & J. A. Sandlin (Eds.), *Promoting critical pratices in adult education* (pp. 85-93). New Directions in Adult and Continuing Education, No. 102. San Francisco: Jossey-Bass.

Hill, R. J. (2006). What's it like to be Queer here? In R. J. Hill (Ed.), *Challenging heterosexism and homophobia: Lesbian, gay, bisexual, transgender and Queer issues in occupational settings* (pp. 7-16). New Directions for Adult and Continuing Education, No. 112. San Francisco: Jossey-Bass.

Hunt, C. (2005). Community education. In L. English (Ed.), *International encyclopaedia of adult education* (pp. 131-136). NY: Palgrave/MacMillan.

Kerka, S. (2001). Adult education and gay, lesbian, bisexual and transgendered communities. *Trends and Issues Alert, 21,* 1-5. Available at http://www.cal-pro-online.org/eric/docs/tia00089.pdf

King, D. L. (2004). *On the down low: A journey into the lives of 'straight' Black men who sleep with men.* Louisville, KY: Broadway Press.

Lynton, R., Pareek, U., & Shepard, H. (1992). Competence, personality and culture: Rules of thumb for change agents. In R. Lynton & U. Pareek (Eds.), *Facilitating development: Readings for trainers, consultants and policy-makers* (pp. 56-58). New Delhi: Sage.

Maheux, B., Haley, N., Rivard, M., & Gervais, A. (1997). Do women physicians do more STD prevention than men? Quebec study of recently trained family physicians. *Canadian Family Physician, 43,* 1089-1095.

Malcolm, N. (1999). *Kosovo: A short history.* NY: New York University Press.

McCormick, J. (2006). Transition Beirut: Gay identities, lived realities. In S. Khalaf & J. Gagnon (Eds.), *Sexuality in the Arab world* (pp. 243-260). London: Saqi.

Mizzi, R. (2008). *Queer eye for the pedagogical guy/girl: Adult education meets sexual difference in foreign contexts.* Paper presented the Canadian Society for the Study of Education, May 31- June 3, Vancouver, British Columbia.

Mizzi, R., & Moo Sang, B. (2007). Developing social sensitivities and insights through social development. In G. Anderson & A. Wenderoth (Eds.), *Facilitating change: Reflections on six years of the educator development program* (pp. 177-203). Ottawa: Universalia.

Moumneh, R. (2008). Sexuality and the politics of development in Lebanon. In R. Mizzi (Ed.), *Breaking free: Sexual diversity and change in emerging nations* (pp. 36-49). Toronto: QPI Publishing.

Patton, M. (2002). *Qualitative research and evaluation methods* (3rd ed.). Thousand Oaks, CA: Sage.

Smith, L. T. (1999). *Decolonizing methodologies: Research and indigenous peoples.* London: Zed Books.

Sommers, M., & Buckland, P. (2004). *Parallel worlds: Rebuilding the education system in Kosovo.* Paris: International Institute for Educational Planning.

Tomlinson, J. (1998). ABC of sexual health: Taking a sexual history. *British Medical Journal, 317,* 1573-1576.

van der Veur, D. (2003). *Homosexuality in south-eastern Europe.* Amsterdam: COC Nederlands.

Whitney, E. (2005). Coming out, youth. In J. Sears (Ed.), *Youth, education, and sexualities: An international encyclopedia* (pp. 193-197). Westport, CT: Greenwood Press.

CHAPTER 13

Posi+ive Prevention for Gay Men: Dismounting Missionary Positions

Francisco Ibáñez-Carrasco

Peter Hall

Posi+ve Prevention (PP+) gets a great deal of lip service but little actual servicing. In other words, professionals involved in HIV prevention practice PP+ all the time, but they still do not have the proper conceptualization to buttress the practice. Thus, we have been elaborating the concept and practice of Posi+ve Prevention since 2003, and our professional experience counterpoints our life experiences: we are contemporaries in age; one of us HIV-positive and one of us HIV-negative. We became friends because we share a love for learning, for gay men, and for our Queer communities. We met in October 2003 after being hired in a similar time frame by the British Columbia Persons with AIDS Society (BCPWA). Our professional backgrounds are in education (Francisco) and psychology (Peter). Francisco continues to work as the HIV/AIDS Community-Based Research Facilitator for the province of British Columbia, which is funded by the Canadian Institutes of Health Research (CIHR). Peter works independently as a psychotherapist in the GLBT community in Toronto. In this article we fuse expertise and experience and bring forward some necessary concepts for prevention practitioners as diverse as frontline and outreach AIDS service organization workers, public health nurses and physicians, epidemiologists, students, social theorists, and activists. In this theoretical inquiry we underline the lives of Canadian gay men. However, it is undeniable that a great deal of the literature consulted comes from the United States and the United Kingdom.

There are academic articles and grey literature (e.g., reports and newsletters) produced by nonprofit agencies in the voluntary sector about PP+ in developing regions such as Africa (see, for example, Bunnell, Mermin, & De Cock, 2006; International HIV/AIDS Alliance [IHAA], 2003; Kalichman, 2007; Morah, 2007). The insurmountable cultural and infrastructural differences between regions impede generalizations about what PP+ ought to be. Indeed, we suggest that such generalizations may work against the best interests of a gay men's health movement in North America. Around the world, HIV has become an issue of social justice manifested in enormous disparities of privilege, power, and access to basic needs (e.g., housing, food), education and outreach (including primary and secondary prevention), treatment (including access to treatment drugs and access to illicit drugs for users), care (including mental health care, aging, and palliative care), and social participation (e.g., in AIDS service organizations [ASOs], old HIV-positive activists are replaced by young graduates in public health, women with HIV in some regions are further victimized, gay men in rural areas often have to hide their status, etc.). Hence we have formulated a central ethical question to guide our thinking and analysis: *Where lies the agency of gay men in their sexual health today?* Furthermore, to operationalize this ethical question, we ask: What are the nonclinical, noninstitutional tools gay men possess to support their sexual health today? We know that there are a number of tested ASO interventions in community settings (Metsch, Gooden, & Purcell, 2005), but they are embedded in cultures, changing motivations, and dynamic relationships we must constantly reassess. We try to resolve both of these questions across what is considered individual (one's body and mind) and collective (both cultural and social—what is normative and institutional such as ASOs, health delivery institutions, or social networks). Our discussion straddles this dialectical relationship, the tensions and harmonies between these two distinctive areas, the individual and the sociocultural. First, we reinscribe the ways we talk about the individual in HIV prevention by adding the necessary words for a PP+ lexicon. Second, our discussion turns to social aspects of PP+, with specific examples in the area.

Defining Posi+ve Prevention (PP+) as Praxis

Often, persons in nonprofit organizations pride themselves on being *doers* and not *theorists*. While this binary distinction is often not true, the self-valuing of frontline workers as doers, not theorists tends to be endemic. Thus, the theoretical work on PP+ continues often to be neglected in ASOs and relinquished to disconnected academics. To start we have refined our definition:

Posi+ive Prevention (PP+) is to affirm the positive in being HIV-positive while reducing the negative impacts of HIV for all gay men (e.g., opportunistic infections, stigmatization, criminalization, reduced social participation).

Our definition emphasizes the empowerment and collective elements in definitions such as the one put together by HIV-positive gay men in the Ontarian Poz Prevention Working Group (2008):

POZ prevention for HIV-POSITIVE gay men aims to empower individuals, promote healthy relations with sexual partners, and improve conditions, to strengthen the sexual health and well being of HIV-POSITIVE gay men and reduce the possibility of new HIV infections and other sexually transmitted infections. (p. 1)

This is one of the few PP+ definitions crafted by gay men in Canada at the time of this writing. However, in a number of nonprofit environments with which we are familiar, this theoretical work is left behind to favor mechanistic programs and campaigns redolent of "safer sex" and "case management," the same old strategies that cancel the reflection aspect of praxis not only at the institutional level but also at the interpersonal level. (For a detailed description of the concept of praxis, see Petronio, 2000.) The result is utterly paradoxical; while organizations across Canada are beginning to change the names of their traditional HIV prevention programs and campaigns to PP+, the actual theory that underwrites it remains unquestioned—thus paying lip service to change.

Our review of the current literature yields some general goals and principles for PP+ that apply to gay men in Canada: intervening with HIV-infected individuals (persons living with HIV/AIDS; henceforth PLWAs) to reduce their likelihood of infecting others and to obtain treatment for HIV; enhancing PLWAs' quality of life, social participation, and psychosocial well-being; and implementing effective HIV programming that includes the expertise and lived experience of diverse PLWAs. The principles of PP+ include the key tenet that PLWAs have the right to live whole lives, including sexual lives, in the face of stigma and discrimination. They also recognize that PLWAs have unique needs and concerns that require targeted approaches, that we should all share the burden of risk equitably because modifying individual behaviors considered risky or noxious (such as smoking, gambling, criminal activity, discrimination, or unprotected sex), and indeed modifying what is considered a risk is a shared responsibility (Lupton, 1999). Most academic and grey literature agrees that there should be greater involvement of people living with AIDS (GIPA) in all areas of HIV-related work (see, for example, UNAIDS, 2007). In sum, our review of the literature indicates that clear goals and principles of PP+ have been set over time (Auerbach, 2004; DiClemente, Wingood, del Rio, & Crosby, 2002; IHAA, 2007; Kalichman, 2005; Palmer, 2004; Ridge, Ziebland, Anderson, Williams, & Elford, 2007); it is our implementation and practice of PP+ and GIPA that have not progressed accordingly .

Gay men know a great deal about HIV, prevention, and sex (Adam, Sears, & Schellenberg, 2000). We know that many PLWAs have continued to be sexually active or to inject drugs all through the pandemic, even after determining their HIV status and even if their perception of risk changes and some behavioral change occurs (Aidala, Lee, Garbers, & Chiasson, 2006; Belcher, Sternberg, Wolitski, Haltikis, & Hoff, 2005; Lightfoot, Swendeman, Rotheram-Borus, Comulada, & Weiss, 2005; Nollen, Drainoni, & Sharp, 2007; Theodore, Durán, Antoni, & Fernandez, 2004). For example, gay PLWAs engage in consensual and negotiated unprotected anal sex and other sexual practices with other PLWAs, thus engaging in unorthodox forms of prevention (Moskowitz & Roloff, 2007). However, at the public-opinion level, we continue to wonder what "the problem" is with gay men and sex; can't they stop having unsafe sex? In this essay, we argue that in many cases of HIV transmission, one HIV-negative person and one HIV-positive person may be involved but not always engaged (e.g., anonymous sexual encounters in bathhouses or truck stops). Moreover, traditional HIV prevention is often not sufficient to re-engage negative and positive gay men with their sexual health and pleasure. We echo Patricia Illingworth's (1990) argument in *AIDS and the Good Society*, where she theorizes that the harm experienced as a consequence of unprotected sex is self-inflicted, voluntary, and based on "unauthentic desires," not autonomous; that is to say, it is fully self-directed, where there is a symmetry between "how they act and how they want to act" (p. 63). There are contested views regarding what constitutes "risk." In this case, Illingworth's definition aligns with a "strong constructionist" approach to risk (Lupton, 1999, p. 35). The main point here is that PP+ must engage HIV-negative as well as HIV-positive men in individual and collective contexts that are nonclinical, such as commercial sex venues (e.g., Internet sites and bathhouses) and LGBTQ community centers. Unless it is understood as a principle for turning reflection into action, affirming what is positive in *being* HIV-positive might seem like a counterintuitive practice that is often challenged by the question: Who chooses to be sick anyway?

This scenario of individual involvement without engagement in sex, that is to say, of having sex with a feeling of limited participation and agency in a community or a sexual micro-culture, is complicated by the frequent situation that a) one or both parties are unaware of or silent about their HIV status and b) the rules of disclosure provided by clinicians and ASOs may often be in dissonance with the rules of disclosure and (non)dialogue at play in sexual, emotional, or cultural environments. In North America, gay men have been historically indoctrinated in the notion of risk. They are told that they are beings susceptible to infection (moral and biological). Here the problem is not that gay men don't know or don't care – we are forcibly made to know and care – but "the problem" with gay men, as we see it, is that we are not often engaged in cultural ways that render us able to protect ourselves and others. Current institutional ways render us invisible to each other or profoundly estranged. We provide gay men, and especially gay PLWAs, direct services (e.g., treatment) without opportunities or spaces where gay men can really use the benefits of those changes (e.g., undetectable viral load) to effect change, reaffirm their agency away from a "nanny state," and disrobe from juvenile stereotypes of reckless behavior. We write this fully aware that agency exists with varying frequency and intensity in gay communities and sexual micro-cultures rifted by disparities and traumatic memories (especially among aging gay PLWAs) and inscribed in a "culture of fear" where the "misanthropy," "reluctance to engage positively with risk," and distancing from one another are "not always…voluntary act[s]" (Furedi, 2006, p. xix). From the consulted literature, we observe in the following sections significant new items in the discourse of sex for gay men, repositories of shame and guilt in gay communities, trends toward criminalization of HIV, the medicalization of HIV prevention, and some hopeful responses that include a PP+ approach for all gay men.

Re-Inscribing Risk into "Safer Sex": The Lexicon of PP+

What used to be called "sex" is now called "unsafe sex"; intimate relationships of gay men have gone from underground and illegal to a discourse of sexual health and sexual rights in the 21st century. These relations are medicalized (Conrad, 2007), and the language used to name these relations glosses over nuances that PP+ needs to include to better capture the entire spectrum of sexual wellness, celebration, and sickness. To say that HIV-positive gay men are selfish and unconcerned about passing HIV to their sexual partners is completely missing the mark. To say that gay men, in general, are caught up in "AIDS optimism" has "acquired many of the trappings of a public health orthodoxy" (Adam, Husbands, Murray, & Maxwell, 2005, p. 245). That gay men have a death wish or bad intentions to infect others is a gross generalization developed over the course of the HIV/AIDS pandemic that perpetuates a strong constructionist notion of risk. This fascination around the ambivalent "desire and disgust" we feel for risk (Lupton, 1999) has led to the label "bugchasers," which is used in urban gay vernacular to describe HIV-negative men who want to become HIV infected. Other labels include "giftgivers," used to describe those who choose to infect others who want to be infected with HIV, and "barebackers," gay men, who may or may not be HIV-positive, who choose to have unprotected anal sex. Research shows a preference for risk taking and uncertainty of someone's HIV status among the bugchaser and barebacker subcultures of gay men. It also shows that barebackers "employ tricks to reduce the likelihood of infection through partner preferences, sexual positioning, etc." (Moskowitz & Roloff, 2007, p. 355). It has also been found that bugchasing is often a narrative fantasy of cultural resistance among gay men who are already HIV-positive (Dean, 2008). Overall, research has shown that "safer sex decision making is caught up in semiotic snares built into government and corporate neoliberal rhetoric, scientific and public health language, autobiographical narratives, status hierarchies, body image, aging and the search for intimacy" (Adam et al., 2005, p. 245). That is to say, gay men are often caught in between the technical calculations of risk as determined by epidemiologists and the need to recreate the unseen, the illicit, the grotesque, and what Graydon (2007), following Bakhtinian theorizing, calls the "carnivalesque" in the gay discourse. This refers to a need to escape from the epidemiological/clinical governmentality over Queer bodies in Western societies (Lupton, 1999). Not all risk taking obeys a "theory of planned action" (Ajzen & Fishbein, 1980) or fits within Rosenstock's (1974) health belief model that fed much of the original 1980s "safer sex" lexicon and prevention approaches.

Pivotal in the new lexicon of PP+ are the seminal signifiers of serosorting and seropositioning, which in vernacular are about the traditional roles of "tops" (anal insertive and stereotypically dominant) and "bottoms" (anal receptive and sometimes, but not always, passive or submissive). Since the advent of highly active antiretroviral therapy (HAART) in 1996, it is not surprising that gay men socialized in the clinical/statistical language of T-cell counts and viral loads have shifted their attention strongly to semen as a meaningful object and metaphor (Schilder, Orchard, Buchner, et al., 2008). Serosorting refers to the controversial practice of choosing sexual partners based on their HIV status (Truong et al., 2006); for example, HIV-positive men, or HIV-negative men, seek men of the same serostatus as sexual partners to enjoy unprotected sex. Serosorting is intended to guide partner selection and may also inform choices regarding condom use. Serosorting is controversial because it is currently unclear whether the practice decreases or increases new HIV infections and other sexually transmitted infections (STIs) (Butler & Smith, 2007). Additionally, serosorting may not prevent reinfection or superinfection of HIV-positive partners. Despite the fact that the impact of serosorting on the lives and health of HIV-positive gay men has yet to be fully explored, serosorting is used as a risk-taking option, a form of risk reduction, by both HIV-positive and HIV-negative individuals. To seroposition oneself is to determine, through spoken or unspoken sexual negotiation, the deliverer of the semen or other bodily fluids that may carry HIV. It has long been held that the man who gets penetrated and receives seminal fluids, the bottom, is at a higher risk of becoming infected with HIV than the top. Above all in PP+, one must be aware of the tremendous fetishistic rise of bodily fluids – in particular, semen – and breeding as initiation/impregnation rites among gay men since the advent of "safer sex" (Dean, 2008; Race, 2007).

HIV Stigma: Shame, Blame, and Guilt

The bodily practices described in the previous section have been mylar wrapped in spectacularity, media sensationalism, and prurient but disengaged public opinion interest that wants to pry without purpose since the 1980s (Watney, 1989). However, gay men have shown great social and personal responsibility at accepting the public consequences of all aspects of our behavior—not only the unprotected sexual practices that transmit HIV—by adopting and promoting the safer sex codex, and by the amazing deployment of activism involving volunteer and professional human resources that create an enduring network of ASOs for all persons infected and affected by HIV. However, it is the deeper layers of motivations, intentions, and repressions that need to be understood in a PP+ approach. HIV/AIDS-related social stigma is a complex, multidimensional concept that refers to prejudice, discrimination, and severe social disapproval directed at persons perceived to have HIV or AIDS. HIV often leads to marginalization and, in the age of "post-gay where sexual identities are being left behind by younger generations as strict and inflexible" (Archer, 2004, p. 25), it magnifies existing social and age inequalities. It may be the case that gay liberation is for those who can afford it, the ones with a great deal of social capital and privilege, and the ones who do not need "passing" as straight any longer and who can comfortably "cover" the unappealing aspects of gayness (e.g., anal sex). However, while "the idea of homosexuality as literal disease (mental illness) has faded, the idea of homosexuality as a figurative disease (a disfavored contagion condition) has endured" (Yoshino, 2006, p. 45). In the latter context, "covering divides *normals* from *queers*" (Yoshino, 2006, p. 77). Similarly, the idea of gay liberation has been identified as a White middle-class idea that tends to exclude the "Other" (Teunis, 2007). Following this reasoning, it may be the case that safer sex is perceived to be for those who can afford it, for example, gay men living in liberal urban environments. It is not surprising that in this partial context of gay liberation, normalization, and assimilation we neglect to look at the underlying memorial, historical grief of gay men—our sense of shame and guilt.

Perception of an individual's HIV-positive status continues to elicit judgments on a person's sexuality, overall behavior, or morality from others and from oneself. Shame, and the accompanying guilt it causes, are psychologically debilitating to HIV-positive persons and is a wholly undeserved consequence of having unprotected sex with another person. Blaming someone or blaming oneself for becoming infected with the virus is akin to blaming someone for becoming pregnant—it is the same bodily fluid after all—and only increases the stigma attached to HIV/AIDS. Blaming oneself for not becoming infected in spite of one's gay sexual practices is probably an even darker and more complex form of survivor's guilt (for having survived the traumatic event of seeing other gay men die of AIDS); it is said to be a contributing factor in a form of "safe sex fatigue," which is the wearing down of resilience in a number of mature gay men getting HIV relatively late in their lives. This fatigue, combined with youthful AIDS optimism, makes for an ambivalent field for gay relationships, to say the least.

Blame is often associated with religion and certainly some organized religions have played a role in stigmatizing illness in general. In the Bible, sickness is the "thorn on the side" of Paul (Cor. 1:2, King James Version), who is caught between good and evil. This is often interpreted to mean that sickness is necessary to learn to overcome evil. Paradoxically, this would make someone like a barebacker wholly necessary to a good society, an argument that echoes social theorist Tim Dean's (2008) assertion that barebackers "are simply not enjoying sex, they are also suffering it on behalf of others" (p. 89). The question is how to transcend blame, shame, and guilt and what to do with spirituality in a prevention framework. It became apparent very early on in the epidemic, as noted through-out this chapter, that HIV is as much a psychosocial, cultural, and environmental condition as it is a physical disease. As such, many PLWAs turned to spirituality in an attempt to come to terms with the emotional aspects brought on by the nonphysical factors associated with being HIV-positive, such as blame, shame, and guilt. Moreover, spirituality becomes a way to find support, kinship, altruism (to sacrifice one's health for others), and reproduction of a culture (breeding) (Dean, 2008; Race, 2007). However, since HIV prevention has been community based, albeit secular and highly medicalized, in Canada, we have rarely figured out what to do with spirituality. However, we know that persons in limiting situa-tions or crisis turn to a number of spiritual practices or organized faith, although there is a paucity of research in this area. In Canada, it is Aboriginal gay men, in particular Two-Spirit persons, who integrate prevention, treatment, traditional medicine, and spirituality.

In addition, a new language and practice of complementary and alternative medicine (CAM) including unconventional faith-based therapies has come to fill this gap somewhat. This is a new-millennium version of the New Age movement sought by gay PLWAs since the early stages of the North American epidemic in the 1980s. CAM allows individuals to integrate body manipulation (e.g., acu-puncture), complementary medicines (e.g., Chinese traditional medicine), tradi-tional healing (e.g., Santeria, an Afro-Cuban spiritual tradition common in parts of Latin America), and mind therapies (e.g., meditation, yoga) to obtain a sense of control over their health without adhering to a strict set of religious command-ments. Francisco participated as a collaborator in the Living Well Lab, a two-year (2006-2008) longitudinal mixed-methods community-based research study at Friends for Life in Vancouver. The research demonstrated that CAM has positive transformational and wellness outcomes for PLWAs, such as developing a sense of wellness and control over their lives and treatment (Jones et al., 2008).

Disclosure and HIV: The Sex Criminals

Canadian law states that it is the legal and ethical responsibility of HIV-pos-itive individuals to disclose their serostatus when sexual activity poses consider-able risk or the likelihood of serious bodily harm (Betteridge & Alexandrova, 2004). Prior to the more recent Canadian legal cases of *R. v. Walkem* and *R. v. Leone,* two earlier Canadian legal cases were cited to address the legal issues regarding responsibility for HIV disclosure: *R. v. Courier* and *R. v. Williams.* The first concerned an HIV-positive man who had multiple sex partners over time but did not disclose his infection. After his death, it was discovered that he was HIV-positive and his estate was successfully taken to court for aggravated assault. Subsequently, it became a legal duty to disclose one's HIV status before engaging in sex. *R. v. Williams* also supported the disclosure of HIV status. Prior to these court decisions, the gay community's view was that one did not have to disclose personal HIV status if one practiced safe(r) sex. However, if there was negotiation around condomless sex, then there should be disclosure. Apparently, ignoring the other complex factors involved in HIV disclosure, Canada's legal system has decided that HIV-positive persons who fail to disclose their serostatus are sex criminals and subject to punishment as other criminals convicted of aggravated sexual assault and possible endangerment of lives.

HIV/AIDS disclosure involves revealing personal information that one has a stigmatized and transmissible infection. Disclosure may lead to a number of outcomes, from feelings of self-acceptance ("I am strong enough to disclose my status and it is rewarding to do so"), abnegation, altruism, and kinship ("I risk likely rejection so others do not get infected with HIV") to shame ("I disclose because I made a mistake when I got infected") and fears of rejection or harm. Nondisclosure raises questions of negotiation, informed decision making, obligation, and responsibility. Most importantly, disclosure has been analyzed as a dialectical process of communication (Petronio, 2000). However, substantial aspects of this analysis are often ignored in clinical and ASO HIV prevention education, programs, and services that more often than not place the onus of "telling" on the gay PLWA as a practice of reasoned action, and even altruism, for the public good.

In Canada federal law is making this dialectical communication process among gay men more difficult by penalizing nondisclosure and the pools of silence that play a traditional cultural function in gay culture (e.g., when hooking up for casual sex). On a personal level, disclosure preceding moderate- and high-risk practices between sexual partners may reduce, but not eliminate, the likelihood of infection. On a societal level, disclosure could eventually normalize discussions about HIV, resulting in decreased difficulty in revealing an HIV-positive status and subsequently decreased stigma.

HIV disclosure has been erroneously conceptualized as a "second coming out." However, declaring one's sexual orientation is not akin to declaring one's HIV status. The underlying systemic risk of criminalizing HIV without having resolved its underlying problems of shame, blame, and guilt is that by forcibly taking away some cultural tools from the inhabitants of a culture (e.g., silence when meeting men for sex), prevention approaches that postulate blanket disclosure policies may be rendering sexual micro-cultures that are emblematic (e.g., barebackers as the totems of gay tribes) and inhabitants that are unintelligible, hence making them de facto sexual criminals. It has been argued that blanket coming out has rendered gay cultures normal and unintelligible to new generations (Archer, 2004). The criminalization of HIV disclosure runs contrary to PP+ approaches.

The Silent Epidemic: Aging with HIV, Loneliness, and Mental Health

Psychological, societal, and environmental factors affecting mental health—such as anxiety, loneliness, depression, low self-esteem, sexual compulsivity, sexual abuse, marginalization, power differences, poverty, and racism (Evans, 1988; Levine, Quick, & Yanez, 1987)—continue to contribute to HIV infection and to barriers to behavior change both for contracting the virus and for overall health once infected (Adam et al., 2000; Gee, 2006). The decision to accept particular kinds of risk may be based on an attempt to satisfy unmet needs, gloss over pain, and deal with grief and loneliness (Torres & Gore-Felton, 2007). Given these powerful factors affecting mental health, the decision to participate in risky sexual behaviors is often complicated.

In community practice in Canada, we find examples of work that connect collective/individual grieving, mental health, psychosocial positionality, and one's individual ability to maintain behavioral changes. The Gay Men and Methamphetamine (GaMMa) Partnership Research Project in 2005-2007 not only yielded data but also built community by training former meth users to be community developers and by sponsoring social activities both in the mainstream and Aboriginal groups to create awareness of the linkages between troubled gay pasts with family and community, use of methamphetamine, history of mental health problems, and unprotected sex. All of these are significant pieces in the puzzle of a gay collective healing process. Tellingly, the final report and conference presentations (Schilder, Orchard, Greatheart, et al., 2008) do not highlight the community development activities; they focus on the data collection and results, the formal aspect. This evidences an endemic and traditional disparity in the significance given to scientific evidence over the achievement of communities. PP+ needs to bring to the fore the undocumented and grey ASO reports and evaluations on the issues of mental health that often surround relationships, sex, and drug use for all gay men, especially for gay PLWAs (Dingwall, 2008). In addition to the silence still existing around mental health connections with prevention, we detected a parallel silence in the useful, nonacademic literature on this topic. This literature is harder to access than the traditional peer-reviewed articles and is often stashed away in grey literature reports of ASOs or public health authorities.

HAART as Prevention

In the complex landscape of words and practices in which seminal signifiers coexist with personal, almost spiritual, ideas of shame, blame, and guilt while being at odds with the law in Canada, today a new clinical/epidemiological approach to prevention may be in the horizon: HAART as prevention. This may be coupled with existing perceptions in gay communities that HAART may reduce harm. In Canada, we have incorporated "harm reduction" in prevention and cure. Once we have accepted risk taking in our lives, such as barebacking, we accept technology and, in particular, the use of pharmaceutical drugs. We also accept that living with HIV (or other voluntarily acquired conditions) is living with (licit and illicit) drug use, and we accept that drug use has nefarious consequences. Nevertheless, has HIV prevention been presenting this harm reduction reasoning to gay men properly? Do gay men understand—or are they even engaged in understanding—the extent of their agency in this approach to gay desire that places technology at its center? Western medical technology overdetermines a great deal of the current approaches to PP+. In industrialized, affluent countries today, an HIV-positive gay man who has minimum coverage of his social and individual determinants of health may make his viral load undetectable (i.e., not enough copies of HIV virus in the bloodstream for a test to find and count). Aviraemia, the absence of virus in the bloodstream of those infected, has been saluted as a default prevention technology (Vernazza, Hirschel, Bernasconi, & Flepp, 2008). This is where prevention precariously begins to meet treatment.

Many reactions have followed the Swiss Declaration at the 15th Conference on Retroviruses and Opportunistic Infections (CROI) in Boston in 2008. In general the declaration states that an HIV-positive individual does not pass on HIV through sexual contact as long as the individual complies with HAART, the viral load has been undetectable for at least six months (i.e., viremia is suppressed), and there are no additional STIs. In a public debate at the 17th Annual Conference on AIDS Research (CAHR), Louise Binder, the chairperson of the Canadian Treatment Action Council (CTAC), verbally summarized some of the difficulties of HAART as prevention. First, in a number of countries, including Canada, gay men are having sex or using drugs in a criminalized environment. The number of legal actions is only bound to increase as gay normalization and gay marriage lead the way to breaking the sort of gay pink code of silence and to bringing about new tribulations such as gay divorce, gay parenthood, and so on. Second, we are seeing the long-term side effects of HAART, including increased osteoporosis, heart failure, lipoatrophy, and depression, to name a few. Third, HIV testing—the cornerstone technology that buttresses disclosure—continues to be cumbersome and not fully supported by existing social services (e.g., counseling, continuum of care). Here HAART as prevention would be introduced in a cultural climate of secrecy and silence. Not all gay men know, or want to know, their serostatus.

HAART as prevention seems to be driven by financial cost-benefit and epidemiologically strong constructionist analyses of risk. However, there are no universal theoretical and ethical guidelines to include treatment wholesale in prevention. HAART in itself is taking a risk over an extended period—we're back to risk. In this regard, some seemingly old-fashioned 1980s maxims coined by the early AIDS activists may still hold true, and they may still fall on deaf ears in our Queer communities. These maxims include: "Treat everyone as if they are HIV-positive." Now that this option has been sanctioned as legitimate in PP+, we should add: "Treat everyone as if they are HIV-positive and make up your mind as to the risks you want to take."

An improved relationship between doctors and patients is a pivotal point in heralding HAART as prevention. Such improvement shows evidence of clinicians, ASOs, and the private sector (pharmaceutical companies) working together, but it may also signal a reverting of the power of medical institutions over bodies, care, treatment, and prevention. Research has shown that health-care providers, in particular physicians, are still the most authoritative and powerful medical actors in the Western medical regime. However, they do not inquire about sexual health in ways that are affirming to the patient or conducive to proper medical diagnosis and treatment. Taking sexual histories from patients in general, and specifically from gay men, has been found to be deficient (Meystre-Agustoni, Jeannin, & Dubois-Arber, 2006; Silenzio, 2003; Verhoeven et al., 2003) in that it assumes monogamy, adopts a heterosexist perspective, adopts a confessional approach to disclosure, and silences sexual micro-cultural practices such as fisting (inserting a hand into the sexual partner's anus), feltching (eating semen that has been deposited in the anus of a sex partner), or booty bumping (using methamphetamine anally for sex).

The outcome of clinical interviews or even ASO conversations between front-line staff and clients that do not include elements of a PP+ approach is often a partial understanding of a gay man's situation that possibly results in lack of referrals to necessary medical tests and adequate support services. It has been confirmed that general practitioners (particularly those in rural areas), male practitioners of any age (Haley, Maheux, Rivard, & Gervais, 2000; Maheux, Haley, Rivard, & Gervais, 1997), and those whose ethnocultural, faith-based, or rural/urban culture differs greatly from the culture of a gay man, do not inquire about sexual health in ways that are affirming to the patient or conducive to proper medical diagnosis and treatment (Meystre-Agustoni et al., 2006; Nicolai & Demmel, 2007). Although this faulty communication cannot always be attributed to homophobia—a difficult correlation to prove or measure—research has shown that poor doctor-patient communication due to a number of factors (e.g., professional training, gender of the physician) has poor health consequences, including a lack of dialogue about sexual health between patients and doctors and lack of adherence to HAART (Gee, 2006; Ingersoll & Heckman, 2005). The coupling of HAART as prevention with still ineffective sexual history taking and sexual health promotion for all PLWAs will and must remain a contested practice and dialogue.

Back to Risk: PP+

We stated at the beginning that Posi+ve Prevention gets a great deal of lip service but little actual servicing; that is to say, we say we practice PP+ but we lack the proper conceptualization about the current prevention discourse, disclosure, HIV criminalization, sex practices, and medical practice. In the work that supports this paper we have conceived of PP+ as an approach to human agency (not necessarily human function/performance); it is not the streamlined system as medical professionals and researchers tend to outline it: sequences of doctor referrals, a number of counseling sessions, and so on (e.g., Aidala et al., 2006; Nollen et al., 2007).

In this section, we pursue the collective and sociocultural answers to the question we posed at the start: Where is the agency of gay men in their sexual health today? In Canada, and likely in all of North America, the collective and sociocultural aspects are immediately narrowed down by a ubiquitous Anglo-based, Judeo-Christian binary of good/evil and patriarchal discourse that permeates the language when spoken in English. And yet in trying to defy old terms such as "coming out," "liberation," or "top/bottom" that harness gay desire these days, we focus on seemingly older terms such as "altruism," "romance," "visibility," "masculinity," and "silence." We argue that these dissonant aspects are shorthand for what is possible within PP+ today. We put forth that the research literature out there, mechanistic as it is, points repeatedly to these aspects by virtue of glossing over them. Altruism is a virtue, romance is a social construct, visibility is the social practice of seeing and being seen, and masculinity is one product of visibility: appearing to be macho, virile, or manly. Silence is one of the effects of masculinity, as in "the strong silent type." In choosing these elements, we keep in mind that "gay" is not a universal archetype, and we make distinctions between identity and practice, between what gay men say we are (and say we do), what we would like to be, and what we indeed do. We do not refuse stereotypes (e.g., gay men as stylish, youthful, and oversexed, etc.), but we work through our stereotypes to find the roots of their cultural lodging. Here we look across race, body ability, and even faith. Teunis (2007) tells us that "not recognizing sexual stereotypes as a social phenomenon maintains the specific manner in which whiteness and racism are stable features in the social life of the gay community" (p. 273). Although antiracism maybe an entirely separate endeavor in Queer communities, we keep this lens while discussing the elements of PP+.

—⋆⋅≡✦≡⋅⋆—

HIV Altruism

Altruism often underlies PP+, the literature we consult, and the anecdotal information we retrieve from our social lives. It also underscores the expertise honed through engaging in private practice (Peter) and participating in the non-profit sphere of action (Francisco). These realms tell us that we hold a collective notion of "altruism" in mind when engaging risk (O'Dell, Rosser, Miner, & Jacoby, 2008) in the good stuff (sex, partying with drugs) or the noxious things (partying in loneliness, addiction)—these are all extremes of a continuum of agency and behavior. The late Eric Rofes (1995) saluted the notion of "reviving the tribe," and who are we to contest such an indisputable notion? However, those who reflect and practice (those who enact the praxis of) PP+ must keep an unsentimental mind that not all gay men have the public good in mind when taking risks and that "personal evaluations and tolerance of risk differ from one person to another" (Belcher et al., 2005, p. 87). We must remain ambivalent about whether risk taking is individual or collective to resist the simplistic resolutions of media figureheads, such as Dan Savage or Sue Johansen, of what gay men should or should not do for each other as individuals. PP+, much like the concept of "disclosure" as conceptualized by Petronio (2000) or the concept of "risk" conceptualized by Lupton (1999), must remain a dialectical and contested space for all gay men. Serosorting and seropositioning are examples of this dialectic process; they may be positive actions or the only possible actions in some contexts or negative and ill-intended in others. In addition, the notion of HIV altruism, that one must protect all others and risk rejection and loneliness, needs to be updated in PP+. Philosopher Ayn Rand (1984) reacted strongly against this ideal of self-abnegation, "that man has no right to exist for his own sake, that service to others is the only justification of his existence, and that self-sacrifice is his highest moral duty, virtue and value," which place "the *self* as a standard of evil, the *selfless* as a standard of the good" (p. 61). A Judeo-Christian hangover of internalized homophobia permeates a great deal of the language and practice of HIV prevention, which are in dire need of revision in PP+ to strengthen self-acceptance, pride, self-control, and the notion that a responsibility to the self can engender care for others. The language of "gay community" may be romantic in itself and confuse altruism with kindness, good will, and respect for the rights of others.

Tainted Love

Romance, confused as romantic courtship and love, is the great confounding factor in prevention. Ibáñez-Carrasco (2003) has written at length elsewhere on this "confusion" and has referred to the powerful metaphor used by Octavio Paz (1996) in *The Double Flame*: "[L]ove is a bet, a wild one, placed on freedom. Not my own; the freedom of the Other" (p. 67). This metaphor suggests that loving is taking risks, not being safe, and that one may be taking risks on the back of the Other. It is not uncommon to see research studies arrive at this point to quickly cough up a couple of awkward sentences then move on to more technical points. There is considerable research fear and cultural fear in this area; it is often impetuously concluded that people engage in irrational and risky behaviors in the name of (romantic) love (Furedi, 2006, p. xvii). For example, Theodore et al. (2004) write:

These findings speak to the importance of understanding why sexual risk continues to occur between primary partners. Are these men uninformed about the potential medical complications associated with HIV reinfection and/or coinfection with other STDs, less concerned because of their preexisting HIV status, or placing greater emphasis on unprotected sex as an expression of love and affection? (p. 328)

Leaving the issue of "love" as a question is telling and happens often in such research papers and in the public opinion. Scientific teams are not in the business of discussing "love," and having a philosopher or other specialist in the area on an interdisciplinary team is very rare. In the public opinion, gay marriage in Canada may have come to enhance the idyllic notion of romantic love and obscure gay sexual/emotional realities of companionship without sex or fuck-buddies. In our view, romance follows "altruism" as the concept to be laid bare in PP+. Romance is seen as an egalitarian and benevolent practice that envelopes the taking of risks: the staunchest "pig play" (sex involving, for example, spit, sweat, feces, and urine) personal advertisements and quick online movies seem to barely sideline the engulfing presence of romance in gay sex. Often we hear from gay men (as well as others, such as sex workers, who tend to be hard-boiled about risk) that one has unprotected sex, tries drugs, or accepts physical abuse or coercion because one is "in love" and is "loved." In the age of liberation and the possible normalization of post-gay, as Bert Archer announces in his 2004 book, two gay men are equal to a man and a woman before the law. Interestingly, marriage-bound romance has resurfaced as a backlash to promiscuity, polyamorous relationships, and open relationships among gay men. Many other unsavory social experiments may be now only seen through the tragic historical lens of AIDS. Research literature gives us repeated clues that risks are taken in the rarefied atmosphere of Harlequin romance that may be largely emotional or even physical *chantage*. Adam et al. (2000) tell us, for example, that some of their participants "attempted to make their sexual lives compatible with the desire to communicate trust in couple relationships," with varying degrees of success (p. 33).

Are we promoting the penetration of sex without feelings? Maybe, but above all we want to elucidate the tangle of feelings that confuse the pragmatism of prevention with romantic love. The research literature we consulted simply does not deal with such a fuzzy area—we don't know what to do with it! Whatever PP+ is able to do, it should unpack this one critical missionary position: romance. By the time two bloodstreams merge, the risk of love has long been accepted, albeit not always understood. It may be the case that gay men have more opportunities to assert their agency when coupled, but the function and form of relationships are diverse (e.g., open sexual relationships, fuck-buddies, polyamory, etc.) and PP+ must consider a wide range of micro-cultures and options in what philosopher Zygmunt Bauman (2003) calls a "liquid modern world" inhabited by "semi-detached couples" (p. ix). To paraphrase Bauman's example, a great number of gay relationships are lived as well as perceived in the ethernet. We are persons worrying about one thing while speaking of another; we say that our passion is to relate, but we are not concerned about how to prevent our relationships from curdling and clotting (Bauman, 2003). It turns out that Eric Rofes's "tribe" has become a "network," and our relationships are replaced by networking that enables us to switch on and off alternately at alarming speed. Paul Virilio (2005) adds to this postmodern scenario by telling us that "speed" creates anxiety and is the result of "fear." In sum, PP+ might even be old-fashioned in trying to slow down the sexual negotiations, the ideas of love and romance, and the time between HIV testing and diagnosis to find space for grappling with what kinds of relationships we are forging as gay men nowadays.

HIV Visibility, Hypermasculinity, and Silence: A Dark Triumvirate

Last, we need to grapple with the performative aspects of being gay (e.g., hypermasculine, twink, etc.) and the significance of these roles and practices for PP+. In particular, we need to grapple with the issue of HIV disfigurement, the face of AIDS in PP+. For gay men, HIV prevention has been often circumscribed in the context of sexual roles, identities, and practices that are both performed socially, politically, in the media, and in the arts. On websites, in person, and in public we "come out" (or not), we define ourselves and tell what we do, and we make it visible or obscure it depending on the degree of agency we have in a given situation or place. However, after the 1980s catastrophe for young, beautiful, White gay men, we have gradually made HIV invisible to others and hypervisible to ourselves in stigmatizing ways. When gay men are "no longer able to conceal or keep their [sero]status private, their bodies turn personal experience into public spectacle" (Persson, 2005, p. 239). This exacting way of seeing HIV is borrowed and enhanced from broader social practices of seeing illness, which

Foucault (1994) describes as the medical gaze and the turning of signals into symptoms. To date, no gay perversion, kink, or radical sexuality seems to be able to help us fully integrate anomaly and disfigurement into our seemingly sheltered lives. We bounce back to what is pristine and untouched—"clean and safe" read the personal ads on websites, which are a prime medium for networking. In contrast, we see a great deal of the new gay pornography that shows semen as fetish, feltching. Players who are muscular, hyper-macho performers take on roles as fuck machines. Seemingly HIV-positive, lipoatrophic performers show telltale signs like sunken cheeks and near total absence of limb fat. "Don't ask, don' tell" seems to be the maxim at work here.

To conclude, we revisit our provocation here that PP+ gets a great deal of lip service but little actual servicing. Thus we invite gay men, ASO staff, academics, all theorists in their own right, to review, reflect, and strategize on specific HIV and gay men's health programs to include a PP+ perspective. The elements we have included here for your reflection are discursive and embodied (e.g., sero-sorting), systemic (e.g., criminalization), medical (e.g., treatment as prevention), psychocultural (e.g., shame, blame, guilt, hypermasculinity, and HIV visibility) and should aid us in assessing where gay men have the most agency to change. Is it in ASOs as they exist today? And where can we find the best tools to affirm living with HIV voluntarily and autonomously? Is it in sero-different relationships or in a different order of things, commercial sex venues (e.g., bathhouses) where all gay men are protected to make their own choices.

References

Adam, B. D., Husbands, W., Murray, J., & Maxwell, J. (2005). AIDS optimism, condom fatigue, or self-esteem? Explaining unsafe sex among gay and bi-sexual men. *Journal of Sex Research, 42*(3), 238-248.

Adam, B. D., Sears, A., & Schellenberg, E. G. (2000). Accounting for unsafe sex: Interviews with men who have sex with men. *The Journal of Sex Research, 37*(1), 24-36.

Aidala, A. A., Lee, G., Garbers, S., & Chiasson, M. A. (2006). Sexual behaviors and sexual risk in a prospective cohort of HIV-positive men and women in New York City, 1994-2002: Implications for prevention. *Aids Education and Prevention, 18*(1), 12-32.

Ajzen, I., & Fishbein, M. (1980). *Understanding attitudes and predicting social behavior.* Englewood Cliffs, NJ: Prentice-Hall.

Archer, B. (2004). *The end of gay: And the death of heterosexuality.* NY: Da Capo Press.

Auerbach, J. D. (2004). Principles of PP+. *Journal of Acquired Immune Deficiency Syndrome, 37*(S2), S122-S125.

Bauman, Z. (2003). *Liquid love: On the frailty of human bonds.* Cambridge, UK: Polity.

Belcher, L., Sternberg, M. R., Wolitski, R. J., Haltikis, P., & Hoff, C. (2005). Condom use and perceived risk of HIV transmission among sexually active HIV-positive men who have sex with men. *AIDS Education and Prevention, 17*(1), 79-89.

Betteridge, G., & Alexandrova, A. (2004, July). *Disclosure of HIV status – Developing resources for community based AIDS service organizations.* Abstract presented at the 15th International AIDS Conference, Bangkok, Thailand.

Bunnell, R., Mermin, J., & De Cock, K. M. (2006). HIV prevention for a threatened continent: Implementing PP+ in Africa. *Journal of the American Medical Association, 296*(7), 855-858.

Butler, D. M, & Smith, D. M. (2007). Serosorting can potentially increase HIV transmissions. *AIDS, 21*(9), 1218-1220.

Conrad, P. (2007). *The medicalization of society: On the transformation of human conditions into treatable disorders.* Baltimore, MD: The Johns Hopkins University Press.

Dean, T. (2008). Breeding culture: Barebacking, bugchasing, giftgiving. *The Massachussets Review, 49*(1/2), 80-94.

DiClemente, R. J., Wingood, G. M., del Rio, C., & Crosby, R. A. (2002). Prevention interventions for HIV-positive individuals: A public health priority. *Sexually Transmitted Infections, 78*, 393-395.

Dingwall, C. (2008). *Trap doors, revolving doors: A mental health and HIV/AIDS needs assessment.* Vancouver, BC: Provincial Health Service Authority.

Evans, P. E. (1988). Minorities and AIDS. *Health Education Research, 3*(1), 113-115.

Foucault, M. (1994). *The birth of the clinic: An archaeology of medical perception* (A. M. Sheridan, Trans.). NY: Vintage Books.

Furedi, F. (2006). *Culture of fear revisited: Risk-taking and the morality of low expectation* (4th ed.). London: Continuum.

Gee, R. (2006). Primary care health issues among men who have sex with men. *Journal of the American Academy of Nurse Practitioners, 18*(4), 144-153.

Graydon, M. (2007). Don't bother to wrap it: Online giftgiver and bugchaser newsgroups, the social impact of gift exchanges and the "carnivalesque." *Culture, Health & Sexuality, 9*(3), 277-292.

Haley, N., Maheux, B., Rivard, M., & Gervais A. (2000). Lifestyle health risk assessment. Do recently trained family physicians do it better? *Canadian Family Physician, 46,* 1609-1616.

Ibáñez-Carrasco, F. (2003). In difference. In G. Wharton (Ed.), *The love that dare not speak its name: Essays on queer sexuality and desire* (pp. 106-115). San Francisco: Boheme Press.

Illingworth, P. (1990). *AIDS and the good society: From philosophy to social policy.* London: Routledge.

Ingersoll, K. S., & Heckman, C. (2005). Patient-clinician relationships and treatment system effects on HIV medication adherence. *AIDS and Behaviour, 9*(1), 89-101.

International HIV/AIDS Alliance. (2003). *Working with men, responding to AIDS: Gender, sexuality and HIV – A case study collection.* Hove, UK: Author.

International HIV/AIDS Alliance. (2007). *Positive prevention: HIV prevention with people living with HIV.* Hove, UK: Author.

Jones, J., Verhoef, M., Mulkins, A., McDonald, J., Towson, J., Hillier, J., et al. (2008). *Complementary and alternative medicine (CAM) shows positive impact on PHAS: Preliminary quantitative data from the Living Well Lab at Friends for Life, B.C.* Abstract presented at the 17th Annual Canadian Conference on HIV/AIDS Research, Montreal, Canada.

Kalichman, S. C. (Ed.). (2005). *PP+: Reducing HIV transmission among people living with HIV/AIDS.* NY: Springer.

Kalichman, S. C. (2007, Spring). PP+: HIV transmission risk reduction interventions for people living with HIV/AIDS. *Southern African Journal of HIV Medicine,* 40-45.

Levine, A., Quick, B., & Yanez, L. (1987). The uneven odds: Minorities are afflicted with AIDS in significantly disproportionate numbers. *U.S. News & World Report, 103*(7), 31-33.

Lightfoot, M., Swendeman, D., Rotheram-Borus, M. J., Comulada, W. S., & Weiss. R. (2005). Risk behaviours of youth living with HIV: Pre- and post-HAART. *American Journal of Health Behavior, 29*(2), 162-171.

Lupton, D. (1999). *Risk.* London: Routledge.

Maheux, B., Haley, N., Rivard, M., & Gervais, A. (1997). Do women physicians do more STD prevention than men? Quebec study of recently trained family physicians. *Canadian Family Physician, 43*, 1089-1095.

Metsch, L. R., Gooden, L. K., & Purcell, D. W. (2005). Interventions in community settings. In S. C. Kalichman (Ed.), *PP+: Reducing HIV transmission among people living with HIV/AIDS* (pp. 193-217). NY: Kluwer Academic/Plenum.

Meystre-Agustoni, G., Jeannin, A., & Dubois-Arber, F. (2006). Talking about sexuality and HIV prevention in medical offices: The situation in Switzerland. *Sexual & Relationship Therapy, 21*(3), 289-301.

Morah, E. U. (2007). Are people aware of their HIV-positive status responsible for driving the epidemic in Sub-Saharan Africa? The case of Malawi. *Development Policy Review, 25*(2), 215-242.

Moskowitz, D. A., & Roloff, M. E. (2007). The existence of a bug chasing culture. *Culture, Health & Sexuality, 9*(4), 347-357.

Nicolai, J., & Demmel, R. (2007) The impact of gender stereotypes on the evaluation of general practitioners' communication skills: An experimental study using transcripts of physician-patient encounters. *Patient Education and Counseling, 69*(1-3), 200-205.

Nollen, C., Drainoni, M. L., & Sharp, V. (2007). Designing and delivering a prevention project within an HIV treatment setting: Lessons learned from a specialist model. *AIDS Behavior, 11*, S84-S94.

O'Dell, B. L., Rosser, B. R. S., Miner, M. H., & Jacoby, S. M. (2008). HIV prevention altruism and sexual risk Behavior in HIV-positive men who have sex with men. *AIDS & Behavior, 12*(5), 713-720.

Palmer, N. B. (2004). "Let's talk about sex, baby": Community-based HIV prevention work and the problem of sex. *Archives of Sexual Behavior, 33*(3), 271-275.

Paz, O. (1996). *The double flame: Love and eroticism* (H. Lane, Trans.). NY: Harvest/HBJ Book.

Persson, A. (2005). Facing HIV: Body shape change and the (in)visibility of illness. *Medical Anthropology, 24*(3), 237-264.

Petronio, S. (2000). The boundaries of privacy: Praxis of everyday life. In S. Petronio (Ed.), *Balancing the secrets of private disclosures* (pp. 37-49). Mahwah, NJ: Lawrence Erlbaum.

Poz Prevention Working Group. (2008, January 25). *Poz prevention definition, values and principles.* Retrieved December 9, 2008, from http://www.health. gov.on.ca/ english/providers/pub/aids/reports/poz_prevention_definition_ values_principles_j.pdf

Race, K. (2007). Engaging a culture of barebacking: Gay men and the risk of HIV prevention. In K. Hannah-Moffat & P. O'Malley (Eds.), *Gendered risks* (pp. 99-126). London: Glasshouse Press.

Rand, A. (1984) *Philosophy: Who needs it?* NY: Signet.

Ridge, D., Ziebland, S., Anderson, J., Williams, I., & Elford, J. (2007). PP+: Contemporary issues facing HIV-positive people negotiating sex in the UK. *Social Science and Medicine, 65*(4), 755-770.

Rofes, E. E. (1995). *Reviving the tribe: Regenerating gay men's sexuality and culture in the ongoing epidemic.* NY: The Haworth Press.

Rosenstock, I. M. (1974). Historical origins of the health belief model. *Health Education Monographs, 2,* 328-335.

Schilder A. J., Orchard, T. R., Buchner, C. S., Miller, M. L., Fernandes, K. A., Hogg, R. S., et al. (2008). "It's like the treasure": Beliefs associated with semen among young HIV-positive and HIV-negative gay men. *Culture, Health & Sexuality, 10*(7), 667-679.

Schilder, A. J., Orchard, T., Greatheart, M., Ibáñez-Carrasco, F., Bayzand, L., Pearson, S., et al. (2008, September). *"I need to talk about methamphetamine and sex": Sexuality and mental health concerns amongst gay men using methamphetamine in Vancouver, Canada.* Abstract presented at the First Global Conference on Meth: Science, Strategies, and Response, Prague, Czech Republic.

Silenzio, V. M. B. (2003). Anthropological assessment of culturally appropriate interventions targeting men who have sex with men. *American Journal of Public Health, 93*(6), 867-871.

Teunis, N. (2007). Sexual objectification and the construction of whiteness in the gay male community. *Culture, Health & Sexuality, 9*(3), 263-275.

Theodore, P. S., Durán, R. E. F., Antoni, M. H., & Fernandez, M. I. (2004). Intimacy and sexual behavior among HIV-positive men-who-have-sex-with-men in primary relationships. *AIDS and Behavior, 8*(3), 321-331.

Torres, H. L., & Gore-Felton, C. (2007). Compulsivity, substance use and loneliness: The loneliness and sexual risk model (LSRM). *Sexual Addiction and Compulsivity, 14,* 63-75.

Truong, H. H. M., Kellogg, T., Klausner, J. D., Katz, M. H., Dilley, J., Knapper, K., et al. (2006). Increases in sexually transmitted infections and sexual risk behavior without a concurrent increase in HIV incidence among men who have sex with men in San Francisco: A suggestion of HIV serosorting? *Sexually Transmitted Infections, 82,* 461-466.

UNAIDS. (2007). *The greater involvement of people living with HIV (GIPA).* Policy Brief JC1299. Geneva, Switzerland: Author.

Verhoeven, V., Bovijn, K., Helder, A., Peremans, L., Hermann, I., Van Royen, P., et al. (2003). Discussing STIs: Doctors are from Mars, patients from Venus. *Family Practice, 20*(1), 11-16.

Vernazza, P., Hirschel, B., Bernasconi, E., & Flepp, M. (2008). Les personnes séropositives ne souffrant d'aucune autre MST et suivant un traitement antirétroviral efficace ne transmettent pas le VIH par voie sexuelle. *Bulletin des médecins suisses, 89*(5), 165-169.

Virilio, P. (2005). *Negative horizon: An essay in dromoscopy* (M. Degener, Trans.). London: Continuum.

Watney, S. (1989). The spectacle of AIDS. In D. Crimp (Ed.), *AIDS: Cultural analysis, cultural activism* (pp. 71-86). Massachusetts: The MIT Press.

Yoshino, K. (2006). *Covering: The hidden assault on our civil rights.* NY: Random House.

CHAPTER 14

Just City Life: Creating a Safe Space for the GLBTQ Community in Urban Adult Education

Tonette S. Rocco

Hilary Landorf

Suzanne J. Gallagher

Gay men and lesbians are everywhere, as evidenced by self-reporting of same-sex couples in 99.3% of all United States counties (Bradford, Barret, & Honnold, 2002). Data from the 2000 United States Census (Bradford et al., 2002) reports a higher concentration of gay- and lesbian-identified people in urban areas. Five metropolitan statistical areas contain more than a quarter of the 600,000 same-sex households reported (Bradford et al., 2002). The five urban areas are New York City (8.9%), Los Angeles (6.6%), San Francisco (4.9%), Washington, D.C. (3.3%), and Chicago (3.1%). The concentration of gays and lesbians in urban areas is further supported by a survey done on voter identification within large cities over 500,000 people. In urban areas, 8.8% of voters identify as gay and lesbian, as compared to 3.7% in suburbs and 2.3% in rural areas with populations between 10,000 and 50,000 (Bradford et al., 2002).

In urban environments, density and diversity cause anonymity and complexity (Daley, Fisher, & Martin, 2000). Density and diversity are determined by incorporated status of an area with a core of 50,000 people and an urbanized area of 100,000 people economically and socially integrated with the core. Anonymity allows people to coexist "without recognizing others as whole persons possessing an identity" (p. 541). Complexity is demonstrated by bureaucratic structures, institutions, cultural enclaves, visible class divisions by neighborhood, and dif-ferential social and economic power. Environments characterized by anonymity and complexity are attractive to GLBTQ people for the safe space to be anony-mous, to facilitate identity development, to find other like people, and to enjoy a sense of belonging. In rural environments, common discourse is that everyone knows everyone else; conformity is the norm, not diversity or complexity; and finding like people is complicated by the need to conform to expected gender roles, which also thwarts identity development. Once drawn into the city, GLBTQ people experience a place where greater opportunity exists alongside oppression. The opportunities include creating welcoming space, pursuing careers that might not have been possible in rural places, and gaining political influence. The op-pression includes violence, discrimination, and marginalization. The purpose of this chapter is to explore urban opportunities and oppressive forces using the four virtues of just city life proposed by Young (1990). First, we present the vir-tues. We follow with a discussion of urban space, leading to a critique of the ideal of community. We end by suggesting Young's vision of a just city life as a means of creating a greater sense of identity, belonging, and justice for GLBTQ people in urban centers and urban adult education.

―+― ﹦◆﹦ ―+―

Creating Safe Space – Developing Identity, a Sense of Belonging, and Justice

The four virtues of just city life proposed by Young (1990) define arenas for creating a dialogical, dynamic, and just experience for GLBTQ people in urban adult education. Young describes her vision of justice in terms of an urban en-vironment where city life is "the being together of strangers" (p. 237). In the just vision of city life, Young identifies four normative virtues: a) social differentiation without exclusion, b) variety, c) eroticism, "in the wide sense of an attraction to the other" (p. 239), and d) publicity or "public places where anyone can speak and anyone can listen" (p. 240). We contend that justice in city life is not neces-sarily the realization of these virtues in individual lives, but rather the degree to which these virtues are embodied and supported by institutional conditions such as urban adult education.

Social Differentiation Without Exclusion

Social differentiation refers to the development of groups in society. The social group is not an ontological entity but the "relational outcome of interactions, meanings, and affinities according to which people identify one another" (Young, 1990, p. 228). The identity of individuals is a product of social relations and is shared with other members of the group. For GLBTQ people, "gaydar" is a term used to describe the process of identifying other GLBTQ people (Nicholas, 2004). Gay men believe they possess this skill (Shelp, 2002), which is learned through an apprenticeship or mentoring (Woolery, 2007). Whether this skill is learned through a mentoring relationship or based on stereotypical attributes, it is a skill that assists GLBTQ people in recognizing each other in urban spaces and in developing community. Once the gaydar is triggered and the identity is affirmed through shared meanings and interactions, the social group of GLBTQ people is affirmed.

Young (1990) goes on to say that differentiation occurs within the social group as well: "Those affirming the specificity of a group affinity should at the same time recognize and affirm the group and the individual differences within the group" (p. 236). This affirms the multiple group identification or polyrhythmic realities that many people have (Sheared, 1994). Differentiation occurs both at the group and the individual levels. Urban environments lend themselves to the development of affinity groups with open and often undecipherable boundaries. The clusters of individuals and their different affinity- group allegiances are diverse and overlapping, creating opportunities for conflict, synergy, indifference, and appreciation.

Variety

As a normative virtue of just city life, variety refers to the differentiated use of social space. Neighborhoods with parks, cafés, schools, homes, businesses, bars, and restaurants draw people out into the public space more readily than neighborhoods with only residences. Neighborhoods with variety tend to have a greater commitment from residents and business owners, tend to be safer, and tend to offer more activities (Young, 1990). Multi-use neighborhoods promote just city life more effectively than single-use neighborhoods by creating opportunities for shared everyday practices without exclusion. Neighborhood borders are often indistinguishable because multiple social groups may share the same space. For instance, a gay neighborhood may be intertwined with Jewish and/or Latino neighborhoods where people live and work.

Eroticism

Eroticism is an attraction to the Other, difference, and the new. Eroticism is "tak[ing] pleasure in being drawn out of oneself to understand that there are other meanings, practices, [and] perspectives on the city, and that one could learn or experience something more and different by interact[ion]" (Young, 1990, p. 240). Eroticism or the concept of being "drawn out of oneself" is critical to engaging and relating to others, unlike exoticism, which objectifies and commodifies the Other. The vision of the just city life affirms the pleasure, and sometimes the fear, of encountering difference. The attractions of urban environments are the unfamiliar foods, music, festivals, and aesthetics generated by different social groups with the full realization of oneself as part of a distinct social group.

While Young's work is delimited by its neglect of rural environments, Young (1990) writes that urban environments, with their mix of social groups and their artifacts, represent "a social and spatial inexhaustibility" (p. 240). The combination and recombination of groups and individuals result in unlimited possibilities or the feeling that there is always something new to see in the city. Imagine an urban adult education program with social and spatial inexhaustibility; the program would be designed to include and affirm, not make learners alike.

The normative virtue of eroticism also affirms the body along with the mind. Eroticism "in the wide sense of an attraction to the other" (Young, 1990, p. 239) is mediated through our senses and our bodies. People feel affirmed because they see themselves reflected in others who share similar goals, values, and appearances. People receive pleasure in encountering the Other, someone who is different and unique. Mediating experience through our bodies forces dominant groups to acknowledge their own bodies, differences, and specificities.

Publicity

The public space of the city is characterized by encounters with those who are different. Young (1990) asserts, "Social justice in the city requires the realization of a politics of difference" (p. 240). Politics depends on the existence of public spaces where everyone has access, open to all. Differences can remain unassimilated, but social groups must be given political representation and opportunities to celebrate their distinctive characteristics. In just city life, it is not required that groups share values nor fully understand one another. The key to justice is acknowledging, listening to, and appreciating other groups.

Urban Space and Everyday Practice

Prior to the nineteenth century, family units remained intact to support the agrarian household for economic survival (D'Emilio, 1993). During the nineteenth century, the Industrial Revolution and the growth of cities allowed individuals to leave the household for jobs in cities. This movement increased after World War II. Up until the 1960s, GLBTQ people formed their identities "in isolation, unaware of others" (D'Emilio, 1993, p. 468), but once identities were formed, the search for others caused many GLBTQ people to move to cities. The "straight" sexual revolution, civil rights, antiwar protests, and the Stonewall Rebellion helped to mobilize gay liberationists into visible and vocal groups (D'Emilio, 1983). Many GLBTQ people have created an identity in a safe urban space and rejected oppressive identities determined by families, religions, and schools that labeled people other than heterosexuals as deviants (Goffman, 1963). The process of identity creation has occurred simultaneously with establishing relationships in gay community centers, gay-friendly churches, and other gay-identified organizations to create a sense of belonging.

The urban space, however, is a contested space like all others. "Geography is about space and place, and the politics of territoriality. Space and place are never neutral, but rather constitute the shifting terrain of cultural conflict" (Grace, Hill, & Wells, 2006, p. 9; see also Chapter 3 above). Space is temporal, physical, and material and can be "produced through public struggle" (Blomley, 2008, p. 158). This public struggle for rights and citizenship creates space for some but denies space for others (Blomley, 2008). At issue in this contested space is "who has the power to determine the meaning of a place" (Sumartojo, 2004, p. 87). Place is understood as the interaction between spatial and social relations (Sumartojo, 2004). Place includes location (distinct point), locale (a bounded area where everyday life occurs), and locus of identity (the center of attraction for individual and group loyalty) (Castree, Featherstone, & Herod, 2008). Social relations include the perceptions and beliefs about a place as well as the everyday practices common in a place. For example, if same-sex couples act affectionately toward one another in open-air cafés on Miami's South Beach (everyday practices), people believe South Beach is a gay neighborhood. Demographically, South Beach has a very diverse population. Still, it is commonly believed to be a gay neighborhood due to these visible everyday practices. Public space is redefined by changing everyday practices, perceptions, and beliefs.

Two men holding hands or two women wearing matching wedding bands challenge the definition of what is normal. When community is defined as het-erosexualized public space, justice for GLBTQ people is limited by the narrow definition and understanding of community as unity and commonality. GLBTQ people have made some progress in redefining public space through participation in politics, business, and culture. By moving into residential areas or neighborhoods en masse, the space becomes redefined. In the Castro District in San Francisco or South Beach in Miami where GLBTQ people and relationships are more visible, heterosexualized public space has been redefined. However, GLBTQ people still suffer from hate crimes and discrimination. The "(hetero) sexualized nature of public space" is a primary determinant of crimes against GLBTQ persons or persons perceived to be GLBTQ (Sumartojo, 2004, p. 87). Public space that reflects a heterosexualized nature defines "normal" exclusively with heterosexual orientation. Other sexual orientations are labeled deviant and are excluded through violence, discrimination, and invisibility. Hate crimes re-inforce the power used to define heterosexualized public space and community.

Contested Space: The Idea of Community

The urban space is defined and redefined by competing ideals of community. Hegel's notion of community as shared ideals has shaped aspirations and actions for the last half-century (Hawkesworth, 2002). Hegel's ideal of community was based on a group of individuals who share ideals and purposes and who strive to infuse these ideals and purposes into institutions and projects (Hegel, 1952). Community may be a bound geographical area where people with common interests and identities live together. A community may be a place and a human system (Flora, 1997, in Ewert & Grace, 2000). Ewert and Grace "see communities as the dynamic, and often contentious, contexts in which people come to know themselves and others and form their interpretations of what is possible to achieve, both individually and collectively" (p.329).

The ideal of community is a unified space, a static entity based on commonality. This ideal of community may be oppressive to people who challenge that unity and/or stability with different values and activities. Stated negatively, "the ideal of community denies and represses social differences" (Young, 1990, p. 227). The unity ideal does not acknowledge the plurality of people's identities, experiences, and practices. Communities are comprised of individuals with complex identities and multiple community memberships that are themselves dynamic and evolving.

GLBTQ people have complex identities. GLBTQ people may be both oppressed and oppressors. For example, a male may be gay and sexist and a female may be lesbian and racist. The GLBTQ community is comprised of people who share one characteristic—a non-heterosexual orientation. Acknowledging diversity within and between people validates the complexity of individual identity. In addition to creating community with complex identities, GLBTQ communities include members who belong to several different communities simultaneously. For example, a gay father is a member of the PTA at his children's school and a member of a local gay-rights advocacy group. His work with the advocacy group for civil protections and rights brings him a sense of belonging; a school board decision to forbid education about gay and lesbian families alienates him from the school system. The ideal of a unified, common community denies the reality of this father's experience.

"Community-making suggests that communities are neither fixed nor given, but are called into being through particular kinds of activities" (Hawkesworth, 2002, p. 331). A particular activity of community making involves excluding some people and including others. A community is more often defined by whom it excludes and who has the power to exclude (Sartwell, 2002). For example, the conservative Christian right excludes people of non-heterosexual orientations. Until the appearance of gay-friendly churches, many GLBTQ people did not define themselves as Christian because to do so would imply acceptance of the conservative Christian right's definition of who is in and who is out. Some GLBTQ people attempted to resolve the dilemma by maintaining their church membership and hiding their sexual differences at church (Sweasey, 1997). Individual memberships in multiple communities belie the reality of a unified, shared community.

Moving from the individual level to the community level, communities are dynamic and constantly redefining themselves (Sartwell, 2002). Neighborhoods traditionally identified with an ethnic or age group may experience gentrification, and a new identity for the neighborhood gradually takes shape. This phenomenon occurred on Miami Beach. During the mid-20th century, Miami Beach was known as a mecca for older Jewish residents. Beginning in the 1970s and 1980s, gay men began arriving in large numbers and eventually transformed the area into a predominantly gay area. Miami-Dade County is also transforming itself from the home of Anita Bryant's initiative to repeal a gay-rights ordinance in 1977 to passing a gay-rights ordinance in 2001 (Bogert, 2002). Recently, Miami-Dade County passed an ordinance extending health benefits to the domestic partners of county employees (Save Dade, 2008). Thus the county "space" is being redefined as more gay-friendly. In addition to communities being dynamic and fluid, membership in multiple, often conflicting, communities challenges the unity ideal of community.

Creating Safe Spaces in Urban Adult Education

In our cities, formal education occurs in institutions of higher education and in business and industry. Informal education occurs regularly during conferences, workshops, and exhibits that are held in urban centers. Nonformal education takes place in grassroots organizations formed to address issues that arise in urban environments. Whether the venue is formal, informal, or nonformal, urban adult education focuses on "learners that are resource rich or resource poor" (Martin & Rogers, 2004, p. 1), in contexts which create "physical, psychological, and socio-cultural distance between and among learners and … providers" (Martin, 2004, p. 3).

Hill (1995) argues that mainstream adult education reproduces heterocentric discourse and homophobia while popular education venues allow GLBTQ people the freedom to define their experiences and identities. The principles of just city life provide mainstream adult education with opportunities to challenge heterocentric discourse and homophobia. Social differentiation, variety, eroticism, and publicity offer practices and meanings that challenge a heterosexualized urban adult education classroom and the ideal of a common community. With the vision of a just city life, difference, multiplicity, and heterogeneity are affirmed, and dominant groups are forced to acknowledge their own specificity. Urban adult educators are challenged to enhance their knowledge and skill base to achieve this vision and create a safe space for GLBTQ learners.

Social differentiation and variety begin with the adult educator's ability to recognize, affirm, and celebrate group affinities and individual differences within those affinities. The assessment of learner needs and the development of instruction should reflect the diversity of group affinities. The adult educator needs to engage in an ongoing process of reflection to ensure the classroom discourse affirms multiple group affinities and identities. Systems for learner feedback regarding affirmation, listening, and celebration should be developed to critique dominant, privileged discourse. Part of establishing social differentiation without exclusion is acknowledging the past of social groups that have been excluded or silenced and bringing this history and voice into the discussions. This includes present practices and future visions of each social group as well.

Adult educators are challenged by the vision of a just city life to create erotic classrooms. We learn through all our senses, and embodied learning activities are appropriate to achieve this virtue. Adult educators must ask the question: How do we promote attraction to the Other? Attraction or eroticism begins with respect for the Other. Then a space is created where heterosexual people and members of other majority communities do not seek to subdue or assimilate the Other, but to experience and appreciate the Other's interactions, meanings, and experiences. Privilege and the patterns and processes that perpetuate privilege destroy eroticism. Adult educators need to be vigilant regarding unjust patterns and processes in the classroom, in admission and graduation policies, and in relationships that create injustice (Rocco & Gallagher, 2004).

Recognizing adult education as a "community maker," educators need to create public pedagogical spaces where anyone may speak and anyone may listen. Educators need to analyze who speaks, about what, and who does not speak. Curriculum, internships, and activities within the classroom, university, or other venues need to be critically analyzed as a heterosexualized space, and constructive alternatives have to be developed and implemented. Here, for example, we should ask: Are significant others mentioned publicly when discussing networking opportunities such as dinners, outings, and college activities? Adult educators have the opportunity and the responsibility to create safe spaces for GLBTQ learners to become full citizens and learners using Young's (1990) alternative to the community ideal and fulfilling the vision of a just city life.

The idea of a just city life is based on the notion that oppressed and marginalized groups must be recognized as having distinct voices and perspectives and be represented in urban policy-making forums (Phillips, 1998). If these groups are not represented as distinct, then policy outcomes will reflect the dominant group's views (Phillips, 1998). The idea of just city life as a "being together of strangers" (Young, 1990, p. 237) may lead to safe spaces for oppressed people if the strangers respect others' distinct voices and perspectives. Pedagogical practices that incorporate the virtues offered by a vision of just city life may facilitate the creation of a safe space for GLBTQ people in urban adult education.

References

Blomley, N. (2008). Making space for law. In K. R. Cox, M. Low, & J. Robinson (Eds.), *The Sage handbook of political geography* (pp. 155-168). Thousand Oaks, CA: Sage.

Bogert, N. (2002). *The gay rights fight: Then and now. Then: Anita Bryant brought celebrity to fight; Now: Most oppose appeal.* South Florida Internet Broadcasting Systems, Inc. Retrieved June 24, 2008, from http://www.nbc6.net/News/1651594/detail.html

Bradford, J., Barret, K., & Honnold, J. A. (2002). *The 2000 census and same-sex households: A user's guide.* NY: The National Gay and Lesbian Task Force Policy Institute, the Survey and Evaluation Research Laboratory, and the Fenway Institute. Available at http://www.ngltf.org

Castree, N., Featherstone, D., & Herod, A., (2008). Contrapuntal geographies: The politics of organizing across sociospatial difference. In K. R. Cox, M. Low, & J. Robinson (Eds.), *The Sage handbook of political geography* (pp. 305-322). Thousand Oaks, CA: Sage.

Daley, B. J., Fisher, J. C., & Martin, L. G. (2000). Urban contexts for adult education practice. In A. Wilson & E. Hayes (Eds.), *Handbook of adult and continuing education new edition* (pp. 539-555). San Francisco: Jossey-Bass.

D'Emilio, J. (1983). *Sexual politics, sexual communities: The making of a homosexual minority in the United States, 1940-1970.* Chicago: The University of Chicago Press.

D'Emilio, J. (1993). Capitalism and gay identity. In H. Abelove, M. A. Barale, & D. M. Halperin (Eds.), *The lesbian and gay studies reader* (pp. 467-476). NY: Routledge.

Ewert, D. M., & Grace, K. A. (2000). Adult education for community action. In A. Wilson & E. Hayes (Eds.), *Handbook of adult and continuing education new edition* (pp. 327-343). San Francisco: Jossey-Bass.

Flint, C. (Ed.). (2004). *Spaces of hate: Geographies of discrimination and intolerance in the U.S.A.* NY: Routledge.

Flora, C. B. (1997). Community. In G. A. Goreham (Ed.), *Encyclopedia of rural America: The land and people.* Santa Barbara, CA: ABC-CLIO, Inc.

Goffman, E. (1963). *Stigma: Notes on the management of a spoiled identity.* NY: Simon and Schuster.

Grace, A. P., Hill, R. J., & Wells, K. (2006). Georgia on our minds: Matters of presence and place for LGBTQ&A participants at AERC. In R. J. Hill & A. P. Grace (Eds.), *Never far away: Separation, subjugation, and violence in LGBTQ lives—Tropes of the fence. Proceedings of the 4th Annual Adult Education Research Conference Lesbian, Gay, Bisexual, Transgender, Queer & Allies (LGBTQ&A) Pre-Conference at the 47th Adult Education Research Conference* (pp. 9-24). University of Minnesota, Minneapolis. Published by the Department of Educational Policy Studies, Faculty of Education, University of Alberta, Edmonton.

Hawkesworth, M. (2002). The university as a universe of communities. In P. Alperson (Ed.), *Diversity and community: An interdisciplinary reader* (pp. 323-334). Malden, MA: Blackwell Publishing.

Hegel, M. (1952). *The philosophy of right.* (T. M. Knox, Trans.). Oxford: Clarendon Press.

Hill, R. J. (1995). Gay discourse in adult education: A critical review. *Adult Education Quarterly, 45*(3), 142-158.

Martin, L. G. (2004). Adult education in the urban context. In L. G. Martin & E. E. Rogers (Eds.), *Crossing borders: Adult education in an urban context* (pp. 3-16). New Directions for Adult and Continuing Education, No. 101. San Francisco: Jossey-Bass.

Martin, L. G., & Rogers, E. E. (2004). New directions for urban adult education. In L. G. Martin & E. E. Rogers (Eds.), *Crossing borders: Adult education in an urban context* (pp. 95-98). New Directions for Adult and Continuing Education, No. 101. San Francisco: Jossey-Bass.

Nicholas, C. L. (2004). Gaydar: Eye-gaze as identity recognition among gay men and lesbians. *Sexuality & Culture, 8*(1), 60-86.

Phillips, A. (1998). *The politics of presence.* Oxford: Clarendon Press.

Rocco, T. S., & Gallagher, S. (2004). Discriminative justice: Can discrimination be just? In L. G. Martin & E. E. Rogers (Eds.), *Crossing borders: Adult education in an urban context* (pp. 29-42). New Directions for Adult and Continuing Education No. 101. San Francisco: Jossey-Bass.

Sartwell, C. (2002). Community at the margin. In P. Alperson (Ed.), *Diversity and community: An interdisciplinary reader* (pp. 47-57). Malden, MA: Blackwell.

Save Dade (2008, May 20). *Domestic partner ordinance now law!* Retrieved June 24, 2008, from http://savedade.readyhosting.com/Newsnewe-mails.htm

Sheared, V. (1994). Giving voice: An inclusive model of instruction—A womanist perspective. In E. Hayes & S. A. J. Colin III (Eds.), *Confronting racism and sexism* (pp. 27-38). New Directions for Adult and Continuing Education, No. 61. San Francisco: Jossey-Bass.

Shelp S. G. (2002). Gaydar: Visual detection of sexual orientation among gay and straight men. *Journal of Homosexuality, 44*(1), 1-14.

Sumartojo, R. (2004). Contesting place: Antigay and -lesbian hate crimes in Columbus, Ohio. In C. Flint (Ed.), *Spaces of hate: Geographies of discrimination and intolerance in the U.S.A.* (pp. 87- 107). NY: Routledge.

Sweasey, P. (1997). *From queer to eternity: Spirituality in the lives of lesbian, gay, and bisexual people.* London: Cassell.

Woolery L. M. (2007). Gaydar: A social cognitive analysis. *Journal of Homosexuality, 53*(3), 9-17.

Young, I. M. (1990). *Justice and the politics of difference.* Princeton, NJ: Princeton University Press.

CHAPTER 15

No End to History: Demanding Civil Quarter for Sexual Minorities in Heteronormative Space

André P. Grace

Robert J. Hill

Blood Red

André P. Grace

I

Polished brass rails

And glistening glasses

A classy bar

A Queer oasis with pretty boys all in a row

Lou smiles from behind

What's your pleasure sweet thing?

SS hats

Leather chaps

A leather vest over a bare chest

Piercing fantasies with boys like me

Nancy boys

II

New York scene 1969

A thirst for justice drives Queers from the oasis into the streets

Gay liberation is the unstoppable response

To the boys in blue and homophobia

To the not so pretty boys of fear in fear

Of Nancy boys and other Queers marching in boots and stilettos

Raging raw and hard

Not everyone loves a man in uniform

The boys in blue can't control it

Each gun is like a penis

Close to shooting

III

Late night scene Montreal 1994

Twenty-five years on gay liberation is a global phenomenon

And yet there is no end to the violence

The boys in blue are still on parade

Battering bleeding Queers

Knocking them to the pavement on another night in another city

There is still no safe civil quarter for Nancy boys and other Queers

What changes in the gay ghetto?

Perhaps only the names of the drag queens

The rainbow banner flutters in the breeze

Blood red remains the color of Queer on the street

Symbolic violence over time (such as using homophobic name-calling and anti-Queer graffiti). Physical violence into the present moment (like assault and battery or worse). The consequences: listlessness, hopelessness, helplessness, malaise. There is no end to the history of violence that seeks an end to us, whether we call ourselves homosexuals, gays and lesbians, Queers (as a contemporary reflection of our diversity and complexity), or some other name that time and tides will generate. Heteronormative ignorance and fear and the violence and nihilism they spawn mark the lives of sexual minorities as un-citizens and seekers of personhood. Fone (2000) locates the origins of Queers as un-citizens in the United States in the period following the first World War:

> *After World War I, diatribes against homosexuality were frequently interwoven with the discourse of patriotism; sexual difference was pictured as un-American, and homosexuals as a threat to the purity of the nation's pioneer traditions. Homosexuality, an offense against the family and social expectations about gender, was also coming to be seen as subverting America itself. (p. 385)*

This heteronormative classification of homosexuality engendered a mainstream homophobic mindset that made way for tragedies like the fascism of McCarthyism that dishonored us as contemptible, limp-wristed communists in the post–World War II period (Fone, 2000). Indeed the 1950s and 1960s proved to be harsh times for sexual minorities. Finally, we were fed up with being indicted "as second-class citizens, as sick, perverted criminals, as undeserving of … [legal] protection" (Fone, 2000, p. 407). And so, Compton's Cafeteria in San Francisco's seedy Tenderloin neighborhood became the site of the first Queer resistance in the United States in the summer of 1966. In response to police harassment, militant hustlers and street queens spilled violently out of the restaurant. Those involved were members of Vanguard, the first known gay youth organization in the United States. This incident was the first recorded public transgender struggle in the United States, but it was eclipsed by the three-day Stonewall rioting that occurred just three years later. On June 28, 1969, at 1:20 a.m., the actions of drag queens, sex hustlers, and street youth generated what is now considered the birthday of a new gay consciousness—the Stonewall Rebellion. It has become the mythic birthday of a new gay consciousness that has since had global impact. Fone (2000) recounts that gay liberation began in New York City with this tumultuous event. He relates that the rebellion marked the emergence of a separatist gay subculture and a new gay sensibility that suggest there might be a shared gay history to be recovered and disseminated.

In this concluding chapter, we consider this history and the status of sexual-minority lives in the contemporary moment. We revisit the emergence of queer theory and its mission to fight heterosexism, homophobia, and transphobia. We also critique that theory for dislocating gay history as it developed new language, new politics, and new understandings of Queer cultural literacy. We then move on to use the more recent history of Queer invisibility at CONFINTEA V, the fifth international adult education conference held in Hamburg, Germany, in 1997, to indicate that there is still history to be made to include sexual minorities as full citizens in social, cultural, political, and economic contexts. Drawing on a pivotal interview with Cornel West, published in the *Harvard Educational Review* (Eisen & Kenyatta, 1996), in which he spoke about heterosexism and transformation, we conclude with a consideration of what might be done to make Queer-inclusive history a reflection of creating place for sexual minorities in the years ahead.

Sharply Conscious of Everything

The responses to oppression in 1969 in New York, in 1994 in Montreal,[7] and in many other times and places are part of a long chain of responses to violence historically perpetrated against Queers. Indeed relentless violence and its repercussions continue to mar many Queer lives in the face of perpetual heterocentric ignorance and fear that place limits on and stall Queer possibilities to be, become, belong, and act in the world. Felt or feared acts of violence, inextricably linked to Queer anxiety and justified anger, are an everyday reality for those of us whose sexual orientations and gender identities fail to fit heteronorms. In writing about this fear as part of his life history and gay history in general, D'Emilio (1992) reminds us of a stark truth: gay history is an unending history of fear as we mediate a dangerous heteronormative world that has historically refused to respect and accommodate us. Consequently, silence, invisibility, stress, illness, and inaction have been common historical markers of hidden homosexual/gay and lesbian/Queer lives. Of course, no hegemony is complete, and so our history also includes resistance and fighting back as in 1966, 1969, and 1994, cited above. D'Emilio writes personally about his own experience of fear and anxiety as a young gay man coming out and coming to terms. For so many of us, it is a wholly

---

7   André s poem remembers such another night of police brutality against Queers that occurred during the summer of 1994 when he was studying at McGill University.

relatable experience in which being closeted is a survival mechanism and identity management tool that enables us to keep jobs and maintain familial and other social relationships. D'Emilio's words speak to our historical social positionality of being the guarded gay outsider:

But the fear stayed. Every moment spent in quest of a homosexual connection remained encased in a mind-numbing terror—of discovery, and of the calamities that would ensue if I were discovered. The terror simultaneously sharpened and dulled my senses. To move ahead, I had to block out as much feeling as I could and, as a result, often saw myself as blanketed by a dense, impenetrable fog. At the same time, whenever I cruised or was in a public space with another gay man, I was acutely, sharply conscious of everything that was happening around me, and absolutely attuned to the finest nuances of behavior. I had to be. (pp. xix-xx, italics in original)

The subtext of D'Emilio's narrative vignette indicates the power of homophobia. In his explication of the politics of homophobia, Fone (2000) describes how the kind of fear that D'Emilio experienced is compounded by the kinds of fear associated with heterosexism, which is the attitude that all people are, or should be, heterosexual. Heterosexism is often "an ideological system that denies, denigrates, and stigmatizes any non-heterosexual form of behaviour, relationship, or community" (Herek, 1990, p. 316). Noting that, in general, heterosexuals have historically perceived homosexuals as disruptors of the heteronormative sexual and gender order, Fone recounts how this perception has tended to induce fear. This fear is exacerbated by another fear: a fear that homosexual social conduct erodes the social, political, ethical, moral, and legal order of society. These entrenched fears are embodied and embedded in homophobia, which Fone describes as constructed, socialized antipathy toward homosexuals that incites violence based on personhood, appearance, social conduct, and/or sexual behavior. As a public pedagogy, homophobia teaches children early to deride fags, dykes, and other Queers.

[H]omophobia has taken various forms and arisen from many sources. Invented, fostered, and supported over time by different agencies of society—religion, government, law, and science—it tends to break out with special venom when people imagine a threat to the security of gender roles, of religious doctrine, of the state and society, or of the sexual safety and health of the individual [as described in sanctioned diagnostic and statistics manuals]. ... So long as it is legitimated by society, religion, and

politics, homophobia will spawn hatred, contempt, and violence, and it will remain our last acceptable prejudice. (Fone, pp. 6-7, 421)

Even though there are laws and legislation to protect us in some nations, violence still takes many forms in contemporary heterosexualizing culture. For example, Janoff (2005), providing an extensive analysis of homophobic violence in Canada in his book *Pink Blood,* concludes that homophobia is "the problem [that] is not going away" (p. 252). Canadian Queers still have to be sharply conscious in their surroundings despite the fact that they have had constitutionally protected equality rights since 1998 (Grace & Wells, 2005). In this regard, what Janoff's study highlights is the pressing need for education based on an encompassing public Queer pedagogy that can be used across age groups in formal, informal, and nonformal educational settings. In particular, we should use this pedagogy to educate youth wherever we find them. As Janoff notes in a Canadian context, 40% of Queer-bashing incidents involve teenage perpetrators. However, carrying out educative work to build Queer knowledge and understanding is a perennial challenge. It is even an uphill battle in teacher-education programs in higher education where aspiring teachers ought to be trained to nurture and support *all* children and youth. However, it seems *all* doesn't always include the Queer ones. Too many instructors ignore sexual-minority children and youth in discussions of context and relationships in their courses (Kissen, 2002). And there is a contingent of undergraduate education students who would prefer not to hear about Queer. Killoran and Pendleton Jiménez (2007) tell a very familiar story:

> *Working as teacher educators, we have experienced extreme resistance, including the refusal to engage in the discourse around LGBT equity, from some of our teacher candidates. How discouraging, for these are the new teachers entering our schools to guide the next generation. While there is a perception that public sentiment and support for LGBT rights has improved, ... [it is clear] that the school community has a long way to go. (p. 5)*

It should be a great source of embarrassment, and even shame, for any teacher to demean, dismiss, or deny sexual-minority children and youth, leaving them behind. After all, as professionals and nurturers, they are expected to be guided by an ethic of care.

In this book we have had an opportunity to explore the history and emerging presence of Queer in another educational context: the Adult Education Research Conference (AERC). Since 1993, the year that Robert J. Hill organized the first Lesbian, Gay, Bisexual, Transgender, Queer, & Allies Caucus at the 34th annual

AERC, there has been a consistent and persistent collective effort to confront the dismissal of Queer in adult education as a replicator of the heteronormative status quo. Importantly, this pioneering work, recounted by Grace and Hill in their chapter and reflected in many other chapters in this collection, has occurred in the same time frame as the emergence of queer theory in the academy. It is this emergence to which we now turn.

⊷⊶⊹⊷⊶

The Emergence of Queer Theory: Vigilance and Vocality in the Face of Heterosexism, Homophobia, and Transphobia

As a post-foundational discourse, queer theory has been under construction as a deterrent to heterosexism and homophobia for about two decades. More recently, queer theory has been emerging as a site to explore gender transphobia, influenced by such pivotal work as Butler's (2004) *Undoing Gender* and Stryker and Whittle's (2006) *The Transgender Studies Reader*. Many Queer and allied academics and graduate students in adult and higher education and other interdisciplinary venues have turned to queer theory, using it as a compass and a medium to energize and inform their own evolving transgressive (and hopefully transformative) work.

> *Queer theory emerged during the 1990s, influenced by Queer social activist aims to expose and transgress heterosexism, homophobia, and [more recently] transphobia. Its interdisciplinary development in academe has been heavily influenced by poststructural feminism and other post-foundational, multi-perspective theoretical discourses....Queer theory continues to develop and build on these discourses. It is a multi-faceted theoretical and creative space for contestation and discovery. Queer theory contests, interrogates, and disrupts systemic and structural relationships of power that are historically caught up in heteronormative attitudes, values, and practices, as well as heteronormative ideological, linguistic, existential, and strategic conventions and constructs. These power relationships have variously defiled or dismissed sexes, sexualities, and genders not sanctioned by heteronormativity. Heteronormativity presumes and values heterosexuality (or the opposite-sex attraction between a biological XY male and a biological XX female) as the norm against which other sexualities have historically been labeled deviant. (Grace, 2008b, p. 718)*

While some locate Eve Kosofsky Sedgwick (1990, 1993) as the founder of queer theory (Gamson, 2000), it might be better to include Sedgwick among several cofounders of queer theory: Teresa de Lauretis (1991), Diana Fuss (1991), Michael Warner (1993), and Judith Butler (1990/1999, 1993) are also prominent in its early theoretical formation (Grace, 2005b, 2008b). Here we will draw on the theorizing of Fuss to provide a synopsis of some of the key emphases in this fluid, tentative, and turbulent theory. Like other Queer theorists, Fuss develops queer theory to confront heterosexism, homophobia, and transphobia. Central to her theorizing is the notion that standard binaries like male/female, heterosexual/homosexual, and public/private are socially, culturally, and historically based on a larger inside/outside binary. In contemporary times, Fuss asserts that this contextually shaped binary locates Queer (as a fluid and encompassing term to name an array of sex, sexual, and gender differences) on the outside "based on a logic of limits, margins, borders, and boundaries" (p. 1). For example, this logic confines sexual identity and desire "variously and in tandem, through acts and experiences of defense, ambivalence, repression, denial, threat, trauma, injury, identification, internalization, and renunciation" (p. 2). As Fuss sees it, heteronormativity assumes that standard binaries are stable and instituted forever so they can continue their work to alienate, diminish, or ignore the diversity and spectral nature of Queer as it marks the human condition. In this regard, the inside/outside construction "encapsulates the structure of language, repression, and subjectivity, [and] also designates the structure of exclusion, oppression, and repudiation" (p. 2). Queer theory ardently interrogates this construct within a politics of transgression and transformation that works to fight heterosexism, homophobia, and transphobia so space, place, respect, and accommodation may be achieved for all who are variously positioned in what Grace (2001) calls "the spectral community of Queer Others" (p. 259).

In developing such a contextually and relationally complex cultural and political theory, Fuss (1991) asks:

> But how, exactly, do we bring the hetero/homo opposition to the point of collapse? How can we work it to the point of critical exhaustion, and what effects – material, political, social – can such a sustained effort to erode and to reorganize the conceptual grounds of identity be expected to have on our sexual practices and politics? (p. 1)

Since the emergence of queer theory, a growing number of Queer theorists have worked to answer these questions. Following Fuss's suggestion, which finds support in the groundbreaking work of other cofounders of queer theory, this contingent has contested the customary cultural status of heterosexuality as a compulsory identity and practice that is legitimate and necessary against tainted homosexuality. As the work of building queer theory continues, it has to continue to persist in forsaking heterosexuality as the only or desired normal while it carries on affirming a spectrum of sex, sexual, and gender differences as well as multiple modes of sexual and gender expression. As well, this work has to traverse more vigorously complex intersections where heterosexism, homophobia, and transphobia meet classism, racism, and other deterrents to living a better life. In sum, the political and cultural work of queer theory is to intensify praxis aimed at increasing protections for and advancing the human and civil rights of those who are degraded, diminished, left out, or made vulnerable by inside/outside categorizations, condoned by heteronormativity and its sense of normalcy that delimit accepted and acceptable desires, differences, positionalities, and expressions. This work would locate Queer within an ecology in which the fluidity and complexity of Queer ontology could continuously challenge the meaning and value of heteronorms.

Much of this chapter is about the importance of turning to history to help us make meaning and sense of the past in order to understand how the present is different (Carr, 1961) and to help us contextualize Queer cultural work to transform the (Queer) human condition. Yet what is perhaps most troubling in the emergence of queer theory is a pervasive dismissal of gay history in the tradition of histories already referenced, like D'Emilio's (1992) *Making Trouble* or Fone's (2000) *Homophobia: A History*. This dismissal can be tied to queer theory's early textual (rather than practical) preoccupation, its inattentiveness to social action, and its (perhaps unwitting) construction of Queer/gay as another inside/outside binary, where Queer is the embraced fluid and expansive descriptor for a host of sex, sexual, and gender differences, and gay is the limited and deposable construct. Strangely, the politics of Queer in the academy has sometimes seemed to be focused on norming Queer, even though queer theory resists norms and normalizing processes. One might say that gay is faggotized in Queer academic culture, pushing gay history and culture to the margins as though they are not important to counterpolitical processes of transgressing and transforming heteronormativity. However, gay history and culture would be better viewed as the antecedents to Queer culture and the history that will be written about it. While the association of gay with often affluent, White, male homosexuals has been used to limit the utility of "gay," the history of "gay" should not be forgotten. Thus it might work better to view "gay" (and its antecedent: "homosexual") as transhistorical categories (Fone, 2000). Those who engage in Queer social activism and cultural work can then turn to homosexual- and gay-oriented histories to learn about counterpraxis and the price sexual and gender outsiders have paid for medical science's long-time diagnosis of us as pathological and deviant, for religion's conservative casting of us as sinful and depraved, and for culture's traditional scapegoating of us in the face of perennial heteronormative ignorance and fear (Grace, 2007, 2008a; Grace & Wells, 2005). They can engage this history as a history of activism and liberation and as a history of resistance to the perpetual violence that has permeated the lives of sexual and gender nonconformists (D'Emilio, 1992). In *Making Trouble*, D'Emilio challenges contemporary gay historians to write gay history as a "collaborative, collective enterprise" (p. xxxix) for the following reason:

> *The vast majority of us in the gay and lesbian movement are saddled with a heavy burden of ignorance about our history of political struggle. The frenzy of activity that envelops us leaves little room for thoughtful reflection; the past vanishes before the image of the next task or crisis. (p. 271)*

While leaving his own historical work open to the scrutiny of others, D'Emilio stresses how urgent it was for him to engage in this work and write the social history of gay life. D'Emilio wants to show how gays have been historically demeaned as un-citizens. He also wants to show that there was a clear link between gay liberation and the gay subculture that produced "cultural workers in a liberation movement" (p. xli) who took risks toward becoming free and full citizens.

⊷ ▨◈▧ ⊶

Still History to Be Made

Earlier we noted the significance of the Stonewall Rebellion, which Fone (2000) linked to the emergence of a separatist gay subculture in the United States. Providing a global perspective, D'Emilio (1992) positions the rebellion as a historical rupture that had worldwide impact, creating a large-scale militant popular social movement that spread throughout the industrialized West and other nations as well. However, there remain significant limits to the impact of this rupture, as a turn to the recent history of events at CONFINTEA V in Hamburg, Germany, in 1997 indicates.[8]

---

8 Some of the material regarding CONFINTEA V has been previously published in Hill (2008). Recognition is given to the international journal, *Convergence*, for its use here.

Throughout this chapter, and indeed throughout this volume, we have been continuously reminded that sexual minorities live in contexts and environments that set up obstacles for us to be, become, belong, and act—both in intimacy and in learning. Here we recognize that certain (heterosexual, dyadic) emotions, feelings, inclinations, orientations, expressions, and behaviors are privileged while others such as those marking the everyday of sexual minorities are disadvantaged, discouraged, or silenced. Hill (2008) has shown how in purportedly democratic states globally we are denied fundamental rights as outlined in the most basic human rights documents, such as the *Charter of the United Nations* (UN, 1945), the *Universal Declaration of Human Rights* (UN, 1948), the *European Convention on Human Rights and Its Five Protocols* (Council of Europe, 1950, 1952, 1963, 1966), the *Vienna Declaration* (OUNHCHR, 1993), the *International Covenant on Civil and Political Rights* (OUNHCHR, 1966a), and the *International Covenant on Economic, Social and Cultural Rights* (OUNHCHR, 1966b). While our lives are rarely proscribed in these documents, the heterocentric language and assumptions specifically refer to heterosexuality, resulting in both planned and unwitting erasure of sexual minorities. In fact, in many nations we still face legal, state-sanctioned discrimination and even death through penalties levied by courts or by extrajudicial actions.

Merrifield (2003) reminds us that "adult education has a strong tradition of education for democracy. We like to think of what we do as promoting good citizenship and involvement in communities" (p. 165). There are, however, exceptions to this maxim. Exploring the Fifth International Conference on Adult Education (CONFINTEA V) at the intersection of gay and lesbian social movement learning is a case in point (CONFINTEA V, 1997a, b). In 1997, more than 1,500 representatives of governments and nongovernmental organizations (NGOs) attended CONFINTEA V in Hamburg, Germany. The result was a groundbreaking strategy for lifelong learning, but one that omitted rights for lesbian, gay, bisexual, transgender, Indigenous/Two-Spirit, and Queer people to learn to be, become, and belong—that is, to assume the avenues that open us to Queer-inclusive learning across the lifespan and that offer physical, spiritual, emotional, and psychological quality of life in a democratic sphere. This omission should be a source of shame to adult education and lifelong learning, since both, historically, have variously placed great value on social education (Grace, 1999, 2000, 2004, 2005a).

Unspoken Words: Precluding Experience, Thought, and Agency

Discourse is not only what is said, but it includes, perhaps insidiously, what remains silent. More than a set of statements, discourse is comprised of the meanings and social relations embedded in those statements. It also includes what remains unsaid in the articulations. Discourse is the "meaningful field that provides the conditions of possibility for experience, thought, and action" (Nash, 2000, p. 274). Scott (1985) suggests that it includes not only specific words and phrases but also a whole set of rules for determining what is true (or not true), what has value (or does not), what is trivial (or meaningful). Discourse as it pertains to CONFINTEA V emerged as a sustained colonial discourse about sexual minorities. It continued a heterosexist process whereby most participants extended authority over us, rarely spoke on behalf of us, and largely perpetuated silences about us. The results of CONFINTEA V are clear: the prospects, possibilities, and systems of validation for sexual minorities were and remain absent because they were deemed irrelevant, even threatening. Mainly, in nuanced and covert ways, we were told to maintain our masked selves and to extinguish the fire in our hearts.

The CONFINTEA V *Agenda for the Future* set "out in detail the new commitment to the development of adult learning… [focused] on common concerns facing humanity.…[It recognized that] profound changes are taking place both globally and locally.…[It called for] ensuring the legitimate right of people to self-determination and to the free exercise of their way of life," and it sought "to ensure accessibility and quality [for learning]" (UNESCO Institute for Education, 1997a, Points 1, 2, 4, 13a, 18; see also UNESCO Institute for Education, 1997b). Oddly, the excitement, foment, and profound changes in society—at least in some places—generated by gay and lesbian social movements were not a part of the *Agenda*'s "new commitment." Regarding the last situation, in Point 18, subtitled "Ensuring Accessibility and Quality," the *Agenda* called for developing and adopting legislation, comprehensive policies, and co-operative mechanisms among adult learning initiatives related to different institutions and sectors of activity. More than a decade after the *Agenda* was penned, we still search for evidence that these have materialized in the formal arena of adult education and training.

Adult Learning, Democracy, Peace, and Critical Citizenship as a Thematic Emphasis at CONFINTEA V: A Situation of Infidelity

Participants at CONFINTEA V asserted that adult education was the key to the 21st century. In this regard, "Adult Learning, Democracy, Peace, and Critical Citizenship" was among themes developed for the CONFINTEA V Mid-Term Review (UNESCO Institute for Education, 2003). This theme has direct relevance to sexual minorities as persons, citizens, learners, and workers. Still, much work remains to be done internationally in policy arenas and in adult and lifelong education either to interpret or apply this theme in consideration of the rights and needs of sexual minorities. In the face of this ongoing neglect, lesbian and gay social movements remain *the* sites of learning, personal growth and transformation, meaning making, and resistance to sexual-minority marginalization and second-class citizenship.

Under the theme of adult learning, democracy, peace, and critical citizenship, sexual minorities clearly fall into the rank of secondary citizens in most countries of the world. Sexual-minority individuals and communities are denied full and equal rights, justice, free will, and the right to organize, as well as opportunities to participate in civil society and open economic development in formal and informal economies. Examples are legion and include being denied the right to marry, the right to have spousal/companion benefits in cases where these are offered to heterosexual couples, the right to adopt or foster children, the right to inherit when our life companions die, the right to hospital visitation, and the right to make medical or legal decisions for life partners when they are incapable of doing so. This list is far from exhaustive. Hill (2003a, b, 2006) provides extensive documentation of these denied rights from the perspective of citizenship rights and the nation-state. This composite exclusion deeply impacts the well-being and the public and personal health of sexual-minority citizens who are disenfranchised from access and accommodation that go hand in hand with the rights and privileges of full citizenship in democratic cultures and societies. It is also critical to point out that heterosexism, homophobia, and transphobia are social ills that affect other citizens in addition to sexual minorities. Many heterosexuals also suffer in societies that have rigid gender and sexuality roles and expectations. Thus, unmarried heterosexuals in long-term, loving relationships may face similar obstacles to those mentioned above.

In Hamburg there was a call for governments to adapt to the realities of a host of marginalized peoples. Civil society, too, was challenged to help individuals express their aspirations and create learning opportunities throughout life. However, sexual minorities were not included in the discussion. There was no space to dream dreams of intimacy and justice or to live full, participatory lives of social inclusion. One exception to this exclusion comes to mind. The CONFINTEA V Mid-Term Review meeting in Bangkok, Thailand, 2003, made a significant move toward establishing the category of *emotional democracy*. The thematic review on democracy positioned multiple layers, including emotional democracy (as a point of gender justice) and recognized the right of sexual minorities to sexual desires. However, it did not develop the latter into the concept of a democracy of intimacy or sexuality. The final Mid-Term Review, to which Robert J. Hill introduced language protecting sexual minorities, affirms, "We therefore call upon Member States, bi- and multilateral agencies, non-governmental and civil society organizations, social movements and the private sector to adopt inclusive policies and take concrete measures and provide adequate resources in support of education programs mainstreaming and catering to the learning demands of persons with disabilities as well as marginalized groups such as…minorities (including sexual minorities, where licit)…" (CONFINTEA V, 2003, p. 19). In 2003, there was slight progress and a glimmer of hope for some. However, the rider "where licit" indicates that there is still much sexual-minority history to be made in inclusive, accommodating contexts.

Lifelong Learning for Nontraditional Actors: Who Decides?

At the close of CONFINTEA V, Esi Sutherland-Addy (from Ghana) declared the "need to…develop human development programmes to *enable adult learning throughout life within and across sectors*; [the need to] maximize opportunities for adult learning by integrating adult learning components into all programmes and projects; [and the need to] *increase capacity of all the non-traditional actors to participate actively in adult learning opportunities*" (CONFINTEA V, 1997a , p. 1, italics added). In most regions of the world this has yet to occur for sexual minorities who live within a heritage of meagerness at best and mean-spiritedness at worst. In keeping with queer theory as exposition of heterosexism, homophobia, and transphobia, it is vital to name all of the irresponsible parties that systematically exclude sexual minorities from the category of nontraditional actors. We must relentlessly ask, "Who are they? How do we change their hearts to step out of the way of our being, becoming, belonging, and acting in the world?"

The joy of learning to be, become, belong, and act, so profoundly and prophetically spelled out at Hamburg in 1997 (Bélanger & Federighi, 2000), awaits realization for sexual-minority communities—at least in the public sphere. Specifically, in the context of lifelong learning, CONFINTEA V has ultimately had little to say to us. For more than a decade, on a global scale, we have been denied the right to ongoing learning processes whereby we can "develop [our] abilities, enrich [our] knowledge, and improve [our]…qualifications…*to meet [our] own needs and those of [our] society*" (CONFINTEA V, 1997b, para. 3, italics added). This is one clear example telling us that there is history yet to be made.

Concluding Perspective: Continuing the Struggle to Make History

Non-Queers who view Queer being, becoming, belonging, and acting through a heterocentric lens where everything is refracted through the optics of the sort of inside/outside binary that Fuss (1991) interrogates ultimately have a limited view of the complexities of the Queer human condition. To continue the struggle to make history that gives sexual minorities space and place, respect and accommodation, and the opportunity to live full and unapologetic lives, Cornel West declares that each of us begin by conceptualizing our own "pain and suffering as it relates to the most visible scars. The most visible source of those scars for … [sexual minorities] has been heterosexism and homophobia" (Eisen & Kenyatta, 1996, p. 361). Then, from the politics of personal locatedness, each of us should move into an intersection—a radical, democratic common space—where we develop strategic coalitions of resistance to counteract the divide-and-conquer approach of the powers that be. Here we need to come to "some overlapping consensus regarding the way in which … [racism, sexism, heterosexism, and other] systems of oppression operate. … [There is a need for] coalitions because the powers that be are so strong" (p. 361). West concludes, "Democracy—radical democracy in all of its forms—tries to accent the variety of institutional and individual forms of evil and constitutes the most formidable threat to the powers that be" (p. 361). This requires trust, which is difficult to build because, "at the psychocultural level, the forms of fear and insecurity and anxiety associated with others from the prevailing systems that socialize us [work] in a way that reinforces the fears and anxieties associated with the 'other'; for example, gay, lesbian, Black, brown, red, and so forth" (p. 362). Yet there is a greater challenge. Those working to counter racism and sexism have to move beyond heterosexist, moralizing discourse that has historically demeaned sexual minorities because

Queer experiences of intimacy lie outside heteronormative understanding. This remains a key challenge globally. It requires a turn to history and much communicative learning and action that emanate from self-critique and cultural critique. West asserts:

> It seems to me that to talk about the history of heterosexism and the history of homophobia is to talk about ways in which various institutions and persons have promoted unjustified suffering and unmerited pain. Hence, the questions become: How do we understand heterosexism? Why is it so deeply seated within our various cultures and civilizations? .... I think it fundamentally has to do with the tendency human beings have to associate persons who are different with degradation, to associate those who have been cast as marginal with subordination and devaluation. (p. 357)

To answer West's questions as a starting point for making history that includes sexual minorities in social, cultural, political, and economic contexts we have to interrogate histories of heterosexism, homophobia, and transphobia that have long set limits to such inclusion. As West sees it, such interrogation is requisite because "evil is inside each and every one of us, in part because of that treacherous terrain called history that has shaped us, and socialized us, and acculturated us" (Eisen & Kenyatta, 1996, p. 360). As we engage history as self-critique and cultural critique, West contends we become both vulnerable and accountable through critical questioning. As a result, we may become open to political possibility so we may make inclusive history to end the history of pain and suffering that has been the lot of sexual minorities for much too long. This is history as transgression. This is history as transformation.

References

Bélanger, P., & Federighi, P. (2000). *Unlocking people's creative forces: A transnational study of adult learning policies.* Hamburg: UNESCO Institute for Education.

Butler, J. (1999). *Gender trouble: Feminism and the subversion of identity.* New York: Routledge.

Butler, J. (1993). *Bodies that matter: On the discursive limits of 'sex.'* New York: Routledge.

Butler, J. (2004). *Undoing gender.* New York: Routledge.

Carr, E. H. (1961). *What is history?* New York: Vintage Books.

CONFINTEA V. (1997a). *Final report.* Retrieved, December 14, 2008, from http://www.unesco.org/education/uie/confintea/repeng.html#A.%20Report%20of%20the%20Conference%20by%20the

CONFINTEA V. (1997b). *Hamburg declaration on lifelong learning.* Retrieved, December 14, 2008, from http://www.unesco.org/education/uie/ confintea/declaeng.htm

CONFINTEA V. (2003, 6-11 September). *Recommitting to adult education and learning: Synthesis report of the CONFINTEA V Mid-Term Review Meeting.* Retrieved, December 14, 2008, from http://www.unesco.org/education/uie/pdf/ recommitting.pdf

Council of Europe. (1950, 1952, 1963, 1966). *European Convention on Human Rights and its five protocols.* Retrieved December 14, 2008, from http://www.hri.org/ docs/ECHR50.html

de Lauretis, T. (Ed.). (1991, Summer). Queer theory. [Special issue]. *Differences: A Journal of Feminist Cultural Studies, 3*(2).

D'Emilio, J. (1992). *Making trouble: Essays on gay history, politics, and the university.* New York: Routledge.

Eisen, V., & Kenyatta, M. (1996). Cornel West on heterosexism and transformation: An interview. *Harvard Educational Review 66*(2), 356-367.

Fone, B. (2000). *Homophobia: A history.* New York: Metropolitan Books, Henry Holt and Company.

Fuss, D. (1991). Inside/out. In D. Fuss (Ed.), *Inside/out: Lesbian theories, gay theories* (pp. 1-10). New York: Routledge.

Gamson, J. (2000). Sexualities, queer theory, and qualitative research. In N. K. Denzin & Y. S. Lincoln (Eds.), *Handbook of qualitative research* (2nd ed., pp. 347-365). Thousand Oaks, CA: Sage Publications.

Grace, A. P. (1999). Building a knowledge base in U.S. academic adult education (1945-1970). *Studies in the Education of Adults, 31*(2), 220-236.

Grace, A. P. (2000). Canadian and U.S. adult learning (1945-1970) and the cultural politics and place of lifelong learning. *International Journal of Lifelong Education, 19*(2), 141-158.

Grace, A. P. (2001). Using Queer cultural studies to transgress adult educational space. In V. Sheared & P. A. Sissel (Eds.), *Making space: Merging theory and practice in adult education* (pp. 257-270). Westport, CT: Bergin & Garvey.

Grace, A. P. (2004). Lifelong learning as a chameleonic concept and versatile practice: Y2K perspectives and trends. *International Journal of Lifelong Education, 23*(4), 385-405.

Grace, A. P. (2005a). Lifelong learning chic in the modern practice of adult education: Historical and contemporary perspectives. *Journal of Adult and Continuing Education, 11*(1), 62-79.

Grace, A. P. (2005b). Queer studies. In L. M. English (Ed.), *International encyclopedia of adult education* (pp. 530-533). New York: Palgrave Macmillan.

Grace, A. P. (2007). In your care: School administrators and their ethical and professional responsibility toward students across sexual-minority differences. In W. Smale & K. Young (Eds.), *Approaches to educational leadership and practice* (pp. 16-40). Calgary, AB: Detselig Enterprises/Temeron Books.

Grace, A. P. (2008a). The charisma and deception of reparative therapies: When medical science beds religion. *Journal of Homosexuality, 55*(4), 545-580.

Grace, A. P. (2008b). Queer theory. In L. M. Given (Ed.), The Sage encyclopedia of qualitative research methods (Vol. 2, pp. 718-722). Thousand Oaks, CA: Sage.

Grace, A. P., & Wells, K. (2005). The Marc Hall prom predicament: Queer individual rights v. institutional church rights in Canadian public education. *Canadian Journal of Education, 28*(3), 237-270.

Herek, G. M. (1990). The context of anti-gay violence. *Journal of Interpersonal Violence, 5*, 316-333.

Hill, R. J. (2003a). Inclusion of sexual minorities in the discussion on gender justice: The GEO Virtual Seminar. In Paz Alonso (Ed.), *Education for inclusion throughout life: The GEO Virtual Seminar* (pp. 130-134). Montevideo, Uruguay: The Gender and Education Office of the International Council for Adult Education.

Hill, R. J. (2003b). Turning a gay gaze on citizenship: Sexual orientation and gender identity—Contesting/ed terrain. In C. Medel-Anonuevo et al. (Eds.), *Citizenship, democracy and lifelong learning* (pp. 99-139). Hamburg, Germany: The United Nations Educational, Scientific, and Cultural Organization (UNESCO) and the Institute for Education (UIE). Also available at http://www.unesco.org/education/ uie/pdf/uiestud35.pdf)

Hill, R. J. (2006). The war on democracy: A perspective from the USA. *Convergence, 38*(2-3), 167-176.

Hill, R. J. (2008). Sexual minority rights (lesbian, gay, bisexual, transgender, Two-Spirit, and Queer): Will comprehensive policy considerations find a voice? *Convergence, 40*(3), 169-179. Available at http://www.icae.org.uy/eng/ convergence34.pdf

Janoff, D. V. (2005). *Pink blood: Homophobic violence in Canada.* Toronto: University of Toronto Press.

Killoran, I., & Pendleton Jiménez, K. (2007). *"Unleashing the unpopular": Talking about sexual orientation and gender diversity in education.* Olney, MD: Association for Childhood Education International.

Kissen, R. (2002). *Getting ready for Benjamin: Preparing teachers for sexual diversity in the classroom.* Lanham, MD: Rowman & Littlefield.

Merrifield, J. (2003). Practicing what we preach: Internal democracy and citizenship in adult education. In P. Coare & R. Johnston (Eds.), *Adult learning, citizenship and community voices* (pp. 165-182). Leicester, UK: NIACE.

Nash, K. (2000). *Contemporary political sociology: Globalization, politics, and power.* Malden, MA: Blackwell.

Office of the United Nations High Commissioner for Human Rights. (1966a). *International covenant on civil and political rights.* Retrieved December 14, 2008, from http://www.unhchr.ch/html/menu3/b/a_ccpr.htm

Office of the United Nations, High Commissioner for Human Rights. (1966b). *International covenant on economic, social and cultural rights.* Retrieved December 14, 2008, from http://www.unhchr.ch/html/menu3/b/a_cescr.htm

Office of the United Nations, High Commissioner for Human Rights. (1993). *Vienna Declaration and programme of action.* World Conference on Human Rights. Retrieved December 14, 2008, from http://www.unhchr.ch/huridocda/ huridoca.nsf/(Symbol)/A.CONF.157.23.En

Scott, J. C. (1985). *Weapons of the weak: Everyday forms of peasant resistance.* New Haven, CT: Yale University Press.

Sedgwick, E. K. (1990). *Epistemology of the closet.* Berkeley: University of California Press.

Sedgwick, E. K. (1993). *Tendencies.* Durham, NC: Duke University Press.

Stryker, S. & Whittle, S. (Eds.). (2006). *The transgender studies reader.* New York: Routledge.

UNESCO Institute for Education. (1997a). *Agenda for the future.* Retrieved December 14, 2008, from http://www.unesco.org/education/uie/confintea/agendeng.htm

UNESCO Institute for Education. (1997b). *The Hamburg Declaration and the Agenda for the Future.* Retrieved December 14, 2008, from www.unesco.org/education/ uie/confintea/publications.html

UNESCO Institute for Education. (2003). *CONFINTEA mid-term review.* Retrieved December 14, 2008, from http://www.unesco.org/education/uie/activities/ CONFVReviewindex.shtml

United Nations. (1945). *Charter of the United Nations.* Retrieved December 14, 2008, from http://www.un.org/aboutun/charter/

United Nations (1948). *Universal declaration of human rights.* Retrieved December 14, 2008, from http://www.un.org/Overview/rights.html

Warner, M. (Ed.). (1993). *Fear of a queer planet: Queer politics and social theory.* Minneapolis, MN: University of Minnesota Press.

ABOUT THE EDITORS

Robert J. Hill is Associate Professor of Adult Education at the University of Georgia, Department of Lifelong Education, Administration, and Policy. In 1993, he co-founded the Adult Education Research Conference Lesbian, Gay, Bisexual, Transgender, Queer, and Allies Caucus and, in 2003, the LGBTQ&A Pre-Conference. He is a past member of the AERC Steering Committee. Bob is editor-in-chief of *Convergence*, the international journal of adult education, and an *ex officio* member of the International Council for Adult Education (ICAE), which he served as Vice President for North America. In 2007, Bob received a UGA Outstanding Teaching Award and, in 2008, the Dr. Martin Luther King, Jr., "Fulfilling the Dream" Presidential Award. Recently he has studied Native American lifeways with two Indigenous elders at the Santa Clara Pueblo, New Mexico, and at Table Mesa, New Mexico, in the Navajo (Diné) Nation. He is an affiliate faculty member in the UGA Institute for Women's Studies and the Qualitative Research Certificate Program. His interests include public and social policy, anti-oppression education, race and gender in the workplace, sexual orientation and gender justice, human rights education, international adult education, environmental justice, activism as the practice of education, diversity instruction, educational work in social movements, and arts-based inquiry. He can be reached at < bobhill@uga.edu >.

André P. Grace is McCalla Research Professor and Director of the Institute for Sexual Minority Studies and Services < www.iSMSS.ualberta.ca > in the Faculty of Education, University of Alberta, Edmonton, Canada. He is Past President of the Canadian Association for the Study of Adult Education and Past Chair of the Steering Committee for the Adult Education Research Conference. André's work in educational policy studies primarily focuses on comparative studies of policies, pedagogies, and practices shaping lifelong learning as critical action, especially in the contexts of countries served by the Organization for Economic Cooperation and Development. Within this research he includes a major focus on sexual minorities and their issues and concerns regarding social inclusion, cohesion, and justice in education and culture. In national research projects, funded by the Social Sciences and Humanities Research Council of Canada, he has used qualitative methodology focused on explorations of the self, others, and culture to examine the positionalities and needs of sexual-minority students and teachers. He has also studied educational interest groups in political analyses of their impacts on sexual-minority inclusion and accommodation in education and culture. André keeps his research and service in dynamic equilibrium. With Kristopher Wells, he is co-founder of Camp fYrefly < www.fYrefly.ualberta.ca >, Canada's largest sexual-minority youth leadership camp, and he sits on the Sexual Orientation and Gender Identity Sub-Committee of the Alberta Teachers' Association's Diversity, Equity, and Human Rights Committee. He can be reached at < agrace@ualberta.ca >.

ABOUT THE CONTRIBUTORS

Thomas V. Bettinger, Ed.D., is an organizational development specialist providing advisory and consultant services regarding organizational culture, knowledge transfer and workplace learning, and change management. Through his affiliation with Penn State University–Harrisburg, Thom's teaching experience includes courses in diversity and social issues, critical media literacy, and pop culture as pedagogy. His two decades as a hospice volunteer underlie both an appreciation of lifelong learning to include the final stages of life as well as a desire to expand hospice services to be more culturally inclusive. Thom's current research interests center on LGBT aging and adult development and on learning in community action and social networking groups. He can be reached at < tbettinger@aol.com >.

Ann Brooks is Professor of Adult, Continuing, and Professional Education and Honorary Professor of International Studies at Texas State University–San Marcos. Her interests include workplace equity, international migration, organizational capacity building, and activist scholarship. Recent publications include *Bringing Community to the Adult ESL Classroom* (with Clarena Larrotta, 2009); *Allies in the Workplace: Adding LGBT to HRD* (with Kathleen Edwards, 2009); and *Where to Now? Race and Ethnicity in Workplace Learning and Development Research: 1980-2005* (with Tamara Clunis, 2007). She is currently working with her doctoral students on a film that explores Mexico-U.S. immigration from the Mexican perspective and, based on her work as a Fulbright Scholar in Cambodia, developing a methodology for mapping university and national research capacity. She can be reached at < abrooks@txsate.edu >.

Debra D. Davis is an award-winning educator, activist, author, college lecturer, and frequent keynote speaker at conferences and conventions throughout the United States. In the last 20 years she has given over 1,000 presentations and workshops. Debra is Executive Director of the Gender Education Center, a Minnesota not-for-profit organization of differently gendered people dedicated to support, advocacy, and education. She consults with employers, law enforcement, human rights agencies, and not-for-profit service providers regarding policies that affect transgender people and is especially effective in coordinating workplace transitions for transgender employees. Debra, a retired high school librarian, came out in May 1998 as a transgender woman at Southwest High School in the Minneapolis Public Schools. This transition was believed to be one of the first successful transitions in the United States of a transgender person working with children in secondary education. More information may be found at Debra's website: <www. debradavis.org >. She can be reached at < debbie@debradavis. org >.

John P. Egan is an adult educator, researcher, and activist whose interests include Queer health, HIV transmission, injection drug use, and community-based research and training. His work has been published in leading adult education journals, such as *Studies in the Education of Adults, Convergence,* and the *Canadian Journal for the Study of Adult Education.* He lives in Vancouver, BC, and can be reached at < john.egan@gmail.com >.

Suzanne J. Gallagher, Ed.D., is Director of Research and Planning at the Children's Services Council of Broward County and an adjunct professor at St. Thomas University, Miami, in their Practical Theology doctorate program. Suzanne is interested in the intersections between theology, social/environmental justice, and service delivery systems. She is challenged to create just intersections using holistic knowledge construction with multiple epistemologies. She can be reached at < sgspirit@comcast.net >.

Julie Gedro is Director of the FORUM Management Program and Assistant Professor of Business, Management, and Economics at Empire State College, State University of New York. Prior to becoming an academic, Julie worked in positions of increasing responsibility in human resource management and development in the finance, technology, and telecommunications sectors. She can be reached at < Julie.Gedro@esc. edu >.

Needham Yancey Gulley is Director of Student Affairs at Athens Technical College in Athens, Georgia, and a doctoral student in the College Student Affairs Administration Program at the University of Georgia. He has worked with LGBT initiatives on a variety of college campuses in North Carolina, California, and Georgia, often in regard to issues around campus climate assessments. Beyond this line of inquiry, Yancey is interested in collaborations between student and academic affairs in terms of enrollment management practices. He can be reached at < nygulley@gmail.com >.

Peter Hall is currently working towards his Ph.D. in the School of Psychology at Northcentral University. His research foci are crisis intervention and emergency mental health, suicide and suicide behavior, and sexual risk-taking practices. Peter is also a Canadian Certified Counselor and has a private mental health counseling and psychotherapy practice with a primarily GLBT focus in Toronto's vibrant GLBT community. He can be reached at < peterhall@me.com >.

Francisco Ibáñez-Carrasco has been, since 2003, the Community-Based Research Facilitator for AIDS service organizations in British Columbia, Canada. He is located at the British Columbia Persons with AIDS Society, funded by the Canadian Institutes of Health Research. In 2004, Francisco co-edited *Public Acts: Disruptive Reading on Making Curriculum Public* with Erica Meiners. He is a faculty member in the Creative Writing Program at Goddard College, Vermont. Arsenal Pulp Press and Suspect Thoughts Press have published his essays and gay erotica in the U.S., U.K., and Canada. He can be reached at < francisco@bcpwa.org >.

Kathleen P. King, Ed.D., is Professor of Adult Education and Human Resource Development at Fordham University's Graduate School of Education in New York City. Kathleen's major areas of research include transformative learning, professional development, distance learning, instructional technology and new media, and diversity issues. She is an award-winning author of 14 books, popular keynote and conference speaker, editor, mentor, and private consultant. Kathleen has been widely recognized for her research, service, and contribution to the field of adult learning. She can be reached at < kpking@fordham.edu > and through her research website: < www.kpking.com >.

Hilary Landorf is Associate Professor of Social Studies/Global Education and Director of the Office of Global Learning Initiatives at Florida International University. She has a Ph.D. in International Education from New York University. Hilary's research focus is inclusive global education. She has written articles examining, modeling, and designing pedagogical strategies helpful in creating an inclusive global learning environment. She is known for her work in using human rights concepts as the philosophical framework for global education. Hilary is consulted regularly as an expert in globalizing curricula. She can be reached at < landorfh@fiu.edu >.

Ronnie Lozano is Associate Professor and Chairman of the Radiation Therapy Program at Texas State University–San Marcos. His role in the baccalaureate degree program involves curriculum development, clinical education, research, and educational scholarship. Ronnie is also a doctoral student in the Adult, Professional, and Community Education Program at Texas State. He can be reached at < RL10@txstate.edu >.

Mitsunori Misawa received his Ph.D. in the Adult Education Program of the Department of Lifelong Education, Administration, and Policy at the University of Georgia. His current research interests include adult bullying; anti-oppressive education; the intersection of race, sexual orientation, and gender; feminist pedagogy; positionality; power dynamics; qualitative research; narrative inquiry; critical race theory; and Queer issues in higher education. Mitsu has presented on these research areas at national and international conferences and has published journal articles and book chapters on these topics. He can be reached at < mmisawa@uga.edu >.

Robert Mizzi is currently working toward his Ph.D. in the Faculty of Education at York University, Toronto. His research foci center on international adult education, sexuality studies in education, teacher training, and intercultural education. Robert is also the founding director of Queer Peace International, a Canadian not-for-profit organization dedicated to creating adult learning opportunities for sexual minorities living in developing countries. In addition to publishing two books related to teacher education in Kosovo, he recently edited *Breaking Free: Sexual Diversity and Change in Emerging Nations* (2008), a book that highlights educational endeavors made by sexual minorities in emerging nations to create change in their communities. Robert resides in Toronto with his partner, Andréw. He can be reached at < Robert_Mizzi@edu.yorku.ca >.

Dawn Robarts is Senior Lecturer in the Department of Health, Physical Education, and Recreation at Texas State University. She has been at Texas State University for more than thirty years, serving as a Health and Wellness Promotion faculty member, a health educator and counselor with the Student Health Center, and an administrator in the Student Affairs Division. Dawn earned both baccalaureate and master's degrees in Health Sciences from Western Illinois University. She is also a doctoral student in the Adult, Professional, and Community Education Program at Texas State University. Her research interests are in the LGBTQ community and LGBTQ retention at Texas universities.

Tonette S. Rocco, Ph.D., is Associate Professor of Adult Education and Human Resource Development at Florida International University. Her research interests include equity and privilege, specifically in terms of race/critical race theory, sexual minorities/LGBT, age, disability, teaching for social justice, employability/career development, and fostering student research and professional writing. She is co-editor of a special issue of *Advances in Developing Human Resources* on sexual-minority issues in HRD (with Julie Gedro and Martin Kormanik, 2009). She is also co-editor of *New Horizons in Adult Education and Human Resource Development*, an electronic journal < http:// education.fiu.edu/newhorizons/ >. She can be reached at < roccot@fiu. edu >.

Kristopher Wells is a Killam Scholar and a Social Sciences and Humanities Research Council of Canada Doctoral Scholar in the Department of Educational Policy Studies, University of Alberta. His research, teaching, and service work center on creating safe, caring, and inclusive schools and communities for sexual-minority youth. With André P. Grace, Kris co-founded Camp fYrefly, Canada's largest leadership retreat for sexual-minority youth < www.fYrefly.ualberta.ca >. Currently, Kris is an associate editor of the *Journal of LGBT Youth* and a researcher at the Institute for Sexual Minority Studies and Services, University of Alberta. Kris has been a consultant to the Canadian Teachers' Federation, the Alberta Teachers' Association, the Alberta Provincial Government, and the Public Health Agency of Canada. He has been an invited presenter to the Canadian Senate Standing Committee on Human Rights and was an invited panelist for an AREA presidential session on LGBT educational research. In 2005, Kris's community service work was recognized with an Alberta Centennial Medallion, bestowed by the Alberta Legislature. Kris can be reached at < kwells@ualberta.ca >.